1,000 Fingerplays & Action Rhymes

A Sourcebook & DVD

Barbara A. Scott

Neal-Schuman Publishers, Inc.

New York   London

Published by Neal-Schuman Publishers, Inc.
100 William St., Suite 2004
New York, NY 10038

Printed and bound in the United States of America.

The paper used in this publication meets the minimum requirements of American National Standard for Information Sciences—Permanence of Paper for Printed Library Materials, ANSI Z39.48-1992.

Library of Congress Cataloging-in-Publication Data

Scott, Barbara A., 1956-
    1,000 fingerplays & action rhymes : a sourcebook & DVD / Barbara A. Scott.
      p. cm.
    Includes bibliographical references and index.
    ISBN 978-1-55570-695-1 (alk. paper)
    1. Children's libraries—Activity programs—United States. 2. Storytelling—United States. 3. Finger play—United States. 4. Rhyming games—United States. I. Title. II. Title: One thousand fingerplays and action rhymes.

Z718.3.S395 2010
027.62'5—dc22

                                        2010017967

This book is dedicated, with all my love, to my husband, Greg. His faith in me throughout this project was strong and steady.

Contents

Preface

I still remember feeling dread and stage fright all too well. I had been a children's librarian for all of a month when my director told me, "You will be responsible for doing preschool storytime." Up until this point, parent volunteers had been filling in for the former children's librarian (who was out on extended sick leave). Fear struck my heart! What did I know about presenting a storytime? My experience with young people, up to that point, had been three years of teaching high school. Next week's audience members would be much smaller and, as far as I was concerned, way more demanding and intimidating!

I am glad to report that I jumped in with both feet and, 20-something years later, am still doing (and loving!) preschool storytime. I consider it a barometer of success (and steel nerves) that instead of running away years ago, I now get the pleasure of telling stories to the children of my first listeners.

Whether you're holding this book because you're looking for some fresh fingerplays or whether, like I was decades ago, you're quivering in fear of presenting your first storytime in front of real live children and their caregivers (not to mention your boss!), don't fear! Storytime preparation is a matter of finding a routine with which you feel comfortable. *1,000 Fingerplays & Action Rhymes: A Sourcebook & DVD* is designed to get you started.

Why Use Fingerplays?

Fingerplays are a staple of library storytime sessions. They:

- increase manual dexterity and muscular control;
- help children develop an understanding of rhythms, size, shape, direction, and number concepts;
- provide fun and relaxation;
- give children a legitimate opportunity to move and wiggle;
- let children express themselves;
- help children learn to follow directions; and
- provide another way for librarians to make the library a fun place children want to visit.

And, as if all of these weren't enough benefits, fingerplays also help increase attention span, foster listening and memory skills, build vocabulary, and aid language development. Fingerplays are key for developing crucial early literacy pre-reading skills.

What's in This Multimedia Resource?

1,000 Fingerplays & Action Rhymes: A Sourcebook & DVD has five components. The Introduction covers what fingerplays are and why we use them. Anyone who needs to convince an administrator that fingerplays aren't just "entertainment" will find convincing ammunition here. It discusses how to organize a storytime; create effective routines, using everything from singing to poetry; use book tie-ins; market storytime programs; and what to do when the storytime is over.

The second and largest part of this book—the "meat" of this publication—contains 42 themed chapters with rhymes. Each one contains fingerplays and action rhymes I've used myself with great success. You'll find not only the words to speak but also the actions to perform as you present and teach the rhyme. Each chapter ends with lists of books to share, musical selections (and where to find them), and the sources reprinted rhymes are drawn from.

Toward the end of this book is " The Source Finder," which has two sections. The first provides sources for ready-made puppets and storysets—everything from felt pieces to hand puppets to finger puppets. The second section lists multimedia resources, ranging from music CDs to parachutes and bean bags. At the very end of the book, the fourth component is a title index of the rhymes that put them all literally "at your fingertips"!

The final, fifth component is the companion DVD you will find on the inside back cover. It is designed especially for those new to storytelling. In one section I'll walk you step-by-step through a typical session. I'll also take you on a visit to my workroom so that you can see how I organize my storyhour themes by folders and check out some of the puppets, props, and other items that I use on a regular basis.

The remainder of the DVD contains demonstrations of 18 fingerplays and action rhymes. These were done with a live audience at my library. You will see me actually doing the movements that accompany the rhymes and see the children do them as well. The rhymes include the following themes: ants, bees, dinosaurs, farms, firefighters, ice cream, kites, outer space (stars), owls, penguins, pigs, pizza, scarecrows, spiders, stir and bake (cookies), teeth, transportation (boats), and the zoo. Look for the DVD icon— ☻—next to the rhyme title in the book.

Fingerplays are an integral part of storytimes. They are opportunities for the librarians, daycare providers, and preschool teachers to interact with children and their caregivers. Anyone who presents early childhood programming on a regular basis is always looking for new activities and themes.

In my own personal storytime planning, I have spent much time looking through multiple sources to find fingerplays on a specific theme that I might be using. Needless to say, this takes a lot of time. I have designed this book and DVD to be a "one-stop" resource for busy librarians and early childhood professionals. I hope both experienced and new children's librarians will find it to be a source of ideas and inspirations throughout the year.

Acknowledgments

When I undertook this project, little did I realize the size and scope of research time that it would entail!

I would like to thank all of the authors who so graciously allowed me to use many of their fingerplays and action rhymes for this book. They are listed below.

My appreciation goes out to my original editor, RoseMary Honnold, my second editor, Mike Kouri, and my current editor, Charles Harmon. All of you have been a tremendous help guiding me along in this long process! Thank you so much!

Finally, to my family and friends, thank you for your patience and encouragement!

"The Ants Go Softly Round and Round," "Four Busy Squirrels," and "The Dinosaur (and Other Ancient Creatures)" are reprinted here with the permission of Linda R.F. Zaletel, KinderNature (kindernature.storycounty.com) and funded by a REAP-CEP grant.

"Dragons," "Squirrels," "Engine on the Track," "Five Little Bees," "Chickadees," "Dinosaurs," "Five Donuts," "Five Yellow Ducklings," Five Little Froggies," "Monkeys in a Tree," "This Little Clown," "Circus Ponies," and "Kites" are reprinted here with the permission of Lynda S. Roberts, author of *Mitt Magic: Fingerplays for Finger Puppets* (Gryphon House, 1985).

"Puppy Dog," "Rags the Dog," "Wiggler (Up, Up, Up)," "The Wheels on My Bike," "This Little Horse," "Ten Little Ponies" (two versions), "How Do You Feed a Dragon?," "All the King's Knights," "Swing Your Dragon Tail," "Dragon Dance," "Did You Ever Find a Dragon?," "Going to the Market," "To Market, To Market," "Round and Round the Market," "The King's in Town," "Where Is the Prince?," "Put Your Crown on Your Head," "Tadpole, Tadpole," "The Horse on the Trail," "Dinosaurs in Motion," "Blast Off!," "We're Flying to the Moon," "I've Got Red Paint," "Here Is the Beehive," "Bumblebee," "Fuzzy Wuzzy Caterpillar," "Ants," and "Queen Bee Says" are reprinted here with the permission of Karen Dravel, Collaborative Summer Library Program (www.cslpreads.org).

"Little Ants" and "Butterfly! Butterfly!" are reprinted here with the permission of Neal-Schuman Publishers from Gail Benton and Trisha Waichulaitis, *Low-Cost, High-Interest Programming: Seasonal Events for Preschoolers* (Neal-Schuman, 2004).

"Bumblebee," "Kitty, Kitty," "Five Little Kittens," "The Circus," "Old Shoes, New Shoes," "Mittens," "The Mitten Song," "Dog Went to Dover," "This Little Doggie," "Doggie's Tail," "Ten Little Firemen," "Five Little Firemen," "My Garden," "Pitter-Pat" (two versions), "Five Little Froggies," "Little Mousie," "Two Mother Pigs," "Raindrops," "The

Boats," "Row, Row, Row Your Boat," "The Train," "Down by the Station," "The Big Train," and "An Airplane" are reprinted here with the permission of Marion Grayson, author of *Let's Do Fingerplays*, and Harold Levine, publisher (R.B. Luce, Inc.,1962).

"I'm a Little Dragon" is reprinted here with the permission of Lisa Dickson (storytimepreschooltoddlers.blogspot.com).

"Scarecrow," "Jingle Jangle Scarecrow," "Scarecrow," "Five Crows All Shiny and Black," "Got My Tooth Brush," "Dinosaurs Walked the Earth," "Dinosaurs Lived Long Ago," "Oh, I Want to Be a Great Big Dinosaur," "Five Enormous Dinosaurs," and "Stomp, Stomp, Stomp" are reprinted here with the permission of Laura Baas (laurabaas.com).

"Chocolate" is reprinted here with the permission of Ava Pavon, author of the Infopeople Workshop "Planning, Doing, & Sustaining a Successful Bilingual Storytime" (infopeople.org/training/past/2008/biling-storytime) and Holly Hinman, Infopeople Project Director.

"Apple Song," "Apples," "Elephant Action Play," "Little Flowers," "The Sleepy Seed," "Vegetables," "Little Seed," and "The Zoo" are reprinted here as found on the website www.alphabet-soup.net with the permission of Kristy Breedlove, webmaster.

"Toothbrush Song" is reprinted here with the permission of Jenny Wanderscheid, Child Fun (www.childfun.com).

"Peek into the Bee Hive," "Bees, Bees, Bees," "Happy Bees," and "Five Little Bees" are reprinted here with permission of Robin Suitt, Learning Wonders (www .learningwonders.com).

"Acrobat," "Elephant," and "Five Queens" are reprinted here with the permission of Mary Jo Ayres, author of the book *Natural Learning from A to Z* (Natural Learning, 1998) and webmaster of www.naturallearning.com.

"Hickory Dickory Dock," "Five Little Mice," and "Little Mousie" are reprinted here with the permission of Karla M. Schmit, Pennsylvania Center for the Book (www .pabook.libraries.psu.edu/familylit).

"The Squirrel" is reprinted here with the permission of JoAnne G. Mondowney, Director, Flint Public Library, Michigan.

"Blast Off," "Ten Little Spaceships," "Row Your Boat Some More," "All Hands on Deck," "A Boxcar Countdown," "Uplifting Experience," "Gas Station Song," and "School Bus Song" are reprinted here with the permission of Jan Irving and Robin Currie, authors of *Full Speed Ahead: Stories and Activities for Children on Transportation* (Teacher Ideas Press, 1988).

"How Many Bubbles in the Bathtub?," "Clown Dress," "Clap for Clothes," "Now You're Getting Dressed," "Buttons, Zippers, Snaps, and Bows," "Pocket Surprise," "Pat-a-Patch," "Work Hats," "Funny Hat," "Where's My Shoe?," "Dirty Feet Song," "The Best Shoes," "This Little Piggy's Piggies," and "Knight Song" are reprinted here with the permission of Jan Irving and Robin Currie, authors of *Glad Rags: Stories and Activities Featuring Clothes for Children* (Libraries Unlimited, 1987).

"Doin' the Chocolate Shake," "The Fudge Song," "Eggs and More Eggs . . . Surprise!," "We're Growing a Little Garden," "How Do You Eat an Ice Cream Cone?," "Hand-Me-Down Food," "Pancakes, What a Treat!," and "Pancake Stack" are reprinted here with the permission of Jan Irving and Robin Currie, authors of *Mudluscious: Stories and Activities Featuring Food for Preschool Children* (Libraries Unlimited, 1986).

"Blankets for My Bed," "Garden Jungle," and "Rain House" are reprinted here with the permission of Jan Irving and Robin Currie, authors of *Raising the Roof: Children's Stories and Activities on Houses* (Teacher Ideas Press, 1991).

"What's Inside" and "Splash! Squish! Smack!" are reprinted here with the permission of Jan Irving and Robin Currie, authors of *Straw into Gold:Books and Activities about Folktales* (Teacher Ideas Press, 1993).

"P-I-Z-Z-A" and "Body Bread" are reprinted here with the permission of Jan Irving and Robin Currie, authors of *Second Helpings: Books and Activities about Food* (Teacher Ideas Press, 1994).

"Under the Circus Tent," "The Circus," "I'm a Great Big Lion," "Leo Lion," "The Lion," "Clowns," "Popcorn," "Scarecrow," "Cookie Jar," "My Teeth," "The Sailboat," "Pumping Gas," "Five Little Kites," "This Little Froggie," "The Anthill," "Roly Poly Caterpillar," "A Rainbow," "My Puppy," "The Old Scarecrow," "The Butterfly," "Budding Flowers," "Take a Little Apple," and "Elephants" are reprinted here with the permission of Rhoda Redleaf, author of *Busy Fingers, Growing Minds: Fingerplays, Verses, and Activities for Whole Language Learning* (Redleaf Press, 1993).

"Five Bad Ants," "Worm in Apple," "Hermie the Worm," "Good Morning, Butterfly," "Flutter, Flutter Butterfly," "Caterpillar to Butterfly Scarf Play," "The Little Caterpillar," "Did You Ever Find a Dragon?," "I'm a Little Dragon," "Five Little Spiders," "Put Your Spider on Your Nose," and "Five Little Cupcakes" are reprinted here with the permission of Stephanie Stokes, LibraryPalooza (www.librarypalooza.net).

"Making Pizza" and "One Elephant" are reprinted here with the permission of Neal-Schuman Publishers from Gail Benton and Trisha Waichulaitus, *Ready-To-Go Storytimes: Fingerplays, Scripts, Patterns, Music, and More* (Neal-Schuman, 2003).

"Rainbow Colors," "Five Little Dinosaurs," "Stomp Stomp Stomp," "The Dinosaur Stomp," "All the Little Doggies," "Five Little Sheep," "Planting Time," "One Little Crocodile," "I'm a Little Crocodile," "Baby Crocodile," "Five Little Cookies," "There's a Cookie on My Plate," "The Little Bitty Cookie," "Ten Little Pancakes," "Where's My Tooth?," "I Have a Loose Tooth," "I'm a Toothbrush," and "Baby Kangaroo" are reprinted here with the permission of Neal-Schuman Publishers from Kay Lincycomb, *Storytimes . . . Plus!* (Neal-Schuman, 2007).

"The Little Baby," "Bedtime," "Buzz, Buzz," "Let's Head to the Circus," "The Colors in My Box," "My Puppy," "Dragons," "The Farmer and His Seeds," "Royalty," "Monkeys," "Off We Go," "Rainwear," "The Rain Comes Down," "The Dentist," "Boats Sail On," "Zoo Antics," "Kangaroo, Kangaroo," "Here We Go Jumping," and "Five Baby Kangaroos" are reprinted here with the permission of Neal-Schuman Publishers from Carolyn Cullum, *The Storytime Sourcebook II: A Compendium of 3,500+ New Ideas and Resources for Storytellers* (Neal-Schuman, 2007).

"Applesauce Chant," "Five Green Apples," "Oh, I See a Butterfly," "Spring Flowers," "One Little Penguin," "Popcorn," "I Love to Take Baths," "Before I Go to Bed," "Kitty Cat, Pounce," "Cats Have Nine Lives," "Winter Clothes," "Searching for My Clothes," "Silly Sally," "Crayon Box," "Wave Your Rainbow," "Fields of Food," "When I Went to the Barnyard," "Little Chicks," "Frog Surprise," "Three Frogs on a Log," "Little Brown Tadpole," "The Wheels on the Bus," "Car Sounds," "I'm a School Bus," "My Bike," "Washing the Car," "We're Going on a Bike Ride," "The Zoo," "I'd Rather Work at the Zoo," "Mama Kangaroo," "Zoo Animals," "Oh, I Work at the Zoo," "Rock-a-Bye Baby," "Some Dogs Bark," "Five Hungry Little Pigs," "Monkeys Swinging," "I Love Pizza,"

"Storm," "One Little Scarecrow," and "Ten Little Cookies" are reprinted here with the permission of Neal-Schuman Publishers from Susan Dailey's two books *Sing a Song of Storytime* (Neal-Schuman, 2007) and *A Storytime Year: A Month-to-Month Kit for Preschool Programming* (Neal-Schuman, 2000).

"Five Elephants in the Bathtub" is reprinted here with the permission of Heidi Anne Heiner (www.surlaunefairytales.com) and Judy Woodworth (www.artfelt.net).

"The Beehive," "Five Busy Bees," "Two Big Beehives," "Hey Bee," "A Bee Is on Me!," "Baby Bumblebee," "The Chocolate Cake," "Five Little Chocolate Chips," "Five Little Tadpoles," "I'm a Little Scarecrow," and "Scarecrow" are reprinted here with the permission of Peggy Drake (www.hummingbirded.com).

Introduction

What Are Fingerplays and Action Rhymes?

Fingerplays and action rhymes are activities that tell stories. They can range from simple rhymes involving just the fingers to full-blown action rhymes that involve the whole body. Rhymes that use the fingers, eyes, or toes help children develop small motor coordination, and the action rhymes work on the larger muscle movements.

Fingerplays and rhymes also expose children to memorization, rhythm, and the concept of rhyming. Not only that, it prepares them to listen to stories by helping them to concentrate and to be actively involved in telling the story. Furthermore, it exposes them to the concept of following directions and to the idea of actions happening in a sequence, which, of course, is one of the important elements of a story.

For toddlers and other young children, exploring language while moving arms, fingers, and sometimes whole bodies is exciting! But what is most exciting are the early literacy concepts that are found wrapped in the rhymes.

Early childhood professionals and much research tell us that exposure to early literacy concepts is the foundation of reading and school success in later years. Children can begin learning six important prereading skills from birth:

Print Motivation	Being interested in and enjoying books
Print Awareness	Figuring out how books "work"; noticing print; knowing how to follow the words on a page (left to right)
Vocabulary	Knowing the names of things
Phonological Awareness	Recognizing the sounds of letters and words; being able to hear and play with the smaller sounds in words (Fingerplays, rhymes, and songs are a great vehicle for teaching this concept. Words are broken up so that there is a note or sound for each word or part of a word!)
Narrative Skills	Learning how to tell a story; being able to describe things and events
Letter Knowledge	Learning what letters are; knowing letters are different from each other and have different names and sounds; being able to recognize letters no matter where they are seen

Fingerplays and action rhymes are wonderful ways to begin helping a child develop these skills.

According to *Helping Your Child Become a Reader*, published by the U.S. Department of Education in January 2000 and revised in 2005, rhyming activities help children to pay attention to the sounds in words.[1] This is the concept of phonological awareness. The authors suggest playing rhyming games and singing rhyming songs with children. And what better type of activity to work with rhyming than fingerplays? Then there's the added benefit of learning numbers as well!

Also, nursery rhymes (which can be in the form of fingerplays) help children to match sounds. Listening for and saying sounds in words will help children to learn that spoken words are made up of sounds, which prepares children to match spoken sounds to written letters—an important first step toward becoming a reader.[2] This covers both the literacy concepts of phonological awareness and letter knowledge. Helping children learn to pay attention to sounds in words can prevent reading problems later on.[3]

But wait! There's more! Think about the different learning styles of children: spatial/visual learners (those children who learn through images); kinesthetic learners (those who are active and find it hard to sit still, learning with the body); and language-oriented learners (they learn through word play). Then, consider the multiple intelligences: musical/rhythmic (children who think and learn in sounds, rhythms, and rhymes); bodily/kinesthetic (children who learn and think in terms of action and movement and can use their bodies in expressive ways); visual/spatial learners (those children who think and learn in pictures and use their imaginations); verbal/linguistic (those children who love everything about stories and storytelling; they think in words and use language well). Acting out a fingerplay allows verbal/linguistic types of learners to express themselves. When children act out a rhyme, they are showing their understanding of what it is about. They are growing as a reader by connecting emotions with written words.[4] And singing of fingerplay songs (and songs in general) help children with rhythm and breaking words into syllables.[5]

Phonological awareness skills are fostered by most of the rhymes, songs, and movements in this book. Hearing the rhythm of language and making animal sounds contribute to phonological awareness.[6] Nursery rhymes are fun to sing and say, and they also expose children to words that are not used in everyday conversation. Researchers have found that children who know rhymes find it easier to learn to read.[7]

The final word on the benefits of fingerplays and rhymes comes from Carolyn Munson-Benson in her article "Making Time for Rhyme" in the May 2007 issue of *Book Links Magazine*,[8] which begins:

> Literary language gives young brains a buzz. This "buzz" results in a boost—growth of synapses in the brain, 90 percent of which develop in the first few years of life. "By repeating the same words and phrases, you rapidly reinforce specific neural pathways," notes Dr. Lise Eliot in *What's Going On In There? How the Brain and Mind Develop in the First Five Years of Life* (Bantam, 2000). Thus, patterns peculiar to poems, nursery rhymes and lullabies are of special value. Repeated rhyming sounds as well as recurring phrases and refrains stimulate brain growth.

A Step-by-Step Guide for Organizing a Storytime

I have found it easier to plan my storytimes when I work with a specific theme. Throughout the year, holidays just beg to be programmed around, so for most months this gives you a good start. Of course, there are the themes that will appeal to preschoolers, such as dinosaurs, colors, counting, and most any type of animal. I also make an effort to do a series focusing on nursery rhymes at least every couple of years. You might think that there is no need for this, but you would be surprised at the number of children who have not been exposed to the traditional rhymes that we baby boomers grew up with! Once you choose your theme, here are some steps that will work for any storytime.

Step 1: Set the Scene

Find a special place to present your storytime. The children's areas of most public libraries may already have an area set aside for storytimes. As with real estate, it's all about location! Preschoolers thrive on routine, and holding your storytime in a certain area time after time makes them feel comfortable.

You may wish to use a special chair. I use a rocking chair in my area. I also leave room for my easel, which holds my flannel/Velcro board, and a cart that holds my CD player, rhythm instruments, bean bags or scarves (if used), and my books and other storytime materials. You may wish to provide carpet squares for the children to sit on. My little ones sit on them during storytime, and it provides an area for them to go back to if we are using instruments or need a specific area to be (e.g., "take your shakers back to your carpet square"). The children choose them prior to the beginning of the session and are responsible (at my prompt at the end of the session) to place them in a pile before leaving the storytime area. Do you have a carpet store in your town? Most times they will donate whatever number you need! Library supply catalogs also supply seating cushions that you may wish to use.

Step 2: Let's Read!

Find one to two books that relate to your theme. Use one book at the beginning of your storytime session. The second can be used later, if needed.

Step 3: My Name Is . . .

What a boon to librarians Ellison dies are! I use these to make the name tags that the storytime participants receive at each session. If you are not familiar with Ellison dies, visit Ellison's website at www.ellison.com. Its catalog boasts die cuts for hundreds of shapes that are just right for storytime name tags, and it sells the Sizzix machine as well. AccuCut also offers dies similar to Ellison's. Visit AccuCut online at www.accucut.com. If you have parent or even teen volunteers, what a great project for them to do for you!

At the beginning of my storyhours, each child receives a personalized name tag. This not only gets me familiar with the children's names but also provides a reference point for their names if I need to call on them during an activity later in the storytime session. You may wish to provide just one name tag that you will laminate and use week after week. I have seen librarians string them on yarn, or you can use inexpensive lanyards. Children are responsible for getting these back to the librarian at the end of the storytime session. Personally, I like the idea of using different name tags each week according to the theme. Many parents will place them on the coloring sheet or craft we have done and then take them home. Sometimes they'll include the name tags in a scrapbook of their child's activities. I have also been told that the name tags decorate refrigerators, bedroom doors, and headboards of beds at home!

Step 4: It's All Routine!

When you are ready to begin your storytime series, it is good to have a structure that is the same time after time. I usually begin by saying, "OK, storyhour friends, if everyone has their carpet square and has a place to sit, it's time to get started!" This alerts children and parents both inside and outside of the specific area that we are ready to get underway.

Ask your participants to identify what their name tag is, if you choose to do the personalized ones every week. Simply query, "Who can tell me what your name tag shape is?" This will result in a chorus of voices. Specifically asking about the shape of the tag most times takes care of the participants just telling you it says their name (which it does). You may wish to ask about the color of the tag, to reinforce that concept.

Step 5: Please Use Poetry!

I love to use poetry in my storytime sessions! I attended a workshop many years ago at which Caroline Feller Bauer spoke. She is a big proponent of using poetry in the classroom. So, I figured why wait until children are in school to expose them to this wonderful use of language! There are just so many great poems out there! Of course, the poem relates to the theme of the week. Where do you find poetry? *Mailbox Magazine* (the preschool edition) is a great source, as well as the poetry section of your juvenile nonfiction area. This might seem a little labor intensive, but it is worth it! Especially around the holidays, there are compilations out there. I always read from a copy of the poem that is typed and illustrated.

Step 6: Everybody Sing!

I am also a big proponent of using music in storytime. Music exposes children to rhythm and rhyme and gives them a chance to get those wiggles out! I use the same song for my opening every week: Jim Gill's "Oh Hey, Oh Hi, Hello," a song that he says he started singing on one of his many trips through Ohio. The lyrics mention specific towns in Ohio (great for Ohio librarians) and gives participants a chance to wave and sing the chorus in a variety of ways (in the library, quietly; outside, very loud; underwater in a swimming pool, very unusual, etc.). At the end of the song, everyone gives themselves a great big hand for doing such a fantastic job. It is unreal the number of parents who say that their little ones sing this song at home all the time, or in the car, sometimes even at church! Some other songs you might want to consider are Debbie Clement's "Jambo Hello" (saying hello in different languages) or "Howdy Song" by Monty Harper, which also teaches children how people around the world say "hello"!

Step 7: Read . . . with Feeling

Once the song is done, I introduce the first book of the session. I begin by saying something like, "This is one of my favorite books" or "This is a very silly (scary, etc.) story about . . ." and introduce the book by title and author. I then proceed to share the book, using a concept called "dialogic" or "hear-and-say" reading. Dialogic reading is a method that helps young children become involved in the story. Although it works best in a one-on-one situation, I have found that it works well in my storytime setting when sharing a book. Literacy research has shown that children learn more from books when they are *actively* involved in the story, and dialogic reading is a powerful means to that end. On tests of language development, young children who are actively involved in the reading process with "hear-and-say" reading have more advanced language and prereading skills!

With dialogic reading, ask "what" questions as you read the story. Examples are "What is that?" or "What's going on here?" or "What color is that?" or "What animal is that?" This will encourage children to speak. Ask more questions. Repeat what the children say. This reinforces! For example: "Yes, that's a cow! What sound does a cow make?" Help children as needed. If they don't know what to say about a picture, say something and have them repeat. If children are pointing and/or commenting on a particular item in a picture, engage on that! There are other ways to engage children too:

- Ask open-ended questions! Preschoolers love guessing what will happen next or giving their opinion on the story!
- When you read, it is important that you read with ENTHUSIASM! Make sound effects, give characters unique voices, use dramatic pauses, or raise and lower your voice. If a character sings, sing the lines! It is a good idea to read through or rehearse your story before presenting it to your storytime group.

Step 8: Use Puppets and Clowns

After sharing the first book, I always do the same two activities each week. The first is a fingerplay that is an abridged version of "Open Them, Shut Them." My version is:

> Open them, shut them,
> Open them, shut them,
> Give a little clap.
> Open them, shut them,
> Open them, shut them,
> Lay them in your lap.

I take this opportunity to use a hand puppet to "help" me do the fingerplay. I keep the puppet hidden behind my flannel/Velcro board until right before we do the fingerplay. I bring it out and introduce it to participants with the patter: "I have someone who is going to help us do our fingerplay. Who can tell me who/what this is?" The puppets that I normally rotate are Ernie, Bert, and Cookie Monster from *Sesame Street*; Clifford, and a giraffe. Basically, any hand puppet that you can manipulate your hand in will work. I also change up the *Sesame Street* ones. For example, Bert has dressed as a bee (with wings and antennae taped on), and Ernie has dressed as a pig, complete with nose and ears to go along with themes. If you can find small hats (perhaps in a local craft store), you can accessorize the puppets for holidays!

The second activity that we do is a counting rhyme that I found called "Five Silly Clowns." I begin with the patter: "All right, it's time to help me count my clowns" as I place them, one by one, on the flannel/Velcro board. Each week, as the theme dictates, I "dress up" these laminated clowns. My clowns have been everything under the sun (including it!). I allow participants to guess what the clowns will be and praise them for being "so smart" when they guess correctly. Once the clowns are on the board and "dressed" (simply a laminated picture of something to do with the theme placed, with Velcro, on top of the clown), and participants are ready with "five fingers up in the air," we begin counting down as follows:

Five silly clowns, jumping all around.	Move arm with five fingers up and down.
Jump so high, then touch the ground!	Move arm up in air; then down to the floor.
One silly clown says, "I can't stay,"	Remove one clown from board; shake head "no."
So she turned and (fill in action) away!	Put clown aside or in pocket.
	Ask participants to count the number of clowns left.
	Continue counting down four, three, two, one.

Depending on the theme, the clowns use all types of locomotion to go "away."

Step 9: Bring in Fingerplays, Action Rhymes, and Flannel Boards

At this point in the storytime, begin introducing fingerplays and action rhymes or flannel or Velcro board stories. A good rule of thumb is to have at least three of each to round out your program. Always plan with more than you think you will need. These flannel/Velcro board stories may come from a variety of sources, as there are a lot of great titles out there. Luckily for me, I "inherited" a good number of stories from the children's librarians who preceded me.

The fingerplays can be done as simply that or with flannel or Velcro board props. The Monkey Mitt and accompanying kits (available from a number of library catalogs and online) is a wonderful prop to use. Simple patterns are also available online to make your own, or you can use something as simple as a gardening glove with Velcro added! If you do not wish to use a large board, small Velcro boards are available (or can be made cheaply). On a personal note, I much prefer the Velcro board to the traditional flannel ones. The added security of the pieces sticking is a big plus! In addition to the Monkey Mitt, great props for fingerplays can be found in catalogs from companies such as Oriental Trading and U.S. Toy. Homemade fingerplay props work well also. Your copy machine and crayons and/or markers will definitely be your friends when creating small characters for fingerplays! What fingerplays to use? That's the purpose of this book: to provide you with a seemingly endless supply on a variety of topics!

Step 10: Let's Play a Game

At this point, we usually play a matching game. Depending on the theme, I use Ellison dies shapes (two of each color) that have been cut and laminated. If you don't wish to use colored paper, wallpaper with distinct patterns is a great alternative! Be sure to make enough shapes so that each participant gets one of the pair. The librarian keeps the other in a pocket of an apron, a basket, or some sort of container. Once everyone has received a shape, tell them you have the matches to the ones that they are holding. One by one, remove a shape from your pocket and ask who has the match. In my experience, participants have a ball with this simple game! Continue until all shapes have been matched by participants. We end with a big round of applause for all. Use this idea if it works for you. I've found it to be very successful!

Step 11: If You Have Time, Use Music and Movement

Many times, I will insert music here. This can be everything from dancing to using rhythm instruments, bean bags, scarves, or a parachute. The sky is the limit here! I try to use music related to the theme. One thing that you will discover once you start using music with your preschoolers is that there is a ton of it available.

Step 12: Share More Books

Share your second book here, if desired.

Finally, After the Story Is Over

Be sure to supply a post-story activity of some sort, and keep it related to the theme. Supplying a coloring sheet is the simplest, but you may wish to do a theme-related craft. We do a craft one time per month and also provide a Snack-and-Play Day one time per month where parent volunteers bring a snack or drink. Afterwards (and for the most part, during), children and parents have a chance to socialize.

A Few Tips

- Always, always, always have books on display that relate to your theme, and encourage parents/caregivers to check them out.
- It is not necessary, but I provide a handout each week for parents detailing books that we own relating to the theme, as well as activities and recipes that they might enjoy doing with their children.
- What about those children who may misbehave during storytime? There are several schools of thought on this. You may wish to discuss appropriate behavior with participants and children before you begin your storytime session. You may also choose to simply correct inappropriate behaviors as they occur. There is much discussion of letting parents sit in on storyhour sessions and, personally, I have no problems with it. If there are behavior problems, most parents are great about taking care of any problems as they occur, leaving you free to continue your activities.
- Don't feel overwhelmed! With practice and sticking to a routine, storytimes are not something to dread! Remember: you, as a children's librarian, are introducing the children of your community to new concepts, new ideas, and, best of all, working on literacy and pre-reading skills by helping them increase their vocabulary and listening skills!

How to Market Your Storytimes

If your library does a great storytime, of course you want to get the word out! Here are some ideas to spread the news:

- Produce in-house fliers and displays detailing days and times storytimes are held.
- If you know your themes well enough in advance, provide a calendar or flier detailing dates and themes. Have these available at both the circulation desk and in the children's area.
- Local radio and television stations are usually glad to support your efforts. Consider doing a Public Service Announcement or television spot highlighting your storytimes. Be available to appear on local radio and TV shows to promote your programming.
- Be a presence at preschool and/or kindergarten registration events. Be sure to have copies of your storytime fliers available! To that end, also be available for parents' nights at local schools. Chances are that parents may have younger ones who would benefit from storytimes.
- Be available to visit local preschools and/or Head Start classrooms. You will be able to tailor the same routine that you do for a storytime to your audience at these locations! No doubt it will be much abbreviated, but you can still share books (remember that dialogic reading) and share simple fingerplays and action rhymes!

Fun . . . movement . . . and brain growth to boot? How can you go wrong?

How to Choose the Right Fingerplay/Action Rhyme

The aim of this book is to provide librarians, teachers, daycare workers, and other educators with a listing of topics and several pages of fingerplays on each of those topics. Fingerplays and action rhymes can be about nearly any subject that is of interest or that your program theme calls for. And, while there are lots of new rhymes out there, don't forget the old tried-and-true Mother Goose rhymes that we have all grown up with.

Personally, I use fingerplays as part of my preschool storytimes as transitions (from opening song and story, then again between flannel or Velcro board stories or games). They are short enough to teach easily and are just that perfect break between longer parts of the storytime.

How to Teach a Fingerplay/Action Rhyme

When teaching a new fingerplay, it is best to repeat the rhyme at least a couple of times. I usually do the rhymes at least twice. The first time through, I go through slowly enough so that the children (and parents who may sit in on storytime) can catch onto the words. I also explain the motions, taking time to help with any motions that are unfamiliar. For example, when we did one of our opening fingerplays and the theme was spiders, I used the American Sign Language (ASL) sign for spider (wrists of hands overlapping, fingers on both hands wiggling). Here are some quick tips for teaching fingerplays and rhymes:

- Be enthusiastic and excited! Your interest will carry over to your audience.
- Be sure to demonstrate actions as you share the words with your group.
- Repeat the rhyme, encouraging the audience to imitate the actions.
- Do the fingerplay again, allowing those who wish to participate with both words and actions to do so.
- Keep the actions and rhythm of the rhyme slow enough so that your audience does not have trouble keeping up. This is important, especially for the first time through. (To see me demonstrating a couple of simple fingerplays, check out Videos 1.1 and 1.2 on the companion DVD.)
- Repeat fingerplays and rhymes often enough for children to become familiar with them. For example, I have a particular opening fingerplay that I do each week at storyhour. You will be surprised what happens if you forget to do it or have someone filling in for you who doesn't know the "drill." The kids will be sure to let you (or your replacement) know!
- Send the words and actions home with parents so that they can be used/practiced at home.
- Always, always, always repeat old favorites!
- Try out some of the new variations of old favorites out there!

Ready? Let's Have Fun!

Now that you know the elements of a successful storytime and what a fingerplay/action rhyme is and how to present it, you are ready for the "meat" of this book: *1,000 Fingerplays & Action Rhymes.* In the following pages, you will find pages of fingerplays and action rhymes on a variety of topics. Each fingerplay/action rhyme includes easy-to-follow motions.

Notes

1. Office of Communications and Outreach. 2005. *Helping Your Child Become a Reader.* Washington, DC: U.S. Department of Education, p. 23.

2. Ibid., p. 24.

3. Ibid.

4. Ibid., p. 25.

5. Ghoting, Saroj. "Storytime Programs Based on Research from Public Library Association and National Institute of Child Health and Human Development's Early Literacy Initiative." Montgomery County Public Libraries. Available: www.ala.org/ala/mgrps/divs/alsc/ecrr/ecrrinpractice/storytimeapplications/researchbasedprograms/prereadersresearch.pdf (accessed May 18, 2010).

6. Ghoting, Saroj, and Pamela Martin-Diaz. 2005. *Early Literacy Storytimes @ Your Library: Partnering with Caregivers for Success.* Chicago: American Library Association, p. 243.

7. Ibid.

8. Munson-Benson, Carolyn. 2007. "Making Time for Rhyme." *Book Links Magazine* (May): 26.

Ants to Bees

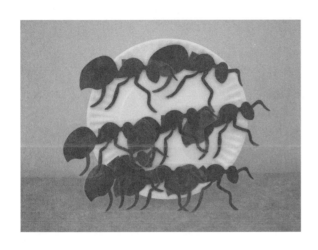

Ants

Off they march, in search of food!

Rhyme

The Ants Go Marching

The ants go marching one by one, hurrah, hurrah.
The ants go marching one by one, hurrah, hurrah.
The ants go marching one by one,
The little one stops to suck his thumb.
And they all go marching down to the ground to get out of
the rain, boom, boom, boom.

ADDITIONAL VERSES:
The ants go marching two by two,
The little one stops to tie his shoe . . .
The ants go marching three by three,
The little one stops to climb a tree . . .
The ants go marching four by four,
The little one stops to shut the door . . .
The ants go marching five by five,
The little one stops to take a dive . . .
The ants to marching six by six,
The little one stops to pick up sticks . . .
The ants go marching seven by seven,
The little one stops to pray to heaven . . .
The ants go marching eight by eight,
The little one stops to shut the gate . . .
The ants go marching nine by nine,
The little one stops to check the time . . .
The ants go marching ten by ten,
The little one stops to say, "The end!"
—Traditional action song

Five Little Ants

Five little ants in an ant hill,
Busily working and never still.
Do you think they are alive?
See them out—
One, two, three, four, five.
These five little ants near an ant hill,
Run as hard and run with a will

Telling Guide

Sung to the tune of "When Johnny Comes Marching Home." This is also a great rhyme to do with puppets or a flannel or Velcro board.
Begin with one finger and gradually add until ten is reached.

Action of sucking thumb.

On the "boom, boom, boom," swing hips from side to side in rhythm.

Action of tying shoe.

Action of climbing a tree.

Action of shutting door.

Action of diving, hands together.

Motion of picking up sticks.

Action of praying.

Action of shutting gate.

Action of looking at wrist to check watch.

Throw hands out to sides.

Close fist, palm down.
Wiggle knuckles.

Bring fingers out one at a time.
Wiggle fingers of one hand toward closed fist of other.

To gather food to keep alive.
Now they go in—
One, two, three, four, five.
　　　　　—From *Let's Do Fingerplays*

Close fingers in fist again.

Little Ants

One little ant climbs up the hill,
Where do you think he will go?
Two little ants walking along,
Looking for food, don't you know?
Three little ants all in a line,
Searching up high and down low.
Four little ants busy at work,
Marching along in a row.
Five little ants spy a fine treat,
Lifting it with a heave-ho.
Bringing the food back to their friends.
HEY! Watch out below!
　　　　　—From *Low-Cost, High-Interest Programming*

This rhyme was originally written as a flannel board story, but can be easily adapted for use with fingers or finger puppets.

Place a plastic vegetable on top of all five ants, holding the vegetable on top of the fingers with the other hand.

Drop the vegetable.

Ants

One ant, two ants, three ants, four.
Our picnic is their grocery store.
Five ants, six ants, seven ants, eight.
They are crawling on my plate!
Eight ants, seven ants,
Stomp around.
Six ants, five ants,
On the ground.
Four ants, three ants,
On the run!
Two ants, one ant,
No more fun.

　　　　　—Author unknown

This rhyme can be done with fingers or with flannel board figures or finger puppets. You can also use a paper plate and attach Velcro to place ants as you do the rhyme.

Five Bad Ants

Five bad ants went out one day,
Out from the anthill and far away.
Inside a house they began to explore.
One fell asleep and then there were four.
Four bad ants went out one day,
Out from the anthill and far away.
One swam in coffee,
And then there were three.

This rhyme was inspired by the book Two Bad Ants by Chris Van Allsburg. It can be used as a fingerplay or with puppets, and it also works well as a flannel board activity.

Three bad ants went out one day,
Out from the anthill and far away.
One was almost cooked all the way through.
He ran for safety and then there were two.
Two bad ants went out one day,
Out from the anthill and far away.
Stuck in a disposal, one spun and spun.
He spun and spun and spun
And then there was one.
One bad ant went out one day,
Out from the anthill and far away.
When he raced back with his sugary treasure,
All five friends were together again.

—Pam Carlson, LibraryPalooza

The Ants Go Softly Round and Round

Sung to the tune of "When Johnny Comes Marching Home."

The ants go softly 'round and 'round
Shhh! Shhh!   Make shushing motion, finger to mouth.
The ants go softly 'round and 'round
Shhh! Shhh!   Make shushing motion again.
The ants go softly 'round and 'round
They creep and crawl upon the ground.   Wiggle fingers around.
And they all move closer,
Eyeing the picnic feast.   Point to eyes.

—From KinderNature

Ants on the Anthill

Sung to the tune of "Skip to My Lou."

Ants on the anthill
One, two, three.   Clap on each number.
Ants on the anthill
One, two, three.   Clap on each number.
When I'm done counting,
What do I see?   Point to eyes.
Ants on the anthill,
One, two, three.   Clap on each number.

—Barbara Scott

Once I Saw an Anthill

Once I saw an anthill   Make fist with left hand.
With no ants about.   Shake head "no."
So I said, "Dear little ants,   Cup hands around mouth.
Won't you please come out?"
Then as if the ants
Had heard my call—   Bring out fingers, one at a time.

One, two, three, four, five came out!
And that is all!

—Traditional rhyme

Counting Ants!

One ant, two ants, three ants, four,
Four ants are knocking at my door.
Five ants, six ants, seven ants, eight,
There are more are the garden gate.
Nine ants . . . one more . . . and then there's ten.
Line them up and begin again!

—Barbara Scott

Hold up four fingers in succession.

Hold up four more fingers.

Hold up last two fingers.

Ants in My Pants

There are ants in my pants!
Ants in my pants, I say!
With those ants in my pants,
I can't sit still today!
My head wiggles and shoulders, too.
My arms and my fingers . . . whew!
My legs wiggle, my knees wiggle, too.
I cvcn have wiggles down in my shoes!
Out, out, ants, get out of my pants!
Get out of my pants, I say!
With no ants in my pants,
I can really sit still today!

—Barbara Scott

This is the perfect rhyme to get those storytime wiggles out of the way!
Wiggle!

Continue to wiggle.
Shake head "no."
Wiggle head and shoulders.
Wiggle arms and fingers.
Wiggle legs and knees.
Wiggle feet and toes.
Making shooing motion.

Shake head "no."

Ants Marching

One by one and two by two,
Ants are marching right on through!
Three by three and four by four,
Ants are marching out the door.
Five by five and six by six,
Ants are marching over sticks.
Seven by seven and eight by eight,
Ants don't have much time to wait!
Nine by nine and ten by ten,
Ants march out and back again!

—Barbara Scott

This fingerplay also works well as a flannel or Velcro board activity.
Hold up fingers as numbers are mentioned in the rhyme.

Shake head "no" while counting.

If You Were an Ant . . .

If you were an ant,
To hear things would be neat!
You'd hear the sounds
Through your feet!

Point to children.
Point to ears.

Point to feet.

If you were an ant,
You'd be really strong!
You could lift a car all day long!
If you were an ant,
You'd leave a special trail.*
To find your food
You'd never fail!

—Barbara Scott

Point to children.
Show muscles.
Motion of lifting something heavy.
Point to children.
Point to ground.
Rub tummy.
Shake head "no."
This special trail is called a pheromone trail. It lets the ant know where it's been!

Ants on a Log

Five little ants and not one more.
One fell off the log and now there are four.
Four little ants spy some food by a tree.
Another ant fell off the log and now there are three.
Three little ants, but before I knew,
Another ant fell off the log and then there were two.
Two little ants know there's work to be done.
Another ant fell off the log, and now there's just one.
One little ant, left all alone.
He fell off the log and now there are none.

—Barbara Scott

Begin rhyme by holding up five fingers. Take away fingers as ants leave.

An Army of Ants

Hup, two, three, four . . .
Ants march off to the grocery store.
Hungry little insects, they.
The march there might take all day!
How they'll push the cart,
I'll never know.
Do you think
That they might grow?
Up and down
The aisles they go,
Moving, oh, so very slow.
Apples, bread, a little cheese,
And some cookies, if you please!
Their shopping's done,
Their cart is full.
Should they push or should they pull?
Never mind,
It's just not funny . . .
The little ants
Forgot their __(money)__!

—Barbara Scott

Pretend to march in place.

Rub tummy.
Point to wrist to indicate watch.

Shake head "no."

Move hands apart to indicate size.
Point up and down.
Motion of pushing cart.
Move in slow motion.
Motion of picking stuff from shelves.
Make small circle in front of body.

Move hands apart to show full cart.
Motions of pushing and pulling.
Shake head "no."

Let children fill in the blank to end the rhyme!

Ants in the Garden

Ants in the garden,
Having lots of fun.
Let's try to count them . . . I see one.

Ants in the garden,
I see one by your shoe.
Please help me count them . . . one, two.

Ants in the garden,
There's another by the tree.
Hurry up and count them . . . one, two, three.

Ants in the garden,
There are more? Are you sure?
Let's get busy counting them . . . one, two, three, four.

Ants in the garden,
Here's the last to arrive.
Let's count again . . . one, two, three, four, five.

—Barbara Scott

This rhyme could be done with finger puppets and works equally well as a flannel or Velcro board activity!

Hold up one finger.

Hold up a second finger.

Hold up a third finger.

Hold up a fourth finger.

Hold up fifth finger.

Books to Share

Becker, Bonnie. 2003. *An Ant's Day Off.* New York: Simon & Schuster Books for Young Readers. ISBN: 978-0689822742.

Martin, David. 2006. *All for Pie, Pie for All.* Somerville, MA: Candlewick Press. ISBN: 978-0763623937.

McDonald, Megan. 2005. *Ant and Honey Bee: What a Pair!* Somerville, MA: Candlewick Press. ISBN: 978-0763612658.

McElliot, Matthew. 2004. *Absolutely Not.* New York: Walker & Company's Books for Young Readers. ISBN: 978-0802788887.

Prince, Joshua. 2007. *I Saw an Ant in the Parking Lot.* New York: Sterling. ISBN: 978-1402738234. (This is the companion book to *I Saw an Ant on the Railroad Track,* another great selection!)

Van Allsburg, Chris. 1988. *Two Bad Ants.* Boston: Houghton Mifflin. ISBN: 978-0395486689.

Musical Selections

"Ants, Ants, Ants" from *Buzzers, Creepers, and Crawlers* by Intelli-tunes. Available: www.songsforteaching.com (accessed March 2, 2010).

"The Ants Go Marching" from *Everybody Sing!* by Sharon, Lois, and Bram. ASIN: B0001NPTN4.

"Ants Go Marching" from *Get Funky and Musical Fun* by The Learning Station. ASIN: B0001CJ8KU.

"The Ants Go Marching" from *Songs for Wiggleworms* by the Old Town School of Folk Music. ASIN: B00004YLUE.

"Ants in My Pants" from *Pizza Pizzazz* by Peter and Ellen Allard. ASIN: B000GETZH4.

"Ants on Parade" from *Songs about Insects, Bugs, and Squiggly Things* by Jane Lawliss Murphy. Kimbo Educational Audio, 1993. ISBN: 978-1563460333.

"Hey, Little Ant" from *Two of a Kind: Connections.* Available: www.songsforteaching.com (accessed March 2, 2010).

Sources

Benton, Gail, and Trisha Waichulaitis. 2004. *Low-Cost, High-Interest Programming: Seasonal Events for Preschoolers*. New York: Neal-Schuman.

Grayson, Marion. 1962. *Let's Do Fingerplays*. Fairfield, CT: R.B. Luce.

KinderNature: A Resource for Early Childhood Educators. Available: kindernature.storycounty .com (accessed March 2, 2010).

LibraryPalooza. Available: www.librarypalooza.net (accessed March 2, 2010).

Poulsson, Emilie. 1893. *Fingerplays for Nursery and Kindergarten*. New York: Lothrop, Lee, and Shepard, reprinted 1921.

Sinclair, Patti, Tami Chumbley, and Kathy Ross. 2005. *Collaborative Summer Library Program Manual*. Mason City, IA: Collaborative Summer Library Program.

Apples
Red, yellow, or green, apples are a yummy treat!

Rhyme

Ten Red Apples

Ten red apples growing on a tree.
Five for you and five for me.
Let me shake the tree just so,
And ten red apples fall down below.
One, two, three, four, five,
Six, seven, eight, nine, ten.

—Author unknown

Look at the Apple

Look at the apple I have found,
So round and rosy on the ground.
Mother will wash it and cut it in two.
Half for me and half for you!

—Martha T. Lyon

Five Red Apples

Five red apples hanging in a tree,
The juiciest apples you ever did see.
The wind came by and gave an angry frown,
And one little apple came tumbling down.

—Author unknown

Five Red Apples

Five red apples at the grocery store.
Bobby bought one and then there were four.
Four red apples on an apple tree.
Susie ate one and then there were three.
Three red apples. What did Alice do?
Why, she ate one and then there were two.
Two red apples ripening in the sun.
Tommy ate one and now there was one.
One red apple and now we are done.
I ate the last one and now there are none!

—Author unknown

All Around the Apple Tree

Here we go 'round the apple tree,
The apple tree, the apple tree.
Here we go 'round the apple tree
On a frosty morning.

Telling Guide

Hold hands high, fingers extended.
Wave one hand, then the other.
Shake body.
Lower hands with fingers extended.
Count fingers on one hand.
Count fingers on other hand.

Sung to the tune of "The Mulberry Bush."
Form circle with hands.

Pretend to wash and cut apple.
Hold out one palm, then the other.

This rhyme also works well as a flannel or Velcro board activity.
Hold up five fingers.

Fingers flutter downward.
One finger falls.
Continue counting down to one.

Begin this rhyme with five fingers.
Take away fingers as rhyme progresses.

Sung to the tune of "The Mulberry Bush."
Mime the motions.

ADDITIONAL VERSES:
This is the way we climb the ladder.
This is the way we pick the apples.
This is the way we wash the apples.
This is the way we peel the apples.
This is the way we eat the apples.

—Author unknown

Here Is an Apple

Here is an apple
And here is an apple
And a great big apple I see.
Now let's count the apples we've made . . .
One, two, three!

—Author unknown

Make circle with thumb and pointer finger. / Make circle with other thumb and pointer finger. / Make circle with arms.

Repeat smaller-to-larger circle-making actions.

Ten Red Apples

Here I have five apples,
And here are five again.
How many apples altogether?
Why, five and five make TEN!

—Author unknown

Hold up five fingers on right hand.
Hold up other hand.

Eat an Apple

Eat an apple;
Save the core.
Plant the seeds,
And grow some more.

—Author unknown

Bring right hand to mouth.
Close right hand into fist.
Bend down; touch hand to ground.
Extend both arms out.

Apples Are Falling

Apples are falling, apples are falling,
From the tree, from the tree.
Pick up all the apples, pick up all the apples.
One, two, three. One two, three.

—Author unknown

Sung to the tune of "Frère Jacques."
Use appropriate motions for actions.

Apple Song

Have you ever seen an apple, an apple, an apple,
Have you ever seen an apple that grows on a tree?
A red one, a yellow one, a red one, a yellow one.
Have you ever seen an apple that grows on a tree?

—From Alphabet Soup

Sung to the tune of "Have You Ever Seen a Lassie?"
Make small circle with hands.
Hands up over head, fingers stretched.
Alternate hands front to back.
Hands up over head, fingers stretched.

Apples

Apples here,
Apples there.

Point to yourself.
Point away.

Apples are growing everywhere.	Form a circle with hands to represent the world. / Point up.
Some are high,	
Some are low.	Point down.
You will see apples wherever you go.	Point to eyes.
Apples on the left,	Extend left arm.
Apples on the right.	Extend right arm.
You will see	Point to eyes again.
Both day and night.	Put hands together at side of head as if sleeping.

—From Alphabet Soup

Apples Green, Apples Red

Apples green,	Show one fist.
Apples red.	Show opposite fist.
Apples falling on my head!	Point to head.
Down they fall	Fingers flutter down.
From way up high.	Point upward.
I'll pick them up	Motion of gathering.
And make a pie!	Make a circle with hands.
Green or red,	
Apples are yummy!	Show one fist and then the other.
And they taste good	
In my tummy!	Rub tummy.

—Barbara Scott

Five Red Apples

Five red apples sweet to the core.	Begin this rhyme with five fingers up. Take away fingers as rhyme progresses.
One fell down, and then there were four.	
Four red apples sitting in a tree.	Hold up four fingers.
One fell down, and then there were three.	
Three red apples, one for you and you and you.	Point to children.
One fell down, and then there were two.	
Two red apples shining in the sun.	Hold up two fingers.
One fell down, and then there was one.	
One red apple left all alone.	Hold up one finger.
One fell down, and then there were none.	

—Author unknown

Two Green Apples

Way up high in an apple tree,	Raise arms high.
Two green apples smiled at me.	Smile.
So I shook that tree as hard as I could!	Pretend to shake tree.
And down fell the apples.	
Mmmmm, they were good!	Rub tummy.

—Adapted traditional rhyme

Apple Poem

Apples big,
Apples small.
Guess what?
I like them all!

—Author unknown

Stretch arms apart to show size.
Put hands close together to show size.
Finger to cheek, tilt head, questioning.
Throw hands out to sides.

Five Little Apples

Five little apples hung on a tree.
The farmer didn't care.
So guess who came to eat?
A CATERPILLAR! . . . MUNCH, MUNCH.
Four little apples hung on a tree.
The farmer didn't care.
So guess who came to eat?
A BIRD! . . . MUNCH, MUNCH.
Three little apples hung on a tree.
The farmer didn't care.
So guess who came to eat?
A PIG! . . . MUNCH, MUNCH.
Two little apples hung on a tree.
The farmer didn't care.
So guess who came to eat?
A HORSE! . . . MUNCH, MUNCH.
One little apple hung on a tree.
The farmer didn't care.
So guess who came to eat?
A SCARECROW! . . . MUNCH, MUNCH.
Now the tree is bare.
There are no apples there.
But when next fall comes around,
Guess who'll be there?
THE CATERPILLAR.
THE BIRD.
THE PIG.
THE HORSE.
And the SCARECROW.

—Author unknown

*This makes a great flannel board activity.
You can use small finger puppets as well!*
Begin rhyme with five fingers up.
Shake head "no."

Opposite hands make munching motions.
Hold up four fingers.

Opposite hands make munching motions.
Hold up three fingers.

Opposite hands make munching motions.
Hold up two fingers.

Opposite hands make munching motions.
Hold up one finger.

Opposite hands make munching motions.
Hold up fist.
Shake head "no."

As each is mentioned, bring back all
five fingers.

Climbing Up the Apple Tree

Climbing up the apple tree,
Swinging on a limb!
If I hear a robin, I may

Climb in place.
Raise arms above head, sway left and right.
Cup hand near ear.

Sing along with him.
And robin, if you fly away
Here's what I think I'll do.
I'll wish a pair of sparrow wings
And fly away with you!

—Author unknown

Sing "tra la la."
Put hands over eyes.
Point with index finger.

Gently flap arms at sides and move around.

Applesauce

Peel an apple,
Cut it up,
Cook it in a pot.
When you taste it,
You will find
It's applesauce
You've got!

—Martha T. Lyon

Sung to the tune of "Yankee Doodle."

Do motions as indicated.

Red Apple

A little red apple
Hung high on a tree.
I looked up at it,
And it looked down at me.
"Come down, please," I called,
And what do you suppose?
That little red apple
Dropped right on my nose!

—Author unknown

Point in the air.
Look upward.
Look downward.
Cup hands around mouth.

Point to nose.

Apple Up High

Apple, apple way up high,
I can reach you if I try.
Climb a ladder
Hold on tight.
Pick you quickly,
Take a bite!

—Author unknown

Sung to the tune of "Twinkle, Twinkle, Little Star."
Point upward.
Reach upward.
Climbing motion.
Hold on to imaginary ladder.
Picking motion.
Motion of biting into apple.

Apples

Apple, apple tree so tall
I can hardly wait 'til fall!
When your apples I can pick
Fill my basket, eat them quick.
Apple, apple tree so tall
I can hardly wait 'til fall!
Apple, apple tree so fair
What do I see growing there?

Chanted or sung to the tune of "Twinkle, Twinkle, Little Star."
Hand in the air to indicate height.
Hug self.
Motion of picking apples.
Motions of gathering and eating.
Indicate size again.
Hug self.

Put index finger to cheek, tilt head, wondering.

Green and round and plump and sweet.

Make circle with hands.

Soon they will be good to eat.

Motion of taking a bite.

Apple, apple tree so fair

What do I see growing there?

Put index finger to cheek, tilt head, wondering.

—Author unknown

A Little Apple Seed

Sung to the tune of "The Itsy Bitsy Spider."

Once a little apple seed was planted in the ground.

Motions of planting, covering up seed.

Down came the raindrops, falling all around.

Flutter fingers down.

Out came the big sun, bright as bright could be.

Make large circle over head with arms.

And that little apple seed grew to be an apple tree!

Raise both arms overhead to represent branches.

—Author unknown

Five Little Apples

Five little apples lying on the floor.

Begin this rhyme with five fingers up.

I'll roll one away, and that leaves four.

Make rolling motion with arms.

Four little apples hanging on a tree.

Hold up four fingers.

I'll pick one off, and that leaves three.

Pick an imaginary apple.

Three little apples, I know what to do!

Hold up three fingers.

I'll put one in my pocket, and that leaves two.

Pretend to put apple in pocket.

Two little apples sitting in the sun.

Hold up two fingers.

I'll pick one up, and that leaves one.

Pretend to pick apple up off the floor.

One little apple waiting in my lunch.

Hold up one finger.

I'll eat it up with a crunch, crunch, crunch!

Pretend to take a big bite.

—Author unknown

Dear! Dear!

Dear! Dear!

Hold face with hands.

What can the matter be?

Sway head back and forth.

Two old women got up

Hold up two fingers.

In an apple tree.

Stretch arms above head to make "tree."

One came down

Hold up one finger on right hand.

And the other stayed up

Hold up one finger on left hand.

'Til Saturday.

—Traditional rhyme

Gathering Apples

Under the apple tree,

Point upward.

Out in the sun,

Make large circle overhead with arms.

Jennie and Kate are

Having their fun.

Harry, above them there

High overhead,

Point overhead again.

Gathers the fruit with care,

Motion of picking fruit.

Apples so red.

See, as he drops them down

Letting them fall,

Wiggle fingers down to represent falling apples.

Jenny or Kate's apron

Catches them all!
Soon the basket is full
Under the tree.
Homeward their cart they pull,
Happy as can be!

—Traditional rhyme

Hold arms out in front as if holding apron.
Make large circle in front of body with arms to indicate basket.

Action of pulling.
Point to a big smile!

Apple Harvest

Up in the green orchard there is a green tree,
The finest of pippins* that ever you see;
The apples are ripe and ready to fall,
And Richard and Robin shall gather 'em all.

—From Kids Nursery Rhymes and Riddles

Stretch arms overhead to represent tree.
Make small circle in front with hands.
Wiggle fingers down.
Action of picking up apples from ground.
What's a pippin? Any of several varieties of apple!

Worm in Apple

This is a great rhyme to do with a small hand puppet I've seen that has a little green worm inside!

I found an apple all shiny and red.
It looks so delicious to me.
I opened my mouth to take a big bite.
Uh-oh! What did I see?
A little hole all soft and brown.
That apple had something inside!
I opened it up and a worm looked at me,
With a grin on his face a mile wide!

—Stephanie Stokes, LibraryPalooza

Make circle with hands.
Rub tummy.
Open mouth.

Make small hole with fingers.

Hold up index finger and wiggle as a worm.
Give a big smile.

Hermie the Worm

Hermie the worm got hungry one day.
He found a sweet apple and nibbled away.
He nibbled and tunneled
Until the day was done.
And then popped his head out
And said, "Isn't this fun?"

—Stephanie Stokes, LibraryPalooza

Hold up index finger for worm.
Close opposite hand in fist for apple.
Allow index finger to work through under fingers in fist.
Pop index finger out of hole by thumb.

Applesauce Chant

First you need apples,
So pick them, pick them.
CHORUS:
 Apple, apple
 Applesauce.
Put them in the sink
And wash them, wash them.

Mimic picking.

Slap legs twice; clap hands twice.
Rub tummy in rhythm.

Pretend to wash.

CHORUS
Then you take the apples
And cut them, cut them.
CHORUS

Make chopping action with one hand against other open palm.

Put them in a pot
And cook them, cook them.
CHORUS

Pretend to stir.

Pour them in a strainer
And squeeze them, squeeze them.
CHORUS

Squeeze hands together.

Take a little sugar
And sprinkle it, sprinkle it.
CHORUS

Pretend to sprinkle.

Then you take the sauce
And eat it, eat it.
CHORUS

Pretend to eat.

Repeat chorus several times at end— first at normal level, then quietly, and finally loudly.

—From *Sing a Song of Storytime*

Five Green Apples

Farmer Brown had five red apples hanging on his tree.
Farmer Brown had five red apples hanging on his tree.
And he plucked one apple
And ate it hungrily,
Leaving four green apples
Hanging on his tree.
Farmer Brown had one green apple hanging on his tree.
Farmer Brown had one green apple hanging on his tree.
And he plucked that apple and gave it just to me.
Leaving no green apples hanging on his tree.

Begin this rhyme with five fingers up. Take away fingers as rhyme progresses.

Take away one finger.

Pretend to eat.

Repeat above verse with four, three, two, and one.

—Adapted from a song by Susan M. Dailey

Let's Count Apples

There's lots of apples, don't you see?
Can you count them now with me?
Here's an apple sitting in the sun.
Let's count! It's apple number one.
Here's an apple by my shoe.
Let's count! It's apple number two.
Here's an apple that fell from the tree.
Let's count! It's apple number three.
Here's an apple by the door.
Let's count! It's apple number four.
Here's an apple, and that's no jive!
Let's count! It's apple number five.

Hold up index finger.

Add middle finger.

Add ring finger.

Add pinkie.

Add thumb.

—Barbara Scott

All Kinds of Apples

Apples tart and apples sweet.
Yummy apples, what a treat!
Red Delicious and Golden, too,
Granny Smith and Winesap,
Just to name a few.
Gala apples taste real fine.
McIntosh is my favorite kind.
Gravenstein and Rome are next on the list.
Fiji and Jonathan can't be missed!
How many apples do you see?
Come on now and count with me!

—Barbara Scott

Clap three times.
Count types of apples on fingers.

Count on ten fingers.

I Love Apples

I love apples,
I love apples,
Yes I do, yes I do.
I would like to share them,
I would like to share them,
Now with you,
Now with you.

—Adapted traditional rhyme

Sung to the tune of "Frère Jacques."
Place one hand over heart.
Place other hand over heart.
Nod head "yes."
Point to self.

Point to children.
Point to more children.

Five Juicy Apples

Five juicy apples at the grocery store.
(_____) bought an apple and then there were four.
Four juicy apples, so yummy can't you see?
(_____) bought an apple and then there were three.
Three juicy apples, what am I to do?
(_____) bought an apple and then there were two.
Two juicy apples ripened by the sun.
(_____) bought an apple and now there's just one.
One juicy apple, I am almost done.
(_____) bought an apple and now there are none.

—Barbara Scott

Begin this rhyme with five fingers up.
Take away fingers as rhyme progresses.
Insert name of child

Insert name of child

Insert name of child

Insert name of child

Insert name of child

Apple Overload

Apple doughnuts, apple tarts.
I love apples with all my heart!
Apple muffins, apple sauce.
I'll show those apples who's the boss!
Apples fried and apples baked.
There are so many things to make!

Count out on fingers.
Place hand over heart.
Continue to count out.
Point to self.
Continue to count out.

Apple cookies, apple bread.
I think that apples have gone to my head!
Apple pie and apple cake.
Oh, no! An apple bellyache!

—Barbara Scott

Continue to count out.
Point to head.
Continue to count out.
Hold tummy and moan.

Over in the Field

Over in the field
Stands a great big apple tree.
It is full of delicious fruit,
As far as the eye can see!
Some of the branches are way up high.
They look like they could touch the sky.
Some of the branches hang very low,
Because of all the apples that grow, grow, grow.
Let's find a basket and climb that tree,
And pick sòme apples for you and me!

—Barbara Scott

Begin this rhyme standing up.
Shield eyes, look.
Stretch arms out to sides to represent tree. / Rub tummy.
Point to eye.
Move arms up into the air.

Move arms lower.

Climbing motion.
Point to children and then yourself.

If You Like to Eat an Apple

If you like to eat an apple, clap your hands.
If you like to eat an apple, clap your hands.
If you like to eat an apple,
Lick your lips and make 'em smackle.
If you like to eat an apple, clap your hands.

ADDITIONAL VERSES:
. . . stomp your feet.
. . . nod your head.
. . . rub your tummy.
. . . shout "hooray"!

—Adapted traditional rhyme

Sung to the tune of "If You're Happy and You Know It."
Clap, clap.
Clap, clap.

Clap, clap.

Apples

Apples are so good to eat!
Some are juicy, some are sweet.
Pick them fresh out of the tree,
By the basketful, don't you agree?
Buy them by the bushel at the store.
Apples, apples, I want more!

—Barbara Scott

Rub tummy.

Motion of picking apples.
Nod head "yes."

Motion of gathering in.

Apples All Around

Apples, apples on the ground.
I see apples all around.
Apples big and apples small,

Point down.
Move hands to show expanse.
Move hands to show size.

I would like to eat them all.	Motion of eating.
Red and yellow, green and brown,	
I see apples all around.	Move hands to show expanse.

—Barbara Scott

Books to Share

Carr, Jan. 2001. *Dappled Apples.* New York: Holiday House. ISBN: 978-0823415830.

Hall, Zoe. 1996. *The Apple Pie Tree.* New York: Blue Sky Press. ISBN: 978-0590623827.

Hutchins, Pat. 2002. *Ten Red Apples.* New York: Red Fox. ISBN: 978-0099413868.

Miller, Virginia. 2002. *Ten Red Apples.* Somerville, MA: Candlewick Press. ISBN: 978-0763619015.

Thompson, Lauren. 2007. *The Apple Pie That Papa Baked.* New York: Simon & Schuster Children's Publishing. ISBN: 1416912401.

Wellington, Monica. 2001. *Apple Farmer Annie.* New York: Dutton Juvenile. ISBN: 978-0525467274.

Winget, Susan. 2006. *Tucker's Apple-Dandy Day.* New York: HarperCollins. ISBN: 978-0060546465.

Musical Selections

"Applepicker's Reel" from *(Almost) Two Much* by Nan Hoffman. Available: www.nanhoffman.com (accessed March 3, 2010).

"Five Green Apples" from *Sing It! Say It! Stamp It! Sway It!*, vol. 1, by Peter and Ellen Allard. ASIN: B000056IIO.

"I Bit an Apple" from *Very Derryberry* by Debi Derryberry. ASIN: B00112XSI2.

"Little Green Apple" from *It's Toddler Time* by Carol Hammet and Elaine Bueffel. ASIN: B0001CVE7A.

"Ten Red Apples" from *Sing Along and Learn* by Ken Sheldon. Available: www.kensheldon.com (accessed March 3, 2010).

Sources

Alphabet Soup. Available: www.alphabet-soup.net/dir2/applesong.html (accessed March 3, 2010).

Cromwell, Liz, Dixie Hibner, and John R. Faitel. 1983. *Finger Frolics: Fingerplays for Young Children.* El Cajon, CA: Partner Press.

Dailey, Susan M. 2007. *Sing a Song of Storytime.* New York: Neal-Schuman.

"Fingerplays." Available: www.thebestkidsbooksite.com/fingerplays-for-kids.cfm (accessed March 3, 2010).

Kids Nursery Rhymes and Riddles. "Index of Rhymes." Available: www.kidsnurseryrhymes.co.uk/rhymes (accessed March 3, 2010).

LibraryPalooza. Available: www.librarypalooza.net (accessed March 3, 2010).

McKinnon, Elizabeth, and Gayle Bittinger. 1994. *Busy Bees Fall: Fun for Two's and Three's.* Everett, WA: Warren Publishing House.

Totline Publications. 1994. *1001 Rhymes and Fingerplays.* New York: McGraw-Hill Children's Publishing.

Warren, Jean, comp. 1989. *Theme-a-Saurus.* Everett, WA: Warren Publishing House.

Wiggin, Kate Douglas, and Nora Archibald Smith. 1907. *Pinafore Palace.* New York: Grosset & Dunlap.

Willett, Edward. 1882. *Around the House.* New York: R. Worthington Publishers.

Bathtime: Glub, Glub in the Tub
Splish, splash! It's bathtime! Don't forget your rubber duck!

Rhyme

Scrub, Scrub in the Tub

Scrub, scrub in the tub,
Getting nice and clean!
Scrub, scrub, scrub.
No dirt can be seen!
Scrub, scrub, scrub my face,
Scrub until it shines!
With all the bubbles in my tub,
It's a scrubbing good time!

—Barbara Scott

Baby's Bath

Baby's ready for his bath.
Here's the baby's tub.
Here's the baby's washcloth.
Here's the way to rub.
Here's the baby's cake of soap.
And here's the towel dry.
Baby's ready for his bed.
Rock-a-bye-lo-bye.

—Maude Burnham

How Many Bubbles in the Bathtub?

Rub a dub dub,
Scrub a dub dub—
Count the bubbles
In my tub!
One, two, three, four, five.
Bubbles, bubbles,
Hop, hop, hop.
Bubbles, bubbles,
Pop, pop, pop!

—Jan Irving

I Love to Take Baths

Put in the water,
First cold, then hot.
Add some soap,

Telling Guide

Sung to the tune of "Row, Row, Row Your Boat."
Scrubbing motions.

Continue scrubbing motions.
Point to eyes.
Scrubbing motions.

"Twinkle" fingers in the air.
Replace the line "scrub my face" with other body parts, such as arms, legs, back, and tummy.

Make circle with arms.
Hold hand up, palm flat.
Pretend to rub face.
Hold hand flat.

Make imaginary cradle and rock it.

This is a slight adaptation of a rhyme by Jan Irving.
Begin the rhyme by having children stand.
Make scrubbing motions.

Count on fingers of one hand.

Everyone hops.

Clap three times and all sit down.

Pretend to turn faucets.
Shiver; fan body with hand.
Pretend to shake box.

A little? No, a lot!
Drop in a washcloth.
Throw in a toy or two.
I really love to take a bath.
How about you?

—Susan M. Dailey

Pretend to drop something.
Pretend to toss two things.
Pretend to wash.
Point to someone.

Bathtime

Sung to the tune of "Shoo Fly."

Bathtime, no, I won't go. — *Shake head "no."*
Bathtime, no, I won't go.
Bathtime, no, I won't go.
I won't even wash my toe. — *Point to toe.*
Mom says I'm too dirty . . . — *Point finger downward.*
But I won't even wash my chin. — *Point to chin.*
Mom says my bath is done . . . — *Pause.*
Do I have to get out? — *Hold up hands in questioning position.*
It's so much fun!

—Susan M. Dailey

Before I Go to Bed

Sung to the tune of "The Wheels on the Bus."

Before I go to bed,
I take a bath.
Splash, splash, splash. — *Make splashing motion.*
Splash, splash, splash.
Before I go to bed,
I take a bath.
Splash, splash, splash.
ADDITIONAL VERSES:
I brush my teeth . . . — *Make scrubbing sound.*
I get a drink . . . Glug, glug, glug.
I read a book . . . Once upon a time.
I sing a song . . . La, la, la.
I give a kiss . . . — *Make kissing sound.*
I whisper goodnight . . . Nighty-night night.
　　　—Adapted from a song by Susan M. Dailey

This Is the Way That I Take a Bath

Sung to the tune of "The Mulberry Bush."

This is the way that I take a bath,
I take a bath, I take a bath.
This is the way that I take a bath
So early in the evening.
This is the way that I fill the tub, — *Motion of turning on faucets.*
Fill the tub, fill the tub.
This is the way that I fill the tub
So early in the evening.

Pour in some bubbles to make it fun,
Make it fun, make it fun.
Pour in some bubbles to make it fun
So early in the evening.

Motion of pouring or shaking in bubble bath.

I get in the tub and I splash around,
I splash around, I splash around.
I get in the tub and I splash around
So early in the evening.

Motion of splashing water.

I scrub and scrub 'til I'm squeaky clean,
Squeaky clean, squeaky clean.
I scrub and scrub 'til I'm squeaky clean
So early in the evening.

Motion of washing all over.

Out of the tub and dry with a towel,
Dry with a towel, dry with a towel.
Out of the tub and dry with a towel
So early in the evening.

Motion of drying off.

—Adapted traditional rhyme

Five Bars of Soap

Five bars of soap and not one more.
One slid away and then there were four.
Four bars of soap for everyone to see.
One slid away and then there were three.
Three bars of soap, we're almost through.
One slid away and then there were two.
Two bars of soap, having lots of fun.
One slid away and then there was one
One bar of soap, sitting all alone.
He slid away and then there were none.

Begin this rhyme with five fingers up. Take away fingers as rhyme progresses.

—Barbara Scott

In the Bathtub

Sung to the tune of "Frère Jacques."

In the bathtub,
In the bathtub,
Splash, splash, splash,
Splash, splash, splash.

Motion of hands splashing water.

It is lots of fun to,
It is lots of fun to

Nod head "yes."

Take a bath,
Take a bath.

Clap three times.
Clap again.

—Adapted traditional rhyme

Five Rubber Duckies

Five rubber duckies on the bathroom floor.
One got put into the tub and now there are four.

Begin rhyme with five fingers up. Take away fingers as rhyme progresses.

Four rubber duckies, happy as can be.
One got left behind the door and now there are three.
Three rubber duckies, just a funny few.
One hid beneath a towel and now there are two.
Two rubber duckies and our rhyme is almost done.
One slid under the sink and now there's just one.
One rubber duckie, not having any fun.
He hid in the closet and now there are none.

—Barbara Scott

Bubbles in the Bathtub

There are bubbles in my bathtub.
Can you see? *Point to eyes.*
Please count the bubbles
Along with me. *Begin counting on fingers.*
One bubble, two bubbles, three bubbles, four,
Five bubbles, six bubbles, seven bubbles more,
Eight bubbles, nine bubbles, and the last bubble, ten.
I can't wait to count them again! *Clap on last three words.*

—Barbara Scott

It's Time for Me to Take My Bath

Sung to the tune of "The Muffin Man."

It's time for me to take my bath, *Point to wrist to indicate time.*
To take my bath, to take my bath.
It's time for me to take my bath.
But the tub needs one more thing.
I'll put my duckie in my bath, *Flap arms like wings.*
In my bath, in my bath.
I'll put my duckie in my bath.
But the tub needs one more thing.
I'll put my big boat in my bath, *Move hands to indicate size.*
In my bath, in my bath.
I'll put my big boat in my bath.
But the tub needs one more thing.
I'll put my bucket in my bath, *Motion of holding bucket and pouring.*
In my bath, in my bath.
I'll put my bucket in my bath.
But the tub needs one more thing.
I'll put my goggles in my bath, *Make circles around eyes with fingers.*
In my bath, in my bath.
I'll put my goggles in my bath.
"Hey! There's no room for me!" *Speak this line; point to self.*

—Adapted traditional rhyme

How Many Toys in the Tub?

It's time for me to take my bath.   Point to wrist to indicate watch.
I'm dirty, don't you see?   Point to eyes.
Before I get into the tub,
I'll need some toys with me.
I'll need . . .   Tap temple with finger, thinking; then count the toys on fingers as the rhyme progresses.
One, a rubber duckie, all shiny and clean.
Two, an army boat that is colored green.
Three, a measuring cup with which to play.
Four, a fish, like the one on my PJs.
Five, a yellow frog, he's not real.
Six, my trusty shovel and pail.
Seven, an orange octopus with lots of legs, you see.
Eight, a plastic horsie that goes everywhere with me.
Nine, an alligator with a mouth that opens wide.
And ten, a squeezy sponge that is sitting on the side.

—Barbara Scott

Rub-a-Dub!

Rub-a-dub!
Scrub-a-dub!
It's time to get into the tub!   Point to wrist to indicate watch.
Fill the water to the top.   Raise hands in the air, palms up.
Don't overflow, know when to stop.   Shake head "no"; put hand up for "stop."
Pour in bubbles,   Pouring motion.
Add some toys.   Pretend to toss a few things.
All a part of bathtime's joys!   Give a big smile!

—Barbara Scott

I Am Dirty

Sung to the tune of "Frère Jacques."

I am dirty,   Point to self.
I am dirty.
What to do?   Shrug.
What to do?
Run a tub of water.   Motion of turning on faucets.
Add some bouncy bubbles.   Motion of pouring.
I'm a scrubbing machine!   Motion of scrubbing all over.
Now I'm clean!   Smile.

—Adapted traditional rhyme

If You're Ready for a Bath

Sung to the tune of "If You're Happy and You Know It."

If you're ready for a bath, clap your hands.   Clap, clap.
If you're ready for a bath, clap your hands.   Clap, clap.

If you're ready for a bath, just follow on my path.	
If you're ready for a bath, clap your hands.	Clap, clap.

ADDITIONAL VERSES:

. . . stomp your feet.

. . . nod your head

. . . shout "glub, glub"!

. . . do all four.

—Adapted traditional rhyme

My Sister's Bath

My little baby sister	Rock arms as if holding baby.
Just loves to take a bath.	Nod head "yes."
It doesn't make her cry.	Nod head "no."
Just watch her splish and splash.	Motion of splashing water.
She's sitting in the tub,	
With all her favorite toys.	Sweep arms out to sides.
Yes, bathtime is a time of day	Point to wrist to indicate watch.
She really does enjoy!	Nod head "yes."

—Barbara Scott

Ten Sudsy Bars of Soap

One sudsy, two sudsy, three sudsy bars of soap,	*Sung to the tune of "Ten Little Indians."*
Four sudsy, five sudsy, six sudsy bars of soap,	Count out on fingers on the first verse; then take away fingers on the second verse.
Seven sudsy, eight sudsy, nine sudsy bars of soap,	
Ten sudsy bars of soap.	
Ten sudsy, nine sudsy, eight sudsy bars of soap,	
Seven sudsy, six sudsy, five sudsy bars of soap,	
Four sudsy, three sudsy, two sudsy bars of soap,	
One sudsy bar of soap.	

—Adapted traditional rhyme

It's Bathtime!

Put some water in the tub,	*Sung to the tune of "London Bridge."*
In the tub, in the tub.	Motion of turning on faucets.
Put some water in the tub.	
Yeah! It's bathtime!	Pump fist in the air.
Take the washcloth	
And scrub, scrub, scrub,	Motion of scrubbing all over.
Scrub, scrub, scrub,	
Scrub, scrub, scrub.	
Take the washcloth	
And scrub, scrub, scrub.	Motion of scrubbing all over.
Yeah! It's bathtime!	Pump fist in air.
Take the shampoo,	

And rub, rub, rub,	Motion of pouring shampoo; then rub head with fingers as if shampooing.
Rub, rub, rub,	
Rub, rub, rub.	
Take the shampoo	
And rub, rub, rub.	Motion of scrubbing all over.
Yeah! It's bathtime!	Pump fist in air.
Take the towel	
And dry, dry, dry,	Motion of drying off.
Dry, dry, dry,	
Dry, dry, dry.	
Take the towel	
And dry, dry, dry.	Motion of drying off.
Yeah! It's bathtime!	Pump fist in air.

—Adapted traditional rhyme

Books to Share

Arnold, Tedd. 1999. *Huggly Takes a Bath.* New York: Scholastic. ISBN: 978-0590918206.

Bruel, Nick. 2008. *Bad Kitty Gets a Bath.* New York: Roaring Brook Press. ISBN: 978-1596433410.

Jarman, Julia. 2004. *Big Red Tub.* London: Orchard Books. ISBN: 978-0439672320.

Neubecker, Robert. 2005. *Beasty Bath.* London: Orchard Books. ISBN: 978-0439640008.

Spinelli, Eileen. 2003. *Bath Time.* Tarrytown, NY: Marshall Cavendish Children's Books. ISBN: 978-0761451174.

Woodruff, Elvira. 1990. *Tubtime.* New York: Holiday House. ISBN: 978-0823407774.

Musical Selections

"Bath Song" from *Super Simple Songs.* ASIN: B000CA8YAG.

"Bubble Bath Blues" from *Music in My Heart* by Rebecca Frezza. ASIN: B00006JIUI.

"I'm Not Getting in That Tub" from *Daniel Kirk and the Chowhounds* by Daniel Kirk. ASIN: B000CA8YZQ.

"I Took a Bath in a Washing Machine" from *Jim Gill Sings the Sneezing Song and Other Contagious Tunes* by Jim Gill. Available: www.jimgill.com (accessed March 3, 2010).

"Shiny Clean Dance" from *Tony Chestnut and Fun Time Action Songs* by The Learning Station. ASIN: B00000GBZ8.

"Splish Splash" from *Bean Bag Rock and Roll.* ASIN: B00015EL2M.

"Take a Bath" from *Good Habits* by Geof Johnson. B00007E8QL.

Sources

Burnham, Maude. 1910. *Rhymes for Little Hands.* East Longmeadow, MA: Milton Bradley Company.

Dailey, Susan M. 2001. *A Storytime Year.* New York: Neal-Schuman.

———. 2007. *Sing a Song of Storytime.* New York: Neal-Schuman.

Irving, Jan, and Robin Currie. 1987. *Glad Rags: Stories and Activities Featuring Clothes for Children.* Santa Barbara, CA: Libraries Unlimited.

Bedtime
Go to bed, you sleepyhead!

Rhyme

This Little Girl

This little girl is ready for bed.
Down on the pillow she lays her head.
Wraps herself in covers so tight,
And this is the way she sleeps all night.

—Traditional rhyme

Blankets for My Bed

A blanket on my bed, a blanket on my bed
Hey ho, I'm cozy-o
A blanket on my bed.
The wind blows tonight, the wind blows tonight.
Hey ho, I'm freezing-o
The wind blows tonight!
Two blankets on my bed, two blankets on my bed.
Hey ho, I'm cozy-o
Two blankets on my bed.
The wind blows and howls, the wind blows and howls.
Hey ho, I'm freezing 'cause
The wind blows and howls.
Three blankets on my bed, three blankets on my bed.
Hey ho, I'm cozy-o
Three blankets on my bed.
Now it starts to snow, now it starts to snow.
Hey ho, I'm freezing 'cause
Now it starts to snow.
Four blankets on my bed, four blankets on my bed.
Hey ho, I'm cozy-o
Four blankets on my bed.
The wind blows the snow, the wind blows the snow.
Hey ho, I'm freezing 'cause
The wind blows the snow.
Five blankets on my bed, five blankets on my bed.
Hey ho, I'm cozy-o
Five blankets on my bed!
The snow doesn't snow,
The wind doesn't blow.
Hey—okey dokey o,
Take the blankets off my bed!

—Jan Irving

Telling Guide

This rhyme can be changed to "boy" or "child" instead of girl.
Hold up thumb.
Put thumb across palm of hand.
Close fingers over thumb.
Put hands up to cheek and close eyes.

Sung to the tune of "The Farmer in the Dell."
Lay arm parallel across chest.
Hug self.

Blow.
Shake all over.
Blow.
Lay other arm over parallel arm.
Hug self.

Blow and howl.
Shake all over.

Lay arm over arm three times.
Hug self.

Wiggle fingers like snow.
Shake all over.

Lay arm over arm four times.
Hug self.

Blow and wiggle fingers.
Shake all over.

Lay arm over arm five times.
Hug self.

The Stars Are Twinkling

The stars are twinkling in the sky.	Wiggle fingers, arms up.
The moon sends silver light.	Move arms to circle head.
They tell us it is time for bed,	"Sleep" on hands.
And so it is. . . . Good night!	Blow kiss in pause.

—Author unknown

Blanket Song

Let's all put a blanket on, blanket on, blanket on.	Motion of hands pulling blanket up to chin.
Let's all put a blanket on, just like this.	
Let's all kick the blanket off, blanket off, blanket off.	Kick off blanket.
Let's all kick the blanket off, just like this.	
Let's all shake the blanket out, blanket out, blanket out.	Motion of shaking blanket.
Let's all shake the blanket out, just like this.	
Let's all fold the blanket up, blanket up, blanket up.	Motion of folding blanket.
Let's all fold the blanket up, just like this.	

—Author unknown

Teddy Bear, Teddy Bear

Teddy bear, teddy, bear,	
Turn around.	Turn in place.
Teddy bear, teddy bear,	
Touch the ground.	Reach down and touch the ground.
Teddy bear, teddy bear,	
Show your shoe.	Hold foot out.
Teddy bear, teddy bear,	
That will do.	Shake finger, admonishing.
Teddy bear, teddy bear,	
Run upstairs.	Run in place.
Teddy bear, teddy bear,	
Say your prayers.	Hands folded in front.
Teddy bear, teddy bear,	
Turn out the light.	Turn off light switch.
Teddy bear, teddy bear,	
Say goodnight.	Wave goodnight.

—Traditional rhyme

When Little Fred Went to Bed

When little Fred went to bed,	Fold hands at side of head, eyes closed.
He always said his prayers.	Fold hands in front.
He kissed mama,	Kiss the back of one hand.
And then papa.	Kiss the back of the opposite hand.
And straightway went upstairs.	March in place.

—Traditional rhyme

Wee Willie Winkie

Wee Willie Winkie
Runs through the town.
Upstairs and downstairs
In his nightgown.
Rapping at the windows,
Crying through the lock,
"Are the children all in bed?
For it's now eight o'clock."

—Traditional rhyme

Run in place.
Point up and then down.

Motion of tapping.
Cup hands around mouth.

Tap on wrist, indicating a watch, or hold up eight fingers.

Good Night, Sleep Tight

Good night, sleep tight.
Wake up bright
In the morning light.
To do what's right
With all your might.

—Traditional rhyme

Place hand to side of head, eyes closed, as if sleeping.

Open eyes and stretch!

Show those muscles!

Angels at the Foot

Angels at the foot,
And angels at the head.
And like a curly little lamb,
My pretty babe in bed.

—Traditional rhyme

Point to feet.
Point to head.

Fold hands at side of head; pretend to sleep.

The Man in the Moon

The man in the moon
Looked out of the moon,
Looked out of the moon and said,
"'Tis time for the children
It's time for all children
To think about getting to bed."

—Traditional rhyme

Make circle around head with hands.
Point to eyes.

Tap wrist to indicate a watch.

Rest head on hands, pretending to sleep.

A Glass of Milk and a Slice of Bread

A glass of milk,
And a slice of bread,
And then good-night,
We must go to bed.

—Traditional rhyme

Pretend to hold glass.
Place hand out in front, palm up.
Wave.
Fold hands at side of head; pretend to sleep.

This is a great rhyme to do with puppets or flannel or Velcro board figures and a big, big bed! This rhyme can be sung or chanted.
Hold up ten fingers.

Ten in the Bed

There were ten in the bed,
And the little one said,

"Roll over! Roll over!"
So they all rolled over,
And one fell out.
There was one in the bed,
And the little one said,
"I'm lonely!"

Roll hands around each other.

Continue down to one.

Make a sad face.

— Traditional rhyme

Sleep

The tree leaves are murmuring hua-la-la.
Baby's very sleepy and wants his mama.
Go to sleep, my baby, and then go to bed,
And any bogie-boo that comes,
I'll knock him on the head!

Raise arms up in air; wiggle fingers for moving leaves. / Rub eyes.

Rock "baby" in arms.

Take fist to head.

— Traditional Chinese rhyme

A Lullaby

The heaven is bright,
The earth is bright,
I have a baby who cries all night.
Let those who pass read what I write,
And they'll sleep all night,
'Til broad daylight.

Point to the sky.

Make circle in front of body with hands.

Rub eyes.

Place hands out in front, palms toward body; move head as if reading.

Make large circle overhead to represent sun.

— Traditional Chinese rhyme

Sleep, Sleepy

Sleep, sleepy,
Sleep, sleep.
My little poppet
Is going to sleep
In the arms of her mommy
Who lulls her tenderly.
Sleep, sleepy,
Sleep, sleep.

Rub eyes.

Fold hands at side of head, eyes closed.

Point to arms.

Rock "baby" back and forth in arms.

Rub eyes, put hands to side of head, and close eyes.

— Traditional French rhyme

Go to Bed Late

Go to bed late,
Stay very small;
Go to bed early,
Grow very tall!

Move hands close together to indicate size.

Stretch hand high above head!

— Traditional rhyme

The Little Baby

Sung to the tune of "Eensy Weensy Spider."

The little tiny baby
Lay on the floor and cried.
In came the Mom and

Lie down and cry.

Hugged her 'til she sighed.

Mom hugs.

Now came the Dad who
Played peek-a-boo 'til she smiled,

Mime peek-a-boo.

And the little tiny baby
Lay down her sleepy head.

Pretend to sleep.

—Carolyn N. Cullum

Bedtime

Sung to the tune of "The Farmer in the Dell." Do motions as the song indicates.

It's time to go to bed; it's time to go to bed.
Let's get ready now.
It's time to go to bed.
I brush my teeth this way; I brush my teeth this way.
Up, down, and rinse it now.
I brush my tecth this way.
I put my PJs on; I put my PJs on.
Pull them up, then over my head.
I put my PJs on.
I pull the covers up; I lay my small head down.
I close my eyes and go to sleep
Until the morning light.

—Carolyn N. Cullum

Bedtime

Up the stairs,

Pretend to walk upstairs.

Turn out the light.

Motion of flipping switch.

It is time to say goodnight.

Point to watch.

Fluff my pillow,

Do motion.

Hop in bed.

Move up and down.

On my pillow, I lay my head.

Lay head on hands.

Pull up the covers,

Do motion.

Close my eyes.

Close eyes.

Oops! Grab my teddy,

Motion of grabbing stuffed animal.

Don't need anything more!
Close my eyes again,

Close eyes.

And begin to snore!

Snore!

—Barbara Scott

Go to Bed

Go to bed, you sleepyhead.

Rub eyes; make tired motion.

On your pillow lay your head.

Lay head on hands.

Close your eyes.

Close eyes.

Breathe in and out,

Breathe deeply.

Oh so deep.
In just a few moments,
You'll be fast asleep.

Snore.

—Barbara Scott

Rock-a-Bye Baby

Rock-a-bye-baby	Pretend to rock baby.
In the treetop.	Point upward.
When the wind blows,	Blow.
The cradle will rock.	Pretend to rock baby.
When the bough breaks,	Hold fists apart; make quick downward motion. / Bring hands to lap.
The cradle will fall,	
And down will come baby	Pretend to rock.
Cradle and all.	

—Adapted traditional rhyme by Susan M. Dailey

Bed Time

The fingers are so sleepy!	Begin with one hand in a fist. Lay fist on opposite hand.
It's time to go to bed.	
Come little Baby Finger	Lay little finger of fist on palm.
You must first tuck in your head.	
Ring Finger creeps in slowly	Lay ring finger of fist on palm.
And who's next but Tallman Straight!	Lay middle finger of fist on palm.
Come, Pointer Finger, hurry,	
For 'tis getting late.	Lay pointer finger of fist on palm.
Now snuggle close, you little men	Wiggle fingers slightly.
There's just one more to come!	
The bed is plenty wide enough for	
Little Master Thumb!	Lay thumb on fist of palm.

—Maude Burnham

Books to Share

Crimi, Carolyn. 2008. *Where's My Mummy?* Somerville, MA: Candlewick Press. ISBN: 978-0763631963.

Dewdney, Anna. 2005. *Llama, Llama, Red Pajama.* New York: Viking Juvenile. ISBN: 978-0670059836.

Grover, Lori Ann. 2009. *Bedtime Kiss for Little Fish.* New York: Cartwheel Books. ISBN: 978-0545128230.

Shea, Bob. 2008. *Dinosaur vs. Bedtime.* New York: Hyperion. ISBN: 978-1423113355.

Sierra, Judy. 2009. *Sleepy Little Alphabet: A Bedtime Story from Alphabet Town.* New York: Knopf Books for Young Readers. ISBN: 978-0375840029.

Willems, Mo. 2006. *Don't Let the Pigeon Stay Up Late!* New York: Hyperion Books for Children. ISBN: 978-0786837465.

Musical Selections

"Down in Sleepytown" from *Hunk-Ta Bunk-Ta Wiggle* by Katherine Dines. ASIN: B000MGTNE6.

"Dream Song" from *Bloom* by Zak Morgan. ASIN: B0001ARHAU.

"Jim Gill's Lullaby" from *Jim Gill Makes It Noisy in Boise, Idaho* by Jim Gill. Available: www.jimgill.com (accessed March 2, 2010).

"Quiet Time" from *We All Live Together*, vol. 1, by Greg and Steve. ASIN: B00000DGMR.

"Ten in a Bed" from *Great Big Hits 2* by Sharon, Lois, and Bram. ASIN: B00007163I.

"Yawn, Yawn, Yawn" from *Yummy Yummy* by The Wiggles. ASIN: B0000AE5YO.

Sources

Anonymous. 2001. *Baby's First Nursery Treasury*. Fairfield, IA: Books Are Fun.

Burnham, Maude. 1910. *Rhymes for Little Hands*. East Longmeadow, MA: Milton Bradley Company.

Cullum, Carolyn N. 2007. *The Storytime Sourcebook II*. New York: Neal-Schuman.

Dailey, Susan M. 2001. *A Storytime Year*. New York: Neal-Schuman.

Headland, Isaac Taylor. 1900. *Chinese Mother Goose Rhymes*. Grand Rapids, MI: Fleming H. Revell.

Index of Rhymes. Available: www.kidsnurseryrhymes.co.uk/rhymes (accessed March 3, 2010).

Irving, Jan, and Robin Currie. 1991. *Raising the Roof: Children's Stories and Activities on Houses*. Santa Barbara, CA: Teacher Ideas Press.

Mama Lisa's World of Children & International Culture. Available: www.mamalisa.com (accessed March 4, 2010).

The Mother Goose Pages. Available: www-personal.umich.edu/~pfa/dreamhouse/nursery (accessed March 4, 2010).

North Central Library Co-operative. n.d. *Storytime Booklet* [out of print].

Rossetti, Christina G. 1893. *Sing-Song: A Nursery Rhyme Book*. New York: Macmillan and Company.

Songs for Teaching: Using Music to Promote Learning. Available: www.songsforteaching.com (accessed March 4, 2010).

Bees
Buzzing here, buzzing there, buzzing bees are everywhere!

Rhyme	Telling Guide
### The Beehive	
Here is the beehive.	Show fist.
Where are the bees.	Raise hands in the air, questioning.
Hidden away where nobody sees.	Point to fist, shake head.
Watch as they come out of their hive—	Wiggle fingers.
One, two, three, four, five.	Show fingers.
They're alive! Bzzzzzzz!	Wiggle fingers.
—Traditional rhyme	
### Five Busy Bees	
Five busy bees on a day so sunny.	Hold up all fingers on one hand.
Number one said, "I'd like to make some honey."	Bend down first finger.
Number two said, "Tell me, where shall it be?"	Bend down second finger.
Number three said, "In the old honey tree."	Bend down third finger.
Number four said, "Let's gather pollen sweet."	Bend down fourth finger.
Number five said, "Let's take it on our feet."	
—From Hummingbird Educational Resources	
### Two Big Beehives	
Two big beehives	Hold out two fists
Closed up tight,	
Protecting sleeping bees	Rest head on hands.
All through the night.	
When the morning sun	Make circle with arms overhead.
Shows its light,	
Ten little bees	Hold up two fists.
Take to flight.	Open hands and wiggle fingers.
—From Hummingbird Educational Resources	
### Hey, Bee	
Looked up to the sky and what did I see.	Look up to the sky, hand to forehead, in a searching motion.
But five little bees buzzin' by me.	Wiggle five fingers in the air.
I said, "Hey bees, hey bees, what are you doing?"	Place hand to mouth, calling.
"We don't know, but we gotta keep movin'."	Wiggle five fingers in the air.
	Look up to the sky, hand to forehead, in a searching motion.
Looked up to the sky and what did I see.	
But four little bees buzzin' by me.	Wiggle four fingers in the air.
I said, "Hey bees, hey bees, what are you doing?"	Place hand to mouth, calling.
"We don't know, but we gotta keep movin'."	Wiggle four fingers in the air.

Looked up to the sky and what did I see.
But three little bees buzzin' by me.
I said, "Hey bees, hey bees, what are you doing?"
We don't know, but we gotta keep movin'."

Look up to the sky, hand to forehead, in a searching motion.
Three fingers wiggling in the air.
Place hand to mouth, calling.
Wiggle three fingers in the air.

Looked up to the sky and what did I see.
But two little bees buzzin' by me.
I said, "Hey bees, hey bees, what are you doing?"
"We don't know, but we gotta keep movin'."

Look up to the sky, hand to forehead, in a searching motion.
Wiggle two fingers in the air.
Place hand to mouth, calling.
Wiggle two fingers in the air.

Looked up to the sky and what did I see.
But one little bee buzzin' by me.
I said, "Hey bee, hey bee, what are you doing?"
I don't know, but I gotta keep movin'."
—From Hummingbird Educational Resources

Look up to the sky, hand to forehead, in a searching motion.
One finger wiggling in the air.

Wiggle one finger in the air.

A Bee Is on Me!

A bee is on my bonnet,
A bee is on my nose.
A bee is on my shoulder,
A bee is even on my toes.
Buzz! Buzz! Buzz!
This bee is bugging me.
Help me! Help me!
How can I be free?
A bee is in my hair,
A bee is in my pants.
A bee is in my ears,
A bee is making me dance.
Buzz! Buzz! Buzz!
This bee is bugging me.
Help me! Help me!
How can I be free?
The bee is near my socks,
The bee is near my shoes.
SPLAT!
Bee, I know how to take care of you!
—From Hummingbird Educational Resources

Point to head.
Point to nose.
Point to shoulder.
Point to toes.

Point to hair.
Point to pants.
Point to ears.
Wiggle all around.

Point to socks.
Point to shoes.
Smack hand onto floor.

Baby Bumblebee

I'm bringing home a baby bumblebee,
Won't my mommy be so proud of me.
I'm bringing home a baby bumblebee.
OUCH! It stung me!

Have lots of fun singing this song!

Cup hands together as if holding bee.

Shake hands as if just stung.

I'm squishing up the baby bumblebee,
Won't my mommy be so proud of me.
I'm squishing up the baby bumblebee.

Squish bee between palms of hands.

Ewwwww . . . it's yucky!

Open hands to look at "mess."

I'm wiping off the baby bumblebee,
Won't my mommy be so proud of me.
I'm wiping off the baby bumblebee.

Wipe hands off on shirt, pants, floor, etc.

Now my mommy won't be mad at me!

Hold hands up to show they are clean.

ADDITIONAL VERSES:
"I'm washin' off the baby bumblebee . . ."
"I'm dryin' off the baby bumblebee . . ."
"I'm sweepin' up the baby bumblebee . . ."
—Traditional rhyme

Peek into the Beehive

Peek into the beehive,
And what do we see . . .

Place hands above eyes, looking.

Buzzing little bees,
Happy as can be!
Count the bees . . . one, two, three.

Count three fingers.

—From Learning Wonders

Bees, Bees, Bees

Bees, bees, bees,
One, two, three.

Count three fingers.

Buzzing around, up and down.

Buzz fingers as words indicate.

In the hive and out they go,

Move fingers in and out.

To the flowers to and fro.

Move fingers in and out again.

Working making honey, you know.
Bees, bees, bees,
One, two, three.

Count three fingers.

—From Learning Wonders

Happy Bees

One happy bee feeling rather blue,

Hold up one finger.

Along came another and then there were two.
Two happy bees buzzing in a tree,

Hold up two fingers.

Along came another and then there were three.
Three happy bees by the front door,

Hold up three fingers.

Along came another and then there were four.
Four happy bees buzzing near a hive,

Hold up four fingers.

Along came another and then there were five.
Five happy bees all having so much fun.

Hold up five fingers.

They buzzed into the hive and then there were none!
—From Learning Wonders

Five Little Bees

One little bee flew near you.
He met a friend and that made two.
Two little bees, busy as could be—
Along came another and that made three.
Three little bees wanted one more,
Found one soon and that made four.
Four little bees going to the hive.
Spied their little brother and that made five.
Five little bees working every hour—
Buzz away, bees, and find every flower.

—From Learning Wonders

Hold up one finger.

Hold up two fingers.

Hold up three fingers.

Hold up four fingers.

Hold up five fingers.

This is a great rhyme to do as a flannel or Velcro board activity.

Ten Buzzing Bees

Ten buzzing bees flying near the gate.
Two flew home. That left only eight.
Eight buzzing bees flying near some sticks.
Two flew home. That left only six.
Six buzzing bees flying near the shore.
Two flew home. That left only four.
Four buzzing bees flying near the canoe.
Two flew home. That left only two.
Two buzzing bees in the sun.
They flew home. Now there are none.

—Robin Suitt

Bumblebee

Bee, bee, bumblebee.
Sting a man upon his knee.
Sting a pig upon his snout,
One, two, three, four, five—you're out!

—From *Let's Do Fingerplays*

Rest index finger on thumb for bee.
"Sting" knee.
"Sting" nose.
Point out each finger.

This action rhyme is done just like "Simon Says . . ." Suit actions to words. If you follow through with all of the actions, it's a great storyhour opener!

Queen Bee Says . . .

Queen Bee says:
. . . buzz.
. . . fly to the wall.
. . . smell a flower.
. . . flap your wings.
. . . jump.
. . . stand on one foot.
. . . sit down.

—Adapted traditional rhyme

Bumblebee, Bumblebee

Bumblebee, bumblebee,
Landing on my nose.
Bumblebee, bumblebee,
Now he's on my toes.
On my arms, on my legs,
On my elbows.
Bumblebee, bumblebee,
He lands and then he goes!

—Adapted traditional rhyme

Sung to the tune of "Jingle Bells."

Point to parts of the body as they are mentioned.

"Buzz, Buzz, Buzz" Says the Great Buzzing Bee

"Buzz, buzz, buzz," says the great buzzing bee.
"Go away, butterfly—this flower's for me!"
"Why? Why? Why?" says the small butterfly.
"If you may sit on this flower, why mayn't I?"

—Traditional rhyme

Move right hand, fingers together, around like a bee.

Dismissing motion; point to self.

Cross hands in front; hook thumbs and flap fingers. / Point to self.

There Was a Bee

There was a bee,
Sat on a wall.

And "buzz" said he,
And that is all.

—Traditional rhyme

This is a great rhyme to do with a finger or hand puppet!

Make right hand the bee.

Hold left arm out in front, bent at elbow, and sit "bee" on top of it.

"Buzz" bee around.

Shrug shoulders.

Five Little Bees 💿

One little bee flew and flew.
He met a friend and that made two.
Two little bees, busy as could be—
Along came another and that made three.
Three little bees wanted one more.
Found one soon and that made four.
Four little bees, going to the hive,
Spied their little brother and that made five.
Five little bees working every hour—
Buzz away, bees, and find another flower.

—Lynda Roberts

This is also a fun rhyme to do with finger puppets or as a flannel or Velcro board activity.

Hold up fingers as the rhyme progresses.

Buzz, Buzz

Buzz, buzz, buzz the bees
All around the hive.

Sung to the tune of "Row, Row, Row Your Boat."

Have children buzz circling a hive.

Making honey all day long
For when the Queen arrives.

—Carolyn N. Cullum

One Little Buzzing Bee

This is also a great rhyme to do as a flannel or Velcro board activity.
Begin rhyme with one finger up, and add fingers as the rhyme progresses.

One little buzzing bee,
Buzzing all around.
Two little buzzing bees
Know there's work to be found.
Three little buzzing bees
With lots of work to do.
Four little buzzing bees
See how far they flew!
Five little buzzing bees
Buzzing 'round the hive.
Let's count those buzzing bees again:
One, two, three, four, five!

—Barbara Scott

A Swarm of Bees

A swarm of bees in May
Is worth a load of hay.   Make mound with hands.

A swarm of bees in June
Is worth a silver spoon.   Pretend to eat.

A swarm of bees in July
Is not worth a fly.   Shake head "no."

—Traditional rhyme

Bumblebee, Bumblebee

Sung to the tune of "Teddy Bear, Teddy Bear" or chanted.

Bumblebee, bumblebee,
Buzz around.   Flap arms; move around in a circle.
Bumblebee, bumblebee,
Land on the ground.   Squat down.
Bumblebee, bumblebee,
Fly up high!   Pretend to fly up.
Bumblebee, bumblebee,
Reach for the sky!   Reach up and stretch!
Bumblebee, bumblebee,
Land on my nose.   Point to nose.
Bumblebee, bumblebee,
Land on my toes.   Point to toes.
Bumblebee, bumblebee,
Flap one wing.   Flap one arm.
Bumblebee, bumblebee,
Please don't sting!   Shake head "no."

—Adapted traditional rhyme

Over in the Meadow

Over in the meadow	
In a snug beehive,	Show fist.
Lived a mother honey bee	Raise index finger of right hand.
And her little bees five.	Raise five fingers of left hand.
"Buzz!" said the mother;	Wiggle index finger.
"We buzz!" said the five.	Wiggle five fingers of left hand.
So they buzzed and they hummed	Buzz and hum.
In the snug beehive.	Show fist.

—Adapted traditional rhyme

Five Little Bees

Five little bees buzzing 'round my back door.	Begin this rhyme with five fingers.
One flew away and then there were four.	Take away fingers as rhyme progresses.
Four little bees buzzing 'round the oak tree.	
One flew away and then there were three.	
Three little bees buzzing in the morning dew.	
One flew away and then there were two.	
Two little bees buzzing in the noonday sun.	
One flew away and then there was one.	
One little bee buzzing 'til the day is done.	
He flew away and then there were none.	

—Barbara Scott

Buzzing Bees

Buzzing bees,	*Sung to the tune of "Jingle Bells."*
Buzzing bees,	Place index finger and thumb together to represent bee.
Buzzing all around.	Fly fingers together.
They land and rest on flowers	Make flower with hands: palms together, cup fingers out.
Where there's nectar to be found.	
Flying here,	Point in one direction.
Landing there,	Point in the opposite direction.
'Round the garden fly.	Make circle with finger.
They drink their fill and then take off	
Flying toward the sky!	Point up.

—Adapted traditional rhyme

Honey Bee

Honey bee, honey bee	*Sung to the tune of "Are You Sleeping?"*
Where are you.	
Where are you?	Place hand over eyes; peer around.
Find a pretty flower,	
Drink up all the nectar.	Make flower with hands: palms together, cup fingers out. / Sucking sound.
Buzz, buzz, buzz!	
Buzz, buzz, buzz!	

—Adapted traditional rhyme

If You're a Busy Bee

If you're a busy bee, flap your wings.
If you're a busy bee, flap your wings.
If you're a busy bee, then sing along with me.
If you're a busy bee, flap your wings.

ADDITIONAL VERSES:
. . . shake your stinger.
. . . do your dance.
. . . do all three!

—Adapted traditional rhyme

Sung to the tune of "If You're Happy and You Know It."
Flap arms.

Wiggle bottom.
Dance in a figure eight motion, just like the bees do!

Hey! A Bee Stung Me!

I saw a pretty yellow rose.
I lifted it up to my nose.
When all of a sudden,
I heard a sound.
That made me drop it
On the ground.
"Ouch!" I yelled. "Oh goodness me!
I've been stung by a bumblebee!"

—Barbara Scott

Point to nose.

Point to ear.

Motion of dropping something.

Shake hand as if smarting from a sting.

Honey

Honey, honey, oh so sweet!
Honey, honey, good to eat!
Good on biscuits,
Good on bread.
In recipes, use for sugar instead!
Honey is such an awesome treat!
Honey, honey, can't be beat!

—Barbara Scott

Clap three times.
Rub tummy.
Make circle with hand.
Hold hand out flat.

Move hands to show excitement.
Clap three times.

How Many Eyes Does a Honeybee Have?

How many eyes does a honeybee have.
A honeybee have, a honeybee have?
How many eyes does a honeybee have.
A honeybee has five eyes!*

—Barbara Scott

Sung to the tune of "The Mulberry Bush."

Point to eyes.

Point to eyes.
Hold up five fingers.

*A honeybee has two compound eyes and three simple eyes. The compound eyes are located on each side of the head, and the simple eyes are located on the top!

I'm a Little Bumblebee

I'm a little bumblebee,
Watch me fly!
First to a flower,
And then to my hive.
I carry nectar
There to make
Honey that tastes really great!

—Adapted traditional rhyme

Bless You, Bless You, Bonny Bee

Bless you, bless you, bonny bee.
Say when will your wedding be.
If it be tomorrow day,
Take your wings and fly away.

—Traditional English rhyme

Counting Bees

Counting bees is so much fun!
Let's begin . . . here's bee number one.
There's a bee that's landed on my shoe.
Let's count . . . that's bee number two.
There's a bee landing up in the tree.
Let's count . . . that's bee number three.
I spy a bee flying out the door.
Let's count . . . that's bee number four.
I see a bee coming out of the hive.
Let's count . . . that's bee number five.
There's a bee on that pile of sticks.
Let's count . . . that's bee number six.
Look, a bee flying up toward heaven.
Let's count . . . that's bee number seven.
There's a bee landing on my plate!
Let's count . . . that's bee number eight.
We're almost done, we're doing fine.
Look! There's bee number nine.
We are almost to the end.
I see a bee and he's number ten!

—Barbara Scott

Sung to the tune of "I'm a Little Teapot."

Flap arms.
Make flower with hands: palms together, cup fingers out. / Make fist.
Cup hands.

Rub tummy.

Place index finger and thumb together to represent bee.
Cock head to side, questioning.

Flap arms.

Count on fingers as the rhyme progresses.

Honey

I know a food that's made by bees,
And honey is its name-o.
H-O-N-E-Y,
H-O-N-E-Y,
H-O-N-E-Y,
And honey is its name-o.

—Adapted traditional rhyme

Sung to the tune of "Bingo." You can place the letters on your flannel or Velcro board or on a glove when they are mentioned; taking away the letters helps in singing the song.

Busy Bees

One, two, three, four, five
Busy bees in the beehive.
Six, seven, eight, nine, ten
Buzzing out and in again.

—Barbara Scott

Count on fingers.
Show fist.
Count on fingers.
Make motions out, fingers spread, and in, making fist.

We Are Busy, Busy Buzzing Bumblebees

We are busy, busy, buzzing bumblebees.
We are busy, busy, buzzing bumblebees.
Oh, we buzz around all day,
First we land, then fly away
We are busy, busy, buzzing bumblebees.
We are busy making honey in our hive,
We are busy making honey in our hive.
Oh, the nectar we will take
And into honey make
We are busy making honey in our hive.

—Adapted traditional rhyme

Sung to the tune of "If You're Happy and You Know It." Encourage children to say "Buzz, buzz" along with you.
"Buzz, buzz" and fly index finger and thumb together around.
"Buzz, buzz."
"Buzz" while flying fingers around.
Motions of landing, flying.
"Buzz, buzz."
"Buzz, buzz."
"Buzz, buzz."

Rub tummy.
"Buzz, buzz."

Five Little Worker Bees

Five little worker bees working very hard.
Buzzing 'round the flowers in my back yard.
Five little worker bees and not one more.
One little worker flew back to the hive and now there are four.
Four little worker bees, as you can plainly see.
One little worker found another flower and now there are three.
Three little worker bees collect nectar like sticky glue.
One little worker stopped to take a nap and now there are two.
Two little worker bees flying in the sun.
One little worker found some shade and now there is one.
One little worker bee, the job is almost done.
That little worker bee flew home and now there are none.

—Barbara Scott

Begin rhyme with five fingers up.
Wiggle fingers.

Take away fingers as rhyme progresses.

One Little Buzzy Bee

One little buzzy bee
To the garden flew.
He met a friend there,
And that makes two.
Two little buzzy bees
Flying 'round the tree,
Were joined by another friend,
And that makes three.
Three little buzzy bees
Into the air they soar,
Were joined by another friend,
And that makes four.
Four little buzzy bees
Buzzing 'round their hive,
Were joined by another friend,
And then there were five.

—Barbara Scott

Hold up index finger.

Add middle finger.

Add ring finger.

Add little finger.

Add thumb.

Oh Honeybee, Oh Honeybee

Oh honeybee, oh honey bee,
How hard you must be working!
Oh honeybee, oh honey bee,
How hard you must be working!
You take the nectar from the flowers
That grow upon the garden bowers.
Oh honeybee, oh honey bee,
How hard you must be working!

—Adapted traditional rhyme

Sung to the tune of "O Christmas Tree, O Christmas Tree."
Place index finger and thumb together to represent bee.

Make flower with hands: palms together, cup fingers out.
Place index finger and thumb together to represent bee.

The Bee's a Busy Little Chap

The bee's a busy little chap.
He cannot stop to talk.
He flits among the flowers
That grow along the walk.
He takes the nectar out of them
And turns it into honey.
Take one look and you'll agree
He's a busy little buggy!

—Barbara Scott

Shake head "no."
Make flower with hands: palms together, cup fingers out.
Pretend to drink.
Rub tummy.
Nod head "yes."

Five Little Bees

Five little bees were having a race.
The first one said, "I want to win first place!"
The second one said, "See how fast I can fly!"

Begin rhyme with five fingers up. Starting with the thumb, point to each in succession.

The third one said, "Watch me streak toward the sky."
The fourth one said, "Don't be so slow."
The fifth one said, "Ready, set, let's go!"

—Barbara Scott

Books to Share

Bentley, Dawn. 2004. *Buzz-Buzz, Busy Bees: An Animal Sounds Book.* New York: Little Simon. ISBN: 978-0689868481.

Carle, Eric. 2001. *The Honeybee and the Robber.* New York: Philomel. ISBN: 978-0399237317.

Hazen, Lynn. 2005. *Buzz Bumble to the Rescue.* London: Bloomsbury Publishing. ISBN: 978-1582349329.

Lewison, Wendy C. 1992. *Buzz, Said the Bee.* New York: Cartwheel Books. ISBN: 978-0590441858.

Smallman, Steve. 2007. *The Very Greedy Bee.* Wilton, CT: Tiger Tales. ISBN: 978-1589250659.

Yorinks, Arthur. 2005. *Happy Bees!* New York: Harry N. Abrams. ISBN: 978-0810958661.

Musical Selections

"Bee Bee Bumblebee" from *One Elephant, Deux Elephants* by Sharon, Lois, and Bram. ASIN: B000068QQ0.

"Bees in the Hive" and "The Bee Bop" from *Songs about Insects, Bugs, and Squiggly Things* by Jane Lawliss Murphy. Kimbo Educational Audio, 1993. ISBN: 978-1563460333.

"Bumblebee" from *Debbie's Ditties 3 at the Library* by Debbie Clement. Available: www.rainbowswithinreach.com (accessed March 4, 2010).

"Bumblebee (Buzz, Buzz)" from *Buzz Buzz* by Laurie Berkner. Available: www.laurieberkner.com (will be forwarded to Two Tomatoes Records' official store; accessed March 4, 2010).

"Jingle Bell Bees" from *Rhythms on Parade* by Hap Palmer. Available: www.happalmer.com (accessed March 4, 2010).

Sources

Cullum, Carolyn N. 2007. *The Storytime Sourcebook II.* New York: Neal-Schuman.

Grayson, Marion. 1886. *Mother Goose's Complete Melodies.* Chicago: M.A. Donohue & Co.

———. 1962. *Let's Do Fingerplays.* Fairfield, CT: R.B. Luce.

Findlay, Diane, Tami Chumbley Finley, Susan Mast, Kathy Ross, and Patti Sinclair. 2008. *Collaborative Library Summer Program Manual.* Mason City, IA: Collaborative Summer Library Program.

Hummingbird Educational Resources. "Lotsa Lesson Plans—Bees." Available: www.hummingbirded.com/bees.html (accessed March 4, 2010).

Learning Wonders: Learning through Play. Available: www.learningwonders.com/cart/home.php?printable=Y&cat=92&js=n (accessed March 4, 2010).

Mama Lisa's World of Children & International Culture. Available: www.mamalisa.com (accessed March 4, 2010).

Nursery Rhymes—Lyrics, Origins & History! Available: www.rhymes.org.uk (accessed March 4, 2010).

Roberts, Lynda. 1985. *Mitt Magic: Fingerplays for Finger Puppets.* Silver Spring, MD: Gryphon House.

Traditional Music Library. Available: www.traditionalmusic.co.uk (accessed March 4, 2010).

Bubbles to Circus

Bubbles
Pop, pop, pop! It's fun to play with bubbles!
Think about having bubble solution or a bubble-making machine to use.

Rhyme	**Telling Guide**
### My Bubble	*Sung to the tune of "My Bonnie Lies Over the Ocean."*
My bubble flew over the ocean,	Make circle with hands; move to right.
My bubble flew over the sea.	Make circle with hands; move to left.
My bubble flew over the rainbow,	Make arc over head with arm.
Oh, come back, my bubble to me!	
Come back, come back,	Beckoning motion.
Oh, come back my bubble, to me, to me!	Point to self.
Come back, come back,	Beckoning motion.
Oh, come back, my bubble, to me.	Point to self.
—Author unknown	
### Blowing Bubbles	
Blowing bubbles every day,	
I blow them all around.	Blow.
Then I watch them float up high,	
Or pop upon the ground.	Clap once.
—Jean Warren	
### Blow, Blow, Blow	
Blow, blow, blow, blow,	Blow into cupped hands.
I blow and then I stop.	Open hands wider.
For if I keep on blowing,	Open hands still wider.
My bubble will surely pop!	Clap once.
—Jean Warren	
### Soap Bubbles	
Fill the pipe!	
Gently blow;	Blow.
Now you'll see	
The bubbles grow!	Make circle with hands and enlarge as you blow.
Strong at first,	
Then they burst,	Clap hands.
And then they go	
To nothing, o!	Shake head "no."
—From *When Life Was Young*	
### Blow, Blow, Bubble!	
Blow, blow, bubble!	Pretend to blow a bubble.
Round and bright.	Make circle with hands.
Blow, blow, bubble!	

Thin and light.
Ev'ry shade the rainbows wear
I have made my bubble bear.
Blow, blow, bubble!
Round and bright.

—From Songs of Childhood

Make arc over head.
Nod head "yes."
Pretend to blow a bubble.
Make circle with hands.

Let's Count the Bubbles!

One bouncy bubble, floating all around.
Two shiny bubbles, floating near the ground.
Three tiny bubbles, very hard to see.
Four slippery bubbles floating over the tree.
Five bouncing bubbles sliding on the floor.
Six silly bubbles heading out the door.
Seven soapy bubbles coming from the tub.
Eight large bubbles, glub, glub, glub.
Nine rainbow bubbles float and cannot stop.
Ten huge bubbles are ready to go POP!

—Barbara Scott

Begin this rhyme with index finger up.
Add fingers as the rhyme progresses.

Clap hands.

Bubble, Bubble

Sung to the tune of "Teddy Bear, Teddy Bear" or chanted.

Bubble, bubble,
Turn around.
Bubble, bubble,
Land on the ground.
Bubblc, bubblc,
Float up high.
Bubble, bubble,
Float toward the sky.
Bubble, bubble,
Float down low.
Bubble, bubble,
Land on my toe.
Bubble, bubble,
Stop, stop, stop!
Bubble, bubble,
Now go POP!

—Adapted traditional rhyme

Turn in place.

Squat down.

Stand up.

Stand on tiptoe and stretch!

Bend down.

Point to or touch toe.

Hand makes "stop" motion.

Clap.

I'm a Bubble

Sung to the tune of "Alouette."

I'm a bubble,
A bright and shiny bubble.
I'm a bubble;
Watch what I can do!
I can float up very high
Reaching almost to the sky.

Make circle with hands.
Bob hands up and down.

Point to eyes.
Point up.
Stretch!

Floating high, to the sky . . . oh
I'm a bubble,
A bright and shiny bubble.
I'm a bubble;
Watch what I can do!
I'm a bubble,
A bright and shiny bubble.
I'm a bubble;
Watch what I can do!
I can float down very low,
Landing now upon your toe.
Floating low, on your toe . . . oh
I'm a bubble,
A bright and shiny bubble.
I'm a bubble;
Watch what I can do!

Make circle with hands.
Bob hands up and down.

Point to eyes.
Make circle with hands.
Bob hands up and down.

Point to eyes.
Point down.
Touch toe.

Make circle with hands.
Bob hands up and down.

Point to eyes.

—Adapted traditional rhyme

My Bubble

My bubble floats way up in the air.
It's floating all around.
Oh no, it's heading down to the ground.
Pop! Goes my bubble!

—Adapted traditional rhyme

Sung to the tune of "Pop Goes the Weasel."

Make circle with hands and float around.

Make circle go down, down, down.
Clap.

Five Little Bubbles

Five little bubbles floating all around.
The first one said, "I'm falling toward the ground!"
The second one said, "I'm spinning . . . I can't stop!"
The third one said, Watch out, or you will pop!"
The fourth one said, "I'm bouncing in the breeze."
The fifth one said, "More bubbles, if you please!"

—Barbara Scott

Hold up five fingers.

Begin with thumb and point to each in succession.

Bubbles Everywhere

There's bubbles everywhere.
There's bubbles everywhere.
See them bouncing all around,
There's bubbles everywhere.
They're landing on my hair.
They're landing on my hair.
See them bouncing all around,
They're landing on my hair.

ADDITIONAL VERSES:
They're landing on my nose . . .
They're landing on my tummy . . .

Sung to the tune of "The Farmer in the Dell."

Make small circles with thumb and index finger of each hand.

Bob hands up and down.

Land "bubbles" on hair.

Land "bubbles" on nose.
Land "bubbles" on stomach.

They're landing on my knees . . .	Land "bubbles" on knees.
They're landing on my toes . . .	Land "bubbles" on toes.

LAST VERSE:

Watch the bubbles pop!	Clap.
Watch the bubbles pop!	Clap.
See them bouncing all around,	
Watch the bubbles pop!	Clap.

—Adapted traditional rhyme

If You'd Like to Blow a Bubble

	Sung to the tune of "If You're Happy and You Know It."
If you'd like to blow a bubble, clap your hands.	Clap, clap.
If you'd like to blow a bubble, clap your hands.	Clap, clap.
If you'd like to blow a bubble, it's not really any trouble.	
If you'd like to blow a bubble, clap your hands.	Clap, clap.

ADDITIONAL VERSES:

. . . stomp you feet.

. . . nod your head.

. . . do all three.

—Adapted traditional rhyme

See My Bubble

See my bubble,	Make circle with hands.
Watch it sparkle in the sun.	Raise arms overhead for sun.
If it pops, I'll blow another.	Clap on the word "pops."
It is so much fun!	

—Barbara Scott

I Love Bubbles

	Sung to the tune of "Are You Sleeping?"
I love bubbles,	Place one hand over heart.
I love bubbles.	Place two hands over heart.
Yes, I do.	Nod head "yes."
Yes, I do.	
I love to catch them,	Motion of catching.
I love to pop them.	Clap.
How 'bout you?	Point to children.
How 'bout you?	Point to other children.

—Adapted traditional rhyme

Bubbles

	Sung to the tune of "Twinkle, Twinkle, Little Star."
Bubbles small and bubbles round,	Make small circles with hands.
Bubbles landing on the ground.	Make "bubbles" land on ground.
Up into the air they fly,	Make "bubbles" go into the air.
Soaring, floating to the sky.	Point up.
I love bubbles, can't you see?	Hands over heart.
I love them, and they love me!	Point to self.

—Adapted traditional rhyme

Books to Share

Bradley, Kimberly B. 2001. *Pop! A Book about Bubbles.* New York: HarperCollins. ISBN: 978-0060287009.
Mahy, Margaret. 2009. *Bubble Trouble.* New York: Clarion Books. ISBN: 978-0547074214.
Woodruff, Elvira. 1990. *Tubtime.* New York: Holiday House. ISBN: 978-0823407774.

Musical Selections

"Bubbles" from *Yes!* by Geof Johnson. ASIN: B002MZXNS2.
"Bubbles of Joy" from *Achoo! Achoo!* by Maureen Conlin. ASIN: B000T5MWOS.
"The Bubble Wrap Stomp" from *Wiggle Worm Workout* by Stephanie Burton. Available: www.songsforteaching.com (accessed March 5, 2010).
"Little Bubbles" by Susan Harrison. Available: www.songsforteaching.com (accessed March 5, 2010).
"One Little Bubble" from *Preschool Rocks* by Wendy Rollin. Available: www.songsforteaching.com (accessed March 5, 2010).

Sources

Dodge, Mary Mapes. 1894. *When Life Was Young.* New York: Century Company.
Giddings, T. 1923. *Songs of Childhood.* Lexington, MA: Ginn and Company.
McKinnon, Elizabeth, and Gayle Bittinger. 1994. *Busy Bees Spring: Fun for Two's and Three's.* Everett, WA: Warren Publishing House.
Totline Staff, comp. 1994. *1001 Rhymes and Fingerplays.* Everett, MA: Warren Publishing House.
Warren, Jean. 1989. *Theme-a-Saurus.* Everett, MA: Warren Publishing House.
———. 1991. *Toddler Theme-a-Saurus.* Everett, MA: Warren Publishing House.
———. 1996. *Four Seasons Movement.* Everett, MA: Warren Publishing House.

Caterpillars and Butterflies
A perfect topic for spring . . . or anytime!

Rhyme	Telling Guide
## Fuzzy Wuzzy Caterpillar	

Fuzzy Wuzzy Caterpillar

Fuzzy wuzzy caterpillar,
Into a corner creeps.
She spins herself a blanket,
And then goes fast asleep.
Fuzzy wuzzy caterpillar,
Wakes up by and by,
And finds that she has sprouted wings,
Look! She's a butterfly!

—Traditional rhyme

Stand with hands out and palms and fingers together. / Use hands and body to wriggle and "creep."

Spin around in place.

Close eyes; rest cheek on palm of hand.

Pop head up and open eyes.

Put hands out, thumbs together and fingers out like wings. / Flap finger-wings and "fly" away.

The Fuzzy Little Caterpillar

The fuzzy little caterpillar
Curled up on a leaf,
Spun her little chrysalis
And then fell fast asleep.
While she was dreaming,
She dreamed that she could fly.
And later when she woke up,
She was a butterfly!

—Elizabeth McKinnon

Make self small.

Rest cheek on folded hands.

Smile.

Pretend to fly around room.

Pretty Butterfly

Here comes a butterfly and lays an egg,
Out comes a caterpillar with many legs.
Now see the caterpillar spin and spin
A little chrysalis to sleep in.
Then from the chrysalis, my oh my,
Out comes a beautiful butterfly!

—Stella Waldron

Fly fingers onto opposite palm.
Crawl fingers on palm.
Circle fingers on palm.
Close fingers and rest hand on palm.
Open fingers slowly.
Fly fingers away.

Flutter, Flutter, Butterfly

Flutter, flutter, butterfly,
Floating in the summer sky.
Floating by for all to see,
Floating by so merrily.
Flutter, flutter, butterfly,
Floating in the summer sky.

—Bonnie Woodward

Wave arms at sides.
"Float" like butterfly.

Butterfly! Butterfly!

Butterfly, butterfly, where did you go?
Fly up high and then down low.
Butterfly, butterfly, where can you be?
Behind my back where I can't see.
Butterfly, butterfly, what did you hear?
Fluttering wings land on my ear.
Butterfly, butterfly, feel the wind blow.
Now you've landed on my toe.
Butterfly, butterfly, be on your way,
Come back soon another day.

—From *Low-Cost, High-Interest Programming*

This rhyme works well with individual butterfly crafts for children to make. Each child can fly his or her own butterfly!
Flutter butterfly in front of self.
Fly butterfly up and then down.
Flutter butterfly in front of self.
Fly butterfly behind back.
Flutter butterfly in front of self.
Fly butterfly to ear.
Flutter butterfly in front of self.
Fly butterfly to toe.
Flutter butterfly in front of self.
Fly butterfly behind back.

Butterfly, Butterfly

Butterfly, butterfly,
Whence do you come?
I know not, I ask not
Nor ever had a home.
Butterfly, butterfly,
Where do you go?
Where the sun shines,
And where the buds grow.

—Traditional rhyme

Cross hands, lock thumbs, and flap fingers as wings.

Shrug shoulders.
Shake head "no."
Same motion as before.

Make circle overhead with arms.
Hands together in front; move upward, opening as a flower.

Brown and Furry

Brown and furry,
Caterpillar in a hurry.
Take your walk
To the shady leaf or stalk,
Or whatnot.
Which will be the chosen spot?
No toad spy you,
Hovering bird of prey pass by you;
Spin and die,
To live again a butterfly.

—Traditional rhyme

Wiggle index finger of right hand on left arm.

Put hands over head to make "shade."

Finger to mouth, tilt head, questioning.
Point to eyes.
Point to sky.
Move index finger in circular motion.
Cross hands in front, thumbs hooked; "flap" fingers for wings.

The Caterpillar

Fuzzy little caterpillar
Crawling, crawling on the ground!
Fuzzy little caterpillar,
Nowhere, nowhere to be found.
Though we've looked and looked and looked

Wiggle index finger.

Shake head "no."

Everywhere around!
When the little caterpillar
Found his furry coat too tight,
Then a snug cocoon he made him
Spun of silk soft and light.
Rolled himself away within it—
Slept there day and night.
See how this cocoon is stirring!
Now a little head we spy—
What! Is this our caterpillar
Spreading gorgeous wings to dry?
Soon the free and happy creature
Flutters happily by!

—Emilie Poulsson

	Hands and arms span wide area.
	Wiggle finger.
	Hug self.
	Rotate the thumb of right hand, then put inside fingers of same hand.
	Weave fist back and forth.
	Bring thumb out of fist.
	Hands out to sides, questioning.
	Cross hands in front, thumbs hooked; flap fingers for wings.

Butterflies Are Pretty Things

Butterflies are pretty things,
Prettier than you or I;
See the color on his wings—
What would hurt a butterfly?
Softly, softly, girls and boys,
He'll come near us by and by.
Here he is, don't make a noise—
We'll not hurt you, butterfly.
Not to hurt a living thing,
Let all good children try;
See, again, he's on the wing,
Goodbye! Pretty butterfly.

—Traditional rhyme

	ASL sign for butterfly: hands crossed, thumbs hooked, wiggle fingers for wings.
	Use ASL sign.
	Point to children, then self.
	Point to eyes.
	Move arms out, tilting head, questioning.
	Tiptoe fingers of one hand on opposite arm.
	Make "Shhh" motion.
	Use ASL sign.
	Wave.

The Butterfly

Away goes the butterfly.
To catch it I will never try;
The butterfly's about to light,
I would not have it, if I might.

—Traditional Chinese rhyme

	Use ASL sign detailed above for this rhyme too.
	Use ASL sign.
	Make "catching" motion.
	Use ASL sign; "land" butterfly on leg.
	Shake head "no."

Fly, Fly Butterfly

Fly, fly, butterfly,
Flutter all around.
Fly, fly, butterfly,
You barely make a sound.
Fly, fly, butterfly

	Sung to the tune of "Jingle Bells" or chanted. Use ASL sign detailed above for this rhyme too.
	Use ASL sign.
	Make hands fly around in front.
	Continue to fly fingers.
	Make "Shhh" motion.
	Use ASL motion again.

On your colorful wings.
You are truly one
Of nature's beautiful things!

—Barbara Scott

Continue ASL motion.
Hold up one finger.

Good Morning Butterfly

Way up in the sky
The butterflies fly.
While down in their nests,
The butterflies rest.
With a wing to the left,
And a wing to the right,
The sweet little butterflies
Sleep all through the night.
Sh-h-h-h-h, they're sleeping.
The bright sun comes up,
The dew falls away.
Good morning, good morning,
The butterflies say.

—Stephanie Stokes, LibraryPalooza

ASL sign for butterfly: hands crossed, thumbs hooked, wiggle fingers for wings.
Use ASL sign; fly hands high.

Fly hands to lap and rest them.

Continue to hold hooked hands on lap.

Make "Shhh" motion.
Hands make circle above head.
Flutter fingers down.

Use ASL sign; flutter fingers away.

Flutter, Flutter Butterfly

Flutter, flutter, butterfly
Floating in the summer sky.
Floating by for all to see,
Floating by so merrily.
Flutter, flutter, butterfly
Floating in the summer sky.

—Stephanie Stokes, LibraryPalooza

Sung to the tune of "Twinkle, Twinkle, Little Star." Use ASL sign detailed above for this rhyme too. Make your butterfly fly all around!

Caterpillar to Butterfly Scarf Play

The caterpillars are wriggling around,
Wriggling around, wriggling around.
The caterpillars are wriggling around,
All around the yard.
The caterpillars are building a cocoon,
Building a cocoon, building a cocoon.
The caterpillars are building a cocoon,
All around the yard.
The butterflies are flying around,
Flying around, flying around.
The butterflies are flying around,
All around the yard.

—Stephanie Stokes, LibraryPalooza

Sung to the tune of "The Wheels on the Bus." Have children lay down on their scarves and then wriggle around like caterpillars trying to keep the scarf under them.

Have children roll into a ball and cover their heads with scarves.

Have children pick up their scarves and fly with them.

The Little Caterpillar

The little caterpillar crawled up into a tree,
Spun his cocoon and slept so quietly.
All through the winter he didn't make a sound.
He dreamt of his new life when he'd be flying all around.
While he was sleeping the snow did gently fall.
Winter came and went, then he heard the robin's call.
"Come on, Mr. Butterfly, out of your cocoon.
Spread your wings and fly for me, while I sing this tune."
—Stephanie Stokes, LibraryPalooza

Sung to the tune of "The Itsy Bitsy Spider."

Wiggle index finger up opposite arm.
Place hands to side of face, eyes closed.
Shake head "no."

Flutter fingers down.

Beckon.
Use ASL sign detailed below; flutter hands all around.
ASL sign for butterfly: hands crossed, thumbs hooked, wiggle fingers for wings.

Oh, I See a Butterfly

Oh, I see a butterfly,
Way up in the sky.
Butterfly
Flying, flying all around,
Landing gently on the ground.
Butterfly
Flying high and flying low,
Flying fast and flying slow.
Butterfly
Landed on my hand and nose,
On my tummy, on my toes.
Butterfly, butterfly, butterfly.
—Adapted from a song by Susan M. Dailey

Point to sky.

Use ASL sign.
Land hands on ground.

Fly up and down.
Flutter fingers fast, then slow.

Land fingers on nose.
Land fingers on tummy, then toes.
Continue to flutter fingers.

Ten Little Caterpillars

Ten little caterpillars crawling in a line.
One wandered off and then there were nine.
Nine little caterpillars crawling on the gate.
One fell off and then there were eight.
Eight little caterpillars crawling up to heaven.
One went to find some food and then there were seven.
Seven little caterpillars crawling over sticks.
One hid away and then there were six.
Six little caterpillars crawled near the hive.
One spun a cocoon and then there were five.
Five little caterpillars crawling on the door.
One blew off and then there were four.
Four little caterpillars crawling on a tree.
One fell asleep and then there were three.
Three little caterpillars crawling toward you.
One went to play and then there were two.

This is a fun rhyme to do with visuals on the flannel or Velcro board!
Begin this rhyme with ten fingers up.
Take away fingers as the rhyme progresses.

Two little caterpillars crawling in the sun.
One scurried away and then there was one.
One little caterpillar, crawling alone is no fun.
He crawled into a hole and now there are none.

—Barbara Scott

Caterpillar

Caterpillar,
Caterpillar,
Crawlin' 'round,
Crawlin' 'round.
First you crawl on my arm.
Then you crawl on my leg.
'Round and 'round,
'Round and 'round.

Wiggle index finger to represent caterpillar.

Crawl index finger on opposite arm.

Crawl index finger on leg.

Continue to let caterpillar crawl all over.

—Adapted traditional rhyme

Five Sleepy Caterpillars

Five sleepy caterpillars were snoozing in a tree.
The first one said, "It feels cold to me."
The second one said, "Let's make a nice, warm bed."
The third one said, "To rest our weary heads."
The fourth one said, "We'll awaken by and by."
The fifth one said, "We will all be butterflies!"

ASL sign for butterfly: hands crossed, thumbs hooked, wiggle fingers for wings.

Begin this rhyme with five fingers up.

Begin with the thumb; point to each in succession.

Use ASL sign.

—Barbara Scott

Crunch, Crunch

Sung to the tune of "Gung Gung Went the Little Green Frog One Day."

Crunch, crunch went the little green bug one day,
Crunch, crunch went the little green bug.
Crunch, crunch went the little green bug one day,
And his tummy went yum, yum, yum!

One hand represents caterpillar; other hand is the leaf for the caterpillar to "munch" on.

Rub tummy.

—Adapted traditional rhyme

Butterfly, Butterfly

This rhyme can be sung to the tune of "Teddy Bear, Teddy Bear" or chanted.

Butterfly, butterfly,
Fly around.
Butterfly, butterfly,
Land on the ground.
Butterfly, butterfly,
Stand and sing.
Butterfly, butterfly,
Flap one wing.
Butterfly, butterfly,
Fly up high!

Fly around in a circle.

Squat down.

Stand and sing a note: la!

Flap one arm.

Flap arms; stand on tiptoes.

Sung to the tune of "Frère Jacques."

Butterfly, butterfly,
Wink one eye.
Butterfly, butterfly,
Day is done.
Butterfly, butterfly,
Sleep 'til the morning sun.

—Adapted traditional rhyme

Wink.

Yawn.

Head on hands; close eyes.

The Sleepy Caterpillar

The caterpillar yawned and said,
"I think it's time I made my bed.
I'll spin a cocoon with all my might,
And wrap myself against the cold so tight.
No longer a caterpillar, but a _____.

—Barbara Scott

ASL sign for butterfly: hands crossed, thumbs hooked, wiggle fingers for wings.
Yawn.
Tap wrist to indicate watch.
Hold up index finger; with other hand, make fist around finger.
Let children guess the word "butterfly." Then use ASL sign.

Caterpillars Crawl

Caterpillars crawl one by one,
Hurrah, hurrah!
Caterpillars crawl one by one,
Hurrah, hurrah!
Caterpillars crawl one by one.
They won't stop until they're done.
And they all go crawling up in the trees,
To get out of the cold.

Sung to the tune of "The Ants Go Marching."

Hold up one finger; add fingers as the rhyme progresses.

ADDITIONAL VERSES:
Caterpillars crawl two by two . . .
  one of them stops to say "Achoo!"
Caterpillars crawl three by three . . .
  one of them stops to look at a tree.
Caterpillars crawl four by four . . .
  one of them stops to look for more.
Caterpillars crawl five by five . . .
  one of them stops to take a dive.
Caterpillars crawl six by six . . .
  one of them stops on a pile of sticks.
Caterpillars crawl seven by seven . . .
  one of them stops to look to heaven.
Caterpillars crawl eight by eight . . .
  one of them stops on the garden gate.
Caterpillars crawl nine by nine . . .
  one of them stops a while to dine.

Caterpillars crawl ten by ten . . .
    one of them stops to say, "The end!"
—Adapted traditional rhyme

Ten Little Butterflies

Sung to the tune of "Ten Little Indians."

One little, two little, three little butterflies,
Four little, five little, six little butterflies,
Seven little, eight little, nine little butterflies,
Ten little butterflies.

Count out on fingers on the first verse.

Ten little, nine little, eight little butterflies,
Seven little, six little, five little butterflies,
Four little, three little, two little butterflies,
One little butterfly.

Take away fingers on the second verse.

—Adapted traditional rhyme

I'm a Little Caterpillar

Sung to the tune of "I'm a Little Teapot."

I'm a caterpillar,
Watch me spin   Move index finger in small circle.
A snug cocoon   Hug self.
That I'll live in.
When the springtime comes,
And snows all melt,   Wiggle fingers to the sides.
A beautiful butterfly   Use ASL sign for butterfly: hands crossed, thumbs hooked, wiggle fingers for wings.
Will come out!

—Adapted traditional rhyme

Butterfly, Butterfly

Sung to the tune of "Jingle Bells." ASL sign for butterfly: hands crossed, thumbs hooked, wiggle fingers for wings.

Butterfly, butterfly   Use ASL sign.
Flying all around.   Do motions as indicated in the rhyme.
First you fly way up high,
And now you're on the ground.
Flying here, flying there,
It seems you never stop.   Shake head "no."
Until you fly way up high   Point up.
And land in the treetops!   Hold arms out to sides to represent tree.

—Adapted traditional rhyme

Creeping, Crawling Caterpillar

Creeping, crawling caterpillar,
Crawl along the ground.   Crawl finger on the ground.
Creeping, crawling caterpillar,
Shhh! Don't make a sound.   Make "Shhh" motion.
Creeping, crawling caterpillar,

All the winter sleep.
Creeping, crawling caterpillar,
In your cocoon so deep.
Creeping, crawling caterpillar,
It's springtime by and by.
Creeping, crawling caterpillar,
You've become a butterfly!

—Adapted traditional rhyme

Place head on hands, eyes closed.

Make fist to represent cocoon.

Move hands to show expanse.

Use ASL sign for butterfly: hands crossed, thumbs hooked, wiggle fingers for wings.

I'm a Caterpillar

Sung to the tune of "The Mulberry Bush."

This is the way I crawl on the ground,
Crawl on the ground, crawl on the ground.
This is the way I crawl on the ground.
I'm a caterpillar.

Use index finger to represent caterpillar; crawl it on your thigh.

This is the way I munch on the leaves,
Munch on the leaves, munch on the leaves.
This is the way I munch on the leaves.
I'm a caterpillar.

One hand represents caterpillar; the other the leaves to munch.

This is the way I spin my cocoon,
Spin my cocoon, spin my cocoon.
This is the way I spin my cocoon.
I'm a caterpillar.

Move index finger in small circles in the air.

This is the way I sleep through the day,
Sleep through the day, sleep through the day.
This is the way I sleep through the day.
I'm a caterpillar.

Place head on hands, eyes closed.

This is the way I fly in the sky,
Fly in the sky, fly in the sky.
This is the way I fly in the sky.

Flap arms; pretend to fly.

"I'm not a caterpillar! What am I? A butterfly!"

—Adapted traditional rhyme

Speak this line.

Butterfly Count

This rhyme is a wonderful one to do on a flannel or Velcro board. A neat touch is to give the butterflies the same number of dots on their wings as those used in the rhyme. It would be easy with a butterfly pattern and ready-made stickers!

So many butterflies I see!
Come and count them now with me!

Beckon.

There's one flying in the sun.
He is butterfly number one.
There's one landing on my shoe.
He is butterfly number two.
Another butterfly I see.
He is butterfly number three.

Hold up one finger; add fingers as the rhyme progresses.

There's one over by the door.
He is butterfly number four.
Watch him swoop and see him dive.
He is butterfly number five.
Look there, on the pile of sticks.
He is butterfly number six.
Flying up as high as heaven,
He is butterfly number seven.
There's one over by the gate.
He is butterfly number eight.
Stopping by a flower to dine,
He is butterfly number nine.
Look there, flying to the glen.
He is butterfly number ten.

—Barbara Scott

Caterpillar, Caterpillar

Caterpillar, caterpillar,
Crawl all around.
Caterpillar, caterpillar,
Crawl on the ground.
Caterpillar, caterpillar,
Look for some lunch.
Caterpillar, caterpillar,
Munch, munch, munch!
Caterpillar, caterpillar,
Now you're fed.
Caterpillar, caterpillar,
Time for bed.
Caterpillar, caterpillar,
Open one eye.
Caterpillar, caterpillar,
Wave bye-bye.

—Adapted traditional rhyme

This rhyme can be sung to the tune of "Teddy Bear, Teddy Bear" or chanted.

Crawl index finger all around.

Crawl index finger on the floor.

Place hand over eyes, searching.

Pretend to eat.

Rub tummy.

Rest head on hands; close eyes.

Open eye.

Wave.

Butterfly

Butterfly,
I am a butterfly.
Butterfly,
Just watch what I can do.
I can fly up high or low.
To the sky, or on your toe.
Flying high, flying low . . . oh

Sung to the tune of "Alouette." ASL sign for butterfly: hands crossed, thumbs hooked, wiggle fingers for wings.
Use ASL sign.

Do motions as indicated.

Butterfly,
I am a butterfly.
Butterfly,
Just watch what I can do!
Butterfly,
I am a butterfly.
Butterfly,
Just watch what I can do!
I can fly here or there.
I can fly most anywhere.
Here or there, anywhere . . . oh
Butterfly,
I am a butterfly.
Butterfly,
Just watch what I can do!

—Adapted traditional rhyme

Continue with ASL motion for butterfly.

Do motions as indicated.

I'm a Sleepy Caterpillar

I'm a sleepy caterpillar,
Just as sleepy as can be.
Winter's coming and I wonder:
What will become of me?
When the snow is flying,
I'm fast asleep in bed.
Spring comes and guess what happens?
I'm a butterfly instead!

—Barbara Scott

Rub eyes and yawn.

Tap temple with finger.
Shrug shoulders.
Wiggle fingers down.
Place head on hands; pretend to sleep.
Use ASL sign for butterfly: hands crossed, thumbs hooked, wiggle fingers for wings.

If You're a Happy Butterfly

If you're a happy butterfly, fly around.
If you're a happy butterfly, fly around.
If you're a happy butterfly and you know it,
Then fly around and show it!
If you're a happy butterfly, fly around.

ADDITIONAL VERSES:
If you're a happy butterfly, fly up high . . .
   then fly up high and show it.
If you're a happy butterfly, fly down low . . .
   then fly down low and show it.
If you're a happy butterfly, do all three . . .
   then do all three and show it.

—Adapted traditional rhyme

Sung to the tune of "If You're Happy and You Know It."
Flap arms and move around.

Butterflies Love Flowers

Butterflies love flowers,	*ASL sign for butterfly: hands crossed, thumbs hooked, wiggle fingers for wings.*
Oh yes indeed, they do!	Use ASL sign.
They drink the nectar from inside,	Nod head "yes."
With their long tongues, they do!	
The nectar gives them energy.	Stick out tongue.
It's just like food for them,	Show muscles.
They stop and eat and gather strength	Rub tummy.
And then can fly again!	
	Flap arms, pretending to fly.

—Barbara Scott

Books to Share

Bentley, Dawn. 2003. *Good Night, Sweet Butterflies.* New York: Little Simon. ISBN: 978-0689856846.

Cain, Sheridan. 2003. *The Munching, Crunching Caterpillar.* Wilton, CT: Tiger Tales. ISBN: 978-1589250253.

Capucilli, Alyssa S. 2009. *Katy Duck Is a Caterpillar.* New York: Little Simon. ISBN: 978-1416960614.

Horacek, Petr. 2007. *Butterfly, Butterfly: A Book of Colors.* Somerville, MA: Candlewick Press. ISBN: 978-0763633431.

Jarrett, Clare. 2008. *Arabella Miller's Tiny Caterpillar.* Somerville, MA: Candlewick Press. ISBN: 978-1844281565.

Swope, Sam. 2000. *Gotta Go! Gotta Go!* New York: Farrar, Straus, and Giroux. ISBN: 978-0374327576.

Musical Selections

"Butterflies Flit" from *Yummy Yummy* by The Wiggles. ASIN: B0000AE5YO.

"Butterfly" from *Animal House* by Recess Monkey. ASIN: B000NQPWUY.

"The Butterfly" from *Bloom* by Zak Morgan. ASIN: B0001ARHAU.

"The Butterfly" from *Dr. Jean Sings Silly Songs* by Dr. Jean. ASIN: B001AZ4MP8.

"Hungry Caterpillar" from *Seasonal Songs in Motion* by The Learning Station. ASIN: B00005TPUN.

"Monarch Butterfly" from *Songs about Insects, Bugs, and Squiggly Things* by Jane Lawliss Murphy. Kimbo Educational Audio, 1993. ISBN: 978-1563460333.

Sources

Anonymous. 1887. *Buds from Every Clime.* Battle Creek, MI: Sperry & Swedberg.

Benton, Gail, and Trisha Waichulaitis. 2004. *Low-Cost, High-Interest Programming: Seasonal Events for Preschoolers.* New York: Neal-Schuman.

Dailey, Susan M. 2007. *Sing a Song of Storytime.* New York: Neal-Schuman.

Findlay, Diane, Tami Chumbley Finley, Susan Mast, Kathy Ross, and Patti Sinclair. 2008. *Collaborative Library Summer Program Manual.* Mason City, IA: Collaborative Summer Library Program.

Headland, Isaac Taylor. 1900. *Chinese Mother Goose Rhymes.* Grand Rapids, MI: Fleming H. Revell.

LibraryPalooza. Available: www.librarypalooza.net (accessed March 3, 2010).

McKinnon, Elizabeth, and Gayle Bittinger. 1994. *Busy Bees Spring: Fun for Two's and Three's.* Everett, WA: Warren Publishing House.

Poulsson, Emilie. 1893. *Fingerplays for Nursery and Kindergarten.* New York: Lothrop, Lee, and Shepard, reprinted 1921.

Rossetti, Christina G. 1893. *Sing-Song: A Nursery Rhyme Book.* New York: Macmillan.

Totline Staff, comp. 1994. *1001 Rhymes and Fingerplays.* Everett, WA: Warren Publishing House.

Warren, Jean, comp. 1989. *Theme-a-Saurus.* Everett, WA: Warren Publishing House.

Cats

Soft and furry, warm and purry . . . kittens to cats!

Rhyme	**Telling Guide**
### Kitty, Kitty	
Kitty, kitty, kitty, kitty,	Extend one hand, palm up, fingers loosely curled.
All my little ones so pretty;	
You, and you, and you, and you,	Point to children.
Let me hear how you can mew,	
Mew, mew, mew, mew.	Children mew.
Kitty, kitty, kitty, kitty,	
All my little ones so pretty.	
Curl up now, just like that,	Curl fingers around thumb.
"Go to sleep," says mother cat,	Close eyes.
"Sleep 'til someone calls out, Scat!"	Open eyes and hand suddenly.
—From *Let's Do Fingerplays*	
### Five Little Kittens	
Five little kittens standing in a row,	Extend left fingers upward, palm out.
They nod their heads to the children, so.	Bend fingers forward.
They run to the left, they run to the right,	Wiggle fingers to left, then to right.
They stand up and stretch in the bright sunlight.	Stretch fingers slowly.
Along comes a dog, who's in for some fun,	Move right fist slowly toward fingers.
M-e-o-w, see those kittens run.	Run left fingers behind back.
—From *Let's Do Fingerplays*	
### This Little Kitty	
This little kitten is as dark as night.	Point to thumb.
This little kitten is black and white.	Point to index finger.
This little kitten loves to sleep.	Point to middle finger.
This little kitten loves to creep.	Point to ring finger.
And this little kitten chases balls of yarn all day!	Point to pinkie finger.
—Barbara Scott	
### I Love Little Pussy	
I love little pussy,	Pretend to hold cat in one arm.
Her coat is so warm.	Pretend to pet cat.
And if I don't hurt her,	Shake head "no."
She'll do me no harm.	Continue to shake head.
I'll sit by the fire,	Wiggle fingers to represent flames.
And give her some food,	Pretend to feed cat.
And Pussy will love me,	Both hands over heart.
Because I am good.	
—Traditional rhyme	

The Three Little Kittens

The three little kittens, they lost their mittens,	Hold up three fingers.
And they began to cry,	Fists to eyes, crying motions.
"Oh mammy dear, we sadly fear our mittens we have lost."	
"What? Lost your mittens? You naughty kittens.	Shake index finger, scolding.
Then you shall have no pie!"	Shake head "no."
The three little kittens, they found their mittens,	Hold up three fingers.
And they began to cry,	
"Oh mammy dear, see here, see here!	Hold up hands, fingers together, thumbs out, to represent mittens.
Our mittens we have found!"	
"What? Found your mittens? You good little kittens.	Mimic patting on head.
Then you shall have some pie."	
The three little kittens put on their mittens,	Hold up three fingers.
And soon ate up the pie.	Pretend to eat.
"Oh mammy dear, see here, see here!	Hold up hands, fingers together, thumbs out, to represent mittens.
Our mittens we have soiled."	
"What? Soiled your mittens? You naughty kittens."	Shake index finger, scolding.
Then they began to sigh.	Big sigh!
The three little kittens, they washed their mittens,	Hold up three fingers.
And hung them up to dry.	Mimic washing and hanging up laundry.
"Oh mammy dear, see here, see here!	
Our mittens we have washed."	
"What? Washed your mittens? You darling kittens.	Place both hands over heart.
But I smell a rat close by!"	Sniff the air.

—Traditional rhyme

Mrs. Pussy's Dinner

Mrs. Pussy, sleek and fat,	Hold up thumb.
With her kittens four,	Hold up four fingers.
Went to sleep upon the mat	Make fist with hand; hold out in front.
By the kitchen door.	
Mrs. Pussy heard a noise—	Hand to ear.
Up she jumped with glee;	Jump hand in the air.
"Kittens, maybe that's a mouse!	
Let us go and see!"	
Creeping, creeping, creeping on,	Creep fingers.
Silently they stole,	Make "Shhh!" motion.
But the little mouse had gone	Stick thumb out of left fist.
Back within its hole.	Put thumb back into fist.
"Well," said Mrs. Pussy then,	
"To the barn we'll go;	Raise hands over head to make roof.
We shall find the swallow there,	
Flying to and fro."	Point to left, then right.
So the cat and kittens four	Hold up five fingers.

Tried their very best;

Paw at the air.

But the swallows flying fast
Safely reached the nest.

Cup hands in front.

Home went hungry Mrs. Puss
And her kittens four.

Hold up five fingers.

Found their dinner on a plate
By the kitchen door.

Thumbs and index fingers make circle
for plate.

Mrs. Puss said, "Meow! To chase birds and mice is fun,

Point to self.

But I'm glad that dinner plates
Cannot fly or run!"

Flap arms; make running motions.

—Traditional rhyme

Pussy-Cat, Pussy-Cat

*ASL sign for cat: make "OK" motion with
fingers, place hand to the side of nose, then
pull the hand out to the side to represent
whiskers.*

Pussy-cat, pussy-cat

Use ASL sign.

Where have you been?

Place hands out to either side, questioning.

I've been to London
To look at the Queen.

Point to top of head to indicate crown.

Pussy-cat, pussy cat,

Use ASL sign.

What did you there?

Place hands out to either side, questioning.

I frightened a little mouse

Wiggle nose.

Under her chair.

—Traditional rhyme

Kitty in Trouble

Kitty, bad kitty,

Shake finger, admonishing.

Come out of the tree.

Come, you bad kitty,

Beckon.

At once to me!

How did you ever

Get up so high?

Point up.

How did you do it, bad kitty,

And why?

Place hands out to sides, questioning.

Only just now

On a cushion you purred.

Make circle with hands.

Then you jumped up,

And went chasing a bird.

Jump.

Did you not know

That you never could fly?

Flap arms.

Ah! 'Tis no wonder

You mew and cry.

Meow plaintively.

Now you are up

And afraid to come down.

Point down.

Worst little kitty

In all the town!
There you must stay, naughty cat,
For a time;
Trees are not made for
Small ladies to climb!

Move hands to indicate size.

Shake finger, admonishing.

Climbing motions.

—Traditional rhyme

Hey, My Kitten

Hey, my kitten, my kitten,
And hey, my kitten, my dear-y!
Such a sweet pet as this
Was neither far nor near-y.

Pretend to hold cat in arms; rock arms back and forth.
Put hands to heart.
Pretend to hold cat in arms.
Point out and then in toward body.

—Traditional rhyme

Cat Ate the Dumplings

ASL sign for cat: make "OK" motion with fingers, place hand to the side of nose, then pull the hand out to the side to represent whiskers.
Use ASL sign.

Pussy cat ate the dumplings,
Pussy cat ate the dumplings!
Mamma stood by, and cried, "Oh fie!
Why did you eat the dumplings?"

Place hands on cheeks; sway head from side to side.

—Traditional rhyme

Kitty Cat, Pounce

Kitty cat, kitty cat
Sneaks out of the house.
Kitty cat, kitty cat
Creeps up to a mouse,
And . . . pounce!
Kitty cat, kitty cat
Creeps up to a bird.
Kitty cat, kitty cat
Is not even heard,
And . . . pounce!
But the mouse ran
And the bird flew away,
So kitty cat, kitty cat found
A ball of yarn
To play . . . pounce!

Creep fingers.

Make "jumping" motion with fingers.
Creep fingers.

Shake head "no."
Make "jumping" motions with fingers.
Make fingers "run."
Flap hands.

Make circle with hands.
Make "jumping" motions with fingers.

—Adapted from a song by Susan M. Dailey

Cats Have Nine Lives

They say cats have nine lives,
And I hope that's true,
For my cats aren't always careful
About the things they do.

Hold up nine fingers.
Cross fingers for "luck."
Shake head "no."

One cat teases the neighbor's dog.
The second one climbs high trees.
The third one stuck his nose once
Into a hive of bees.
They never check for traffic
Before dashing across the street.
And they've fallen from high places
But always landed on their feet.

—Susan M. Dailey

Hold up one finger; "Bark."
Hold up two fingers; pretend to climb.
Hold up three fingers; stick nose out.
Move index finger through air; "Buzz."
Look in both directions.

Point upward.
Lightly touch hands to lap.

Five Little Kittens

This kitty said, "I smell a mouse!"
This kitty said, "Let's hunt through the house!"
This kitty said, "Let's play we're asleep."
This kitty said, "Let's go creepity-creep."
This kitty said, "Meow! Meow! Meow!
I saw him run in his hole just now!"

—Maude Burnham

Begin rhyme with five fingers up. Start with the thumb and point to each in succession.

Oh! Pussy Cat

Oh! Pussy cat, pussy cat,
Where did you go?
I've hunted most every place,
Both high and low.
Now where can I find you?
Oh! What shall I do?
But just then I spied her,
Inside an old shoe.

—From *Golden Playdays*

Use ASL sign for cat: make "OK" sign with fingers; begin with hand by nose; pull out as if pulling on whiskers.

Place hand over eyes, looking around.
Point up, then down.

Shrug.
Point to eyes.
Point to shoe.

One Little Kitten, One

One little kitten, one
Playing with yarn and having fun.
Two little kittens, two
They are playing with a shoe.
Three little kittens, three
They are climbing up a tree.
Four little kittens, four
They are lying by the door.
Five little kittens, five
Running, playing, so alive!

—Barbara Scott

Hold up pointer finger.

Add middle finger.

Add ring finger.

Add pinkie finger.

Add thumb.
Wiggle all fingers.

Pussy Cat, Pussy Cat

Pussy cat, pussy cat,
Turn around.

This rhyme can be sung to the tune of "Teddy Bear, Teddy Bear" or chanted.

Turn in place.

Pussy cat, pussy cat,
Sit on the ground.
Pussy cat, pussy cat,
Lick your paws.
Pussy cat, pussy cat,
Show those claws!
Pussy cat, pussy cat,
Stretch in the sun.
Pussy cat, pussy cat,
Run, run, run!
Pussy cat, pussy cat,
See the moonlight.
Pussy cat, pussy cat,
Say goodnight.

—Adapted traditional rhyme

Sit.

Pretend to lick paws.

Show claws.

Stretch.

Run in place.

Make circle in the air for moon.

Close eyes; place head on hands.

If You're a Kitty and You Know It

If you're a kitty and you know it, say meow.
If you're a kitty and you know it, say meow.
If you're a kitty and you know it, then your face will surely show it.
If you're a kitty and you know it, say meow.

ADDITIONAL VERSES:
. . . lick your paws.
. . . show your claws.
. . . swish your tail.
. . . do all four.

—Adapted traditional rhyme

Sung to the tune of "If You're Happy and You Know It."
"Meow."
"Meow."
Stroke whiskers.

"Meow."

Five Little Kitty Cats

Five little kitty cats sitting by the door.
One went to chase a mouse and now there are four.
Four little kitty cats sitting by the tree.
One went to chase a bird and now there are three.
Three little kitty cats with nothing much to do.
One went to chase some yarn and now there are two.
Two little kitty cats were lying in the sun.
One decided to take a nap and now there's just one.
One little kitty cat sitting all alone.
He went off to find some food and now there are none.

—Barbara Scott

Begin this rhyme with five fingers up.
Take away fingers as the rhyme progresses.

Where Are You Hiding, Kitty?

Where are you hiding, kitty?
I've looked everywhere.

Place hand above eyes, peering around.
Move arms to show expanse.

In the hamper, under the table,
Even behind the chair.
You'll never believe where I found him.
He wasn't having fun.
He was stretched out,
Sleeping in the sun!

—Barbara Scott

Open hamper; look under and behind.

Shake head "no."

Place head on hands; pretend to sleep.

Cats Are Purring

Sung to the tune of "Alouette."
Pretend to hold cat and pet.

Cats are purring,
Kitty cats are purring.
Cats are purring
All around the house.
Purring here and
Purring there.
Purring, purring everywhere.
Everywhere, everywhere, oh. . . .
Cats are purring,
Kitty cats are purring.
Cats are purring
All around the house.
ADDITIONAL VERSES:
Cats are slinking . . .
Cats are pouncing . . .
Cats are napping . . .

—Adapted traditional rhyme

Spread arms to show expanse.
Point in one direction.
Point in the opposite direction.
Spread arms to show expanse.
Point both ways.
Repeat same motions as beginning.

Sneaking motion.
Pouncing motion.
Pretend to nap.

Ten Little Kittens

Sung to the tune of "Ten Little Indians."
Count out on fingers for the first verse.

One little, two little, three little kittens,
Four little, five little, six little kittens,
Seven little, eight little, nine little kittens,
Ten little kitty cats!
Ten little, nine little, eight little kittens,
Seven little, six little, five little kittens,
Four little, three little, two little kittens,
One little kitty cat!

—Adapted traditional rhyme

Remove fingers for the second verse.

Five Little Kittens

Five little kittens were playing in the grass.
The first one said, "I saw a mouse run past."
The second one said, "Which way did he go?"
The third one said, "I don't know."
The fourth one said, "I see a nose that is pink."
The fifth one said, "Caught him! Quick as a wink!"

—Barbara Scott

Begin rhyme with five fingers up.
Point to each in succession, beginning with the thumb.

Where Is Kitty?

Where is kitty?
Where is kitty?
Here I am!
Here I am!
How are you today, sir?
Very well, I thank you.
Run and play,
Run and play.

—Adapted traditional rhyme

Sung to the tune of "Where Is Thumbkin?"
Hide hands behind back.

Bring out one thumb.
Bring out other thumb.
Wiggle thumbs as if talking.

Put one thumb behind back.
Put other thumb behind back.

Five Little Cats

Five little cats went out to play,
In the backyard one fine day.
Mama Cat said, "Mew, mew, mew, mew!"
Only four little cats came back, that's true.

No little cats went out to play
In the backyard one fine day.
Mama Cat said, "Mew, mew, mew, mew!"
And all the little cats came back, that's true!

—Adapted traditional rhyme

Sung to the tune of "Five Little Ducks."
Hold up five fingers; take away as rhyme progresses.

Continue with four, three, two, one, until . . .
Shake head "no."

Bring all five fingers back and wiggle them.

Gray Cat, Gray Cat

Gray cat, gray cat,
Swish your fluffy tail.
Gray cat, gray cat,
Swish your fluffy tail.
Silky ears and velvet paws,
When you're mad,
You show your claws.
Gray cat, gray cat,
Swish your fluffy tail.

—Adapted traditional rhyme

This rhyme can be sung to the tune of "Gray Squirrel, Gray Squirrel" or chanted.

Move bottom back and forth.

Move bottom back and forth.
Point to ears, then hold out hands.

Show claws.

Move bottom back and forth.

One Cat

One cat, two cats,
Three cats, four.
Five cats, six cats,
Seven cats more!

—Adapted traditional rhyme

Chanted in the style of "One Potato, Two Potato."
Count on fingers as the rhyme progresses.

Five Little Kittens

Five little kittens were climbing a tree.
The first one said, "A nest do I see."
The second one said, "Are there birds nearby?"

Begin rhyme with five fingers up.
Starting with the thumb, point to each in succession.

The third one said, "To catch them, we must try."
The fourth one said, "I think they flew away."
The fifth one said, "We will try another day."

—Barbara Scott

One Kitten

One kitten, two kittens, three kittens, four
Kittens hiding behind the door.
Five kittens, six kittens, seven kittens, eight
Kittens sitting on top of the gate.
Nine kittens and finally ten
Kittens chase after a mouse again!

—Barbara Scott

Count on fingers as rhyme progresses.

Wiggle all fingers and hide them behind back.

The Cats Are Creeping

The cats are creeping,
Creeping 'round the house.
The cats are creeping everywhere,
In search of a little mouse.
They have looked in places low
And even places high.
But as they're creeping all around,
Not one mouse do they spy!
That's because that little mouse
Is one smart, furry fellow!
He's asleep inside HIS house
His head upon his pillow!

—Barbara Scott

Creeping, sneaky motion.
Raise hands over head to make roof.
Creep.
Use fingers to show size.
Point down.
Point up.
Creep.
Shake head "no."

Tap head at temple.
Raise hands over head to make roof.
Lay head on hands; pretend to sleep.

How Do Kittens Take a Bath?

How do kittens take a bath,
Take a bath, take a bath?
How do kittens take a bath?
Tell me, tell me.
They lick their fur with their tongue,
With their tongue, with their tongue.
They lick their fur with their tongue.
That's how they do it!

—Adapted traditional rhyme

Sung to the tune of "London Bridge."
Shrug, questioning look.

Clap four times.
Pretend to lick fur.

Clap five times.

All Kinds of Cats

There are fat cats,
Skinny cats,
Tall cats,
Small cats.
When it comes to things cat,
I love ALL cats!

—Barbara Scott

Move hands to indicate size on all.

Move arms to show expanse.

I Love My Little Kitty

I love my little kitty.	Put one fist on lap to represent cat.
Her fur is soft as silk.	Pretend to pet "cat."
I feed her good food every day,	Rub tummy.
And she drinks lots of milk.	Motion of lapping milk from a bowl.

—Barbara Scott

Books to Share

Ehlert, Lois. 1998. *Top Cat.* Boston: Harcourt Children's Books. ISBN: 978-0152017392.

Numeroff, Laura J. 2008. *If You Give a Cat a Cupcake.* New York: HarperCollins. ISBN: 978-0060283247.

Powell, Richard. 2003. *The Black Cat.* Somerville, MA: Candlewick Press. ISBN: 978-0763621087.

Scotton, Rob. 2008. *Splat the Cat.* New York: HarperCollins. ISBN: 978-0060831547. (This is one of a series of books about this character.)

Thomas, Jan. 2007. *What Will Fat Cat Sit On?* Boston: Harcourt Children's Books. ISBN: 978-0152060510.

Turner, Ann Warren. 2004. *Pumpkin Cat.* New York: Hyperion Books for Children. ISBN: 978-0786804948.

Musical Selections

"Cool Cat" from *Counting Sheep* by Collin Raye. ASIN: B0000488U9.

"Copy Cat 1" and "Copy Cat 2" from *Kidding around with Greg and Steve.* ASIN: 6307799595.

"Fred (The Tabby Cat)" from *Animal House* by Recess Monkey. ASIN: B000NQPWUY.

"Here, Kitty, Kitty" and "Five Little Cats" from *Get Ready, Get Set, Sing* by Sarah Barchas. ASIN: B0020SQRRK.

"Pussycat, Pussycat" and "Three Little Kittens" from *Pop Go The Wiggles: Nursery Rhymes and Songs* by The Wiggles. ASIN: B0012OVFSE.

"Three Little Kittens" from *Toddler Favorites, Too!* ISBN: 978-1566283229.

Sources

Anonymous. *Denslow's Mother Goose.* Available: www.gutenberg.org/etext/18546 (accessed March 6, 2010).

Burnham, Maude. 1910. *Rhymes for Little Hands.* East Longmeadow, MA: Milton Bradley Company.

Dailey, Susan M. 2001. *A Storytime Year.* New York: Neal-Schuman.

——. 2007. *Sing a Song of Storytime.* New York: Neal-Schuman.

Dorsey, C.J. 1922. *Golden Playdays.* Baltimore, MD: Children's Publishing Company.

Grayson, Marion. 1962. *Let's Do Fingerplays.* Fairfield, CT: R.B. Luce.

Index of Rhymes. Available: www.kidsnurseryrhymes.co.uk/rhymes (accessed March 6, 2010).

Lang, Andrew, ed. 1897. *The Nursery Rhyme Book.* London: Frederick Warne & Co.

Moffat, Alfred. 1911. *Our Old Nursery Rhymes.* New York: G. Schirmer.

Poulsson, Emilie. 1893. *Fingerplays for Nursery and Kindergarten.* New York: Lothrop, Lee, and Shepard, reprinted 1921.

Wiggin, Kate Douglas, and Nora Archibald Smith. 1907. *Pinafore Palace.* New York: Grosset & Dunlap. Available: www.gutenberg.org/files/29378/29378-h/29378-h.htm (accessed March 6, 2010).

Willet, Edward. 1882. *Around the House.* New York: R. Worthington.

Chocolate

It's one of the four food groups . . . isn't it?

Rhyme	**Telling Guide**

Doin' the Chocolate Shake

You squat right down,

Up you stand.

Stamp your feet,

Shake your hands.

Wiggle all over,

And mix real well.

Doin' the Chocolate Shake!

YUM!

—Jan Irving and Robin Currie

Sung to the tune of "The Hokey Pokey."

Squat.

Stand up.

Stamp feet.

Shake hands.

Wiggle.

Roll hands over and over.

Clap hands.

Reach high.

The Fudge Song

Oh, give me a pan,

And a spoon if you can,

Pour some milk and sugar right in.

Then add choc-o-lot

And the good stuff you've got,

Now you know how to begin.

Stir, stir 'round and 'round.

Sneak a lick whenever you can.

Oh, give me a taste,

But try not to waste,

My fudge that's stuck in the pan.

Fudge, fudge is the best.

I eat it whenever I can.

Now caramel's OK,

But I'd vote every day,

To lick the fudge out of the pan!

—Jan Irving and Robin Currie

Sung to the tune of "Home on the Range."

Hold out right hand.

Hold out left hand.

Pouring motion.

Pouring motion.

Stirring motion.

Pretend to lick spoon.

Pretend to taste.

Eating motion.

Licking motion.

The Chocolate Cake

Ten little candles on a chocolate cake.

Wh! Wh! Now there are eight.

Eight little candles on candlesticks.

Wh! Wh! Now there are six.

Six little candles and not one more.

Wh! Wh! Now there are four.

Four little candles, red, white, and blue.

This rhyme also works well as a flannel or Velcro board rhyme by attaching candles to a cake.

Start rhyme with ten fingers up.

Each time you blow, put down two fingers.

Wh! Wh! Now there are two.
Two little candles standing in the sun.
Wh! Wh! Now there are none.

—From Hummingbird Educational Resources

Chocolate

One, two, three, CHO,   Put three fingers in the air and count.
One, two, three, CO,
One, two, three, LA,
One, two, three, TE . . .
Chocolate, chocolate!
Stir, stir, the chocolate!   Stirring motion.

—Ana-Elba Pavon

Chocolate, Chocolate

Chocolate, chocolate!
It's a treat!   Clap hands.
Chocolate is so
Good to eat!   Rub tummy.
Chocolate cookies and
Chocolate pie!
I love chocolate!   Hug self.
Don't ask why!   Shake head "no."
Chocolate ice cream,
Chocolate cake,
Chocolate, chocolate
Milk, milk shake!   Shake all over.
Chocolate candy
In a box.   Make heart with fingers.
No doubt about it—   Shake head "no."
Chocolate rocks!

—Barbara Scott

Chocolate Cheer!

Because the majority of your preschoolers will not know how to spell, have them echo the letters and lines below. Use pom-poms if you have them or give each child two colored scarves to shake instead.
Have children echo each letter.

Give me a C!
Give me an H!
Give me an O!
Give me a C!
Give me another O!
Give me an L!
Give me an A!
Give me a T!
Give me an E!

That spells chocolate! | Say the word for the children.
What does it spell? | Have the children echo the word.

—Barbara Scott

Continue with echo as many times as you wish!

From the Tall Cacao Tree

From the tall cacao tree | Raise hands up above head; stretch fingers to represent branches.
In the great rainforest, |
Comes a treat that's really sweet, | Flutter fingers down to represent rain.
And can be good for us. |
The beans are picked and dried by hand, | Nod head "yes."
Then sold to factories. | Show hands.
They make chocolate goodies |
Just for you and me! | Point to children, then self.

—Barbara Scott

Books to Share

Cali, Davide. 2009. *I Love Chocolate.* Toronto, Canada: Tundra Books. ISBN: 978-0887769122.

Henkes. Kevin. 2003. *Lily's Chocolate Heart.* New York: Greenwillow Books. ISBN: 978-0060560669.

Rey, H.A., and Margaret Rey. 1998. *Curious George Goes to a Chocolate Factory.* Boston: Houghton Mifflin. ISBN: 978-0395912140.

Slonim, David. 2003. *Oh, Ducky! A Chocolate Calamity.* San Francisco: Chronicle Books. ISBN: 978-0811835626.

Wells, Rosemary. 1999. *Max's Chocolate Chicken.* New York: Viking Juvenile. ISBN: 978-0670887132.

Musical Selections

"The Candy Man" and "I Want Candy" from *Easter Bunny's Favorite Songs.* ASIN: B00005YDFP.

"The Chocolate Milk Train" from *Milk and Me Sing-a-Long Milk Melodies.* ASIN: B000XY9O46.

"How Sweet It Is" from *How Sweet It Is* by The Sugar Beats. ASIN: B000009SEW.

"Lechita Chocolate" from *Very Derryberry* by Debi Derryberry. ASIN: B00112XSI2.

"Milkshake Song" from *Songs for Wiggleworms.* ASIN: B00004YLUE.

Sources

"Birthdays." Hummingbird Educational Resources. Available: www.hummingbirded.com/birthdays .htm (accessed March 6, 2010).

Irving, Jan, and Robin Currie. 1986. *Mudlucious: Stories and Activities Featuring Food for Preschool Children.* Santa Barbara, CA: Libraries Unlimited.

Pavon, Ana-Elba. 2007. "Planning, Doing, & Sustaining a Successful Bilingual Storytime." An Infopeople Workshop. Infopeople Project. Available: infopeople.org/training/past/2008/ biling -storytime/ (accessed April 9, 2010).

Circus: Acrobats, Big Cats, and Clowns
Ladies and gentlemen, boys and girls, direct your attention to the center ring!

Rhyme	**Telling Guide**
## The Circus	
Going to the circus to have a lot of fun:	Hold up closed fists.
The animals parading, one by one.	Raise fingers to indicate each new number.
Now they're walking two by two,	
A great big lion and a caribou.	
Now they're walking three by three,	
The elephants and the chimpanzee.	
Now they're walking four by four,	
A stripy tiger and a big old boar.	
Now they're walking five by five,	
Makes us laugh when they arrive.	
Now they're walking six by six,	
Little dogs jumping over sticks.	
Now they're walking seven by seven,	
Zebras stamping on to Devon.	
Now they're walking eight by eight,	
Running and jumping over the gate.	
Now they're walking nine by nine,	
Scary rabbit and the porcupine.	
Now they're walking ten by ten,	
Ready to start all over again.	

—From *Let's Do Fingerplays*

Under the Circus Tent

What wondrous things you're sure to see,	Walk in circle.
If you enter the circus tent with me.	Hold up three fingers.
Three big rings on the circus floor,	
With animals, acrobats, clowns, and more.	
As the fancy horses begin to prance,	Prance in place.
The dressed-up dogs do a little dance.	Children dance.
The drums and trumpets are loudly playing,	Imitate playing.
"Watch ring number one," the announcer is saying.	Cup hands over mouth.
Some people are balancing on a high wire,	Pretend to balance.
Sliding and riding on top of a little tire.	
Under the circus tent is an amazing place	
But if I get scared, I cover my face.	Cover face with hands.

—From *Busy Fingers, Growing Minds*

The Circus

We went to the circus and what did we see?
Clowns doing tricks as silly as could be.
Lions and monkeys jumping through hoops.
Trapeze artists doing loop de loops.
We went to the circus and what did we do?
We ate cotton candy and hot dogs, too.
                    —From *Busy Fingers, Growing Minds*

Do floppy clown acts.
Jump through pretend hoops.
Pretend to fly through air.

Pretend to eat.

Acrobat

One little acrobat swinging through the air.
He flips and he flops as we stare.
And suddenly he's caught by another with flare!
He didn't even know that he gave me a scare!
One little acrobat swinging through the air.
He lands and bows with the greatest of care!
                    —From *Natural Learning*

Hold index finger up and swing from side to side. / Make index finger bend up and down.

Excitement in voice, lock both index fingers together. / Shake head, wipe brow.

Hold index finger up and swing from side to side. / With left palm facing up, place right hand with index finger up on the left palm and bend it as to bow.

I'm a Great Big Lion

I'm a great big lion,
You can hear me roar!
I've had my dinner but I
Want some more!
                    —From *Busy Fingers, Growing Minds*

"Roar."

Pretend to eat.

Leo Lion

I'm a little bit afraid when I hear
Leo Lion roar!
But I like him when he's sleeping
'Cuz he doesn't even snore!
                    —From *Busy Fingers, Growing Minds*

Have children roar.

Put head on hands, as if asleep.

The Lion

The lion is a ferocious beast,
His roaring makes me hide.
I'm glad he's locked up in a cage
And we are all outside!
                    —From *Busy Fingers, Growing Minds*

Act fierce and roar like a lion.
Hide behind hands.
Pretend to lock up cage like a lion tamer.
Fold arms and smile.

Five Little Clowns

This little clown is jolly and fat,
This little clown wears a big red hat.
This little clown is strong and tall,
This little clown likes to fall.

Point to thumb.
Point to index finger.
Point to middle finger.
Point to ring finger.

This little clown is wee and small,

But he does the funniest tricks of all.

—Paula C. Foreman

Clowns

Clowns are marching in the circus parade.

They wear the funniest clothes ever made.

Watch those floppy, floppy clowns.

They make funny faces

From smiles to frowns.

They do a lot of silly tricks.

Some are even doing flips.

They seem to have lots of ups and downs.

—From *Busy Fingers, Growing Minds*

Clown Dress

The clown puts on his clown face.

First he paints it white,

Then he draws around his eyes,

Big and round and bright.

He paints his mouth and nose

A rosy, rosy red.

His wig is green that he pulls on

His old round head.

His shoes are enormous.

His suit is immense.

It looks like he's wearing

A whole circus tent!

—Jan Irving and Robin Currie

Clowns

Clowns have big ears

And funny feet.

They smile at everyone they meet.

The clowns jump high,

The clowns jump low.

They make a face

And down they go!

—Author unknown

It's Very Plain

It's very plain.

A tightrope makes

A roadway rather narrow

On which to travel

Back and forth

And trundle a wheelbarrow.

Action column:

Point to little finger.

Wiggle little finger.

Pretend to march.

Let bodies do floppy things.

Make funny faces.

Do tricks.

Bend up and down.

Jump and fall down.

Point to the parts of the body when mentioned.

Put hands behind ears.

Kick feet.

Point to big smile.

Jump, arms up.

Jump, then squat.

Make a face.

Sit down.

Point to eyes.

Put hands close together to show size.

Point left, then right.

Pretend to push wheelbarrow.

So, I am sure
You'll not dispute   Shake head "no."
The acrobat shows well
His talents   Point to self.
When thus with ease,
He promenades and always   Pretend to walk tightrope, arms out
Keeps his balance!   to either side.

—Traditional rhyme

This Little Clown

The first little clown is fat and gay.   Begin rhyme with thumb up.
The second little clown does tricks all day.   Add fingers as the rhyme progresses.
The third little clown is tall and strong.
The fourth little clown sings a funny song.
The fifth little clown is wee and small.
But he can do anything at all.

—Lynda Roberts

Circus Ponies

Five circus ponies all in a row—   Begin rhyme with five fingers up.
One jumped through a hoop,
And now there are four.   Take away fingers as the rhyme
Four circus ponies standing by a tree—   progresses.
One walked away, and now there are three.
Three circus ponies waiting for their cue—
One danced about, and now there are two.
Two circus ponies thought they were done.
One dashed away, and now there is one.
One circus pony standing all alone—
He took a bow, and went on home.

—Lynda Roberts

Let's Head to the Circus

The circus train is coming to town,   *Sung to the tune of "London Bridge."*
Coming to town, coming to town.
The circus train is coming to town.
Let's have some fun!
The circus clowns jump and fall,   Do motions as indicated.
Spray some water, make some noise.
The circus clowns make me laugh.
Let's have some fun!
The elephants march side to side,
Side to side, side to side.
The elephants trumpet load and clear.
Let's have some fun.   Repeat first verse.

—Carolyn N. Cullum

We're Going to the Circus

We're going to the circus, the circus, the circus.
We're going to the circus, the circus today.
We'll see elephants at the circus,
The circus, the circus.
We'll see elephants at the circus, the circus today.

ADDITIONAL VERSES:
We'll see clowns at the circus . . .
We'll see horses at the circus . . .
We'll see acrobats at the circus . . .

We'll see lions at the circus . . .

—Barbara Scott

March in place.

Lean over, hand at nose to represent trunk; swing arm and sway back and forth.

Point to big smile.
Gallop in place.
Roll hands over each other or pretend to balance on a high wire.
Show claws.

This rhyme can be sung to the tune of "Teddy Bear, Teddy Bear" or chanted.

Funny Clown, Funny Clown

Funny clown, funny clown,
Jump all around!
Funny clown, funny clown,
Touch the ground.
Funny clown, funny clown,
Show your clown shoe.
Funny clown, funny clown,
That will do!
Funny clown, funny clown,
Run in place.
Funny clown, funny clown,
Happy face!
Funny clown, funny clown,
Turn out the light.
Funny clown, funny clown,
Say goodnight.

—Adapted traditional rhyme

Jump.

Bend and touch the ground.

Show shoe.

Shake finger, admonishing.

Run.

Make a big smile!

Motion of turning off light.

Put head on hands; pretend to sleep.

Five Funny Clowns

Five funny clowns were standing by the door.
One fell down and now there are four.
Four funny clowns, as silly as can be!
One went to find his hat and now there are three.
Three funny clowns, doing tricks as they do.
One made himself disappear and now there are two.
Two funny clowns having so much fun.
One drove away in a little car and now there's just one.
One little clown didn't want to be a hero.
He ran away and now there are zero!

—Barbara Scott

Begin this rhyme with five fingers up.
Take away fingers as the rhyme progresses.

The Circus Is Coming to Our Town

The circus is coming to our town,
Hurrah! Hurrah!
The circus is coming to our town,
Hurrah! Hurrah!
We'll see acrobats and lions there,
Some jugglers and a big trained bear!
And we'll all have fun,
The circus is coming to our town!

—Adapted traditional rhyme

Sung to the tune of "When Johnny Comes Marching Home."

Pump arm in the air.

Pump arm in the air.

Count out on fingers.
Point to self and children.

Down at the Circus

Down at the circus
Early in the morning,
See the circus animals
Standing in a row.
There's elephants and lions,
Monkeys, seals, and tigers.
All of them are ready
To put on a show!

—Adapted traditional rhyme

Sung to the tune of "Down by the Station."

Raise arms above head to make sun.

Hold up five fingers.

Count off the five types on fingers.

Clap three times.

Five Silly Clowns

Five silly clowns standing in the circus ring.
The first clown said, "Just listen to me sing."

The second clown said, "That note was very flat."
The third clown said, "I have a funny hat."
The fourth clown said, "I'll juggle all these balls."
The fifth clown said, "I'll do a funny fall."

—Barbara Scott

Begin this rhyme with five fingers up.
Starting with the thumb, point to each in succession. Sing a note . . . "la"!
Make a "raspberry" sound.

I'm a Clown

I'm a clown,
A silly circus clown.
I know tricks,
I'll do some for you now.
I can juggle lots of balls,
Or I can do a funny fall.
Juggle balls, funny fall . . . oh.
I'm a clown,
A silly circus clown.
All my tricks will
Make you laugh and laugh!

—Adapted traditional rhyme

Sung to the tune of "Alouette."

Point to self.

Tap temple twice.

Pretend to juggle.
Pretend to fall.

Point to self.

Hold stomach as if laughing.

Circus Hokey Pokey

You put your elephant ears in,
Your put your elephant ears out.
You put your elephant ears in,
And you shake them all about.
You do the circus pokey,
And you turn yourself around.
That's what it's all about!

ADDITIONAL VERSES:
 . . . seal nose
 . . . acrobat toes
 . . . magician's hands
 . . . horse's tail

—Adapted traditional rhyme

Sung to the tune of "The Hokey Pokey."

Place hands on either side of the head; move back and forth as if flapping.

Shake head.

Turn in a circle.
Clap!

Point to nose and stick in.
Stick toes in.
Hands in, wiggle fingers.
Wiggle bottom.

Ten Little Clowns

One little, two little, three little clowns,
Four little, five little, six little clowns,
Seven little, eight little, nine little clowns,
Ten little laughing clowns!
Ten little, nine little, eight little clowns,
Seven little, six little, five little clowns,
Four little, three little, two little clowns,
One little laughing clown!

—Adapted traditional rhyme

Sung to the tune of "Ten Little Indians."
Count out on fingers for first verse.

Take away fingers on second verse.

Five Little Acrobats

Five little acrobats hear the crowd roar.
One flies off the trapeze and now there are four.
Four little acrobats, balancing you see.
One falls into the net and now there are three.
Three little acrobats with lots of stunts to do.
One slides down the pole and now there are two.
Two little acrobats ready for some fun.
One does a double flip and now there's just one.
One little acrobat, his act is almost done.
He stands and takes a bow and now there are none.

—Barbara Scott

Begin this rhyme with five fingers up.
Take away fingers as the rhyme progresses.

Five Prancing Ponies

Five prancing ponies dancing in the circus ring.
The first pony said, "I'm so happy I could sing!"
The second pony said, "Just watch how I dance!"
The third pony said, "We made a good entrance!"

Begin this rhyme with five fingers up.
Starting with the thumb, point to each in succession.

The fourth pony said, "We'll take lots of bows."
The fifth pony said, "Just listen to that crowd!"

—Barbara Scott

If You Play in the Circus Band

If you play in the circus band, clap your hands.
If you play in the circus band, clap your hands.
If you play in the circus band, give yourself a great big hand!
If you play in the circus band, clap your hands.
ADDITIONAL VERSES:
If you play in the circus band, toot your horn . . .
If you play in the circus band, crash your cymbals . . .
If you play in the circus band, do all three! . . .

—Adapted traditional rhyme

Sung to the tune of "If You're Happy and You Know It."
Clap, clap.
Clap, clap.

Clap, clap.

Toot, toot.
Make chh, chh sound.

Circus Animal Count

One enormous elephant parading 'round the ring.
Two beautiful parrots who can't wait to sing.
Three silly chimps doing tricks up a tree.
Four waltzing bears dancing for all to see.
Five little puppy dogs doing stunts all day.
Six rambunctious seals find their horns to play.
Seven roaring lions let all know who is king.
Eight striped tigers, just watch their tails swing.
Nine dancing horses, see them balance on two feet.
Ten furry camels, their nodding keeps the beat.

—Barbara Scott

This is also a great rhyme to do as a flannel or Velcro board presentation using pictures of the animals!
Count the animals on fingers as they are mentioned.

At the Circus

At the circus,
At the circus,
We'll have fun,
We'll have fun.
Acrobats are tumbling,
Circus clowns are juggling.
Come along!
Come along!

—Adapted traditional rhyme

Sung to the tune of "Frère Jacques."

Clap three times.
Clap three times.
Roll hands.
Pretend to juggle.
Beckon.
Beckon.

Five Trapeze Artists

Five trapeze artists are ready to swing.
The first one said, "I'll catch the open rings."
The second one said, "You will catch me with your hands."

Begin this rhyme with five fingers up.
Starting with the thumb, point to each in succession.

The third one said, "Hear the roar from the stands!"
The fourth one said, "I'll do a double flip!"
The fifth one said, "Be careful! Don't slip!"

—Barbara Scott

Books to Share

Bronson, Linda. 2001. *The Circus Alphabet.* New York: Henry Holt and Company. ISBN: 978-0805062946.

Davenport, Meg, and Lisa V. Werenko. 1998. *Circus! A Pop-Up Adventure.* New York: Little Simon. ISBN: 978-0689820939.

Downs, Mike. 2005. *You See a Circus, I See. . . .* Watertown, MA: Charlesbridge Publishing. ISBN: 978-1580890977.

Keret, Etgar. 2004. *Dad Runs Away with the Circus.* Somerville, MA: Candlewick Press. ISBN: 978-0763622473.

Rex, Adam. 2006. *Tree-Ring Circus.* Boston: Harcourt Children's Books. ISBN: 978-0152053635.

Rey, H.A. 1998. *See the Circus.* Boston: Houghton Mifflin Books for Children. ISBN: 978-0395906958.

Musical Selections

"Bean Bag Balance" and "Bean Bag Juggle" from *Me and My Bean Bag.* ASIN: B0001Z8VYQ.

"Crazy Shoes Theme" from *Jim Gill Sings Moving Rhymes for Modern Times* by Jim Gill. Available: www.jimgill.com (accessed March 3, 2010).

"It's Showtime" from *Get Funky and Musical Fun* by The Learning Station. ASIN: B0001CJ8KU.

"The Marching Band" from *Rockin' Rhythm Band.* ASIN: B000ZSZ0IY.

Sources

Anonymous. 1898. *Circus Friends.* New York: McLoughlin Brothers.

Cullum, Carolyn N. 2007. *The Storytime Sourcebook II.* New York: Neal-Schuman.

"Fingerplays." Natural Learning. Available: www.naturallearning.com/fingerplays.html (accessed March 6, 2010).

Grayson, Marion. 1962. *Let's Do Fingerplays.* Fairfield, CT: R.B. Luce.

Irving, Jan, and Robin Currie. 1987. *Glad Rags: Stories and Activities Featuring Clothes for Children.* Santa Barbara, CA: Libraries Unlimited.

North Central Library Co-operative. n.d. *Storytime Booklet* [out of print].

Redleaf, Rhonda. 1983. *Busy Fingers, Growing Minds.* St. Paul, MN: Redleaf Press.

Roberts, Lynda. 1985. *Mitt Magic: Fingerplays for Finger Puppets.* Silver Spring, MD: Gryphon House.

Totline Staff, comp. 1994. *1001 Rhymes and Fingerplays.* Everett, WA: Warren Publishing House.

Warren, Jean, comp. 1989. *Theme-a-Saurus.* Everett, WA: Warren Publishing House.

Chapter 3

Clothing to Dragons

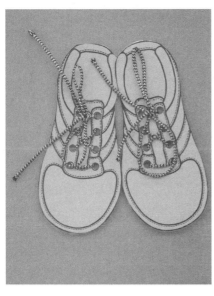

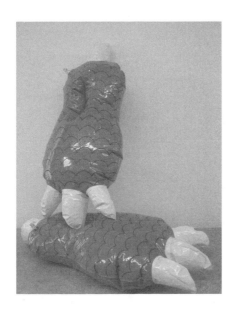

Clothing (Hats, Shoes, and More!)
Clothes, clothes, all kinds of clothes!

Rhyme

Telling Guide

Clap for Clothes

We wear some shoes.	Point to shoes.
They come in twos.	
One, two,	Point to one shoe, then the other.
Clap your hands.	Clap two times.
We wear a shirt.	Point to shirt.
Brush off the dirt.	
Brush, brush.	Brush shirt.
One, two,	
Clap your hands.	Clap two times.
We wear some pants.	Point to pants.
To do a dance.	
Dance, dance.	Dance.
Brush, brush,	Brush shirt.
One, two,	
Clap your hands.	Clap two times.
We wear some socks.	Point to socks.
To jump on rocks.	
Jump, jump.	Jump.
Dance, dance.	Dance.
Brush, brush.	Brush shirt.
One, two,	
Clap your hands.	Clap two times.
Now we're all dressed.	
We look our best!	
Jump, jump.	Jump.
Dance, dance.	Dance.
Brush, brush.	Brush shirt.
One, two,	
Clap your hands.	Clap two times.

—Jan Irving

Now You're Getting Dressed

First put on your underwear,
Underwear, underwear.
First put on your underwear.
Now you're getting dressed.
Stick your arms down in your shirt,

Sung to the tune of "Mary Had a Little Lamb."

Pretend to put on each item as it is mentioned.

In your shirt, in your shirt.
Stick your arms down in your shirt.
Now you're getting dressed.
Pull your pants up to your waist,
To your waist, to your waist.
Pull your pants up to your waist.
Now you're getting dressed.
Wiggle toes down in your socks,
In your socks, in your socks.
Wiggle toes down in your socks.
Now you're getting dressed.
Slip your shoes on, tie them tight,
Tie them tight, tie them tight.
Slip your shoes on, tie them tight.
Now you're getting dressed.
Now you can go out and play,
Out and play, out and play.
Now you can go out and play.
You got yourself all dressed.
YES!

—Jan Irving

Run or jump in place for last verse.

Buttons, Zippers, Snaps, and Bows

Buttons, zippers, snaps and bows,
Snaps and bows, snaps and bows.
Buttons, zipper, snaps and bows.
That's the way we close our clothes!

Sung to the tune of "The Mulberry Bush." Older children will enjoy singing the last verse very fast.

Buttons poke in button holes,
Button holes, button holes.
Buttons poke in button holes.
That's the way we close our clothes!

Form circle with one hand; point finger through hole.

Zippers run along a track,
'Long a track, 'long a track.
Zippers run along a track.
That's the way we close our clothes!

Run thumb from belt to chin.

Snaps together pop and snap,
Pop and snap, pop and snap.
Snaps together pop and snap.
That's the way we close our clothes!

Snap fingers.

Make two loops to tie a bow,
Tie a bow, tie a bow.
Make two loops to tie a bow.
That's the way we close our clothes!

Wiggle fingers by shoes.

Buttons, zippers, snaps, and bows,

Do all four actions.

Snaps and bows, snaps and bows.
Buttons, zippers, snaps and bows.
That's the way we close our clothes!

—Jan Irving

Pocket Surprise

Right here in my pocket	Place hands over shirt pocket.
Is a surprise for you.	Point to children.
It isn't an umbrella,	Touch fingers overhead; bend elbows.
Or a monster who says "Boo!"	Circle eyes with fingers.
It's not a wiggle spider,	Wiggle fingers in air.
Or a snake that likes to hiss.	Wiggle body and "Hissss."
Right here in my pocket	Place hands over shirt pocket.
Is a big two-handed kiss!	Hold up both hands in air.
Mmmmm-wah!	Touch hand to mouth; spread arms wide.

—Jan Irving

Pat-a-Patch: An Action Rhyme

Patches, patches	Clap twice.
On your knees.	Tap your knees twice.
Up,	Reach up.
Down,	Reach down.
Turn around.	Turn around.
I love patches.	Clap three times.
Patches, patches	
On your knees.	
On your elbows.	Tap your elbows twice.
Up,	
Down,	
Turn around.	
I love patches.	
Patches, patches	
On your knees,	
On your elbows,	
On your toes.	Tap toes twice.
Up,	
Down,	
Turn around.	
I love patches.	
Patches, patches	
On your knees,	
On your elbows,	
On your toes,	
On your eye.	Touch eyes twice.

Up,
Down,
Turn around.
I love patches.
Patches, patches
On your knees,
On your elbows,
On your toes,
On your eye,
On your seat.   Tap seat of pants.
Up,
Down,
Turn around.
I love patches.

—Jan Irving

My Hat Has Three Corners

My hat it has three corners.   Point to head; hold up three fingers.
Three corners has my hat.   Hold up three fingers; point to head.
And had it not three corners,   Hold up three fingers.
It wouldn't be my hat.   Shake head "no"; point to head.

—Traditional German rhyme

A Tall Hat

A tall hat,   Hold right hand high above head; put
A small hat,   left hand on head. / Lower right hand
A big hat,   to just above left hand.
A cap.   Hold both hands wide from head.
Now I take my hats off,   Touch fingers above head.
And put them in my lap.   Fold hands.
                                                         Put in lap.

—Author unknown

Work Hats

An astronaut's hat
Is worn out in space.   Hands up, walk as if in space.
A lifeguard's visor
Keeps the sun off her face.   Shield eye with hand.
Quarterbacks wear helmets
To protect their heads.   Bend knees; place hands on them.
Firefighters wear hats
All bright and red.   Mime using fire hose.
Police wear hats
With a shiny shield.   Put hand up as if stopping traffic.
Farmers wear brimmed hats

Out in the field.
These hats help people
Get their work done.
But, sometimes, hats
Are just for fun.

—Jan Irving

Funny Hat

On my head I wear a hat.
It is such a funny hat,
That my head will wiggle, wiggle to and fro.
Where else can my fun hat go?
On my knee I wear a hat.
It is such a funny hat,
That my knee will wiggle, wiggle to and fro.
Where else can my fun hat go?
On my hands I wear a hat.
It is such a quiet hat.
My hands don't wiggle, they just go clap,
Then I put them in my lap.

—Jan Irving

Caps for Sale

Caps for sale, caps for sale,
Caps upon my head.
Caps for sale, caps for sale,
Yellow, blue, and red.

—Jean Warren

Where's My Shoe?

One, two
Where's my shoe?
Three, four
On a kangaroo?
Five, six
On a slippery snake?
Seven, eight
On a fish in a lake?
Nine, ten
Look and see.
Here they are—
Right on me!

—Jan Irving

Mime hoeing field.

Put hands out, palms up.

Clap three times.

Sung to the tune of "This Old Man." After children understand how the actions and words go together, let them suggest other parts of the body for using the hat. For extra fun, use a real hat!
Put hands on head.
Shake head.
Wiggle head.
Put hands shoulder high, palms up.
Point to knee, then do actions as in last verse.

When all the wiggles are out, use this last verse to get settled for the next activity.

Touch head.

Have fun with this activity by clapping on each number and doing the actions indicated.

Put palms up, shoulder high.

Jump.

Wiggle body.

Put palms together; move hands in zigzag fashion.

Circle eyes with fingers.

Point to shoes, then self.

Dirty Feet Song

I don't want to wear my shoes,
Wear my shoes, wear my shoes.
I don't want to wear my shoes,
So I have dirty feet.
March in puddles, splash and splash,
Splash and splash, splash and splash.
March in puddles, splash and splash,
So I have dirty feet.
Run in tall grass, run and run,
Run and run, run and run,
Run in tall grass, run and run,
So I have dirty feet.
Jump in mud holes, jump and jump,
Jump and jump, jump and jump.
Jump in mud holes, jump and jump,
So I have dirty feet.
Now I'd better wash them off,
Wash them off, wash them off.
Now I'd better wash them off,
I don't want dirty feet!

—Jan Irving

Sung to the tune of "The Mulberry Bush."
Shake head or take off shoes.

March in place.

Run in place.

Jump.

Rub feet or put on shoes.

The Best Shoes

Shiny party shoes go squeak.
Squeak, squeak, squeak.
Squeak, squeak, squeak.
Shiny party shoes go squeak.
They are not the best.
Sunny summer sandals flap.
Flap, flap, flap.
Flap, flap, flap.
Sunny summer sandals flap.
They are not the best.
I like sneakers best of all.
Best of all.
Best of all.
I like sneakers best of all.
They run and run and run!
Run and run and run and run.
Run and run.
Run and run.
Run and run and run, and run.
Sneakers are the best—YES!

—Jan Irving

Sung to the tune of "Mary Had a Little Lamb."
Walk on tiptoe.

Walk in place, ankles limp.

Run in place.
Continue to run in place.

This Little Piggy's Piggies

This little piggy wears toe shoes.	Point to big toe.
This little piggy wears slippers.	Point to next toe.
This little piggy wears sandals.	Point to next toe.
This little piggy wears flippers.	Point to next toe.
This little piggy lost his tennies,	Point to little toe.
So his little piggies don't wear any!	

—Jan Irving

Stockings On

Deedle, deedle, dumpling,	Walk in stocking feet.
Shoes all gone.	
We went to town	
With our stockings on.	
Shoes all gone,	
Stockings on.	
Deedle, deedle, dumpling,	
Shoes all gone.	

—Adapted traditional rhyme

Right Shoe, Left Shoe

Tap your right shoe,	Do actions as indicated.
All of you.	
Tap your left shoe,	
We're not through!	
Right shoe,	
Left shoe,	
Tap, tap, tap!	
Hands together,	
Clap, clap, clap!	

—Traditional rhyme

Old Shoes, New Shoes

Old shoes, new shoes,	Point to child's shoes, first one, then the other.
Black and brown and red shoes.	
One, two, three, four,	Show four fingers.
Tapping softly on the floor.	Tap fingers on floor.

—From *Let's Do Fingerplays*

Mittens

Slide your fingers into the wide part,	Hold right hand forward, palm down.
Make your thumb stand alone and tall.	Keep fingers together, thumb apart.
When you put your mittens on,	Slide left hand over grouped fingers, then over thumb.
You won't feel cold at all.	

—From *Let's Do Fingerplays*

The Mitten Song

"Thumb in the thumb place,
Fingers all together!"
This is the song we sing in mitten weather.
When it's cold,
It doesn't matter whether
Mittens are wool
Or made of finest leather.
This is the song we sing in mitten weather;
"Thumbs in the thumb place,
Fingers all together!"

—From *Let's Do Fingerplays*

Hold one hand up, fingers together, thumb apart; point to thumb and then to fingers.

Rub hands together.

Hold two hands up, fingers together, thumbs apart.

Hold one hand up, fingers together, thumb apart; point to thumb and then to fingers.

Put on Your Mittens

Put on your mittens—it's cold, I fear,
Now that winter snow is here.
Play in the yard and when you're done,
Pull off your mittens one by one.

—Barbara Paxson

Pretend to put on mittens.
Hug self and shiver.
Pretend to make and toss snowballs.
Pretend to remove mittens.

Color Mittens

My poor little kitten lost her mitten
And started to cry, "Boohoo."
So I helped my kitten look for her mitten,
Her beautiful mitten of blue.
I found a mitten just right for a kitten
Under my mother's bed.
But, alas, the mitten was not the right mitten,
For it was colored red.
I found a mitten just right for a kitten
Under my father's pillow.
But, alas, the mitten was not the right mitten,
For it was colored yellow.
I found a mitten just right for a kitten
Under the laundry so clean.
But, alas, the mitten was not the right mitten,
For it was colored green.
I found a mitten just right for a kitten
Inside my favorite shoe.
And this time the mitten was just the right mitten,
For it was colored blue!

—Jean Warren

Pretend to cry.
Cup hand above eye and glance around.

Pretend to peek under bed.
Shake head.

Pretend to peek under pillow.
Shake head.

Pretend to peek under folded laundry.
Shake head.

Pretend to peek inside shoe.
Nod head and smile.

Cobbler, Cobbler

Cobbler, cobbler, mend my shoe.

Get it done by half past two.

Half past two is much too late.

Get it done by half past eight.

Stitch it up and stitch it down,

And I'll give you half a crown.

—Traditional rhyme

Pound fist of one hand on palm of other.

Show two fingers.

Shake head "no."

Tap wrist to indicate watch or show eight fingers.

Sewing motions up and then down.

Motion of handing over money.

A Big Shoe

Said little Sue

To little Pete,

"I can't see you

For your big feet."

Said little Pete

To little Sue,

"'Tis not my feet;

'Tis but my shoe."

—Traditional rhyme

Have both thumbs "talk" to each other.

Shake head "no."

Wiggle feet.

Thumbs "talk" again.

Shake head "no."

Point to shoes.

Winter Clothes

Three layers of shirts on top,

And two pairs of pants below,

A winter coat with a zipper,

To play out in the snow.

One, two, three pairs of socks

And warm boots for my feet.

A scarf to wrap around my neck

To keep in my body heat.

Two pairs of mittens for my hands,

A stocking cap for my head.

With any more clothes, I couldn't walk in the snow.

I'd have to roll around instead.

—Susan M. Dailey

Hold up three fingers; point to chest.

Hold up two fingers; point to lower body.

Pretend to zip.

Point with finger.

Count with fingers; point to feet.

Pretend to pull on boots.

Pretend to wrap.

Hug self and shiver.

Hold up hands with fingers in mitten shape. / Pretend to pull down cap.

Shake head "no."

Roll hands around each other.

Searching for My Clothes

It's time to go!

It's time to go!

Where are my socks?

I don't know!

I searched high and I searched low.

Where are my socks?

I don't know!

I searched by the computer

Tap wrist.

Hold hands out in questioning motion.

Shake head.

Put hand above eyes; look upward, then downward.

Pretend to type on keyboard.

And by the rocking chair.	Pretend to rock.
I finally looked in the toy box.	Pretend to lift lid.
What are they doing there?	Shrug shoulders.
I pulled them on,	Pretend to put on.
Found a hole in the toe.	
So who cares?	Shrug shoulders.
I'm ready to go.	Nod head.
"You mean I have to wear shoes?"	Speak this line.
It's time to go!	Tap wrist.
It's time to go!	
Where are my shoes?	Hold out hands in questioning motion.
I don't know!	Shake head.
I searched high and I searched low.	Put hand above eyes; look upward, then downward.
Where are my shoes?	
I don't know!	
I searched by the computer	Pretend to type on keyboard.
And by the rocking chair.	Pretend to rock.
I finally looked in the freezer.	Pretend to open door.
What are they doing there?	Shrug shoulders.
I put them on.	Pretend to put on.
Tied the laces in a bow.	Pretend to tie.
My shoes are on.	
I'm ready to go.	Nod head.
"You mean I have to wear a coat?"	Speak this line.
It's time to go!	Tap wrist.
It's time to go!	
Where is my coat?	Hold out hands in questioning manner.
I don't know!	Shake head.
I searched high and I searched low.	Put hand above eyes; look upward, then downward.
Where is my coat?	
I don't know.	
I searched by the computer	Pretend to type on keyboard.
And by the rocking chair.	Pretend to rock.
I finally looked in the closet.	Pretend to open door.
What is it doing there?	Shrug shoulders.
I put it on,	Pretend to put on.
Zipped it up just so.	Pretend to button or zip.
I'm finally ready.	
Come on, let's go!	Nod head.

—Adapted from a song by Susan M. Dailey

Silly Sally

Silly Sally tried to get dressed.	Pretend to put on clothes.
Silly Sally was a mess.	
Silly Sally put her shirt on her toes.	Point to toes.

Silly Sally put her socks on her nose.

Silly Sally put her pants on her head.

Silly Sally, just go back to bed!

—Susan M. Dailey

This Is the Way: An Action Rhyme

Point to nose.

Point to head.

Rest head on hands; snore.

This rhyme is excerpted from the rhyme "The Mulberry Bush." These stanzas deal directly with clothing and make a great rhyme on their own! Of course, they are sung to the traditional tune.

This is the way we wash our clothes,

Wash our clothes,

Wash our clothes.

This is the way we wash our clothes,

So early in the morning.

Motion of washing clothes.

This is the way we iron our clothes,

Iron our clothes,

Iron our clothes.

This is the way we iron our clothes,

So early in the morning.

Motion of ironing.

This is the way we mend our clothes,

Mend our clothes,

Mend our clothes.

This is the way we mend our clothes,

So early in the morning.

Motion of sewing.

This is the way we get dressed up,

Get dressed up,

Get dressed up.

This is the way we get dressed up,

So early in the morning.

Motion of putting clothing on.

—Adapted traditional rhyme

Hats, Hats, Hats

Sung to the tune of "Three Blind Mice."

Point to head.

Hats, hats, hats.

Hats, hats, hats.

I love hats.

I love hats.

Place one hand over heart.

Place both hands over heart.

Hats to wear

For work or play.

On work, pretend to hammer; for play, wiggle fingers in the air.

Hats for night

And hats for day.

Arms make circle low to represent moon.

Arms make circle above head to represent sun.

Hats from here

And far away.

I love hats.

Point to ground.

Point away.

Point to self.

—Adapted from a song by Jean Warren

I Can Do It Myself

Hat on head, just like this,
Pull it down, you see.
I can put my hat on
All by myself, just me.
One arm in, two arms in,
Buttons, one, two, three.
I can put my coat on
All by myself, just me.
Toes in first, heels push down,
Pull and pull, then see—
I can put my boots on
All by myself, just me.
Fingers here, thumbs right here,
Hands warm as can be.
I can put my mittens on
All by myself, just me.

—Adapted traditional rhyme

Do actions as rhyme indicates.

In My Pockets

The things in my pockets are lots of fun,
I will show you one by one.
In my first pocket is a frog,
I found him sitting on a log.
In my second pocket is a car,
It can race off very far.
In my third pocket is a ball,
I can bounce it on a wall.
In my fourth pocket is a bunny,
She twitches her nose and looks so funny.
In my fifth pocket is a dog,
He's a friend of my little frog.

—Sue Schliecker

Hold up five fingers.

Point to thumb.

Point to index finger.

Point to middle finger.

Point to ring finger.

Point to little finger.
Touch little finger to thumb.

Our Mittens

These are our mittens,
What are they for?
They keep our hands warm
When we go out the door.

—Beverly Qualheim

Pretend to put on mittens.

Five Little Hats

Five little hats hanging by the door.
Daddy took one, and then there were four.
Four little hats, so nice and warm, you see.

Begin this rhyme with five fingers up.
Take away fingers as the rhyme progresses.

Mommy took one, and then there were three.
Three little hats, one of them is new.
Brother took one, and then there were two.
Two little hats, our rhyme is almost done.
Sister took one, and now there is one.
One little hat, not having any fun.
That hat is mine, and now there are none.

—Barbara Scott

We Are Going Out to Play

We are going out to play,
Out to play, out to play.
We are going out to play.
Let's get dressed!

First our coat we button up,   *Action of buttoning coat.*
Button up, button up.
First our coat we button up.
Let's get dressed!

Next we put on a warm scarf,   *Motion of wrapping scarf around neck.*
A warm scarf, a warm scarf.
Next we put on a warm scarf.
Let's get dressed!

We put a hat upon our head,   *Action of putting on a hat.*
On our head, on our head.
We put a hat upon our head.
Let's get dressed!

Next we pull on both our boots,   *Action of pulling on boots.*
Both our boots, both our boots.
Next we pull on both our boots.
Let's get dressed.

We put our hands into our gloves,   *Motion of putting hand in gloves.*
Into our gloves, into our gloves.
We put our hands into our gloves.
"Now, let's go outside!"   *Speak this line.*

—Adapted traditional rhyme

Five Little Pairs of Shoes

Five little pairs of shoes sitting in the store.   *Begin this rhyme with five fingers up.*
The first pair said, "We are sitting on the floor." *Take away fingers as the rhyme progresses.*
The second pair said, "We're bright and shiny blue."
The third pair said, "We are shiny, too."
The fourth pair said, "A family I see."
The fifth pair said, "Buy me! Buy me!"

—Barbara Scott

Sung to the tune of "London Bridge."

Ten Little Pair of Socks

One little, two little, three little pair,
Four little, five little, six little pair,
Seven little, eight little, nine little pair,
Ten little pair of socks.
Ten little, nine little, eight little pair,
Seven little, six little, five little pair,
Four little, three little, two little pair,
One little pair of socks!

—Adapted traditional rhyme

Sung to the tune of "Ten Little Indians." This is also a fun rhyme to do on a flannel or Velcro board. Another fun approach is to have two children hold a clothesline and pin actual pairs of socks to it!

Count out fingers for the first verse.

Take away fingers for the second verse.

Books to Share

Beaton, Clare. 2005. *Daisy Gets Dressed*. Cambridge, MA: Barefoot Books. ISBN: 978-1841487939.
Blankenship, LeeAnn. 2005. *Mr. Tuggle's Troubles*. Honesdale, PA: Boyds Mills Press. ISBN: 978-1590781968.
Kuskin, Karla. 2004. *Under My Hood I Have a Hat*. New York: HarperCollins. ISBN: 978-0060572426.
Moss, Miriam. 2005. *Bare Bear*. London: Hodder Children's Books. ISBN: 978-0340882023.
Parnell, Robyn. 2005. *My Closet Threw a Party*. New York: Sterling. ISBN: 978-1402712982.
Shea, Bob. 2007. *New Socks*. New York: Little, Brown Young Readers. ISBN: 978-0316013574.

Musical Selections

"Blue Suede Shoes" from *Bean Bag Rock and Roll*. ASIN: B00015EL2M.
"Bring Your Clothes" from *Whaddya Think of That?* by Laurie Berkner. ASIN: B00004SR1J.
"Crazy Shoes Theme" from *Jim Gill Sings Moving Rhymes for Modern Times* by Jim Gill. Available: www.jimgill.com (accessed March 4, 2010).
"Goofy Hat Dance" from *Greg and Steve: Fun and Games* by Greg and Steve. ASIN: B0000A8XP9.
"I Got a Hat" from *Seasonal Songs in Motion* by The Learning Station. ASIN: B00005TPUN.
"Look at My New Shoes" from *Don't Forget the Donut* by Wayne Potash. ASIN: B000BP2Y26.
"Old Sock Stew" from *Jim Gill Sings The Sneezing Song and Other Contagious Tunes* by Jim Gill. Available: www.jimgill.com (accessed March 4, 2010).

Sources

Dailey, Susan M. 2001. *A Storytime Year*. New York: Neal-Schuman.
———. 2007. *Sing a Song of Storytime*. New York: Neal-Schuman.
Grayson, Marion. 1962. *Let's Do Fingerplays*. Fairfield, CT: R.B. Luce.
Index of Rhymes. Available: www.kidsnurseryrhymes.co.uk/rhymes (accessed March 6, 2004).
Irving, Jan, and Robin Currie. 1987. *Glad Rags: Stories and Activities Featuring Clothes for Children*. Santa Barbara, CA: Libraries Unlimited.
McKinnon, Elizabeth, and Gayle Bittinger. 1994. *Busy Bees Fall: Fun for Two's and Three's*. Everett, WA: Warren Publishing House.

———. 1994. *Busy Bees Spring: Fun for Two's and Three's*. Everett, WA: Warren Publishing House.

———. 1994. *Busy Bees Winter: Fun for Two's and Three's*. Everett, WA: Warren Publishing House.

"The Mother Goose Pages." Mama Lisa's World of Children & International Culture. Available: www.mamalisa.com (accessed March 4, 2010).

North Central Library Co-operative. n.d. *Storytime Booklet* [out of print].

Totline Staff, comp. 1994. *1001 Rhymes and Fingerplays*. Everett, WA: Warren Publishing House.

Traditional Music Library. Available: www.traditionalmusic.co.uk (accessed March 6, 2010).

Warren, Jean, comp. 1990. *Theme-a-Saurus II*. Everett, WA: Warren Publishing House.

Warren, Jean. 1991. *Toddler Theme-a-Saurus*. Everett, WA: Warren Publishing House.

Colors
Colors, colors, they're all around!

Rhyme

I've Got Red Paint

I've got red paint.
You've got blue.
What would happen if we mixed the two?
Pour out some red paint,
Pour out some blue.
What's gonna happen when we mix the two?
Purple is the color that we made!
Now we're ready to paint today!
I've got yellow paint.
You've got blue.
What would happen if we mixed the two?
Pour out some yellow paint.
Pour out some blue.
What's gonna happen when we mix the two?
Green is the color that we made!
Now we're ready to paint today!
I've got yellow paint.
You've got red.
What would happen if we mixed the two?
Pour out some yellow paint.
Pour out some red.
What's gonna happen when we mix the two?
Orange is the color that we made!
Now we're ready to paint today!

—Kathy Ross

Rhyme of Colors

The rainbow is celebrating
For it wears on its head
A bow with all the colors
The same as my little sister's.
Violet, indigo,
Blue, green, yellow, orange, and red.
The rainbow is celebrating
The colors are on its head.

—Traditional French rhyme

Telling Guide

Sung to the tune of "Shortnin' Bread."

Point to self.
Point to children.

Pouring motion.
Pour again.
Place hand under chin, wondering.
Clap.
Use above motions for the following verses.

Make arch overhead for rainbow.
Point to head.

Count out colors on fingers.
Make arch overhead.
Point to head.

The Colors in My Box

There's colors in my box,
There's colors in my box.
Hi ho the cherrio
There's colors in my box.
The yellow takes the blue,
The yellow takes the blue.
They hug together merrily,
And now there's green too.
The white takes the red,
The white takes the red,
They hug together merrily,
And pink appears instead.

—Carolyn N. Cullum

Rainbow Colors

If you know the colors of the rainbow, step right up.
If you know the colors of the rainbow, step right up.
If you know the colors of the rainbow,
    well just step right up and say so.
If you know the colors of the rainbow, step right up.
If you see the color red, just nod your head.
If you see the color red, just nod your head.
If you see the color red,
    well just step up and nod your head.
If you see the color red, just nod your head.
If you see the color black, just hop right back.
If you see the color black, just hop right back.
If you see the color black,
    well just step up and hop right back.
If you see the color black, just hop right back.
If you see the color yellow, act like Jell-O.
If you see the color yellow, act like Jell-O.
If you see the color yellow,
    well just step up and act like Jell-O.
If you see the color yellow, act like Jell-O.
If you see the color blue, just stomp your shoe.
If you see the color blue, just stomp your shoe.
If you see the color blue,
    well just step up and stomp your shoe.
If you see the color blue, just stomp your shoe.
If you see the color white, go fly a kite.
If you see the color white, go fly a kite.
If you see the color white,
    well just step up and fly a kite.
If you see the color white, go fly a kite.

Sung to the tune of "The Farmer in the Dell."

Repeat first verse.

Sung to the tune of "If You're Happy and You Know It."
Stomp each foot.

Stomp each foot.
Nod.

Nod.
Hop backward.

Hop backward.
Shake all over.

Shake all over.
Stomp foot.

Stomp foot.
Hold hand up, as if flying a kite.

Hold hand up, as if flying kite.

If you see the color pink, give a wink.
If you see the color pink, give a wink.
If you see the color pink,
   well just step up and give a wink.
If you see the color pink, give a wink.

—Kay Lincycomb

Crayon Box

One big crayon, two big crayons,
Three big crayons, four big crayons,
Five big crayons, six big crayons,
Seven, eight big crayons.
Red one, yellow one, blue one, green one,
Orange one, purple one, black and brown ones,
Many colors of the rainbow
In my crayon box.

—Susan M. Dailey

Wave Your Rainbow

Red and orange and yellow and green,
Then there's blue and purple.
Wave your rainbow, wave your rainbow,
Wave your pretty rainbow.

CHORUS:
Hold your rainbow way up high.
Wave your pretty rainbow.
Make it arc across the sky.
Yes, wave your pretty rainbow.
Rain your rainbow to one side.

—Adapted from a song by Susan M. Dailey

I See Blue

I see blue, I see the color blue.
I see blue, please come and look with me!
I see blue up in the sky,
And on the bluebird flying high.
In the sky . . . flying high . . . oh.
I see blue, I see the color blue
I see blue, please come and look with me!

—Adapted traditional rhyme

If You're Wearing . . .

If you're wearing red today, nod your head.
If you're wearing red today, nod your head.

Wink.

Wink.

Sung to the tune of "Ten Little Indians." Hold up fingers for the number of crayons.

Use same fingers for the colors named below.

Sung to the tune of "Yankee Doodle." Make up visual aids for children, such as pieces of paper in the colors named, or use scarves of the colors! Have children point to appropriate color.

Move as indicated.

Sung to the tune of "Alouette." Point to eyes.
Point to self.
Point up.
Flap arms.
Point up; then flap arms.

Point to self

Sung to the tune of "If You're Happy and You Know It." Have children do responses if they are wearing the color mentioned. Nod head "yes."

If you're wearing red today, go ahead and nod away!
If you're wearing red today, nod your head.
If you're wearing green today, pat your back.   *Pat back.*
If you're wearing green today, pat your back.
If you're wearing green today, go ahead and pat away!
If you're wearing green today, pat your back.
If you're wearing white today, stomp your feet.   *Stomp feet.*
If you're wearing white today, stomp your feet.
If you're wearing white today, go ahead and stomp away.
If you're wearing white today, stomp your feet.
If you're wearing blue today, shout "hooray."   *Shout and pump fist in the air.*
If you're wearing blue today, shout "hooray."
If you're wearing blue today, go ahead and shout "hooray"!
If you're wearing blue today, shout "hooray."

—Adapted traditional rhyme

Hunting for Colors

When doing this rhyme, you may want to pause a moment before naming the color and let the children guess the color from the rhyming word before!

Hunting for colors,   *Hold up index finger.*
The first I've seen
Was the grass in the front yard.
It was colored green.
The second was the flower.   *Hold up index and middle fingers.*
In the vase by my bed,
A beautiful rose,
And it was colored red.
The third was the grapes,   *Hold up index, middle, and ring fingers.*
So good I want to burp-le.
Yummy and sweet,
And they were colored purple.
The fourth was the sun,   *Hold up index, middle, ring, and pinkie fingers.*
So shiny and mellow.
Way up in the sky,
And it was colored yellow.
The fifth was a car,   *Hold up all five fingers.*
All shiny and new
With four round tires,
And it was colored blue.

—Barbara Scott

Rainbow Colors

The rainbow is so beautiful,   *Make arc in the air with hand.*
Way up in the sky.   *Point up.*
It has such brilliant colors;
To name them, let us try: *Count out the seven colors on fingers.*
Red is first, followed by orange,

Yellow, green, and blue.
Last, there's indigo,
And a color called violet, too!

—Barbara Scott

I See Colors

I see blue, I see blue,
In our room, in our room.
Quickly, can you find it,
Quickly, can you find it?
Zoom, zoom, zoom.
Zoom, zoom, zoom.

—Adapted traditional rhyme

Sung to the tune of "Frère Jacques." Have children point to or call out where they see the color. Continue with other colors for as long as there is interest. Point to eyes.

Pump arms back and forth as if running.

Books to Share

Beaumont, Karen. 2005. *I Ain't Gonna Paint No More.* Boston: Harcourt Children's Books. ISBN: 978-0152024888.

Catalanotto, Peter. 2005. *Kitten Red, Yellow, Blue.* New York: Atheneum. ISBN: 978-0689865626.

Dodd, Emma. 2001. *Dog's Colorful Day: A Messy Story about Colors and Counting.* New York: Dutton Juvenile. ISBN: 978-0525465287.

Ficocelli, Elizabeth. 2007. *Kid Tea.* Tarrytown, NY: Marshall Cavendish. ISBN: 978-0761453338.

Schachner, Judith B. 2007. *Skippyjon Jones: Color Crazy.* New York: Dutton Juvenile. ISBN: 978-0525477822.

Wood, Audrey. 2005. *The Deep Blue Sea: A Book of Colors.* New York: Blue Sky Press. ISBN: 978-0439753821.

Musical Selections

"Color Farm" from *Sing to Learn with Dr. Jean.* ASIN: B000F8R7J4.

"Color Game" from *Jim Gill Sings Do Re Mi on His Toe Leg Knee* by Jim Gill. Available: www.jimgill.com (accessed March 4, 2010).

"Colors" from *Dance and Sing: The Best of Nick Jr.* ASIN: B00005Q3AT.

"Over the Rainbow" from *Musical Scarves and Activities.* ASIN: B0001AC3KO.

"Rainbow of Colors" from *We All Live Together*, vol. 5, by Greg and Steve. ASIN: B00000DGMT.

"Who's Wearing Yellow?" from *Get Ready, Get Set, Sing!* By Sarah Barchas. ASIN: B0020SQRRK.

Sources

Cullum, Carolyn N. 2007. *The Storytime Sourcebook II.* New York: Neal-Schuman.

Dailey, Susan M. 2001. *A Storytime Year.* New York: Neal-Schuman.

———. 2007. *Sing a Song of Storytime.* New York: Neal-Schuman.

Findlay, Diane, Tami Chumbley Finley, Susan Mast, Kathy Ross, and Patti Sinclair. 2008. *Collaborative Summer Library Program Manual.* Mason City, IA: Collaborative Summer Library Program.

Lincycomb, Kay. 2007. *Storytimes . . . Plus!* New York: Neal-Schuman.

Mama Lisa's World of Children & International Culture. Available: www.mamalisa.com (accessed March 4, 2010).

Dinosaurs
This theme is a favorite one for children of all ages!

Rhyme	**Telling Guide**

Dinosaurs

Dinosaurs
Lived long ago.
Some walked,
Some swam,
Some flew, you know.
Some were big,
Some were small.
Some were gigantic, don't you know?

—From Laurabaas.com

Telling Guide:
Stomp.
Swim with arms.
Flap arms.
Stretch up high.
Crouch down low.
Stand tall, arms stretched wide.

Dinosaurs

Dinosaurs used to stomp.
They used to roar and moan.
But now they are quiet,
And quite still,
Because they've turned to stone.

—Author unknown

Telling Guide:
This is a great rhyme for opening a dinosaur storytime. It prepares children to listen to the book that will follow!
Stomp feet.
Roar.
Put finger to lips.
Sit down.
Arms quiet, ready to listen.

Five Enormous Dinosaurs

Five enormous dinosaurs, letting out a roar,
One went away and then there were four.
Four enormous dinosaurs, munching on a tree,
One went away and then there were three.
Three enormous dinosaurs didn't know what to do,
One went away and then there were two.
Two enormous dinosaurs having lots of fun,
One went away and then there was one.
One enormous dinosaur afraid to be a hero,
He [she] went away and then there were zero.

—From Laurabaas.com

Telling Guide:
Begin rhyme with five fingers up; roar.
Take away fingers as rhyme progresses.
Munching motion with arms and hands.

Scratch head.

Smile and laugh.

Hide face.

Stomp, Stomp, Stomp

The first big dinosaur went stomp, stomp, stomp.
I said to the first dinosaur, "Stop, stop, stop!"
The second big dinosaur went run, run, run.
I said to the second dinosaur, "Fun, fun, fun!"
The third big dinosaur went thump, thump, thump.
I said to the third dinosaur, "Jump, jump, jump!"

Telling Guide:
Begin with one finger up.

Add fingers as the rhyme progresses.

The fourth big dinosaur went whack, whack, whack.
I said to the fourth dinosaur, "You stay back!"
The fifth big dinosaur went creep, creep, creep.
I said to the fifth dinosaur, "It's time to sleep!"

—From Laurabaas.com

All Around the Swamp

The dinos in the swamp go stomp, stomp, stomp,
Stomp, stomp, stomp,
Stomp, stomp, stomp.
The dinos in the swamp go stomp, stomp, stomp
All around the swamp.

Sung to the tune of "The Wheels on the Bus."
Stomp feet.

ADDITIONAL VERSES:
The necks on the dinos move back and forth . . .
The wings on the dinos go flap, flap, flap . . .
The tails on the dinos go swish, swish, swish . . .
The mouth of the dino goes chomp, chomp, chomp . . .

Sway head from one side to the other.
Flap arms.
Move bottom from side to side.
Make chomping motion with hands.

—Barbara Scott

Five Little Dinos

Five little dinosaurs, listen to them roar.
One stomped away and then there were four.
Four little dinosaurs, eating leaves from a tree.
One stomped away and then there were three.
Three little dinosaurs, one of them is blue.
One stomped away and then there were two.
Two little dinosaurs enjoying the sun.
One stomped away and now there is one.
One little dinosaur, he's a lonely one.
He stomped away and now there are none.

Begin this rhyme with five fingers up.
Stomp feet and take fingers away as
the dinos leave.

—Barbara Scott

Dinosaur Dance

If you like to boogie, if you like to prance,
Let's all do the dinosaur dance!
Stomp your feet from side to side.
Swing your neck out big and wide!
Flap your wings like you're going to soar.
Swish that tail and dance some more!

Move around.
Clap.
Stomp feet.
Swing neck from side to side.
Flap arms.
Move your bottom from side to side.

—Barbara Scott

Dinosaurs in Motion

Harriet Hadrosaur loves to hop.
Danny Deinonychus dances.
Terrance Tyrannosaur walks on tiptoe.
While Steggie just spins and can't stop!

Hop on one foot.
Dance around.
Walk on tiptoe.
Spin around in a circle.

—Kathy Ross

Dinosaurs Walked This Earth

Dinosaurs walked on this earth,
On this earth, on this earth.
Dinosaurs walked on this earth,
A long, long time ago.

Sung to the tune of "Mary Had a Little Lamb."
Stomp feet from side to side.

Tyrannosaurus Rex was the king,
Was the king, was the king.
Tyrannosaurus Rex was the king,
A long, long time ago.

Hands in front, fingers make claws;
swish claws in air.

Tyrannosaurus [child's name] was the king,
Was the king, was the king.
Tyrannosaurus [child's name] was the king,
A long, long time ago.

Point to child named.

—From Laurabaas.com

Oh, I Want to Be a Great Big Dinosaur

Oh, I want to be a great big dinosaur,
That is what I really want to be!
For if I were a great big dinosaur,
Everyone would run away from me. . . .
Ahhhhhhhhh!

*Sung to the tune of "I Wish I Was an
Oscar Mayer Wiener."*
Put hand in the air to show height.

Show height again.
Run in place.
Cup hands around mouth.

ADDITIONAL VERSES:
Stomp away from me . . .
Crawl away from me . . .

Slither away from me . . .

Stomp feet from side to side.
Move hands back and forth in front,
as if crawling.
Hands with palms together, move
right and left in a slithering motion.

—From Laurabaas.com

Dinosaurs

Five enormous dinosaurs
Letting out a roar—
One went away, and
Then there were four.

Begin this rhyme with five fingers up.

Four enormous dinosaurs
Crashing down a tree—
One went away, and
Then there were three.

Take away fingers as rhyme
progresses.

Three enormous dinosaurs
Eating tiger stew—
One went away, and
Then there were two.
Two enormous dinosaurs
Trying to run—
One ran away, and
Then there was one.

One enormous dinosaur,
Afraid to be a hero—
He went away, and
Then there was zero.

—Lynda Roberts

Five Little Dinosaurs

Five little dinosaurs in the forest one night,
Heard a noise that gave them an awful fright.
The dinosaurs heard a loud and mighty roar,
One ran away, and now there are four.
Four little dinosaurs in the forest one night,
Heard a noise that gave them an awful fright.
The dinosaurs heard a roar and then one did flee,
One ran away, and now there are three.
Three little dinosaurs in the forest one night,
Heard a noise that gave them an awful fright.
The dinosaurs heard a roar and away another flew.
One ran away, and now there are two.
Two little dinosaurs in the forest one night,
Heard a noise that gave them an awful fright.
The dinosaurs heard a roar and one more began to run.
One ran away, and now there is only one.
One little dinosaur in the forest one night,
Heard a noise that gave him an awful fright.
He jumped into his bed, trembling with all his might.
That roar was Papa saying, "Turn out that light!"

—Kay Lincycomb

Begin this rhyme with five fingers up.

Take away fingers as rhyme progresses.

Stomp, Stomp, Stomp

Stomp! Stomp!
Roar! Roar!
There's a dinosaur at my door!
I see a dinosaur big and green.
He's the biggest dinosaur you've ever seen.
Stomp! Stomp!
Roar! Roar!
There's a dinosaur at my door!
I see a dinosaur and he's yellow.
My, oh, my, he's a scary fellow.
Stomp! Stomp!
Roar! Roar!
There's a dinosaur at my door!

This would make a great flannel or Velcro board activity, using dinosaurs of the different colors mentioned!
Stomp feet.
Raise hands and roar.

Stomp feet.
Raise hands and roar.

Stomp feet.
Raise hands and roar.

I see a dinosaur with wings of blue.
He doesn't scare me, does he scare you?
Stomp! Stomp!
Roar! Roar!
There's a dinosaur at my door!
I see a dinosaur and he's red.
I sure hope that he's been fed.
Stomp! Stomp!
Roar! Roar!
There's a dinosaur at my door!
I see a dinosaur that is tall and gray.
I think now I'll run away.
Stomp! Stomp!
Roar! Roar!
There's a dinosaur at my door!
I see a purple dinosaur and he loves me.
I think I like this one, because it's Barney!

> Stomp feet.
> Raise hands and roar.
>
> Stomp feet.
> Raise hands and roar.
>
> Stomp feet.
> Raise hands and roar.

—Kay Lincycomb

The Dinosaur Stomp

Put your right claws in, put your right claws out,
Put you right claws in, and swish them all about.
Do the dinosaur stomp, and stomp yourself around.
That's what it's all about.

> *Sung to the tune of "The Hokey Pokey."*
> Do motions as indicated.
>
> Clap, clap.

ADDITIONAL VERSES:
Put your left claws in . . . and swish them all about.
Put your sharp teeth in . . . and snap them all about.
Put your long tail in . . . and shake it all about.
Put your wings in . . . and flap them all about.
Put your whole scary body in . . . and stomp it all about.

—Kay Lincycomb

Dinosaur Stomp!

Dinosaur stomp!
Dinosaur run!
Come on!
Let's have some dinosaur fun!
Dinosaur twist,
Dinosaur glide.
Dinosaur seek,
Dinosaur hide.
Dinosaur fly,
Dinosaur swim.
Dinosaur wide,

> *Begin this rhyme with children standing.*
> Stomp feet.
> Run in place.
> Beckon with hand.
>
> Do the Twist!
> Slide feet side to side.
> Put hand above eyes, searching.
> Put hands in front of face.
> Flap arms.
> Swimming motion.
> Spread hands far apart.

Dinosaur slim.
Dinosaur wave,
Dinosaur hop.
This dinosaur fun
Never stops!

—Barbara Scott

Counting Dinosaur Eggs

One dinosaur egg, one.
Counting them is so much fun!
Two dinosaur eggs, two.
One for me, and one for you.
Three dinosaur eggs, three.
I found this one in a tree.
Four dinosaur eggs, four.
Did you hear a dinosaur roar?
Five dinosaur eggs, five.
Watch them jump and watch them jive!
Six dinosaur eggs, six.
They are doing lots of tricks.
Seven dinosaur eggs, seven.
We are counting up to heaven!
Eight dinosaur eggs, eight.
Hurry, hurry, don't be late!
Nine dinosaur eggs, nine.
Almost done, you're doing fine!
Ten dinosaur eggs, ten.
Waiting to hatch, who knows when!

—Barbara Scott

I'm a Little Dinosaur

I am a dinosaur,
Small and green.
I've got the sharpest claws
You have ever seen!
When I swish my tail,
And stomp my feet,
The neighbors hear me
Down the street!

—Barbara Scott

Dinosaur, Dinosaur

Dinosaur, dinosaur,
Flying all around,
Looking, searching very hard

Bring hands close together.
Wave hand.
Hop in place.

Shake head "no."

This rhyme also works well as a flannel or Velcro board activity!
Hold up a finger for each egg mentioned.

Sung to the tune of "I'm a Little Teapot."

Move hands indicate size.

Show hands as claws.
Wiggle bottom.
Stomp feet.
Put hand to ear.

Sung to the tune of "Jingle Bells."

Flap arms; move around.
Put hand over eyes, looking.

For food to be found.
When you find what you want,
Swoop down to the ground,

Gobble up your food and then
Leave without a sound!

Pretend to fly, swooping low.

Motion of "Shhh!"

—Barbara Scott

I Dig Dinosaurs

When it comes to bones,
I dig deepest.
I'm a paleontologist!
With my shovel and my pick,

I do a pretty nifty trick!
I brush away the dirt,
Drill some holes.
Dinosaur bones
I do expose!

Digging motion.
Put thumbs to shoulders; act proud.
Hold out one hand to side, then the opposite hand.
Nod head "yes."
Pretend to use brush.
Pretend to drill.

Point to self.

—Barbara Scott

Spike

I know a dinosaur who has
Big bones on his tail.
S-P-I-K-E, S-P-I-K-E, S-P-I-K-E,
And Spike is his name—yeah!

Sung to the tune of "Bingo."

Continue to sing, taking away letters from the end and substituting with clapping hands.

—Adapted traditional rhyme

T. Rex, T. Rex

T. Rex, T. Rex, turn around.
T. Rex, T. Rex, shake the ground!
T. Rex, T. Rex, show those claws!
T. Rex, T. Rex, snap those jaws!
T. Rex, T. Rex, run in place.
T. Rex, T. Rex, scary face!
T. Rex, T. Rex, don't be a fright.
T. Rex, T. Rex, say goodnight.

Stomp feet.
Show fingers as claws.
Chomp teeth.
Run.
Make a scary face.
Shake head "no" and shake finger, admonishing. / Put hands to side of head; pretend to sleep and snore loudly!

—Barbara Scott

Lots of Dinosaurs

A long, long time ago,
Dinosaurs lived, don't you know.
Some were smooth
And some were scaly.
Some had spikes on their tail-y!

Point index finger in the air.
Rub arm for "smooth.
Make face for "scaly."
Hold one hand up, fingers spread out to represent spikes.

Some were tiny, very small.
Some could be 100 feet tall!
Some had plates upon their back.
These made them hard to attack!
Some ate plants and some ate meat.
Some dinosaurs had great big feet!
Some had mouths just like a duck.
Some dinosaurs lived in the muck.
Some dinosaurs were very scary.
Some, like the mammoth, were very hairy.
There are no dinosaurs today,
But if there were, I'd run away!

—Barbara Scott

Put thumb and index finger close together to represent size.
Put hands far apart to represent size.
Hold hands side by side in front of body.

Pretend to eat.
Point to feet.
Point to mouth.
Put hands on thighs, and bring up as if pulling out of mud. / Make scary face.

Point to hair.

Run in place.

Run, Dinosaur, Run!

Triceratops, stegosaurus, brontosaurus, run!
Now is no time to be having fun.
Spinosaurus, velociraptor, pteradon, fly!
Raise those wings up to the sky!
Dimetrodon, iguanadon, seismosaurus, stomp!
Make your way back through the swamp.
Apatosaurus, allosaurus, brachiosaurus, roar!
You're being chased by the king of the dinosaurs!

—Barbara Scott

This is a great rhyme to do using a Tyrannosaurus Rex puppet!
Run in place.
Shake head "no."

Flap arms.
Stomp feet.
Sway side to side as if moving through water or grass. / "Roar!"

Ask children who this would be . . .
Tyrannosaurus Rex, of course!

Dino-Roar

Dino-roar, dino-roar!
I'm a great big dinosaur.
With a long, long neck,
And a long tail, too.
Huge footprints,
I have made a few!
Leaves from the trees,
I love to eat.
Green and yummy,
And oh, so sweet.
You can hear me coming,
That's for sure!
I'm a great big dinosaur!

—Barbara Scott

"Roar!"

Point to neck and stretch.
Wiggle bottom.
Point to feet.
Nod head "yes."

Chewing motion.
Rub tummy.

Point to ears.
"Roar!"

Dinosaurs

Dinosaurs lived a long time ago,
Long time ago, long time ago.
Dinosaurs lived a long time ago.

Sung to the tune of "The Mulberry Bush."

The earth was pretty new then. | Make circle with hands for earth.
Some dinosaurs, they ate lots of meat, | Eating and chewing motions.
Ate lots of meat, ate lots of meat.
Some dinosaurs, they ate lots of meat,
Like Tyrannosaurus Rex! | Roar and show claws.
Some dinosaurs, they ate lots of plants, | Hand makes chewing motion.
Ate lots of plants, ate lots of plants.
Some dinosaurs, they ate lots of plants,
Just like the brontosaurus! | Raise hand in the air for long neck.
Some dinosaurs could swim like a fish | Swimming motion.
Swim like a fish, swim like a fish.
Some dinosaurs could swim like a fish,
Just like the ichthyosaurus!
Some dinosaurs could fly way up high, | Flap arms.
Fly way up high, fly way up high.
Some dinosaurs could fly way up high,
Just like the pterodactyl!

—Adapted traditional rhyme

If You're a T. Rex

Sung to the tune of "If You're Happy and You Know It." Remember, this dinosaur has short, stubby arms . . . have fun with the clapping!

If you're a T. Rex and you know it, clap your hands. | Clap, clap.
If you're a T. Rex and you know it, clap your hands. | Clap, clap.
If you're a T. Rex and you know it, then your face will | Point to face.
surely show it.
If you're a T. Rex and you know it, clap your hands. | Clap, clap.

ADDITIONAL VERSES:
. . . stomp your feet.
. . . show your claws.
. . . wag your tail.
. . . roar real loud!
. . . do all five!

—Adapted traditional rhyme

Five Sleepy Dinosaurs

Five sleepy dinosaurs, much too tired to roar. | Begin this rhyme with five fingers up.
One went to sleep and then there were four. | Take away fingers as the rhyme progresses.
Four sleepy dinosaurs, rubbing eyes, you see.
One went to sleep and then there were three.
Three sleepy dinosaurs, tired through and through.
One went to sleep and then there were two.
Two sleepy dinosaurs, much too tired to run.
One went to sleep and then there was one.

One sleepy dinosaur when the day is done.
He went to sleep and now there are none.

—Barbara Scott

I'm a Stegosaurus

Sung to the tune of "I'm a Little Teapot."

I'm a stegosaurus,
Short and fat.

Move hands to indicate size.

The plates on my back
Go this way and that.

Put hands in front, side by side, as they appear on the dinosaur.

On my tail I have
A set of spikes.

Put fingers on one hand up to represent spikes. / Point to eyes.

One look at them,
And you'll say "Yikes!"

Put hands on face, scared look.

—Adapted traditional rhyme

Five Rowdy Dinosaurs

Five rowdy dinosaurs walking through the swamp.

Begin this rhyme with five fingers up.

The first one said, "I'm ready to romp!"
The second one said, "Get ready for some noise!"

Starting with the thumb, point to each in succession.

The third one said, "Let's go, boys!"
The fourth one said, "I can roar really loud!"
The fifth one said, "We're quite a crowd!"

—Barbara Scott

Five Little Dinos Went Out to Play

Five little dinos went out to play,
Deep in the forest one fine day.

Begin this rhyme with five fingers up.

Mama Dino, she let out a roar.
Only four little dinos came back . . . no more.

Take away fingers as rhyme progresses.

No little dinos went out to play,
Deep in the forest one fine day.

Continue with four, three, two, one, until . . .

Mama Dino, she let out a roar.
All five little dinos came back, no more!

—Adapted traditional rhyme

Ten Little Dinosaurs

Sung to the tune of "Ten Little Indians."

One little, two little, three little dinosaurs,
Four little, five little, six little dinosaurs,

Count out on fingers for the first verse.

Seven little, eight little, nine little dinosaurs,
Ten little dinosaurs roar!
Ten little, nine little, eight little dinosaurs,

Take away fingers on the second verse.

Seven little, six little, five little dinosaurs,
Four little, three little, two little dinosaurs,
One little dinosaur roar!

—Adapted traditional rhyme

Sleepy Dinosaur

Are you sleeping,
Are you sleeping,
Dinosaur, dinosaur?
Stretch and yawn and sigh.
Close your sleepy eyes.
Snore, snore, snore.
Snore, snore, snore.

—Adapted traditional rhyme

Sung to the tune of "Frère Jacques."
Move head to the side, questioning.

Do motions.
Close eyes.
Snore!

I Can Walk Like a Dinosaur

I can walk like a dinosaur.
Watch my feet as they stomp the floor.
Watch my tail as it swings to and fro.
Walk like a dinosaur, go, go, go!

—Barbara Scott

Point to self.
Stomp feet.
Move hips back and forth.
Stomp and sway.

Ten Huge Dinosaurs

Ten huge dinosaurs were standing in a line.
One tripped on a cobblestone, and then there were nine.
Nine huge dinosaurs were trying hard to skate.
One cracked right through the ice, and then there were eight.
Eight huge dinosaurs were counting past eleven.
One counted up too far, and then there were seven.
Seven huge dinosaurs learned some magic tricks.
One did a disappearing act, and then there were six.
Six huge dinosaurs were learning how to drive.
One forgot to put in gas, and then there were five.
Five huge dinosaurs joined the drum corps.
One forgot the drumsticks, and then there were four.
Four huge dinosaurs were wading out to sea.
One waded too far out, and then there were three.
Three huge dinosaurs went to the Amazon.
One sailed in up to his head, and then there was one.
One lonesome dinosaur knew her friends had gone.
She found a big museum, and then there were none.

—Adapted from an old English rhyme

This is also a great rhyme to do as a flannel or Velcro board activity.
Begin this rhyme with ten fingers up.
Take away fingers as the rhyme progresses.

Books to Share

Bendall-Brunello, John. 2009. *Snore, Dinosaur, Snore*. Tarrytown, NY: Marshall Cavendish. ISBN: 978-0761456261.
Donaldson, Julia. 2008. *Tyrannosaurus Drip*. New York: Feiwel and Friends. ISBN: 978-0312377472.

Foreman, Michael. 2003. *A Trip to Dinosaur Time.* Somerville, MA: Candlewick Press. ISBN: 978-0763621049.
Heidbreder, Robert. 2006. *Drumheller Dinosaur Dance.* Tonawanda, NY: Kids Can Press. ISBN: 978-1553379829.
Lewis, Kevin. 2006. *Dinosaur, Dinosaur.* London: Orchard Books. ISBN: 978-0439603713.
Waddell, Martin. 2009. *The Super Hungry Dinosaur.* New York: Dial. ISBN: 978-0803734463.

Musical Selections

"Alley Oop" from *A Child's Celebration of Rock and Roll.* ASIN: B000002M7T.
"Dino Beat" from *Walt Disney Dancin' Tunes.* ASIN: B00005B6CJ.
"Dinosaur Romp" from *Debbie's Ditties 4: Come Dance S'More!* by Debbie Clement. Available: www.rainbowswithinreach.com (accessed March 6, 2010).
"Dinosaur Tap" from *Rhythm Sticks Rock* by Georgiana Stewart. ASIN: B000QUU6GM.
"Dinosaurs" from *Monster Teaching Times: Songs and Learning Fun.* ASIN: B000BYCV16.
Once Upon a Dinosaur by Jane Murphy. This CD has 13 dino-riffic songs! Available: www.kimboed.com (accessed March 6, 2010).

Sources

Findlay, Diane, Susan Mast, Kathy Ross, and Patti Sinclair. 2007. *Collaborative Summer Library Program Manual.* Mason City, IA: Collaborative Summer Library Program.
Flora, Sherrill B. 1987. *The Preschool Calendar.* Minneapolis: T.S. Denison & Co.
Laurabaas.com. Available: laurabaas.com/2007/10/02.time-for-stories-dinosaurs-storytime-plan/.
Lincycomb, Kay. 2007. *Storytimes . . . Plus!* New York: Neal-Schuman.
North Central Library Co-operative. n.d. *Storytime Booklet* [out of print].
Roberts, Lynda. *Mitt Magic: Fingerplays for Finger Puppets.* Silver Spring, MD: Gryphon House, 1985.
Scott, Louise B. 1983. *Rhymes for Learning Times.* Minneapolis: T.S. Denison & Co.

Dogs
After all, they are man's best friend!

Rhyme	**Telling Guide**

Mother Hubbard Rhyme

Old Mother Hubbard went to the cupboard
To fetch her poor dog a bone.
But when she got there the cupboard was bare,
And so the poor dog had none. — Form a zero with fingers.
Old Mother Hubbard went to the butcher
To get a bone, all alone.
When she got home, she put in the bone,
And now her cupboard has one. — Hold up one finger.
Old Mother Hubbard went to the butcher
For another bone, it's true.
When she got home, she put in the bone,
And now her cupboard has two. — Hold up two fingers.
Old Mother Hubbard went to the butcher
To get another, you see.
When she got home, she put in the bone,
And now her cupboard has three. — Hold up three fingers.
Old Mother Hubbard went to the butcher
And asked for just one more.
When she got home, she put in the bone,
And now her cupboard has four. — Hold up four fingers.

—Jean Warren

Call Your Dog

Call your dog, — Cup hands around mouth.
Give him a bone, — Extend hand.
Take him for a walk, — Pretend to hold leash.
Then put him in his home. — Form a roof shape with fingers.

—Traditional rhyme

Dog Went to Dover

Leg over leg — Hold arm forward; "step" fingers of other hand toward arm.
As the dog went to Dover,
He came to a stile,
And jump—he went over. — Jump fingers over arm.

—From *Let's Do Fingerplays*

This Little Doggie

This little doggie ran away to play,
This little doggie said, "I'll go too some day."
This little doggie began to dig and dig,
This little doggie danced a funny jig.
This little doggie cried, "Ki! Yi! Ki! Yi!
I wish I were big."

—From *Let's Do Fingerplays*

Hold up fingers of one hand; point to each finger in turn.

Doggie's Tail

A little doggie all brown and black,

Wore his tail curled on his back.

—From *Let's Do Fingerplays*

Make fist with one hand; extend thumb and index finger touching each other for head.
Curl other index finger and hold against back of fist for tail.

Puppy Dog

Puppy dog, puppy dog, turn around.
Puppy dog, puppy dog, touch the ground.
Puppy dog, puppy dog, wag your tail.
Puppy dog, puppy dog, drink from the pail.
Puppy dog, puppy dog, sit and beg.
Puppy dog, puppy dog, hold up one leg.
Puppy dog, puppy dog, take a walk.
Puppy dog, puppy dog, try to talk.
Puppy dog, puppy dog, try to lick.
Puppy dog, puppy dog, fetch the stick.
Puppy dog, puppy dog, go upstairs.
Puppy dog, puppy dog, look for bears.
Puppy dog, puppy dog, turn off the light.
Puppy dog, puppy dog, say goodnight!

—Kathy Ross

Have children do actions as in "Teddy Bear, Teddy Bear."

Rags the Dog

I have a dog and his name is Rags.
He eats so much that his tummy sags.
His ears flip-flop,
And his tail wig-wags.
And when he walks, he goes zig-zag.
He goes flip-flop, wig-wag, zig-zag.
He goes flip-flop, wig-wag, zig-zag.
He goes flip-flop, wig-wag, zig-zag.
I love Rags and he loves me.
My dog Rags, he loves to play.
He rolls around in the mud all day.

Hang hands by your ears.
Hold hands in front of tummy.

Flop hands by ears and wag your tail!
Cross arms in front to zig, open up to zag.
Put motions together now and repeat.

Hang hands by your ears.
Roll hands.

I whistle but he won't obey.	Whistle.
He always runs the other way.	
He goes flip-flop, wig-wag, zig-zag.	Repeat motions above for this verse.
He goes flip-flop, wig-wag, zig-zag.	
He goes flip-flop, wig-wag, zig-zag.	

—Kathy Ross

Five Little Puppies

Five little puppies were playing in the sun.	Hold up hand, five fingers extended.
This one saw a rabbit and he began to run.	Bend down first finger.
This one saw a butterfly and he began to chase.	Bend down second finger.
This one saw a cat and he began to chase.	Bend down third finger.
This one tried to catch his tail and he went 'round and 'round.	Bend down fourth finger.
This one was so quiet, he never made a sound.	Bend down fifth finger.

—Traditional rhyme

The Puppy and the Kitty Cat

Here is a little puppy.	Hold up left fist.
Here is a kitty cat.	Hold up right fist.
Puppy goes to sleep,	
Curled up on his mat.	Put left fist, fingers down, on lap.
Kitty creeps up softly,	Move fingers of right hand slowly toward left hand.
Tickles puppy's chin.	Tickle thumb of left hand with finger of right hand.
Puppy wakes up quickly!	Jump left fist up.
See the chase begin!	Have left fist chase right, rolling hands around and around each other.

—Author unknown

The Puppy

Call the puppy	Beckon with hand or finger.
And give him some milk.	Pretend to pour milk into bowl.
Bush his coat,	Pretend to brush dog.
'Til it shines like silk.	
Call the dog	Beckon with hand or finger.
And give him a bone.	Hold two fingers as though holding bone.
Talk him for a walk,	Pretend to hold leash.
Then put him in his home.	Put fingertips together to form roof of doghouse.

—Traditional rhyme

Some Dogs Bark

Some dogs bark,	Bark.
Some dogs growl.	Growl.
Some dogs yip,	Make yipping sound.
Some dogs howl.	Howl!
And some dogs just wag their tail.	Wiggle bottom.

—From *A Storytime Year*

Oh Where, Oh Where Has My Little Dog Gone?

Oh where, oh where has my little dog gone?
Oh where, oh where can he be?
With his ears cut short and his tail cut long.
Oh where, oh where can he be?

—Traditional rhyme

Put hands on either side of face; sway head back and forth.
Put hands out to each side, questioning.
Use hands to indicate sizes: short and long. / Put hands on either side of face; sway head back and forth.

A Dog and a Cat Went Out Together

A dog and a cat went out together,
To see some friends just out of town.
Said the cat to the dog,
"What d'ya think of the weather?"
"I think, ma'am, the rain will come down,
But don't be alarmed, for I've an umbrella
That will shelter us both," said this amiable fellow.

—Traditional rhyme

This is a great rhyme to do with finger or hand puppets!
Make one hand the dog, the other the cat.
Point to eyes.

Point to head, questioning.
Wiggle fingers for rain.
Put hands overhead, fingertips together, to form an umbrella. Bring fists of both hands close together.

Four Little Doggies

Four little doggies
All in their best.
One little doggy
Sings for the rest.

Two little doggies
Talking so low.
What they are saying,
None of us know.

—Traditional rhyme

Hold up four fingers.
Pat clothing.
Hold up one finger.
Place one hand on chest; hold the other arm out to the side as if singing.
Hold up two fingers.
Act as if whispering.

Shake head "no."

Caesar's Song

Bow, wow, wow!
Whose dog art thou?
Little Tommy Tinker's dog.
Bow, wow, wow!

—From *The Nursery Rhyme Book*

Clap three times.
Shrug shoulders.

Clap three times.

All the Little Doggies

Five little doggies out in the snow,
Five little tails wagged to and fro.
Soon the front door opened wide,
And a little boy said, "Come on inside!"

Begin this rhyme with five fingers up; take away fingers as the rhyme progresses.
Wag finger.
Spread hands.
Gesture.

And the doggie went, "Bark!" Then the doggie went in.
No little doggies out in the snow,
No little tails wagging to and fro.
The little boy let them in and when they had been well fed,
All the little doggies were asleep inside their bed.

         —Kay Lincycomb

Repeat verse, counting down four, three, two, one, increasing barks.

Wag finger.

My Puppy

My puppy chewed up my new sneakers,
My puppy chewed up my new pants.
My puppy made a puddle in the kitchen.
Oh he tries to be good, but he can't.
Oh please, oh please,
Help my new puppy be good, be good.
Oh please, oh please,
Help him learn clothes are not food.

         —Carolyn N. Cullum

Sung to the tune of "My Bonnie Lies Over the Ocean."
Point to sneakers.
Point to pants.
Hold your nose.

Put hands together to plead.

Bingo

There was a farmer had a dog and Bingo was his name-o.
B-I-N-G-O,
B-I-N-G-O,
B-I-N-G-O,
And Bingo was his name-o.

         —Traditional rhyme

This is a well-known traditional song. Once sung through, start taking away letters from the name and clap instead!

Puppy Dog, Puppy Dog

Puppy dog, puppy dog,
Turn around.
Puppy dog, puppy dog,
Sit on the ground.
Puppy dog, puppy dog,
Sit and beg.
Puppy dog, puppy dog,
Stand on one leg!
Puppy dog, puppy dog,
Bark and wail!
Puppy dog, puppy dog,
Chase your tail!
Puppy dog, puppy dog,
Into your bed creep.
Puppy dog, puppy dog,
Go to sleep!

         —Adapted traditional rhyme

This rhyme can be sung to the tune of "Teddy Bear, Teddy Bear" or chanted.

Turn in place.

Sit.

Motion of sitting and begging.

Stand on one leg.

Bark and then "aroooo!"

Run around in a circle.

Walk softly.

Close eyes; put head on hands.

Ten Little Puppies

One little, two little, three little puppies,
Four little, five little, six little puppies,
Seven little, eight little, nine little puppies,
Ten little puppy dogs!
Ten little, nine little, eight little puppies,
Seven little, six little, five little puppies,
Four little, three little, two little puppies.
One little puppy dog!

—Adapted traditional rhyme

Sung to the tune of "Ten Little Indians."

Count out on fingers for the first verse.

Take fingers away on second verse.

Dogs Are Barking

Dogs are barking,
Hear the dogs a' barking.
Dogs are barking,
All around the town.
Dogs are barking over here
Dogs are barking over there
Over here, over there . . . oh . . .
Dogs are barking,
Here the dogs a' barking.
Dogs are barking,
All around the town.

—Adapted traditional rhyme

Sung to the tune of "Alouette." ASL sign for dog: hold hand out in front of body, palm up, snap fingers.
Use ASL sign.
Put hand to ear.
Use ASL sign.
Make large circle with hands.
"Arf!"; point to the right.
"Arf!"; point to the left.
Point in both directions.
Use ASL sign.
Put hand to ear.
Use ASL sign.
Make large circle with hands.

If You're a Doggie and You Know It

If you're a doggie and you know it, bark out loud.
If you're a doggie and you know it, bark out loud.
If you're a doggie and you know it and you really want to show it.
If you're a doggie and you know it, bark out loud.

ADDITIONAL VERSES:
. . . sit and beg.
. . . wag your tail.
. . . shake your head.
. . . do all four.

—Adapted traditional rhyme

Sung to the tune of "If You're Happy and You Know It."
"Arf! Arf!"
"Arf! Arf!"

"Arf! Arf!"

Sit with hands in front, pant.
Move hips back and forth.
Shake head back and forth.
Bark, sit, move hips; shake head.

Five Little Puppies

Five little puppies were waiting by the door.
One went to chase a cat and now there are four.
Four little puppies digging by the tree.
One got tired and now there are three.

Begin this rhyme with five fingers up.
Take away fingers as the rhyme progresses.

Three little puppies crowding 'round a bowl of food.
One got full and now there are two.
Two little puppies playing in the sun.
One went to take a nap and now there's just one.
One little puppy sitting all alone.
He went off to find a bone and now there are none.

—Barbara Scott

Five Little Doggies

Five little doggies went out to play

In the doggie park one day.

Mama Dog said, "Bark, bark, bark, bark!"

Only four little doggies came back to the park.

No little doggies went out to play

In the doggie park one day.

Mama Dog said, "Bark, bark, bark, bark!"

And all the little doggies came back to the park!

—Adapted traditional rhyme

Sung to the tune of "Five Little Ducks."

Start out with five fingers up.

Take away fingers as rhyme progresses.
Continue four, three, two, one, until . . .

Wiggle five fingers.

I Have a Dog

I have a dog.

He likes to play

With his bouncy ball

The live-long day!

I throw the ball

And catch he will!

He runs and runs

And never sits still!

—Barbara Scott

ASL sign for dog: hold hand out in front of body, palm up, snap fingers.
Use ASL sign.
Nod head "yes."
Make circle with hands.
Move hands to show expanse.
Motion of throwing.
Nod head "yes."
Run in place.
Shake head "no."

I'll Give My Dog a Bath

Sung to the tune of "The Farmer in the Dell." This is cute with a stuffed dog, or you could simply do as an action rhyme!

I'll give my dog a bath,
I'll give my dog a bath.
Heigh-ho the derry-o,
I'll give my dog a bath.
I'll scrub his little tail,
I'll scrub his little tail.
Heigh-ho the derry-o,
I'll scrub his little tail.
I'll scrub his dirty paws,
I'll scrub his dirty paws.
Heigh-ho the derry-o,
I'll scrub his dirty paws.
I'll scrub behind his ears,

Scrub tail.

Scrub paws.

Scrub ears.

I'll scrub behind his ears.
Heigh-ho the derry-o,
I'll scrub behind his ears.
I'll scrub his furry back, — Scrub back.
I'll scrub his furry back.
Heigh-ho the derry-o,
I'll scrub his furry back.
Now my dog's all clean,
Now my dog's all clean.
Heigh-ho the derry-o,
Now my dog's all clean!

—Adapted traditional rhyme

Five Little Puppies

Five little puppies were sitting in the sun. — Hold up five fingers.
The first one said, "Let's have some fun!" — Starting with the thumb, point to each in succession.
The second one said, "Let's go chase a cat!"
The third one said, "I don't know about that."
The fourth one said, "Let's go dig for bones!"
The fifth one said, "Wait! Don't leave me all alone!"

—Barbara Scott

I'm a Little Puppy Dog

Sung to the tune of "I'm a Little Teapot."

I'm a little puppy dog
Short and fat. — Use hands to indicate size.
I can wag my tail
Just like that! — Wiggle hips back and forth.
My ears they go flop — Point to ears.
From side to side, — Move head back and forth.
And my nose sniffs bones — Point to nose.
That try to hide! — Sniff . . . sniff!

—Adapted traditional rhyme

Sleepy Puppy

I like to hold my sleepy puppy
Right here in my lap, — Use fist as dog; hold in lap.
And when I pet him,
He goes to sleep — Pet fist; close eyes to sleep.
Just like that! — Snap fingers.

—Barbara Scott

Here Is My Dog's Doghouse

Here is my dog's doghouse — Form roof over head with hands.
And inside is his bed. — Close eyes to sleep.
Outside are his bowls of food — Make circle with hands.

When he's ready to be fed. | Rub tummy.

                              —Barbara Scott

Books to Share

Beaumont, Karen. 2006. *Move Over, Rover!* Boston: Harcourt Children's Books. ISBN: 978-0152019792.

Bluemle, Elizabeth. 2008. *Dogs on the Bed.* Somerville, MA: Candlewick Press. ISBN: 978-0763626082.

Catalanotto, Peter. 2007. *Ivan the Terrier.* New York: Atheneum. ISBN: 978-1416912477.

Dodd, Emma. 2002. *Dog's ABC: A Silly Story about the Alphabet.* New York: Dutton Juvenile. ISBN: 978-0525468370.

Grogan, John. 2007. *Bad Dog, Marley!* New York: HarperCollins. ISBN: 978-0061171147.

Heiligman, Deborah. 2005. *Fun Dog, Sun Dog.* Tarrytown, NY: Marshall Cavendish Children's Books. ISBN: 978-0761451624.

Musical Selections

"I Love My Dog" from *Animal Rock* by Walt Disney. ASIN: B00005B6CG.

"I Wanna Be a Dog" from *(Almost) Two Much* by Nan Hoffman. Available: www.nanhoffman.com (accessed March 7, 2010).

"My Dog Rags (My Little Puppy)" from *Sing Along with Bob #1.* ASIN: B00000DAO4.

"Seis Perritos" [Six Dogs] from *Songs for Wiggleworms.* ASIN: B00004YLUE.

"Walkin' the Dog" from *Catch That Train!* by Dan Zanes. ASIN: B000EXZ2JW.

Sources

Anonymous. n.d. *The Comic Picture Book.* Chicago: W.B. Conkey.

Anonymous. 1902. *Nursery Rhymes from Mother Goose with Alphabet.* Philadelphia: W.W. Houston. Available: www.childrenslibrary.org (accessed March 7, 2010).

"Baby and Preschool Fingerplays and Songs." Fun Baby Games Online. Available: www.fun-baby-games-online.com/preschool-fingerplays-and-songs.html (accessed March 7, 2010).

Cullum, Carolyn N. 2007. *The Storytime Sourcebook II.* New York: Neal-Schuman.

Dailey, Susan. 2001. *A Storytime Year.* New York: Neal-Schuman.

Grayson, Marion. 1962. *Let's Do Fingerplays.* Fairfield, CT: R.B. Luce.

Lang, Andrew, ed. 1897. *The Nursery Rhyme Book.* London: Frederick Warne & Co.

Lincycomb, Kay. 2007. *Storytimes . . . Plus!* New York: Neal-Schuman.

Moffat, Alfred. 1911. *Our Old Nursery Rhymes.* New York: G. Schirmer.

Perry Public Library. n.d. "Perry Public Library Storytime." Available: www.perrypubliclibrary .org/Kids/Programs/Storytimes/Dogs.pdf (accessed April 9, 2010).

Scott, Barbara. 2003. *Celebrate Ohio: 1803*–2003. Columbus, OH: State Library of Ohio.

Totline Staff, comp. 1994. *1001 Rhymes and Fingerplays.* Everett, WA: Warren Publishing House.

Traditional Music Library. Available: www.traditionalmusic.co.uk (accessed March 7, 2010).

Dragons

There's no need to fear these dragons! They like to have fun!

Rhyme

Dragons

Five enormous dragons
Letting out a roar—
One went away, and
Then there were four.
Four enormous dragons
Crashing down a tree—
One went away, and
Then there were three.
Three enormous dragons
Eating tiger stew—
One went away, and
Then there were two.
Two enormous dragons
Trying to run—
One ran away, and
Then there was one.
One enormous dragon
Afraid to be a hero—
He went away, and
Then there was zero.

—Linda Roberts

Swing Your Dragon Tail

Turn around once
And swing your dragon tail.
Turn around twice
And flap your wings like sails.
Turn around three times
Then stomp your foot and roar.
Jump up high, then sit down on the floor.

—Kathy Ross

How Do You Feed a Dragon?

How do you feed a dragon
Who is tall, tall, tall?
When you're just a little kid
Who is small, small, small.

Telling Guide

Begin rhyme with five fingers up.

Take away fingers as rhyme progresses.

"Whee . . ."
Wiggle bottom.
"Whee . . . whee . . ."
Flap arms.
"Whee . . . whee . . . whee . . ."
Stomp feet; roar.
Jump, then sit.

Have children reach up and stretch to become as tall as possible.

Have children crouch down to be as small as possible.

If you could stand on tiptoes,
Even though you are little,
The dragon could bend down
And meet you in the middle!

—Kathy Ross

Have children stand up on tiptoes.

Have children bend down.
Do this a few times, going a little faster each time.

Dragon Dance

If you want to be a dragon,
Here's your chance,
Because everyone's doing the dragon dance.
You just stamp your feet,
And you growl and roar.
Then your twirl around and
Jump on the floor.
Flap those wings and start to prance.
That's how you do the dragon dance.

—Kathy Ross

Suit actions to words.

Did You Ever Find a Dragon?

Did you ever find a dragon?
A dragon? A dragon?
Did you ever find a dragon all scaly and green?

With blazing eyes and fiery breath,
And swishy tail and green toes?

Did you ever find a dragon all scaly and green?

—Stephanie Stokes, LibraryPalooza

Sung to the tune of "Did You Ever See a Lassie?"

Walk in circle.

Have children stop and point to their eyes. / Have children wiggle their behinds and toes.
Walk in circle.

I'm a Little Dragon

I'm a little dragon, strong and stout.
Here is my tail and here is my snout.
If you get me upset, you better watch out!
I'll give you something to shout about!

—Stephanie Stokes, LibraryPalooza

Sung to the tune of "I'm a Little Teapot."

Point to tail and then to nose.

Roar loudly and show claws.

As the Sun Came Up

As the sun came up, a ball of red,
I followed my friend wherever he led.
My teacher rode on his horse ahead,
While I followed close on my dragon steed.
He thought his fast horse would leave me behind,
But I rode a dragon as swift as the wind.

—Traditional Chinese rhyme

Arms make large circle overhead.

Action of riding, bouncing up and down.
Action of swaying from side to side.
Point to head and tap temple.
Repeat action of swaying from side to side.

Dragons

Dragons, dragons in the air.
Breathing fire here and there.

Up above the castle walls,
Fighting knights as they brawl.
Dragons, dragons in the air.
Breathing fire here and there.

—Carolyn N. Cullum

Sung to the tune of "Twinkle, Twinkle, Little Star."
Point up.
Point in one direction, then in the opposite.
Put hands together to make wall.
Pretend to fight with sword.
Point up.
Point in one direction, then in the opposite.

Five Hungry Dragons

Five hungry dragons sitting on the floor.
One found some popcorn, then there were four.
Four hungry dragons, as hungry as could be.
One found some candy, then there were three.
Three hungry dragons, wishing for some stew.
One found some cookies, then there were two.
Two hungry dragons waiting for the sun.
One found some pizza, then there was one.
One hungry dragon sitting all alone.
He found some potato chips, and then there were none.

—Barbara Scott

Begin this rhyme with five fingers up.
Take away fingers as the rhyme progresses.

Flying with Dragons

Dragons fly up,
Dragons fly down.
Dragons are flying all around.
Fly to the left,
Fly to the right.
Flap those arms with all your might!
It's time to land,
Our flying's done.
Flying with dragons is
Lots of fun!

—Barbara Scott

Flap arms and move up on tiptoes.
Flap arms and squat down.
Fly around in a circle.
Flap arms and move left.
Flap arms and move right.
Flap arms.

Sit.

Clap three times on last line.

Counting Dragons

Dragon one and dragon two,
They have wings that are shiny and new.
Dragon three and dragon four,
Get ready for a dragon roar!
Dragon five and dragon six,
They are doing silly tricks.
Dragon seven and dragon eight,

Begin rhyme with one finger up; add fingers as the rhyme progresses.

Roar!

Hurry up and don't be late.
Dragon nine and dragon ten,
Are all the dragons in the dragon den!

—Barbara Scott

Dancing Dragons

Dragons are dancing!	Dance!
Dancing all around.	Dance around!
There are no happier	Shake head "no."
Dragons to be found!	
The dragons dance left,	Dance to the left.
The dragons dance right.	Dance to the right.
Flapping wings so hard,	Flap those arms!
They might take flight!	
They nod their heads.	Nod head.
Their tails they sway.	Wiggle bottom.
I think they could	
Dance all day!	Continue to dance.
They stomp their feet.	Stomp feet.
They turn around.	Turn in a circle.
And last of all,	
They sit right down!	Sit.

—Barbara Scott

Little Dragon, Little Dragon

Little dragon, little dragon, fly around.	Do motions as indicated in the rhyme.
Little dragon, little dragon, stomp on the ground.	
Little dragon, little dragon, show your claws.	
Little dragon, little dragon, snap those jaws!	
Little dragon, little dragon, blow smoke rings.	
Little dragon, little dragon, stand and sing!	
Little dragon, little dragon, climb the castle wall.	
Little dragon, little dragon, do not fall.	

—Adapted traditional rhyme

Dragons on Parade

Dragons are marching,	March in place.
Marching through the town.	
One of those dragons	
Is dressed like a clown.	Make a funny face or point to a BIG smile! / Continue to march in place.
Dragons are marching	
Down the street.	
Flapping their wings,	Flap arms.
And stomping their feet.	Stomp feet.
One of those dragons	Hold up one finger.

Is playing a drum.	Pretend to play.
One of those dragons	Hold up one finger.
Has a guitar to strum.	Pretend to strum guitar.
Look now, here comes	Put hand over eyes, searching.
The rest of the band!	
Everyone give them	
A great big hand!	Clap hands.

—Barbara Scott

Books to Share

Banks, Kate. 2008. *Max's Dragon*. New York: Farrar, Straus, and Giroux. ISBN: 978-0374399214.

Broach, Elise. 2005. *Hiding Hoover*. New York: Dial. ISBN: 978-0803727069.

Ellery, Amanda. 2006. *If I Had a Dragon*. New York: Simon & Schuster Children's Publishing. ISBN: 978-1416909248.

Morgan, Mary. 2008. *Dragon Pizzeria*. New York: Knopf Books for Young Readers. ISBN: 978-0375823091.

Nash, Ogden. 1995. *The Tale of Custard the Dragon*. New York: Little, Brown. ISBN: 978-0316598804.

Thomas, Shelley M. 2008. *A Cold Winter's Good Knight*. New York: Dutton Juvenile. ISBN: 978-0525479642. (This is part of a series of books by this author about the little dragons and their friend, the Knight.)

Musical Selections

"Do the Dragon" from *Castles, Knights, and Unicorns* by Ronno. ASIN: B00019PVO0.

"Dragon Achoo" from *Monster Teaching Time: Songs and Learning Fun*. ASIN: B000BYCV16.

"Dragon Dance" from *Jump and Jive with Hi-5*. ASIN: B0002O06X0. (This is what is called just a "songlet," but cute, nonetheless!)

"The Giggling Dragon" from *The Giggling Dragon* by Dan Crow. ASIN: B000EOU3BI.

"Nine-Foot Dragon and a Four-Foot Boy" from *What Kind of Cat Are You?* by Billy Jonas. ASIN: B00007BJZX.

"Puff the Magic Dragon" from *Songs My Family Taught Me* by John Storms-Rohn. ASIN: B00008OLY4.

Sources

Cullum, Carolyn N. 2007. *The Storytime Sourcebook II*. New York: Neal-Schuman.

Headland, Isaac Taylor. 1900. *Chinese Mother Goose Rhymes*. Grand Rapids, MI: Fleming H. Revell.

LibraryPalooza. Available: www.librarypalooza (accessed March 3, 2010).

Roberts, Lynda. 1985. *Mitt Magic: Fingerplays for Finger Puppets*. Silver Spring, MD: Gryphon House.

Sinclair, Patti, Tami Chumbley, and Kathy Ross. 2005. "Dragons, Dreams, and Daring Deeds." *Collaborative Summer Library Program Manual*. Mason City, IA: Collaborative Summer Library Program.

Storytime Source Page: Storytimes for Babies, Toddlers, Preschool, and Kindergarten. Available: storytimepreschooltoddlers.blogspot.com (accessed March 7, 2010).

Chapter 4

Ducks to Flowers and Gardens

Ducks: Just Ducky

Have fun shaking your tail with these rhymes about our fine-feathered friends!

Rhyme	**Telling Guide**

Little Duck

Little duck swimming to and fro,	Bend elbow and wrist; form hand into duck head.
Sees a fish and down he goes;	Drop hand to side.
Eats that fish for a morning snack,	Make fingers "chew."
And up he comes with a "Quack, quack, quack."	Raise arm to original position; move fingers to simulate quacking.

—Author unknown

Six Little Ducks

Six little ducks that I once knew.	Hold up six fingers.
Fat ones, skinny ones, tall ones too.	Make motions showing fat, skinny, tall.
But the one little duck with the feather on his back,	Move arm up and down behind back.
He led the others with a "Quack, quack, quack, Quack, quack, quack."	Open and close hand.
He led the others with a "Quack, quack, quack!"	
Down to the river they would go,	
Wiggle-waggle, wiggle-waggle, all in a row.	Wiggle body like a waddle.
But the one little duck with the feather on his back,	Move arm up and down behind back.
He led the others with a "Quack, quack, quack, Quack, quack, quack."	Open and close hand.
He led the others with a "Quack, quack, quack!"	
Up from the river they did come.	
Wiggle-waggle, wiggle-waggle, ho-hum-hum-hum.	
But the one little duck with the feather on his back,	Move arm up and down behind back.
He led the others with a "Quack, quack, quack, Quack, quack, quack."	Open and close hand.
He led the others with a "Quack, quack, quack!"	

—Traditional rhyme

Five Yellow Ducklings

Five little ducklings	Begin rhyme with five fingers up.
Went swimming one day,	
Across the pond	
And far away.	
Old mother duck said,	
"Quack, quack, quack."	Take away fingers as rhyme progresses.
Four yellow ducklings	
Came swimming back.	Continue until there is one left.

One yellow duckling
Went swimming one day,
Across the pond
And far away.
Old mother duck said,
"Quack, quack, quack."
No yellow ducklings
Came swimming back.
Old mother duck said,
"Quack, quack, quack!"   Say this very loud.
Five yellow ducklings
Came swimming back.

—Lynda Roberts

Little Ducklings

All the little ducklings   Have children act out the movements
Lined up in a row.   described.
"Quack, quack, quack,"
And away they go.
They jump in the water
And bob up and down.
"Quack, quack, quack,"
They all swim around.

—Elizabeth Vollrath

The Ducks

"Quack! Quack!"
See the ducks go waddling   Waddle.
Down to the brook in
A jolly little row!
"Quack! Quack!"
See the ducks go waddling!   Waddle.
Splash in the water   Pretend to splash.
And swim to and fro.   Swimming motions.

—Adapted from a song by Helen Call

Ten Little Ducklings

                                          Sung to the tune of "Ten Little Indians."
One little, two little, three little ducklings,   Count off on fingers for the first
Four little, five little, six little ducklings,   verse.
Seven little, eight little, nine little ducklings,
Ten little ducklings quack!
Ten little, nine little, eight little ducklings,   Take away fingers on the second
Seven little, six little, five little ducklings,   verse.
Four little, three little, two little ducklings,
One little duckling quacks!

—Adapted traditional rhyme

If You'd Like to Be a Duck

If you'd like to be a duck, say "Quack, quack."
If you'd like to be a duck, say "Quack, quack."
If you'd like to be a duckie, well then you are very lucky!
If you'd like to be a duck, say "Quack, quack."

ADDITIONAL VERSES:
. . . waddle around.
. . . shake your tail.
. . . flap your wings.
. . . do all four.

Sung to the tune of "If You're Happy and You Know It."
Quack twice.

Waddle.
Shake your bottom.
Flap arms.
Quack, waddle, shake, and flap.

—Adapted traditional rhyme

Five Sleepy Ducks

Five little ducks were swimming in the lake.
The first one said, "I can hardly stay awake."
The second one said, "I am very sleepy, too."
The third one said, "Well, what should we do?"
The fourth one said, "Let's all take a nap."
The fifth one said, "Until Mother calls quack, quack."

Begin this rhyme with five fingers up.
Starting with the thumb, point to each in succession.

—Barbara Scott

Two Little Ducks

Two little ducks
With feathers on their backs.
One named Quick,
And the other named Quack.
Waddle away, Quick.
Waddle away, Quack.
Come back, Quick.
Come back, Quack.

Holding out two hands in front, thumbs up.

Wiggle one thumb.
Wiggle other thumb.
Move one thumb behind back.
Move other thumb behind back.
Return first thumb to front.
Return second thumb to front.

—Adapted traditional rhyme

Five Little Ducks

Five little ducks were wading by the shore.
One chased a fish and then there were four.
Four little ducks were resting by the tree.
One fell asleep and then there were three.
Three little ducks find mud to waddle through.
One got really stuck and then there were two.
Two little ducks were playing in the sun.
One wandered off and then there was one.
One little duck, no one to share his fun.
He waddled off and now there are none.

Begin this rhyme with five fingers up.
Take away fingers as rhyme progresses.

—Barbara Scott

I'm a Yellow Duckie

I'm a yellow duckie,
Feathered and sleek.
Here is my tail,
And here is my beak.
When the rain falls on me,
It's OK.
Because the raindrops
Just roll away!

—Adapted traditional rhyme

Sung to the tune of "I'm a Little Teapot."
Point to self.

Wiggle bottom.
Point to mouth.
Wiggle fingers down for rain.
Nod head "yes."

Roll hands.

Oh, Mother Duck

Oh, Mother Duck,
Oh, Mother Duck,
How many are your ducklings?
Oh, Mother Duck,
Oh, Mother Duck,
How many are your ducklings?
There's one, two, three, four, five, and six,
Seven, eight, nine, and finally ten.
Oh, Mother Duck,
Oh, Mother Duck,
How many are your ducklings?

—Adapted traditional rhyme

Sung to the tune of "O, Christmas Tree."

Shrug, wondering look.

Count out on fingers.

Reinforce numbers by counting fingers a second time.

The Little Duck Goes Quack

The little duck goes "Quack,"
The little duck goes "Quack."
Hi-ho the derry-o,
The little duck goes "Quack."
He waddles all around,
He waddles all around.
Hi-ho the derry-o,
He waddles all around.
He flaps his little wings,
He flaps his little wings.
Hi-ho the derry-o,
He flaps his little wings.
His beak is long and flat,
His beak is long and flat.
Hi-ho the derry-o,
His beak is long and flat.
His feet are big and wide,
His feet are big and wide.

Sung to the tune of "The Farmer in the Dell."
Quack.

Waddle.

Flap arms as wings.

Make duck head with hand.

Point to feet.

Hi-ho the derry-o,
His feet are big and wide.

—Adapted traditional rhyme

Five Little Ducklings

Five little ducklings to the water dash.   Wiggle five fingers.
In they jump with a big ker-splash!   Clap hands.
They paddle their feet . . . just look at them go!   Move hands up and down as if paddling.
    Swimming motion.
See them swimming to and fro!

—Barbara Scott

Quack, Quack

Sung to the tune of "Gung Gung Went the Little Green Frog One Day."

"Quack, quack" went the little brown duck one day,   Make duck's head with hand; move fingers for mouth.
"Quack, quack" went the little brown duck.
"Quack, quack" went the little brown duck one day,
And his tail went swish, swish, swish!   Move hips from side to side in rhythm.

—Adapted traditional rhyme

Ducks Love Rain

Ducks love rain.   Wiggle fingers down for rain.
Oh yes, we do!   Nod head "yes."
We play and play   Wiggle fingers side to side.
The whole day through!
We swim and splash,   Swimming motion; clap on the word "splash."

And paddle 'round   Paddle hands.
No happier ducks   Smile broadly.
Will ever be found!   Shake head "no."

—Barbara Scott

I'm a Duck

Sung to the tune of "Frère Jacques."

"Quack, quack, quack, quack,   One hand makes duck's head; move fingers to "talk."
Quack, quack, quack, quack."
I'm a duck,
I'm a duck.
When I walk, I waddle,   Waddle hand and arm back and forth.
When I walk, I waddle.
"Quack, quack, quack,   Make hand "talk" again.
Quack, quack, quack."

—Adapted traditional rhyme

Little Duck, Little Duck

This rhyme can be sung to the tune of "Teddy Bear, Teddy Bear" or chanted.

Little duck, little duck,   Waddle.
Waddle around.
Little duck, little duck,

Sit on the ground.	Sit.
Little duck, little duck,	
Swish your tail.	Wiggle bottom.
Little duck, little duck,	
Through the water sail.	Swimming motions.
Little duck, little duck,	
Paddle your feet.	Paddle hands up and down.
Little duck, little duck,	
Quack so sweet.	Quack!
Little duck, little duck,	
No more light.	Shake head "no."
Little duck, little duck,	
Say goodnight.	Put head on hands; close eyes.

—Adapted traditional rhyme

Swimming Ducks

The first little duck decided to take a swim.	Begin this rhyme with five fingers up.
The second little duck joined right in.	Starting with the thumb, point to each in succession.
The third little duck just stuck in a toe.	
The fourth little duck cried, "No, no, no!"	
The fifth little duck decided to play	
and go for a swim another day.	

—Barbara Scott

Little Ducks

Little ducks go "Quack, quack, quack,	*Sung to the tune of "London Bridge."*
Quack, quack, quack,	Hand and arm make duck's head; move fingers to "talk."
Quack, quack, quack."	
Little ducks go "quack, quack, quack,"	
Swimming all day.	Swimming motion.
With their feet, they paddle, paddle, paddle,	Paddle hands up and down.
Paddle, paddle, paddle,	
Paddle, paddle, paddle.	
With their feet, they paddle, paddle, paddle,	
Swimming all day.	Swimming motion.
With their tails, they swish, swish, swish,	Move bottom side to side.
Swish, swish, swish,	
Swish, swish, swish.	
With their tails, they swish, swish, swish,	
Swimming all day.	Swimming motion.

—Adapted traditional rhyme

Ducks Are Swimming

Ducks are swimming to and fro	*Sung to the tune of "Camptown Ladies."*
Quack-quack, quack-quack.	Swimming motion.

Watch their little feet go, go!

Quack-quack-quack-quack-quack!

Gonna swim all night,

Gonna swim all day.

Ducks are swimming to and fro.

Quack-quack-quack all day!

—Adapted traditional rhyme

Paddle hands up and down.

Swimming motion.

One Little Duck

One little duck flew and flew.

He found a friend and now there are two.

Two little ducks swimming on the sea

Found another friend and now there are three.

Three little ducks wading by the shore

Found another friend and now there are four.

Four little ducks getting ready to dive

Found another friend and now there are five.

—Barbara Scott

Begin this rhyme with one finger up.

Add fingers as the rhyme progresses.

.

The Ducks Go Waddling

The ducks go waddling one by one,

Hurrah, hurrah.

The ducks go waddling one by one,

Hurrah, hurrah.

The ducks go waddling one by one,

The little duck stops to say "Well done."

And they all go waddling down to the pond,

To play in the rain.

ADDITIONAL VERSES:

Two by two . . . the little duck stops to say "Achoo!"

Three by three . . . the little duck stops, a bug to see.

Four by four . . . the little duck stops to shut the door.

Five by five . . . the little duck stops to take a dive.

Six by six . . . the little duck stops to pick up sticks.

Seven by seven . . . the little duck stops to look to heaven.

Eight by eight . . . the little duck stops to say "Too late."

Nine by nine . . . the little duck stops to read a sign.

Ten by ten . . . the little duck stops to say "The end!"

—Adapted traditional rhyme

Sung to the tune of "The Ants Go Marching."

Begin with one finger up.

Add fingers for each verse.

Ducks Are Swimming

Ducks are swimming,

Ducks are swimming,

In the pond,

Sung to the tune of "Frère Jacques."

Swimming motion.

Make circle in front of body with hands.

In the pond.
Can you hear them singing,
Can you hear them singing?
"Quack, quack, quack,
Quack, quack, quack!"

—Adapted traditional rhyme

Put hand to one ear.
Put other hand to opposite ear.

Books to Share

Alborough, Jez. 2003. *Captain Duck*. New York: HarperCollins. ISBN: 978-0060521233. (This book is part of a series by this author.)

Berry, Lynne. 2009. *Duck Tents*. New York: Henry Holt and Company. ISBN: 978-0805086966. (This is one of a series of books by this author.)

Freedman, Claire. 2009. *A Cuddle for Little Duck*. New York: Cartwheel Books. ISBN: 978-0545077972.

Grindley, Sally. 2005. *Mucky Duck*. New York: Bloomsbury Children's. ISBN: 978-1582348216.

Hills, Tad. 2007. *Duck, Duck, Goose*. New York: Schwartz and Wade Books. ISBN: 978-0375840685. (This is part of a series of books by this author.)

Urbanovic, Jackie. 2008. *Duck Soup*. New York: HarperCollins. ISBN: 978-0061214417. (This is one of a series of books by this author.)

Musical Selections

"Be Kind to Your Web-Footed Friends" from *A Child's Celebration of Silliest Songs*. ASIN: B00000JZB8.

"I Speak Duck" from *Making Faces* by Rick Scott. Available: www.songsforteaching.com (accessed March 10, 2010).

"Mama Duck" from *Sing It! Say It! Stamp It! Sway It!*, vol. 3, by Peter and Ellen Allard. ASIN: B00007EEFF.

"Six Little Ducks" from *Sing Along with Bob*, vol. 1. ASIN: B00000DAO4.

"Three Little Ducks" from *Songs for Wiggleworms*. ASIN: B00004YLUE.

"The Ugly Duckling" from *We All Live Together,* vol. IV, by Greg and Steve. ASIN: B000KZCZ9O.

Sources

Giddings, T. 1923. *Songs of Childhood*. Lexington, MA: Ginn and Company.

McKinnon, Elizabeth, and Gayle Bittinger. 1994. *Busy Bees Spring: Fun for Two's and Three's*. Everett, WA: Warren Publishing House.

North Central Library Co-operative. n.d. *Storytime Booklet* [out of print].

Roberts, Lynda. 1985. *Mitt Magic: Fingerplays for Finger Puppets*. Silver Spring, MD: Gryphon House.

Warren, Jean. 1990. *Theme-a-Saurus II*. Everett, WA: Warren Publishing House.

Elephants

Add these rhymes to circus, jungle, or zoo storytimes for lots of fun!

Rhyme

Telling Guide

Five Big Elephants

Five big elephants—oh, what a sight,
Swinging their trunks from left to right!
Four are followers, and one is the king.
But they all walk around in the circus ring.

—Author unknown

Choose four children to be elephants who follow one chosen to be king. Have them walk around the room several times as the rhyme is recited. Keep choosing children until all have had a chance to participate.

Crouch over and clasp hands; move arms left and right.

Swing trunks as the walk continues around the room.

An Elephant Goes Like This and That

An elephant goes like this and that.
He's terrible big,
And he's terrible fat.
He has no fingers,
And he has no toes,
But goodness gracious, what a nose!

—Author unknown

Pat knees.

Put hands up high.

Put hands out wide.

Wriggle fingers.

Touch toes.

Make curling movement away from nose.

Five Gray Elephants

Five gray elephants marching through a glade,
Decide to stop and play, they are having a parade.
The first swings his trunk and announces he'll lead,
The next waves a flag, which of course they need.
The third gray elephant trumpets a song,
The fourth beats a drum as he marches along.
While the fifth makes believe he's the whole show,
And nods and smiles to the crowd as they go.
Five gray elephants marching through the glade,
Having a lot of fun during their parade.

—Author unknown

March fingers of right hand.

Swing arm like trunk.

Wave hand over head.

Blow through hand.

Beat a drum.

Nod head to left and right; smile.

The Elephant's Trunk

The elephant has a great big trunk,
That goes swinging, swinging so.
He has tiny, tiny eyes that show him where to go.
His huge long ears go flapping, flapping up and down.
His great feet go stomping, stomping on the ground.

—Author unknown

Pretend an arm is the trunk.

Swing trunk.

Point to eyes.

Pretend hands are ears.

Stomp with feet.

Five Little Elephants

Five little elephants
Rowing toward the shore.
One fell in
And then there were four.
Four little elephants
Climbing up a tree.
One slid down,
Then there were three.
Three little elephants
Living in the zoo.
One walked off,
Then there were two.
Two little elephants
Playing in the sun.
One fell asleep,
Then there was one.
One little elephant
Isn't any fun.
Abra ca da bra!
Then there were none!

Begin rhyme with five fingers up.

Take away fingers as rhyme progresses.

—Author unknown

Elephant

A circus elephant I went to see.
He had four legs and was bigger than me.
He had two ears big and around,
And one long nose that made a sound. Eeeeeeeeeeeeeeeee!

Hold hand over eyes.
Hold up four fingers and point to self.
Show two fingers and make a circle with hands. / Put arm like trunk and make elephant noise.

—From Natural Learning

Elephant Action Play

Who is the animal baggy and gray,
That walks in the forest with a sway?
Who runs around on big, big toes,
And feeds himself with his nose?
The elephant!

Circle both arms.
Sway both arms.
Point to toes.
Point to nose.
Clap hands one time.

—From Alphabet Soup

Five Elephants in the Bathtub

One elephant in the bathtub going for a swim.
Knock, knock.
Splash, splash.
Come on in!
Five elephants in the bathtub

This rhyme makes a fun flannel or Velcro board story!

Clap twice on "knock, knock."
Slap knees twice on "splash, splash."
Motion with both hands to come in.
Continue up through five.

Going for a swim.
Knock, knock.
Splash, splash.
They all fell in!

—From SurLaLune Storytime

Elephants at Work and Play

As five little elephants	Hold up five fingers.
Marched through the grass,	March in place.
They decided to stop and	
Have a music class.	
The first blew his trumpet	Point to thumb.
And announced he'd be teacher.	
The next gave a call of the	
Wild jungle animal.	Point to index finger.
The third and fourth elephants	
Trumpeted a song.	Point to middle and ring fingers in succession.
But the last little elephant	
Just followed along.	Point to little finger.
Then he left the others,	
As he didn't care to play,	Hold up only little finger.
And he carried tree logs	Motion of carrying something heavy.
The rest of the day.	

—Author unknown

An Elephant

An elephant is big and gray.	Hold hands far apart to show size.
To both sides he likes to sway.	Sway from side to side.
He stomps his feet upon the ground	Stomp feet.
And makes a very noisy sound!	Put hands over ears.

—Barbara Scott

Elephant

Said Madame Elephant: "O dear,	Lean over; put arm to nose; swing back and forth to represent elephant's trunk.
I'd love to stay at home this year!	
This circus work is very hard,	Wipe brow.
I should enjoy my own back yard."	Pretend to pick flowers.

—From *Four-Footed Folk*

A Balancing Elephant

An elephant was balancing	Begin rhyme with one finger up.
On a spider web.	Add fingers as the rhyme progresses.
Since he saw he didn't fall,	
He found another elephant to call.	Continue with two, three, four, five.

—Traditional Spanish rhyme

Trunk

The elephant has a long, long nose,
And it is called a trunk.
T-R-U-N-K,
T-R-U-N-K,
T-R-U-N-K,
And it is called a trunk!

—Adapted traditional rhyme

Five Enormous Elephants

Five enormous elephants were talking one day.
The first one said, "I love to eat hay."
The second one said, "I am big and strong."
The third one said, "My trunk is very long."
The fourth one said, "Many tricks I can do."
The fifth one said, "I want to be friends with you."

—Barbara Scott

Elephant, Elephant

Elephant, elephant,
Turn around.
Elephant, elephant,
Stomp on the ground!
Elephant, elephant,
Trunk up high!
Reach the sky!
Elephant, elephant,
Never fear.
Elephant, elephant,
Flap those ears.
Elephant, elephant,
Sway left and right.
Elephant, elephant,
Say goodnight.

—Adapted traditional rhyme

One Elephant Went Out to Play

One elephant went out to play,
Upon a spider's web one day.
He thought it was such enormous fun,
That he called for another elephant to come!

— Traditional rhyme

Sung to the tune of "Bingo." Have a visual of some sort for this rhyme, either letters to put on your flannel board or smaller letters that would fit on a hand glove. Point to nose.

Proceed with rhyme, taking away letters and clapping to replace the letter not said.

Begin this rhyme with five fingers up.
Starting with the thumb, point to each finger in succession.

This rhyme can be sung to the tune of "Teddy Bear, Teddy Bear" or chanted.

Turn in place.

Stomp feet.

Hands and arms make trunk.
Reach up with "trunk."

Shake head "no."

Put hands to sides of head to represent ears; move back and forth.

Sway back and forth.

Put head on hands; pretend to sleep.

Sung to the tune of "Five Little Ducks." Do this rhyme with just five fingers or flannel or Velcro board characters, or use a long piece of rope or string for children to stand on. Continue singing until you have included all of the children in your storytime session!

This Is the Way, Elephant Style!

This is way I stomp my feet,
Stomp my feet, stomp my feet.
This is the way I stomp my feet,
'Cause I am an elephant!
This is the way I stand and sway,
Stand and sway, stand and sway.
This is the way I stand and sway,
'Cause I am an elephant!
This is the way I move my trunk,
Move my trunk, move my trunk.
This is the way I move my trunk,
'Cause I am an elephant!

—Adapted traditional rhyme

Sung to the tune of "The Mulberry Bush."
Stomp feet.

Sway back and forth.

Clasp hands in front to form trunk.
Move them back and forth and up and down.

Five Elephants

Five elephants went out to play
In the jungle one fine day.
Mama Elephant trumpeted loud and deep.
Only four elephants came back to sleep.
No elephants went out to play
In the jungle one fine day.
Mama Elephant trumpeted loud and deep,
And all the elephants came back to sleep!

—Adapted traditional rhyme

Sung to the tune of "Five Little Ducks."
Begin rhyme with five fingers up.

Take away fingers as rhyme progresses.
Continue with four, three, two, one, until . . .

One Little Elephant

One little, two little, three little elephants,
Four little, five little, six little elephants,
Seven little, eight little, nine little elephants,
Ten little elephants play!
Ten little, nine little, eight little elephants,
Seven little, six little, five little elephants,
Four little, three little, two little elephants,
One little elephant plays!

—Adapted traditional rhyme

Sung to the tune of "Ten Little Indians." This rhyme makes a great flannel or Velcro board presentation as well!
Count out on fingers for the first verse.

Wiggle ten fingers in the air!
Take away fingers on the second verse.

Wiggle one finger.

Five Huge Elephants

Five huge elephants
Jumping all around!
They look like they are having fun,
But oh, what a sound!

—Barbara Scott

Hold up five fingers.
Jump fingers up and down.
Nod head "yes."
Hold hands over ears and shake head.

Elephants

Elephants swing their long trunks,
Their long trunks, their long trunks.
Elephants swing their long trunks
While they're walking.
Elephants flap their big ears,
Their big ears, their big ears.
Elephants flap their big ears
While they're walking.
Elephants move to and fro,
To and fro, to and fro.
Elephants move to and fro
While they're walking.

Sung to the tune of "London Bridge."
Clasp hands in front for "trunk";
move arms back and forth.

Put open hands to ears; move back
and forth.

Sway from side to side.

—Adapted traditional rhyme

Five Gray Elephants

Five gray elephants were standing by the door.
One went to find some food and now there are four.
Four gray elephants stood underneath a tree.
One saw a tiny mouse (eek!) and now there are three.
Three gray elephants with lots of things to do.
One went to move some logs and now there are two.
Two gray elephants were standing in the sun.
One drifted off to sleep and now there's just one.
One gray elephant standing all alone.
He went home to take a bath and now there are none.

Begin this rhyme with five fingers up.
Take away fingers as the rhyme
progresses.

—Barbara Scott

Five Little Elephants

Five little elephants were having a parade.
The first little elephant marched in the shade.
The second little elephant trumpeted loud and long.
The third little elephant sang a silly song.
The fourth little elephant was tired and sat down.
The fifth little elephant began to dance around!

Begin rhyme with five fingers up.
Starting with the thumb, point to each
finger in succession.

—Barbara Scott

The Elephant

The elephant looks like a giant.
He is wrinkled and he is strong.
He has two big floppy ears
And a nose that's oh so long.
He sways back and forth.
Through the jungle he goes,
With his big floppy ears,

Move hands far apart to indicate size.
Show muscles.
Hold up two fingers.
Point to nose.
Sway.

Put hands to either side of head to
represent ears.

And his hose of a nose.

—Folk rhyme

The Elephant Has a Great Big Trunk

The elephant has a great big trunk

Clasp hands in front; move arms up and down for trunk.

That goes swinging to and fro.

Clasp hands to make trunk swing.

And he has teeny, tiny eyes

That show him where to go.

Point to eyes.

His great big ears go flopping,

Put hands to ears.

While his great big feet go stomping, stomping, stomping.

Stomp feet.

—Author unknown

What Am I?

My feet go stomp, stomp, stomp.

Stomp feet.

My mouth goes chomp, chomp, chomp.

Motion of chewing.

My trunk swings slap, slap, slap.

Swing arms, hands clasped together, side to side.

My ears move flap, flap, flap.

Put hands to ears; move back and forth.

What am I?

—Barbara Scott

Achoo!

The elephant has
A trunk for a nose.

Clasp hands together in front to form trunk.

When he has to sneeze,

Put index finger under nose, stifling a sneeze.

It has a long way to go!

Move hands apart to indicate length.

—Barbara Scott

Slowly, Slowly

Slowly, slowly the elephant walks.

Take big, quiet steps in place.

His feet don't make a sound.

Make "Shhh" motion.

But when he lifts his trunk up high,

Clasp hands together in front; raise arms into the air.

It makes a trumpet sound!

Trumpet like an elephant!

—Barbara Scott

Go, Elephant!

See me walking down the street.

Point to eyes.

Hear the sound of my big feet.

Point to ears.

I walk fast, and sometimes slow

Walk fast, then slow.

Anywhere I go, go, go!

Move hands to show expanse.

—Barbara Scott

If You're an Elephant and You Know It

Sung to the tune of "If You're Happy and You Know It."

If you're an elephant and you know it, stomp your feet!

Stomp feet.

If you're an elephant and you know it, stomp your feet.

If you're an elephant and you know,
Really shake the ground and show it.
If you're an elephant and you know, stomp your feet.
If you're an elephant and you know it, wave your trunk!
If you're an elephant and you know it, wave your trunk.
If you're an elephant and you know it,
Swing your trunk around and show it.
If you're an elephant and you know it, wave your trunk.
If you're an elephant and you know it, trumpet loud!
If you're an elephant and you know it, trumpet loud!
If you're an elephant and you know it,
Blow a trumpet sound and show it.
If you're an elephant and you know it, trumpet loud.

— Adapted traditional rhyme

Clasp hands in front; move arms side to side, up and down.

Clasp arms in front of nose for trunk; raise arms; make trumpeting sound!

Books to Share

D'Amico, Carmela. 2008. *Ella Sets Sail.* New York: Arthur A. Levine Books. ISBN: 978-0439831550. (This is part of series of books by this author.)

Judge, Lita. 2009. *Pennies for Elephants.* New York: Hyperion Books. ISBN: 978-1423113904.

Lewis, Kim. 2006. *Hooray for Harry.* Somerville, MA: Candlewick Press. ISBN: 978-0763629625.

McKee, David. 2009. *Elmer's Special Day.* London: Andersen Press. ISBN: 978-0761351542.

Monroe, Chris. 2009. *Monkey with a Tool Belt and the Noisy Problem.* Minneapolis: Carolrhoda Books. ISBN: 978-0822592471.

Willems, Mo. 2009. *Elephants Cannot Dance.* New York: Hyperion Books. ISBN: 978-1423114109. (This is part of series of books about Elephant and his friend, Pig.)

Musical Selections

"An Elephant Named Ed" from *Animals at the Zoo* by Bobby Susser. ASIN: B00005BABL.

"The Elephant Parade" by Ashley De La Rocha. Available: www.songsforteaching.com (accessed March 7, 2010).

"Elephant Party Jam" from *Let's Dance* by Sharon, Lois, and Bram. ASIN: B00000DCJW.

"An Elephant's Trunk" from *Jump and Jive with Hi-5.* ASIN: B0002O06X0.

"One Elephant" from *Great Big Hits* by Sharon, Lois, and Bram. ASIN: B000008KML.

"One Elephant, Deux Elephants" and "Elephant Rhyme" from *One Elephant, Deux Elephants* by Sharon, Lois, and Bram. ASIN: B000068QQ0.

Sources

Briggs, Diane. 1999. *101 Fingerplays, Stories, and Songs to Use with Finger Puppets.* Chicago: American Library Association.

———. 2007. *Preschool Favorites: 35 Storytimes Kids Love.* Chicago: American Library Association.

Cromwell, Liz, Dixie Hibner, and John R. Faitel. 1983. *Finger Frolics,* rev. ed. El Cajon, CA: Partner Press.

Davis, Robin Works. 1998. *Toddle on Over.* Fort Atkinson, WI: Alleyside Press.

"Fingerplays." Natural Learning. Available: www.naturallearning.com/fingerplays.html (accessed March 7, 2010).

Gordon, Elizabeth. n.d. *Four-Footed Folk.* Available: www.childrensbooksonline.org/Four_Footed _Folk/index.htm (accessed March 7, 2010).

Hansen, Charles, and Cynthia Stilley. 1996. *Ring a Ring O'Roses,* 10th ed. Flint, MI: Flint Public Library.

Holley, Cynthia. 1993. *First Time Circle Time: Shared-Group Experiences for Three, Four, and Five-Year-Olds.* Torrance, CA: Fearon Teacher Aids.

Lit2Go. n.d. "Elephants at Work and Play." Available: etc.usf.edu/lit2go/contents/2900/2988/ 2988.pdf (accessed April 9, 2010).

Maddigan, Beth. 2003. *The Big Book of Stories, Songs, and Sing-Alongs.* Santa Barbara, CA: Libraries Unlimited.

Mama Lisa's World of Children & International Culture. Available: www.mamalisa.com (accessed March 4, 2010).

Matterson, Elizabeth, comp. 1971. *Games for the Very Young: Fingerplays and Nursery Games.* New York: McGraw-Hill.

Redleaf, Rhoda. 1993. *Busy Fingers, Growing Minds.* St. Paul, MN: Redleaf Press.

Scott, Louise B. 1983. *Rhymes for Learning Times.* Minneapolis: T.S. Dennison & Co.

SurLaLune Storytime. Available: www.surlalunefairytales.com/storytime/elephants/index.html (accessed March 7, 2010).

Totline Staff, comp. 1994. *1001 Rhymes and Fingerplays.* Everett, WA: Warren Publishing House.

Wilmes, Liz, and Dick Wilmes. 1983. *Everyday Circle Times.* Elgin, IL: Building Blocks.

"Zoo Songs, Poems, and Fingerplays." Alphabet Soup. Available: www.alphabet-soup.net/dir7/ zoosong.html (accessed March 7, 2010).

Farms

Let's have loads of fun, down on the farm!

Rhyme

Make a Noise

Make a noise like a rooster.
Make a noise like a hen.
Make a noise like a chick.
Make a noise like an unhatched egg.
Good! And now you're ready to listen.

—Author unknown

Little Chick

Snuggled down inside
An egg that was white,
Was a tiny chick
With its head tucked in tight.
Then it lifted its head,
Tapped the egg with its beak,
And quickly popped out,
Cheep, cheep, cheep!

—Colraine Pettipaw Hunley

Eggs and More Eggs—Surprise!

Turkeys make big ones,
Robins make small
Bright blue eggs,
The prettiest of all.
Duck eggs are dandy,
Owl eggs are round,
The ostrich lays an egg
That weighs three pounds.
Teeny is a hummingbird,
Great is a goose,
They lay eggs.
How about a moose?

But a chicken-sized egg
Seems just about right.
Crack it open.
Surprise! Delight!

—Jan Irving

Telling Guide

This is a great rhyme to begin your storytime!
Everyone crows.
Everyone clucks.
Everyone peeps.
Silence.

Do actions as rhyme indicates.

Stretch arms out wide.
Place hands close together.
Touch fingers to form circle.

Place arms under armpits to form wings.
Circle eyes with fingers.
Hold arms straight out, fingers locked.
Bend knees to show weight of egg.
Form circle with finger and thumb.
Touch fingers to form circle.
Nod.
Touch thumbs to head; spread fingers for antlers; shake head "no."
Cup hands for nest.
Nod.
Clap.
Put arms in air; wave fingers.

This Little Cow

This little cow eats grass,
This little cow eats hay.
This little cow drinks water,
And this little cow runs away.
This little cow does nothing,
But just lie down all day

—Traditional Chinese rhyme

Hold up one hand; bend down one finger, then others in succession as rhyme progresses.

Gallop-a-Gallop

Gallop-a-gallop-a-gallop around,
Riding my horse all over town.
Gallop-a-gallop-a-gallop again,
Riding my horse back home again.

—Traditional rhyme

Gallop in circle to left.

Gallop in circle to right.

Ten Little Ponies

Ten little ponies in a meadow green,
Friskiest ten little ponies I've ever seen.
They go for a gallop, they go for a trot,
They come to a halt in the big feed lot.
Ten little ponies fat and well fed,
Curl up together in a soft straw bed.

—Kathy Ross

Hold up ten fingers.
Wiggle fingers.
Motion of hands galloping, then trotting.
Keep hands still.

Close fingers in hands.

This Little Horse

This little horse eats grass.
This little horse eats hay.
This little horse drinks water.
This little horse runs away.
This little horse does nothing at all,
But switches his tail all day.

—Kathy Ross

Point to each finger in sequence, beginning with the thumb.

Ten Little Ponies

One little, two little, three little ponies,
Four little, five little, six little ponies,
Seven little, eight little, nine little ponies,
Ten little ponies in a herd.

—Kathy Ross

This rhyme can be sung to the tune of "Ten Little Indians" or chanted.
Hold up fingers as the rhyme progresses.

The Horse on the Trail

The horse on the trail goes trot, trot, trot,
Trot, trot, trot,
Trot, trot, trot.
The horse on the trail goes trot, trot, trot,
All around the ranch.

Sung to the tune of "The Wheels on the Bus." Stand in a circle, and follow the leader's motions while going around the circle.

ADDITIONAL VERSES:
The horse on the trail goes gallop, gallop, gallop. . . .
The horse on the trail goes walk, walk, walk . . .
The horse on the trail goes stop, stop, stop . . .

—Kathy Ross

Horsie, Horsie, Don't You Stop

Horsie, horsie, don't you stop.
Just let your feet go clippety-clop;
Your tail goes swish,
And the wheels go 'round—
Giddyup, you're homeward bound.

—Traditional rhyme

Shake head "no."
Clip-clop cupped hands on thighs.
Bend arm at elbow; wave back and forth.
Roll hands.
Pretend to hold reins and snap them.

Hickety, Pickety

Hickety, pickety, my black hen.

She lays eggs for the gentlemen.

Sometimes nine and sometimes ten.

Hickety, pickety, my black hen.

—Traditional rhyme

Pretend to hold hen in one arm; pet with the other hand.
Form oval shape with thumbs and index fingers together.
Hold up nine, then ten fingers.
Pretend to hold hen in one arm; pet with the other hand.

Baa, Baa, Black Sheep

Baa, baa, black sheep,
Have you any wool?
Yes sir, yes, sir,
Three bags full.
One for the master,
And one for the dame,
And one for the little boy
Who lives down the lane.

—Traditional rhyme

Put hands out to sides, questioning.
Nod head "yes."
Hold up three fingers; point to each in succession.

Ride Away, Ride Away

Ride away, ride away,
Johnny shall ride.
He shall have a pussy cat
Tied to one side.
He shall have a little dog
Tied to the other.
Johnny shall ride
To see his grandmother.

—Traditional rhyme

Bounce up and down, pretending to ride horse.

Point to the left.

Point to the right.
Bounce up and down, pretending to ride horse.

Charley Warley Had a Cow

Charley Warley had a cow,
Black and white about the brow.
Open the gate and let her through,
Charley Warley's old cow.

—Traditional rhyme

ASL sign for cow: thumb and little finger extended, other three tucked, thumb up next to temple.
Use ASL sign for cow.
Point to forehead.
Motion of opening gate.
Use ASL sign for cow.

The Lambs

This is the meadow where all the long day,
Ten frolicsome lambs are at play.
These are the measures the good farmer brings,
Salt in, or oatmeal, and other good things.
This is the lamb's own big water-trough.
Drink, little lambs, and then scamper off!
This is the rack where in winter, they feed.

Hay makes a very good dinner indeed.
These are the big shears to shear the old sheep;
Dear little lambs their soft wool may keep.
Here with its big double doors shut so tight;
This is the barn where they sleep at night.

—Emilie Poulsson

Make circle in front of body with arms.
Wiggle all ten fingers.
Hold out cupped hand in front.
Cup hands together in front.
Wiggle fingers away.
Put hands together, fingers spread, to make an "X."
Nod head "yes."
Index and middle fingers make scissor motion.
Clasp hands clasped in front, thumbs side by side.

The Pigs

Piggy Wig and Piggy Wee
Hungry pigs as pigs could be!
For their dinner had to wait
Down behind the barnyard gate.

Piggy Wig and Piggy Wee
Climbed the barnyard gate to see,
Peeking through the gate so high
But no dinner did they spy.
Piggy Wig and Piggy Wee
Got down sad as pigs could be;
But the gate soon opened wide

And they scampered forth outside.
Piggy Wig and Piggy Wee
What a delight to see
Dinner ready not far off;
Such a full and tempting trough.
Piggy Wig and Piggy Wee
Greedy pigs as pigs could be.

Hold up both thumbs.
Put hands together, fingertips to fingertips.
Hold up both thumbs.
Climbing motion.
Point to eyes.
Shake head "no."
Hold up both thumbs.
Begin with fingertips together, then open as a gate.
Wiggle thumbs.
Hold up both thumbs.
Clap hands.
Cup hands to represent trough.
Hold up both thumbs.

For their dinner ran pell-mell.
In the trough both piggies fell!

—Emilie Poulsson

Down in the Barnyard 💿

When the farmer's day is done,
In the barnyard, ev'ry one,
Beast and bird politely say,
"Thank you for my food today."
The cow says, "Moo!"
The pigeon, "Coo!"
The sheep says, "Baa!"
The lamb says, "Maa!"
The hen, "Cluck, cluck!"
"Quack" says the duck;
The dog, "Bow wow!"
The cat, "Meow!"
The horse says, "Neigh, I love sweet hay!"
The pig nearby, grunts in his sty.
When the barn is locked up tight,
Then the farmer says "Good night!"
Thanks his animals, ev'ry one,
For the work that has been done.

—Maud Burnham

Hens and Chickens

Chicky, chick, chick
Come to me quick,
And see what a worm I have found.
Come, while I scratch
In the strawberry patch,
And dig them up out of the ground.
Chicky, chick, chick,
Scramble and pick,
And talk as you run to and fro.
Scratch with your claws,
And fill up your craws,
For that is the way you must grow.
Chicky, chick, chick,
Worms arc so thick

Turn thumbs down.

This is a great rhyme to use with a flannel or Velcro board if you have figures for all farm animals mentioned.

Hold up ten fingers.
Wiggle each one as animal is mentioned.

ASL sign for chicken: Begin with hand by mouth, thumb and index finger slightly apart to form "beak," with other fingers tucked. Then take "beak" and do a downward movement into the open palm of the other hand.
Use ASL sign for chicken.

Beckon.

Use index finger for a wiggly worm!

Pretend to scratch at the ground with one hand.

Scratch at ground with both hands.
Use ASL sign for chicken.

Point to the left, then right.
Scratching motion.

Use ASL sign for chicken.
All fingers in the air, wiggle them.

That you can have plenty today.
Bustle about,
And dig them all out,
And eat and grow fat while you may!

— From *Around the House*

Scratch with both hands.
Rub tummy.

There's a Cow

There's a cow on the mountain,
The old saying goes.
On her legs are four feet,
On her feet are eight toes.
Her tail is behind
On the end of her back,
And her head sticks out front
At the end of her neck.

— Traditional Chinese rhyme

ASL sign for cow: thumb and little finger extended, other three tucked, thumb up next to temple.
Use ASL sign for cow.

Hold up four fingers.
Hold up eight fingers.
Wiggle hips.
Point to back.
Point to head.
Point to neck.

The Farmer's Guide

In spring, plant the turnip.
In summer, the beet.
When harvest is over,
We sow the buckwheat.

— Traditional Chinese rhyme

Motion of hoeing.
Motion of planting.

Motion of swinging sickle back and forth.

Chickadees

Five little chickadees, sitting by the door—
One flew away, and then there were four.

CHORUS:
Chickadees, chickadees, happy and gay,
Chickadees, chickadees, fly away.

Four little chickadees, sitting in a tree—
One flew away, and then there were three.
CHORUS

Three little chickadees, looking at you—
One flew away, and then there were two.
CHORUS

Two little chickadees, sitting in the sun—
One flew away, and then there was one.
CHORUS

One little chickadee, sitting all alone—
That one flew away, and then there were none.

— Lynda Roberts

Begin this rhyme with five fingers up.
Take away fingers as the rhyme progresses.
Repeat the chorus between each number verse.

Five Little Sheep

There were five little sheep in the meadow one day.
One ran off because he wanted to play.
Well that farmer went looking behind the barn door,
But that little sheep was gone and there were only four.
There were four little sheep in the meadow one day.
One ran off because he wanted to play.
Well the farmer went looking, he checked behind a tree,
But that little sheep was gone and there were only three.
There were three little sheep in the meadow one day.
One ran off because he wanted to play.
Well the farmer went looking, behind a truck of blue,
But that little sheep was gone and there were only two.
There were two little sheep in the meadow one day.
One ran off because he wanted to play.
Well the farmer went looking and he started to run,
But that little sheep was gone and there was only one.
There was one little sheep in the meadow one day,
And that sheep ran off because he wanted to play.
Well the farmer went looking, but he was done,
Since that last sheep was gone, now there were none.
There were no more sheep in the meadow that day.
They had all run off because they wanted to play.
But when the sun went down, and the day was gone,
Those little sheep came back to sleep until the dawn.

—Kay Lincycomb

Begin this rhyme with five fingers up.

Look around.
Take away fingers as rhyme progresses.

Pretend to look behind tree.

Pretend to look.

Run in place.

Shrug shoulders.

The Farmer and His Seeds

The farmer plants his seeds.
The farmer plants his seeds.
Hi, ho, the dairy-o.
The farmer plants his seeds.

ADDITIONAL VERSES:
The sun comes out to shine . . .
The rain begins to fall . . .
The plant begins to grow . . .
The farmer cuts them down . . .
And now he grinds it up . . .
And now he bakes the bread . . .

—Carolyn N. Cullum

Sung to tune of "The Farmer in the Dell."
Do the motions as indicated.

Bend and pretend to plant.

Make circle with arms.
Fingers flutter up and down.
Slowly raise up.
Cutting motion.
Grinding motion.
Put in oven.

Fields of Food

Plow the fields.	Turn hand over from palm up to palm down to show ground being turned.
Plant the seeds.	Pretend to plant.
Wait for the sun.	Make circle above head with hands.
And rain they need.	Flutter fingers like rain.
Hoe the weeds.	Pretend to hoe.
Watch the plants grow.	Cup hands together; move upward.
Fields of food	Pretend to eat.
In long, long rows.	Start with hands together, then move outward.

—Susan M. Dailey

Sung to the tune of "The Bear Went Over the Mountain."

When I Went to the Barnyard

When I went into the barnyard,
When I went into the barnyard,
When I went into the barnyard,
What do you think I saw?
I saw a cow and her baby,
I saw a cow and her baby,
I saw a cow and her baby,
And what do you think I heard?   Make cow noises.

ADDITIONAL VERSES:
I saw some little pink piglets . . .
I saw a big fat turkey . . .
I saw a fluffy white sheep . . .
I saw an old gray donkey . . .

—Susan M. Dailey

Little Chicks

Tiptoe to the hen house,	Creep fingers.
Peek in the door.	Put hand above eyes and look around.
See the little eggs,	
One, two, three, four.	Hold up fingers while counting.
But when will they hatch?	Hold out hands in questioning gesture.
When will they appear?	
Listen! Listen!	Cup hand around ear.
And you will hear . . .	
Peck, peck, peck	Pinch thumb and index finger together; make up and down motion.
And pick, pick, pick,	
And out of an egg	Cup hands, then open them up.
Comes one little chick!	
Peck, peck, peck	
And pick, pick, pick.	Cup hands, then open them up.

Peck, peck, peck
And pick, pick, pick.
Peck, peck, peck
And pick, pick, pick.
And out of the egg
Comes the last little chick!

—Adapted from a song by Susan M. Dailey

Five Little Farmers

Five little farmers arise with the sun.

The first little farmer knows there's plowing to be done.

The second little farmer feeds the hungry pigs.
The third little farmer has fence holes to dig.
The fourth little farmer goes to fix his tractor now.
The fifth little farmer goes to milk the cow.

—Barbara Scott

Make circle overhead with arms; hold up five fingers.
Beginning with thumb, point to each in succession.

All Around the Farm

The cows on the farm go "Moo, moo, moo,
Moo, moo, moo,
Moo, moo, moo."
The cows on the farm go "Moo, moo, moo,"
All around the farm.

ADDITIONAL VERSES:
The horses . . . "Neigh, neigh, neigh."
The pigs . . . "Oink, oink, oink."
The chicks . . . "Peep, peep, peep."
The sheep . . . "Baa, baa, baa."

—Adapted traditional rhyme

Sung to the tune of "The Wheels on the Bus." You can augment this rhyme using pictures of all the animals mentioned on a flannel or Velcro board.

Make large circle in the air with hand.

The length of this rhyme is limited only by the number of animals you wish to use!

Ten Little Farmers

One little, two little, three little farmers,
Four little, five little, six little farmers,
Seven little, eight little, nine little farmers,
Ten little farmers plow.
Ten little, nine little, eight little farmers,
Seven little, six little, five little farmers,
Four little, three little, two little farmers,
One little farmer plows.

—Adapted traditional rhyme

Sung to the tune of "Ten Little Indians."

Count out on fingers for the first verse.

Take away fingers in the second verse.

The Farmer in the Dell

The farmer in the dell,
The farmer in the dell.
Heigh-ho, the derry-o,
The farmer in the dell.
The farmer takes a wife . . .
The wife takes a child . . .
The child takes a nurse . . .
The nurse takes a cow . . .
The cow takes a dog . . .
The dog takes a cat . . .
The cat takes a rat . . .
The rat takes the cheese . . .
The cheese stands alone . . .

—Traditional rhyme

This is the traditional action song. If you have more children than characters, add other farm animals, such as horse, pig, sheep, etc. Have your farmer stand in the middle of a circle, and move around him or her as you sing.

Five Little Cows

Five little cows and not one more.
One cow ran away and then there were four.
Four little cows enjoy the shade of the tree.
One cow fell asleep and then there were three.
Three little cows with nothing much to do.
One cow wandered off and then there were two.
Two little cows standing in the sun.
One cow went to find some hay and then there was one.
One little cow, being alone is no fun.
He walked back to the barn and now there are none.

—Barbara Scott

Begin this rhyme with five fingers up.
Take away fingers as the rhyme progresses.

Animals on the Farm

Pigs that oink,
And cows that moo,
Horses, sheep, and duckies, too.
Kittens, dogs, and fish that swim,
Chickens, roosters, gather in.
All of these friends you will see
If you come to the farm with me!

—Adapted traditional rhyme

Sung to the tune of "Twinkle, Twinkle, Little Star." You can augment this rhyme by using pictures of the animals mentioned.

Point to eyes.
Point to self.

Farm Sounds

The cow, she goes "Moo, moo."
The cow, she goes "Moo, moo."
It's a sound heard on the farm.
The cow, she goes "Moo, moo."

Sung to the tune of "The Farmer in the Dell." It's up to you to decide if the animals are hes or shes when you sing!

Hold hand to ear.

ADDITIONAL VERSES:

The horse . . . "Neigh, neigh."

The pig . . . "Oink, oink."

The sheep . . . "Baa, baa."

The duck . . . "Quack, quack."

The chicken . . . "Cluck, cluck."

—Adapted traditional rhyme

Five Little Chicks

Five little chicks went out to play

In the barnyard one fine day.

Mother Hen said, "Cluck, cluck, cluck, cluck."

Only four little chicks came back . . . what luck.

No little chicks went out to play

In the barnyard one fine day.

Mother Hen said, "Cluck, cluck, cluck, cluck."

And all the little chicks came back . . . what luck!

—Adapted traditional rhyme

Sung to the tune of "Five Little Ducks."

Begin rhyme with five fingers up.

Take away fingers as rhyme progresses.
Continue four, three, two, one, until . . .
Shrug shoulders.

Bring all five fingers wiggling back!

Five Little Chickens

Said the first little chicken,

With a queer little squirm,

"I wish I could find

A fat little worm."

Said the next little chicken,

With an odd little shrug,

"I wish I could find

A fat little slug."

Said the third little chicken,

With a sharp little squeal,

"I wish I could find

Some nice yellow meal."

Said the fourth little chicken,

With a small sigh of grief,

"I wish I could find

A little green leaf."

Said the fifth little chicken,

With a faint little moan,

"I wish I could find

A wee gravel stone."

"Now see here," said the mother

From the green garden patch,

"If you want your breakfast,

Just come here and scratch."

—Traditional English rhyme

Begin this rhyme with one finger up.

Add fingers as the rhyme progresses.

Books to Share

Bateman, Teresa. 2001. *Farm Flu.* Morton Grove, IL: Albert Whitman & Co. ISBN: 978-0807522745.

Krosoczka, Jarrett J. 2005. *Punk Farm.* New York: Knopf Books for Young Readers. ISBN: 978-0375824296. (You will also enjoy the sequel: *Punk Farm on Tour!*)

Kutner, Merrily. 2005. *Down on the Farm.* New York: Holiday House. ISBN: 978-0823419852.

Reynolds, Adrian. 2005. *Chicks and Salsa.* New York: Bloomsbury Children's. ISBN: 978-1582349725.

Sauer, Tammi. 2009. *Chicken Dance.* New York: Sterling. ISBN: 978-1402753664.

Tekavec, Heather. 2004. *What's That Awful Smell?* New York: Dial. ISBN: 978-0803726604.

Musical Selections

"Baby Chickie" from *So Big: Activity Songs for Little Ones* by Hap Palmer. ASIN: B0000690AD.

"The Chicken Dance" and "The Mack Chicken Dance" from *Big Fun* by Greg and Steve. ASIN: B00000AG60.

"Down by the Barnyard" from *Sing It! Say It! Stamp It! Sway It!*, vol. 3, by Peter and Ellen Allard. ASIN: B001YW7Y7A.

"Down on Grandpa's Farm" from *Five Little Monkeys: Songs for Singing and Playing.* ASIN: B00004SVH2.

"Farm Families" from *On the Farm with Ronno.* ASIN: B00019PVNQ. (This CD has lots of other fun farm songs as well!)

"The Farmer in the Dell" from *Sing Along with Bob*, vol. 1. ASIN: B00000DAO4.

Sources

Anonymous. 2001. *Baby's First Nursery Treasury.* Fairfield, IA: Books Are Fun.

Briggs, Diane. 1999. *101 Fingerplays, Stories, and Songs to Use with Finger Puppets.* Chicago: American Library Association.

Cullum, Carolyn N. 2007. *The Storytime Sourcebook II.* New York: Neal-Schuman.

Dailey, Susan M. 2001. *A Storytime Year.* New York: Neal-Schuman.

———. 2007. *Sing a Song of Storytime.* New York: Neal-Schuman.

Headland, Isaac Taylor. 1900. *Chinese Mother Goose Rhymes.* Grand Rapids, MI: Fleming H. Revell.

Irving, Jan, and Robin Currie. 1986. *Mudlicious: Stories and Activities Featuring Food for Preschool Children.* Santa Barbara, CA: Libraries Unlimited.

Lincycomb, Kay. 2007. *Storytimes . . . Plus!* New York: Neal-Schuman.

McKinnon, Elizabeth, and Gayle Bittinger. 1994. *Busy Bees Spring: Fun for Two's and Three's.* Everett, WA: Warren Publishing House.

"The Mother Goose Pages." Mama Lisa's World of Children & International Culture. Available: www.mamalisa.com (accessed March 4, 2010).

North Central Library Co-operative. n.d. *Storytime Booklet* [out of print].

Poulsson, Emilie. 1893. *Fingerplays for Nursery and Kindergarten.* New York: Lothrop, Lee, and Shepard, reprinted 1921.

Roberts, Lynda. 1985. *Mitt Magic: Fingerplays for Finger Puppets.* Silver Spring, MD: Gryphon House.

Sinclair, Patti, Tami Chumbley, Geri Cupery, Diane Findlay, and Jerri J. Heid. 2004. *Collaborative Summer Library Program Manual.* Mason City, IA: Collaborative Library Summer Program.

Sinclair, Patti, Tami Chumbley, Geri Ceci Cupery, and Kathy Ross. 2006. *Collaborative Summer Library Program Manual.* Mason City, IA: Collaborative Library Summer Program.

Totten, Kathryn. 1998. *Storytime Crafts.* Fort Atkinson, WI: Alleyside Press.

Traditional Music Library. Available: www.traditionalmusic.co.uk (accessed March 10, 2010).

Warren, Jean, comp. 1990. *Theme-a-Saurus II.* Everett, WA: Warren Publishing House.

Wiggin, Kate Douglas and Nora Archibald Smith. 1907. *Pinafore Palace.* New York: Grosset & Dunlap.

Willet, Edward. 1882. *Around the House.* New York: R. Worthington. Available: www.gutenberg.org/wiki/Main_Page (accessed March 10, 2010).

Firefighters

These community helpers may be male or female, so feel free to substitute the word "firefighters" for "firemen"!

Rhyme	Telling Guide
### Ten Little Firemen	
Ten little firemen Sleeping in a row;	Extend both hands, fingers curled, to represent sleeping men.
Ding, dong goes the bell,	Pull bell cord with one hand.
And down the pole they go.	Close both fists; put one on top of other; slide them down pole.
Off on the engine, oh, oh, oh,	Steer engine with hands.
Using the big hose, so, so, so.	Make nozzle with fist.
When all the fire's out, home so-o slow.	Steer engine with hands.
Back to bed, all in a row. —From *Let's Do Fingerplays*	Extend both hands, fingers curled.
### The Wheels on the Truck	*Sung to the tune of "The Wheels on the Bus."*
The wheels on the fire truck go round and round,	Roll hands.
Round and round, round and round. The wheels on the truck go round and round. All through the town!	Make motion of large circle.
ADDITIONAL VERSES:	
The bell on the fire truck goes clang, clang, clang . . .	Motion of pulling cord and ringing bell.
The ladder on the fire truck goes up and down . . .	Move arm up in the air, then down.
The water from the fire hose goes spray, spray, spray . . .	Motion of spraying water with hose.
The axes on the truck go chop, chop, chop . . . —Adapted traditional rhyme	Chopping motion.
### Firefighters	*Sung to the tune of "Down by the Station."*
Down at the firehouse Early in the morning, You can see our clothes Hanging in a row. When there is a fire We can dress real fast.	
Boots, jackets,	Touch feet, then shoulders.
Hats, gloves,	Touch head, then hands.
Off we go! —Jean Warren	

Five Little Firemen

Five little firemen sit very still	Hold up five fingers.
Until they see a fire on top of the hill;	
Number one rings the bell, ding-dong;	Bend down thumb.
Number two pulls his big boots on;	Bend down pointer finger.
Number three jumps on the fire engine red;	Bend down middle finger.
Number four puts a red fire hat on his head;	Bend down ring finger.
Number five drives the red fire truck to the fire,	Bend down little finger.
As the big yellow flames go higher and higher.	Spread arms.
"Whooooo-ooooo! Whooooo-ooooo!" hear the fire truck say,	Imitate siren.
As all of the cars get out of the way.	
Shhh! goes the water from the fire hose spout,	Rub palms together.
And quicker than a wink the fire is out!	Clap hands.

—From *Let's Do Fingerplays*

Brave Little Firefighter 💿

Brave little firefighter, turn around.	Turn in place.
Brave little firefighter, touch the ground.	Touch ground.
Brave little firefighter, climb up high,	Pretend to climb ladder.
Until a fire you chance to spy.	Look around.
Brave little firefighter, put on your gear.	Motion of putting on coat, hat, boots.
Brave little firefighter, never fear!	Shake head "no."
Brave little firefighter, drive your truck.	Pretend to drive.
Brave little firefighter, don't get stuck!	
Brave little firefighter, hurry with the hose,	Hold imaginary fire hose; pretend to spray water.
'Cause with the water, out the fire goes!	

—Adapted traditional rhyme

The Fireman Pokey

	Sung to the tune of "The Hokey Pokey."
You put your helmet in,	Move head in.
You put your helmet out.	Move head out.
You put your helmet in,	Move head in.
And you shake it all about.	Shake head.
You do the fireman pokey and you turn yourself around.	Turn in a circle.
That's what it's all about!	Clap.

ADDITIONAL VERSES:

. . . gloves in.	Move hands.
. . . boots in.	Move feet.
. . . bunker pants in.	Move bottom.

—Adapted traditional rhyme

The Sleepy Firefighters

The sleepy firefighters climb into bed.	Yawn and stretch.
Down on their pillows they lay their heads.	Put head on hands; pretend to sleep.

Off goes the alarm,
And down the pole they slide.
They jump in the truck
And to the fire they ride!

—Barbara Scott

Clap.
Motion of sliding down.
Jump.
Pretend to drive truck.

Five Firefighters

Five firefighters heard the siren roar.
One slid down the pole and now there are four.
Four little firefighters, a fire they want to see.
One slid down the pole and now there are three.
Three firefighters, there's lots of work to do.
One slid down the pole and now there are two.
Two firefighters get dressed on the run.
One slid down the pole and now there's just one.
One firefighter, no need to be a hero.
He slid down the pole and now there are zero!

—Barbara Scott

Begin rhyme with five fingers up.
Take away fingers as the rhyme progresses.

Ten Little Firemen

One little, two little, three little firemen,
Four little, five little, six little firemen,
Seven little, eight little, nine little firemen,
Ten little firemen brave!
Ten little, nine little, eight little firemen,
Seven little, six little, five little firemen,
Four little, three little, two little firemen,
One little fireman brave!

—Adapted traditional rhyme

Sung to the tune of "Ten Little Indians."
Count out on fingers for first verse.

Take away fingers on second verse.

Five Brave Firefighters

Five brave firefighters were ready for the day.
The first one said, "Here's a hose I can spray."
The second one said, "We'll be busy, with some luck."
The third one said, "I want to drive the truck."
The fourth one said, "We are waiting for the alarm."
The fifth one said, "We will keep you safe from harm."

—Barbara Scott

Begin rhyme with five fingers up.
Starting with thumb, point to each finger in succession.

If You'd Like to Be a Fireman

If you're like to be a fireman, slide down the pole.
If you'd like to be a fireman, slide down the pole.
If you'd like to fight a fire,
And spray the hose is your desire.
If you'd like to be a fireman, slide down the pole.

Sung to the tune of "If You're Happy and You Know It."
Motion of sliding.

ADDITIONAL VERSES:

. . . drive the truck.

. . . spray the hose.

. . . shout "Hooray, the fire's out!"

. . . do all four.

—Adapted traditional rhyme

Motion of driving.

Motion of holding nozzle and spraying back and forth.

Motion of pumping fist in the air.

Slide, drive, spray, and shout.

Stop, Drop, and Roll

Stop, drop, and roll,

Stop, drop, and roll.

That's what we do,

That's what we do.

If our clothes catch on fire,

Don't run around or the flames will get higher.

Putting the fire out is our goal.

Just stop, drop, and roll!

—Adapted traditional rhyme

Sung to the tune of "Three Blind Mice."

Do motions.

Point to self with one hand.

Point to self with other hand.

Point to clothes.

Shake head "no."

Do motions.

I'm a Great Big Fire Truck

I'm a great big fire truck,

It is true.

I carry water, hoses, and ladders, too.

When there is a fire,

I'm on the run.

Fighting fires is so much fun!

—Adapted traditional rhyme

Sung to the tune of "I'm a Little Teapot."

Point to self.

Nod head "yes."

Count on fingers.

Wiggle fingers for flames.

Pretend to drive.

Clap three times on last three words.

Firefighter

Firefighter,

Firefighter,

Never fear!

Never fear!

When I see a fire,

I spray it with some water.

Out it goes!

Out it goes!

—Adapted traditional rhyme

Sung to the tune of "Frère Jacques."

Point to self.

Shake head "no."

Point to eyes.

Pretend to spray water with hose.

Clap three times.

Clap three times.

Firefighter, Firefighter

Firefighter, firefighter,

Turn around.

Firefighter, firefighter,

Hear that sound?

Firefighter, firefighter,

Drive your truck.

This rhyme can be sung to the tune of "Teddy Bear, Teddy Bear" or chanted.

Turn in place.

Put hand to ear, listening.

Pretend to drive.

Firefighter, firefighter,
Don't get stuck!   Shake head "no."

Firefighter, firefighter,
Swing your axe about.   Pretend to swing axe.

Firefighter, firefighter,
Spray the fire out.   Pretend to use hose and spray.

Firefighter, firefighter,
Turn out the light.   Motion of clicking off light.

Firefighter, firefighter,
Say goodnight.   Put head on hands; pretend to sleep.

—Adapted traditional rhyme

All the Little Firemen

All the little firemen,   Hold up both hands.
Sound asleep in bed.   Put head on hands; sleep and snore.
The alarm bell sounds,   Motion of ringing bell.
And to the pole they head!   Run in place.
They jump in the truck,   Jump.
And to the fire race.   Pretend to drive.
When their work is done,   Brush hands together.
They're asleep, all in their place.   Hold up both hands as before.

—Barbara Scott

This Is the Way I Dress for a Fire

Sung to the tune of "The Mulberry Bush."

This is the way I dress for a fire,   Point to clothes.
Dress for a fire, dress for a fire.
This is the way I dress for a fire,
Because I'm a fireman!   Point to self proudly.

This is the way I put on my pants,   Motion of putting on pants.
Put on my pants, put on my pants.
This is the way I put on my pants,
Because I'm a fireman!   Point to self proudly.

ADDITIONAL VERSES:
. . . boots.   Motion of putting on boots.
. . . coat.   Motion of putting on coat.
. . . helmet.   Motion of putting on helmet.
. . . mask.   Motion of sliding mask over face.
. . . pack.   Motion of sliding arms in on each side and adjusting.

—Adapted traditional rhyme

This Little Firefighter

This little firefighter stacks hose just so.   Begin this rhyme with five fingers up;
This little firefighter is ready to go!   starting with thumb, point to each in
This little firefighter exercises for fun.   succession.

This little firefighter sits out in the sun.
And this little firefighter fixes dinner for everyone!

—Barbara Scott

One Brave Firefighter

One brave firefighter with lots of work to do.
He met another firefighter and now there are two.
Two brave firefighters use a ladder to climb a tree.
They met another firefighter and now there are three.
Three brave firefighters heard the siren roar.
They met another firefighter and now there are four.
Four brave firefighters all wanting to drive.
They met another firefighter and now there are five.
Five brave firefighters race to the fire,
And put out all the flames before they get much higher!

—Barbara Scott

Begin this rhyme with one finger up.
Add fingers as the rhyme progresses.

Wiggle all five fingers.
Pretend to spray fire with hose

Ten Busy Firefighters

Ten busy firefighters standing in a line.
One went to get his gear and now there are nine.
Nine busy firefighters and now it's getting late.
One went to bed and now there are eight.
Eight busy firefighters looking up to heaven.
One spots some flames and now there are seven.
Seven busy firefighters with dinner left to fix.
One went to the grocery store and now there are six.
Six busy firefighters glad to be alive.
One went to wash the truck and now there are five.
Five busy firefighters standing by the door.
One went to get his boots and now there are four.
Four busy firefighters, two and two you see.
One went to take out the trash and now there are three.
Three busy firefighters, there's always work to do.
One went to test some hose and now there are two.
Two busy firefighters, the day is almost done.
One went to brush his teeth and now there's just one.
One busy firefighter, see that great big yawn.
He went to bed and now there are none.

—Barbara Scott

This is a fun rhyme to do with figures on a flannel or Velcro board.
Begin this rhyme with ten fingers up.
Take away fingers as rhyme progresses.

I'm a Fireman

I'm a fireman
Strong and brave.
Rrr, rrr, there goes the siren.
Off the truck

Sung to the tune of "Pop Goes the Weasel."
Point to self.
Show muscles.
Make siren sound.
Pretend to pull.

Comes the hose.   Pretend to spray.
Out goes the fire!   Clap.
                              —Adapted traditional rhyme

The Fire Chief Says . . .

                                                             Perform this rhyme like "Simon Says."
The fire chief says . . .   *Suit actions to words.*
. . . climb the ladder.
. . . spray the hose.
. . . swing the axe.
. . . drive the fire truck.
                              —Adapted traditional rhyme

                                                             Sung to the tune of "Pop Goes the Weasel."
One Simple Rule!

If your clothes catch on fire,   Point to clothes.
There's one simple rule.   Hold up one finger.
Don't get scared and don't run around.   Shake head "no."
Stop! Drop! And roll!   Motions.
                              —Adapted traditional rhyme

Books to Share

Bond, Felicia. 2003. *Poinsettia and the Firefighters.* New York: HarperCollins. ISBN: 978-0060535094.

Demarest, Chris L. 2000. *Firefighters A to Z.* New York: Margaret K. McElderry. ISBN: 978-0689837982.

Greene, Rhonda G. 2005. *Firebears: The Rescue Team.* New York: Henry Holt and Company. ISBN: 978-0805070101.

Hubbell, Patricia. 2007. *Firefighters: Speeding! Spraying! Saving!* Tarrytown, NY: Marshall Cavendish Children's Books. ISBN: 978-0761453376.

Mitton, Tony. 1998. *Flashing Fire Engines.* Ashmore City, Qld: Kingfisher Publishing. ISBN: 978-0753451045.

Rex, Michael. 1999. *My Fire Engine.* New York: Henry Holt and Company. ISBN: 978-0805053913.

Musical Selections

"Drive the Fire Truck" from *Songs for Wiggleworms.* ASIN: B00004YLUE.

Fire Safety Songs by Futoro. Available: www.songsforteaching.com (accessed March 10, 2010).

"Fire Truck" from *Songs from the Big Hat: A Community Helper Album* by Geof Johnson. Available: www.songsforteaching.com (accessed March 10, 2010).

"The Firefighters" from *Early Years.* Available: www.songsforteaching.com (accessed March 10, 2010).

Sparky and the Firehouse 5. ASIN: B000CAF84Q. (Sixteen songs and instrumental sing-a-longs are included on this CD!)

Sources

Grayson, Marion. 1962. *Let's Do Fingerplays.* Fairfield, CT: R.B. Luce.

Totline Staff, comp. 1994. *1001 Rhymes and Fingerplays.* Everett, WA: Warren Publishing House.

Warren, Jean. 1991. *Alphabet Theme-a-Saurus.* Everett, WA: Warren Publishing House.

Flowers and Gardens
Enjoy this bouquet of rhymes!

Rhyme	**Telling Guide**

Ten Little Leaf Buds

Ten little leaf buds growing on a tree,
Curled up as tightly as can be.
See them keeping snug and warm,
During the winter's cold and storm.
Now along comes windy March,
With his breath now soft, now harsh.
First he swings them roughly so,
Then more gently to and fro.

—Author unknown

Use fingers as buds.
Curl fingers up into fists.

Snuggle fist under fist.

Swing fists back and forth.
Swing tenderly.

My Garden

This is my garden.
I'll rake it with care.
And then some flower seeds
I'll plant in right there.
The sun will shine
And the rain will fall
And my garden will blossom
And grow straight and tall.

—Author unknown

Extend one hand forward, palm up.
Raking motion with fingers.
Planting motion.

Make circle with hands.
Let fingers flutter down to lap.
Cup hands together; extend upward slowly.

Flower Play

If I were a little flower,
Sleeping underneath the ground,
I'd raise my head and grow and grow,
And stretch my arms and grow and grow,
And nod my head and say,
"I'm glad to see you all today."

—Author unknown

Curl up.
Raise head and begin to grow.
Stretch arms.
Nod head.

Relaxing Flowers

Five little flowers standing in the sun.
See their heads nodding, bowing one by one?

Down, down, down comes the gentle rain,
And the five little flowers lift their heads up again!

—Author unknown

Hold up five fingers.
Bend fingers several times.
Raise hands; wiggle fingers and lower arms to simulate rain.
Hold up five fingers.

The Flower

Here's a green leaf,	Show hand.
And here's a green leaf;	Show other hand.
That, you see, makes two.	
Here is a bud	Cup hands together.
That makes a flower;	
Watch it bloom for you!	Open cupped hands gradually.

—Author unknown

Purple Violets

One purple violet in our garden grew;	Hold up one finger.
Up popped another, and that made two.	Hold up two fingers.
Two purple violets were all that I could see,	
But Billy found another, and that made three.	Hold up three fingers.
Three purple violets—if I could find one more,	
I'd make a wreath for Mother, and that would make four.	Hold up four fingers.
Four purple violets—sure as you're alive!	
Why, here is another! And now there are five!	Hold up five fingers.

—Author unknown

Dig a Little Hole

Dig a little hole,	Pretend to dig.
Plant a little seed.	Pretend to drop in seed.
Pour a little water,	Pretend to pour.
Pull a little weed.	Pretend to pull up weed.
Chase a little bug,	Flick hand to one side.
Oh! There he goes!	Cup hand above eye.
Give a little sunshine,	Lower spread fingers slowly.
Grow a little rose!	Pretend to smell sweet flower.

—Adapted traditional rhyme

My Garden

This is my garden;	Extend one hand forward, palm up.
I'll rake it with care,	Make raking motion on palm with three fingers of other hand.
And then some flower seeds	Make "planting" motion with thumb and index finger of same hand.
I'll plant in there.	
The sun will shine	Make circle above head with hands.
And the rain will fall,	Let fingers flutter down to lap.
And my garden will blossom	Cup hands together; extend upward slowly.
And grow straight and tall.	

—From *Let's Do Fingerplays*

Making a Garden

Dig, dig, dig,	Do actions as rhyme indicates.
Rake just so.	

Plant the seeds,
Watch them grow.
Chop, chop, chop,
Pull up weeds.
Sun and rain
My garden needs.
Up, up, up,
Green stems climb.
Open wide,
It's blossom time!

—Adapted traditional rhyme

Little Plants

Out in the garden early in the morning,
See the little plants bending to and fro.
See the gentle breeze help them lift their arms,
Swish-swish, swish-swish, wave hello!

—Jean Warren

Sung to the tune of "Down by the Station."
Stand straight and tall.
Bend body back and forth.
Raise arms out at sides.
Wave arms gently up and down.

Pitter-Pat

Pitter-pat, pitter-pat, oh so many hours,
Although it keeps me in the house,
It's very good for flowers.

—From *Let's Do Fingerplays*

Let fingers patter on floor, table, hand, etc.

Cup hands and extend slowly upward.

Four Little Flowers

Four little flowers I did see.
I picked one, then there were three.
Three little flowers, pretty and new.
I picked another, then there were two.
Two little flowers out in the sun.
I picked one more, then there was one.
One little flower left in the sun.
I picked it too, then there were none.

—Jean Warren

Hold up four fingers.
Hold up three fingers.

Hold up two fingers.

Hold up one finger.

My Little Garden

In my little garden bed,
Raked so nicely over,
First the tiny seeds I plant,
Then with soft earth cover.
Shining down, the great round sun
Smiles upon it often;
Little raindrops, pattering down,
Help the seeds to soften.

Extend one hand, palm up.
Use three fingers for rake.

Using planting and covering motions.
Circle with arms.

Flutter fingers.

Then the little plant awakes—
Down the roots go creeping,
Up it lifts its little head
Through the brown earth peeping.
High and higher still it grows,
Through the summer hours,
'Til some happy day the buds
Open into flowers.

—Author unknown

Little Flowers

Little flowers swaying in the breeze,
Turning our faces up to sun and trees,
When night comes each one nods and sleeps.

—From *Alphabet Soup*

The Sleepy Seed

A tiny seed
Slept on the ground
Beneath a leafy cover.
Until one day
The sun did say,
"Wake up, it's time for summer!"
The seed was tired
So he snuggled up
Close beside his brothers.
The sun got mad
And called the wind,
Who blew off all the covers!

—From *Alphabet Soup*

Vegetables

I'm a tomato, red and round,
Red and round, red and round.
I'm a tomato, red and round,
Seated on the ground.
I'm a corn stalk, tall and straight,
Tall and straight, tall and straight.
I'm a corn stalk, tall and straight,
And I taste just great!

—From *Alphabet Soup*

Little Seed

A little seed so soft and round
I'll dig and lay you down.

Move fingers downward.

Hold fingers close together; point upward.

Raise arms, fingers still cupped.

Spread fingers.

For this rhyme, children may stand and sway back and forth, turn faces to the sun, then nod, droop head, and close eyes.

Rest closed left hand.

Hold right fist, as sun, over left hand.
Pretend to knock.

Wiggle fingers on left hand.

Wave right hand for wind.
Remove "covers"; wiggle the left hand fingers.

Sung to the tune of "Mary Had a Little Lamb." Do actions as indicated.

Form a circle with fingers.
Make a digging motion.

And you may rest beneath the ground
Until your leaves come up
And your roots go down.

—From Alphabet Soup

We're Growing a Little Garden

We're growing a little garden here,
Dig in, dig in.
We're growing a little garden here,
Dig in, dig in.
Oh, we'll dig the ground
And then we'll hoe.
We'll plant the seeds
In rows and rows.
Then we'll all clap hands
To make our garden grow.
We're growing a little garden here,
Dig in, dig in.
We're growing a little garden here,
Dig in, dig in.
Oh the corn will grow ears
And the cabbage, heads.
Sweet potatoes root
In their beds.
And we'll all clap hands
To make our garden grow.
We're growing a little garden here,
Dig in, dig in.
We're growing a little garden here,
Dig in, dig in.
The beans will grow up
And the turnips down.
We'll eat our harvest
All year round.
And we'll clap our hands
The day our garden grows.

—Jan Irving

Garden Jungle

Who lives out in the garden,
Under the flowers and trees?
Who lives out in the back yard,
Feeling the sun and the breeze?

Cup one hand; lay other over it.
Point up.
Point down.

Sung to the tune of "When Johnny Comes Marching Home." Do this in a circle.
Extend arms, palms up.

Make digging action.
Wipe brow.

Wiggle fingers to plant seeds.

Clap.

Point to ears.
Point to head.

Sleep on hands.

Clap.

Point up.
Point down.
Rub tummy.

Clap.

This is a cumulative action rhyme.

There's a creeping ant
Crawling up a plant.
It's a jungle garden home.

     Wiggle fingers up arm.

There's a wiggly worm
Watch him squirm.

     Wiggle all over.

There's a creeping ant
Crawling up a plant.
It's a jungle garden home.
There's a digging mole
Scooting into his hole.

     Put palms together in front; wiggle wrists.

There's a wiggly worm
Watch him squirm.
There's a creeping ant
Crawling up a plant.
It's a jungle garden home.
There's a buzzing bee
Hey! Don't sting me!

     Wiggle fingers by ear.
     Clap on the word "Hey."

There's a digging mole
Scooting into his hole.
There's a wiggly worm
Watch him squirm.
There's a creeping ant
Crawling up a plant.
It's a jungle garden home.
That's who lives in the garden
Under the sky so blue.
It's a jungle out there in the garden.
Watch out or they'll get you!

                        —Jan Irving

The Little Plant

In my little garden bed
Raked so nicely over,

     Put hands out, fingertips together. / Fingers of one hand make raking motion.

First the tiny seeds I sow,

     Action of planting seeds.

Smiles upon in often;

     Smile.

Little raindrops pattering down

     Flutter fingers down.

Help the seeds to soften.
Then the little plant awakes!
Down the roots go creeping.

     "Walk" fingers down leg.

Up it lifts its little head

     Make fist with thumb inside, then bring thumb out and up.

Through the brown mould peeping.

High and higher still it grows
Through the summer hours.
'Til some happy day, the buds
Open into flowers.

—Emilie Poulsson

Elevate the arm; raise the thumb from hand.

Open hand.

Mary, Mary Quite Contrary

Mary, Mary, quite contrary,
How does your garden grow?
"With silver bells and cockle shells,

And pretty maids all in a row!"

—Traditional rhyme

Shake finger, admonishing.
Put hands out to sides, questioning.
Pretend to ring bell with one hand; cup other hand for cockle shell.
Hold up ten fingers.

Bright-Eyed Daisies

Where innocent bright-eyed daisies are,

With blades of grass between.

Each daisy stands up like a star
Out of a sea of green.

—Traditional rhyme

Put left arm up, hand in fist, palm facing out.
Put right hand up, palm out, fingers apart.
Put left arm up; open up fist slowly.

Annie's Garden

In little Annie's garden,
Grew all sorts of posies.
There were pinks, and mignonette,
And tulips and roses.
Sweet peas and morning glories,
A bed of violets blue,
And marigolds and asters
In Annie's garden grew.
There the bees went for honey,

And the hummingbirds, too;
And there were pretty butterflies
And the lady-birds flew.
And there among her flowers
Every bright and pleasant day,
In her own pretty garden,
Annie went to play.

—Eliza Lee Follen

Put hands out in front, palms up.
Count out the nine kinds of flowers on fingers.

Hold one palm out for garden; fly other hand to it.
Nod head "yes."
Cross hands in front; hook thumbs.

Put hands out in front, palms up.
Hands make large circle overhead to represent sun.

Five Little Marigolds

Five little marigolds
Standing in a row.
Now, isn't that the best way
For marigolds to grow?
Each with a green stalk
And all five had got
A bright yellow flower
And a new red pot.

Hold up five fingers.

Nod head "yes."

Put right arm in air; make fist.

Slowly open fist.
Make a small circle with both hands.

—From *Under the Window*

In Our Pretty Garden Green

This is how we plant a bean,
In our garden, in our garden.
This is how we plant a bean,
In our pretty garden green.
Now we plant it with our foot,
In our garden, in our garden.
Now we plant it with our foot,
In our pretty garden green.
Now we plant it with our hand,
In our garden, in our garden.
Now we plant it with our hand
In our garden green.
Now we plant it with our elbow,
In our garden, in our garden.
Now we plant it with our elbow,
In our pretty garden green.
Now we plant it with our knee,
In our garden, in our garden.
Now we plant it with our knee,
In our pretty garden green.
Now we plant it with our chin,
In our garden, in our garden.
Now we plant it with our chin,
In our pretty garden green.

"Dig" a hole in the ground.

While standing, "plant" bean with foot.

Kneel down and "plant" bean with hand.

Crouch down and "plant" bean with elbow.

While kneeling, "plant" bean with knee.

On all fours, "plant" bean with chin.

—From Anglik.net

Flower Pot

Wee little flower pot,
Very deep green,
With just the sweetest flowers
That ever were seen.
Mother with her babies
Playing very funny,

Make small circle with hands.

Pretend to sniff flowers.

Wiggle all fingers.

Father doing business, Making lots of money.	Motion of gathering money toward you.
Grandpa very old, But never going to die,	Shake head "no."
Grandma just as bright As a star in the sky.	Point to sky.

—Traditional Chinese rhyme

Watering the Flowers

I water the flowers, I water the flowers,	Motion of watering flowers with watering can.
I water them morning and evening hours.	Point to wrist to indicate watch.
I never wait 'til the flowers are dry,	Shake head "no."
I water them e'er the sun is high.	Arms make large circle over head for sun.
A basin of water, a basin of tea,	Hold out one hand, then the opposite hand.
I water the flowers, They're op'ning, you see.	Put hands in front, palms together; move palms apart slightly.
A basin of water, another beside, I water the flowers, They're opening wide.	Put hands in front as above; move palms farther apart.

—Traditional Chinese rhyme

There Once Was a Flower

There was once a flower.	Put hand out, palm up, fingers together.
It opens a little, then a lot.	Spread fingers a little, then a lot.
A butterfly comes and rests on the flower.	With second hand, mimic butterfly landing on the flower.
Mmmmm, that smells nice!	
The butterfly flies away, out of sight.	Hide second hand behind back.
The flower closes up, withers, and disappears.	Join fingers, palm down; hide hand behind back.

—Traditional French rhyme

Planting Time

	Sung to the tune of "Here We Go Looby Loo."
Here we go planting beans.	Do motions as the rhyme indicates.
Here we go planting corn. Here we go planting peas.	
We're out in the sun so bright.	Arms make circle above head.
Here we go weeding here. Here we go weeding there. Here we go weeding here. We're weeding with all of our might. Now we water our beans. Now we water our corn. Now we water our peas. We're watering with all of our might.	

Here we go gathering beans.
Here we go gathering corn.
Here we go gathering peas.
Our garden is such a delight.

—Kay Lincycomb

Spring Flowers

It is spring!
Let's plant some seeds.

Here comes the sun
And rain they need.
Wait awhile and they will grow
Pretty blue flowers
In a row.

—Adapted from a song by Susan M. Dailey

Hold out one hand, palm up; pretend to plant seeds in it.
Make circle with hands above head.
Flutter fingers downward.
Bring hands upward.

Repeat with pink and white flowers, or whatever colors you desire!

Flowers Are Blooming

Flowers are blooming
Everywhere.
Everywhere, everywhere.
Flowers are blooming
Everywhere.
What a lovely day!

Flowers are blooming
Everywhere,
Everywhere, everywhere.
Flowers are blooming
Everywhere,
In the month of May.

—Jean Warren

Sung to the tune of "Mary Had a Little Lamb." To show flowers blooming, put hands in front, palms together, and slowly bring palms away from each other.
Blooming flower motion.

Blooming flower motion.

Hands make circle above head to represent sun.
Blooming flower motion.

Blooming flower motion.

Hold up five fingers to represent the fifth month.

Five Little Flowers

Five little flowers all standing in a row.
The first flower said, "Water would help us grow."
The second flower said, "The rain is falling down."
The third flower said, "It's soaking in the ground."
The fourth flower said, "It's watering our roots."
The fifth flower said, "Be ready for new shoots!"

—Barbara Scott

Begin this rhyme with five fingers up.
Starting with thumb, point to each in succession.

Five Beautiful Flowers

Five beautiful flowers just outside my door.
Daddy came and picked a flower and now there are four.
Four beautiful flowers, two and two you see.
Mommy came and picked a flower and now there are
   three.
Three beautiful flowers, but before I knew,
Sister came and picked a flower and now there are two.
Two beautiful flowers in the noonday sun.
Brother came and picked a flower and now there's just one.
One beautiful flower standing all alone.
I picked the very last flower and now there are none.

               —Barbara Scott

Begin this rhyme with five fingers up.
Take away fingers as rhyme progresses.

When We Plant Our Garden

This is the way we hoe the ground,
Hoe the ground, hoe the ground.
This is the way we hoe the ground,
When we plant our garden!

Sung to the tune of "The Mulberry Bush."
Motion of hoeing.

ADDITIONAL VERSES:
. . . rake the ground.
. . . plant the seed.
. . . pack the soil.
. . . watch it grow.

           —Adapted traditional rhyme

Motion of raking.
Motion of dropping seed into ground.
Motion of patting down soil over seed.
Head cupped in hands, watching.

I Plant Some Little Seeds

I plant some little seeds in the ground,
And wait for springtime showers.
A little sun, a little rain,
Up pop the flowers!

           —Adapted traditional rhyme

Sung to the tune of "Pop Goes the Weasel."
Motion of planting.
Wiggle fingers down for rain.
Make circle for sun; wiggle fingers for rain. / Put palms together, then open as a flower.

Little Flower, Little Flower

Little flower, little flower,
Twist around.
Little flower, little flower,
Planted in the ground.
Little flower, little flower,
Spread your petals wide.
Little flower, little flower,
Now you hide.
Little flower, little flower,

This rhyme can be sung to the tune of "Teddy Bear, Teddy Bear" or chanted.

Twist at the waist.

Point down.

Start with arms together overhead, then spread them side to side.

Bring arms back together overhead, as if flower is closing.

Stretch toward the sun.   Stretch up.
Little flower, little flower,
In the wind, have fun!   Sway from side to side.
Little flower, little flower,
No more light.   Shake head "no."
Little flower, little flower,
Say goodnight.   Put head on hands; pretend to sleep.

—Adapted traditional rhyme

Ten Little Daisies

Sung to the tune of "Ten Little Indians."

One little, two little, three little daisies,   Count out on fingers for first verse.
Four little, five little, six little daisies,
Seven little, eight little, nine little daisies,
Ten little daisy flowers!
Ten little, nine little, eight little daisies,   Take away fingers on second verse.
Seven little, six little, five little daisies,
Four little, three little, two little daisies,
One little daisy plant!

—Adapted traditional rhyme

I'm a Tiny Seedling

Sung to the tune of "I'm a Little Teapot."

I'm a tiny seedling,   Show size.
Stuck in the ground.   Point down.
Waiting for the sun,
All warm and round.   Make circle overhead with arms.
A little bit of rain   Wiggle fingers downward.
Gives me water to drink,   Pretend to drink.
And up I sprout,   Point up.
Quick as a wink!   Clap three times on last three words.

—Adapted traditional rhyme

Five Little Seeds

This is a fun rhyme to do as a flannel or Velcro board presentation!

Five little seeds and not one more.   Begin this rhyme with five fingers up.
One turned into a pumpkin and now there are four.   Take away fingers as rhyme
Four little seeds, just waiting to see.   progresses.
One turned into a stalk of corn and now there are three.
Three little seeds, just a mystery few!
One turned into a watermelon and now there are two.
Two little seeds, our rhyme is almost done.
One turned into a pod of peas and now there's just one.
One little seed, the very last one.
It turned into an asparagus and now there are none!

—Barbara Scott

My Garden in the Spring

My garden in the spring,
My garden in the spring.
Hi ho the derry-o,
My garden in the spring.

I rake the garden well,
I rake the garden well.
Don't want the weeds to grow,
I rake the garden well.

The sun comes out each day,
The sun comes out each day.
It warms the ground, you know.
The sun comes out each day.

The rain comes falling down,
The rain comes falling down.
Rain helps the seeds to grow.
The rain comes falling down.

The little seeds soon sprout,
The little seeds soon sprout.
Watch them grow and grow and grow.
The little seeds soon sprout.

—Adapted traditional rhyme

Sung to the tune of "The Farmer in the Dell."

Motion of raking.

Shake head "no."

Make circle above head with arms for sun.

Wiggle fingers down for rain.

Put palms together to make flower.

Hold hands up; pull palms apart for blooming flower.

I Am a Seed

I am a seed
Planted in the ground.
Waiting for rain
And the sun so round.
Both of these help me
To grow strong and tall.
I'll grow up to be
A flower after all!

—Barbara Scott

Move fingers to indicate size.

Wiggle fingers down for rain.
Make circle above head with arms.

Move hands to indicate size.

Nod head "yes."

One Little Rose

One little rose in the garden grew.
Another one bloomed and now there are two.
Two little roses grew underneath the tree.
Another one bloomed and now there are three.
Three little roses with petals galore.
Another one bloomed and now there are four.
Four little roses, so red and alive!
Another one bloomed and now there are five.

—Barbara Scott

Begin rhyme with one finger up.
Add fingers as the rhyme progresses.

Five Little Potatoes

Five little potatoes   Hold up five fingers.
Were growing in the ground.
Covered up with rich soil,   Place other hand over fingers.
Not making a sound.
Down came the rain   Flutter fingers downward.
One stormy summer day.
The five little potatoes   Rest cheek on folded hands.
Slept the day away.
Out came the sun,   Walk in place.
The farmer came out too.
He dug up those potatoes
To give to me and you.

—Mildred Hoffman

Mister Carrot

Nice Mr. Carrot
Makes curly hair.   Put hands on head.
His head grows underneath the ground,   Bob head.
His feet up in the air.   Raise feet.
And early in the morning,
I find him in his bed,   Close eyes; lay head on hands.
And give his feet a great big pull   Stretch legs out.
And out comes his head!

—Author unknown

My Flower Bed

See the blue and yellow blossoms
In the flower bed.
The daisy spreads it petals wide   Hold palm up, fingers open.
The tulip bows its head.

—Author unknown

Watch It Bloom

Here is a green leaf   Hold out one palm.
And here is a green leaf.   Hold out other palm.
That, you see, makes two.   Hold up two fingers.
Here is a bud   Cup hands together.
That makes a flower.   Slowly start opening hands.
Watch it bloom for you.   Open hands wide.

—Author unknown

Tulips in My Garden

One red tulip in my garden grew.   Begin this rhyme with one finger up.
Up popped another, and that made two.   Add fingers as rhyme progresses.
Two red tulips were all that I could see.

But Mommy found another, and that made three.
Three red tulips, if I could find one more,
I'd put them in a flower vase, and that would make four.
Four red tulips, goodness sakes alive.
Oh, here's another one, now that makes five.

—Traditional folk rhyme

Harvest Time

Harvest time is here again,	
In the garden we will dig.	Motion of digging.
Carrots, onions, radishes,	
And sweet potatoes, oh so big!	Move hands to show size.

—Kristine Wagoner

A Little Plant

In the heart of a seed,	Make a fist to represent seed.
Buried down so deep,	
A little plant lay fast asleep.	
"Awake," said the sun,	Circle arms overhead.
"Come up through the earth."	
"Awake," said the rain,	Flutter fingers downward.
"We are giving you birth."	
The little plant heard	
With a happy sigh,	
And pointed its petals	Open hand and turn up fingers.
Up to the sky.	Raise hand to indicate growth.

—Author unknown

I Dig, Dig, Dig

I dig, dig, dig,	Pretend to dig.
And I plant some seeds.	Stoop down and plant seeds.
I rake, rake, rake,	Pretend to rake.
And I pull some weeds.	Pull up weeds.
I wait and watch,	Stoop down and watch ground intently.
And soon I know.	
My garden sprouts	Raise hands from ground as if sprouting.
And starts to grow.	

—Author unknown

Five Plump Peas

Five plump peas in a peapod pressed.	Press two fists together.
One grew, two grew, so did the rest.	Have fingers gradually pop up from fist.
They grew and they grew and did not stop,	Slowly move hands apart.
Until one day the pod went pop!	Bring hands together with a great big clap!

—Author unknown

One Pretty Flower

One pretty flower in the morning dew.	Begin rhyme with one finger up.
Up popped another and now there are two.	Add fingers as rhyme progresses.
Two pretty flowers growing under the oak tree.	
Up popped another and now there are three.	
Three pretty flowers attract bees galore.	
Up popped another and now there are four.	
Four pretty flowers growing next to the hive.	
Up popped another and now there are five.	
Five pretty flowers dance in the breeze.	Wiggle fingers; sway hands.
Dance all day with grace and with ease!	Continue wiggling and swaying.

—Barbara Scott

Books to Share

Boyd, Lizi. 1998. *Lulu Crow's Garden.* New York: Little, Brown. ISBN: 978-0316104197.

Dahl, Michael. 2004. *From the Garden: A Counting Book about Growing Food.* Mankato, MN: Picture Window Books. ISBN: 978-1404811164.

Hall, Zoe. 1998. *The Surprise Garden.* New York: Scholastic. ISBN: 978-0590100755.

Mallett, David. 1995. *Inch by Inch: The Garden Song.* New York: HarperCollins. ISBN: 978-0060243036.

Park, Linda Sue. 2005. *What Does Bunny See? A Book of Colors and Flowers.* New York: Clarion Books. ISBN: 978-0618234851.

Ward, Jennifer. 2002. *Over in the Garden.* Flagstaff, AZ: Rising Moon. ISBN: 978-0873587938.

Musical Selections

"Captain Vegetable" from *Sesame Street Silly Songs.* ASIN: B0013D8J74.

"City Garden Rap" from *Wonder Pets!* by Wonder Pets ASIN: B000NOKBF2.

"Dandelion" and "The Garden Song" from *(Almost) Two Much* by Nan Hoffman. Available: www.nanhoffman.com (accessed March 10, 2010).

"English Country Garden" from *Pop Go The Wiggles: Nursery Rhymes and Songs* by The Wiggles. ASIN: B0012OVFSE.

"Garden of Plenty" and "Seeds" from *Plant a Little Seed* by Prairie Orchid. ASIN: B001R0KB6U.

"Plant a Seed" from *Sing It! Say It! Stamp It! Sway It!,* vol. 2, by Peter and Ellen Allard. ASIN: B000056IIN.

Sources

Briggs, Diane. 1997. *52 Programs for Preschoolers.* Chicago: American Library Association.

———. 1999. *101 Fingerplays, Stories, and Songs to Use with Finger Puppets.* Chicago: American Library Association.

Cromwell, Liz, Dixie Hibner, and John R. Faitel. 1983. *Finger Frolics,* rev. ed. El Cajon, CA: Partner Press.

Dailey, Susan M. 2007. *Sing a Song of Storytime.* New York: Neal-Schuman.

Grayson, Marion. 1962. *Let's Do Fingerplays.* Fairfield, CT: R.B. Luce.

Greenaway, Kate. 1879. *Under the Window.* London: Frederick Warne & Co.

Hansen, Charles, and Cynthia Stilley. 1996. *Ring a Ring O'Roses*, 10th ed. Flint, MI: Flint Public Library.

Headland, Isaac Taylor. 1900. *Chinese Mother Goose Rhymes*. Grand Rapids, MI: Fleming H. Revell.

Herr, Judy, and Yvonne Libbey. 1990. *Creative Resources for the Early Childhood Classroom*. Clifton Park, NY: Delmar Publishers.

Hogstrom, Daphne. 1966. *Little Boy Blue: Fingerplays Old and New*. Racine, WI: Golden Press.

Irving, Jan, and Robin Currie. 1986. *Mudlicious: Stories and Activities Featuring Food for Preschool Children*. Santa Barbara, CA: Libraries Unlimited.

———. 1991. *Raising the Roof: Children's Stories and Activities on Houses*. Santa Barbara, CA: Teacher Ideas Press.

Mama Lisa's World of Children & International Culture. Available: www.mamalisa.com (accessed March 4, 2010).

McKinnon, Elizabeth, and Gayle Bittinger. 1994. *Busy Bees Spring: Fun for Two's and Three's*. Everett, WA: Warren Publishing House.

Moffat, Alfred. 1911. *Our Old Nursery Rhymes*. New York: G. Schirmer.

"Plants and Flowers." Alphabet Soup. Available: www.alphabet-soup.net/mini/plant.html (accessed March 10, 2010).

Poulsson, Emilie. 1893. *Fingerplays for Nursery and Kindergarten*. New York: Lothrop, Lee, and Shepard, reprinted 1921.

Redleaf, Rhoda. 1993. *Busy Fingers, Growing Minds*. St. Paul, MN: Redleaf Press.

Rosetti, Christina G. 1893. *Sing-Song: A Nursery Rhyme Book*. New York: Macmillan and Company.

Scott, Louise B. 1960. *Rhymes for Fingers and Flannelboards*. New York: McGraw-Hill Book Company.

Sitarz, Paula. 1990. *More Picture Book Story Hours*. Santa Barbara, CA: Libraries Unlimited.

Stavros, Sally, and Lois Peters. 1987. *Big Learning for Little Learners*. El Cajon, CA: Partner Press.

Totline Staff, comp. 1994. *1001 Rhymes and Fingerplays*. Everett, WA: Warren Publishing House.

Traditional Songs from English Speaking Countries. Available: www.anglik.net/songs.htm (accessed March 10, 2010).

Warren, Jean, comp. 1984. *More Piggyback Songs*. Everett, WA: Warren Publishing House.

———. 1989. *Theme-a-Saurus*. Everett, WA: Warren Publishing House.

———. 1990. *Theme-a-Saurus II*. Everett, WA: Warren Publishing House.

Warren, Jean, and Susan Shroyer. 1992. *Piggyback Songs to Sign*. Everett, WA: Warren Publishing House.

Wiggin, Kate Douglas, and Nora Archibald Smith. 1907. *Pinafore Palace*. New York: Grosset & Dunlap. Available: www.gutenberg.org (accessed March 10, 2010).

Wilmes, Liz, and Dick. 1984. *Circle Time Book for Holidays and Seasons*. Elgin, IL: Building Blocks.

Chapter 5

Frogs and Toads to Mice

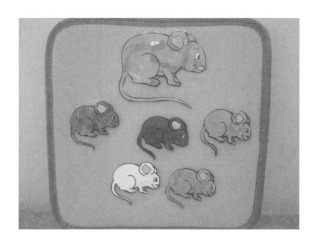

Frogs and Toads
These rhymes will make you hop with joy!

Rhyme

Telling Guide

Five Little Frogs

Five little frogs sit by a pool,
Dive down where it's nice and cool.
Jump, little froggies, up, up, up.

Croak, croak, croak, croak.

Brrrrup!

—Traditional rhyme

Hold up five fingers.

Make fist; drop fist down.

Raise fist in three steps.

Beginning with index finger, raise one at a time for each "croak."

Lift thumb.

What's Inside?

There's a big bull frog
With two bulgy eyes
And a long, long tongue
For catching flies.
If I had green skin
I'd run and hide.
Maybe he thinks
He's a prince inside.

—Jan Irving and Robin Currie

Sit with legs folded, hands on knees.

Circle eyes with fingers.

Stick out tongue.

Clap several times in air.

Point to skin.

Hide face in hands.

Point to head.

Bow.

Splash! Squish! Smack!

Around the pond and into the lake,
Tell me the sounds a frog can make.
Splash, crash.
Around the pond and into the lake,
Tell me sounds a frog can make.
Splash, crash.
Glide, slide.

—Jan Irving

Use this two-line rhyme to encourage children to brainstorm sounds a frog can make. Make a list of the possible sounds; then set a rhythm by slapping hands on knees and clapping. Repeat the rhyme and combine sound words to create as much internal rhyme as you can (e.g., splash–crash or glide–slide).

I Am a Little Toad

I am a little toad,
Hopping down the road.
Just listen to my song,
I sleep all winter long.
When spring comes, I peep out,
And then I jump about.
And now I catch a fly,
And now I wink my eye,

Make fingers hop in time to verses.

Put palms together at side of head.

Peep behind hands.

Make arms jump.

Clap hands.

Wink one eye.

And now and then I hop,

And now and then I stop.

—Traditional rhyme

Make hands hop.

Fold hands.

Five Little Froggies

Five little froggies sat on the shore,

One went for a swim and then there were four.

Four little froggies looked out to sea,

One went swimming and then there were three.

Three little froggies said, "What can we do?"

One jumped in the water and then there were two.

Two little froggies sat in the sun,

One swam off and then there was one.

One lonely froggie said, "This is no fun."

He dived into the water and then there was none.

—From *Let's Do Fingerplays*

Open hand; extend fingers.

Push down one finger as each frog leaves.

Five Little Froggies

Five little froggies sitting on a well—

One looked up, and down he fell.

Froggies jumped high,

Froggies jumped low.

One little froggy sitting on a well—

He looked up and down he fell.

—Lynda Roberts

This rhyme can also be done using finger puppets!

Begin with five fingers up.

Take away fingers as rhyme progresses.

Jump fingers in the air.

Jump fingers to the floor. Continue with four, three, two, until . . .

Five Green and Speckled Frogs

Five funny speckled frogs sitting on a hollow log,

Eating the most delicious bugs. Yum! Yum!

One jumped into the pool, where it was nice and cool.

Then there were four speckled frogs.

ADDITIONAL VERSES:

Four green and speckled frogs . . .

Three green and speckled frogs . . .

Two green and speckled frogs . . .

FINAL VERSE:

One green and speckled frog sitting on a hollow log,

Eating the most delicious bugs. Yum! Yum!

He jumped into the pool, where it was nice and cool.

Then there were no more speckled frogs!

—Traditional rhyme

For extra fun, add a "glub, glub" to the end of each verse!

Hold out arm; place five fingers of other hand on top.

Rub tummy.

Jump with hand into a pool.

Return hand with the appropriate number of fingers for each verse.

Five Little Tadpoles

Five little tadpoles	Hold up five fingers.
Swimming near the shore.	
The first one said "Let's swim some more."	Starting with thumb, point to each in succession.
The second one said, "Let's rest awhile."	
The third one said "Swimming makes me smile."	
The fourth one said "My legs are growing long."	
The fifth one said "I'm getting very strong!"	
Five little tadpoles	
Will soon be frogs.	
They'll jump from the water.	Jump fingers down
And sit on logs.	Sit five fingers on arm of opposite hand.

—From Hummingbird Educational Resources

Tadpole, Tadpole

Tadpole, tadpole,	
Swimming in my pail.	Make swimming motions with arms.
Big round head,	Form circle above head with arms.
And wiggly tail.	Wiggle bottom.
Some day soon,	
Four legs will sprout.	Hold up four fingers.
And then, small frog,	
You'll hop right out!	Hop around, then sit down.

—Anonymous

"Croak!" Said the Toad

Just what are the "pales" mentioned in this rhyme? They are fences!

"Croak!" said the toad.	Hold up right fist.
"I'm hungry, I think;	Rub stomach.
Today I've had nothing	Shake head "no."
To eat or to drink.	
I'll crawl to a garden	Crawling motion with arms.
And jump through the pales.	Jump hand.
And there I'll dine nicely	Pretend to eat.
On slugs and snails."	
"Ho, ho!" said the frog.	Hold up left fist.
"Is that what you mean?	
Then I'll hop away to	Hop hand.
The next meadow green.	Put hands in front, side by side.
There I will drink, and	
Eat worms and slugs, too,	Pretend to eat and drink.
And then I shall have a	
Good dinner like you."	Point to opposite fist.

—Traditional rhyme

This Little Froggy

This little froggy took a big leap.
This little froggy took a small.
This little froggy leaped sideways,
And this little froggy not at all.
And this little froggy went
Hippety, hippety, hippety, hop all the way home.

—Traditional rhyme

Begin this rhyme with five fingers up.
Point to each as the rhyme progresses.

Hop hand.

Yaup, Yaup, Yaup

"Yaup, yaup, yaup,"
Said the frogs.
"It's charming weather.
We'll come and sup,
When the moon is up,
And we'll all of us
Croak together."
"Yaup, yaup, yaup,"
Said the frog as he
Splashed about.
"Good neighbors all,
When you hear me call,
It is odd you do not
Come out."

—Traditional rhyme

Point to sky.
Pretend to eat.
Make circle overhead with fingers.

Hands fan out to indicate a large group.

Hands to the sides, pretend to splash water.
Hands cupped around mouth.

Shake head "no."

Froggie

Froggie, old froggie,
Come over to me.
You'll never go back
To your home in the sea.
You're an idle old croaker
As ever I saw,
And if not calling papa,
You're calling mama.

—Traditional Chinese rhyme

Beckon.
Shake head "no."

Point to eyes.
Cup hands around mouth.

Frog Surprise

Late last night, I had a surprise!
It was green with bulgy eyes,

With hopping legs.
"Ribbit, ribbit," it said.
I found a frog on my bed.
And it went hop, hoppity, hop.

Throw hands in air.
Make circles with hands and put in front of eyes.
Point to legs.
Make "ribbit" sounds.

Hop fingers.

Yes, it went hop, hoppity hop.	Continue to hop fingers.
And it went hop, hoppity hop.	Frown; shake head.
Yes, it went hop, hoppity hop.	Shake finger.
I frowned at the frog and shook my head.	Point backward with thumb over shoulder.
"You don't belong on my bed!	Hop fingers.
Go back home!" I told that frog.	
So it hopped right back to its bog.	

—Adapted from a song by Susan M. Dailey

Three Frogs on a Log

Three frogs on a log,	Hold up three fingers of one hand.
One fly in the sky:	Hold thumb and index finger on opposite hand together for "fly."
Buzzzzzzzzzz.	
The one fly flew nearby	Move "fly" down toward three fingers.
Those three frogs on a log.	Make gulp exaggerated swallow.
Then, zip, zap, gulp!	Clap hands. Repeat with two, then one.
Splash!	

—Adapted from a song by Susan M. Dailey

Little Brown Tadpole

Little brown tadpole	Put hands together with palms flat, making wiggling motion.
Swims around like a fish.	
He swims to the left.	Move hands as indicated.
He swims to the right.	
He swims down deep.	
He swims to the light.	
But slowly, slowly	
Brown tadpole changes . . .	
He grows two legs in front,	Put hands in front of body.
He grows two legs in back,	Put hands behind body.
And his tail grows shorter and shorter	Put one hand behind body; move it toward body.
Until a tail he lacks.	
Then one day he climbs out of the bog.	
A big, fat, hoppy frog.	Hop around.

—Teresa Dustman

A Little Frog

A little frog in a pond am I,	
Hippity, hoppity, hop.	Hop fist up and down.
Watch me jump in the air so high,	
Hippity . . . hoppity . . . hop!	Hop fist as high as possible.

—Adapted traditional rhyme

Listen to the Frog

Listen to the frog,
Croaking on a log.
He croaks about this
And he croaks about that.
It seems very clear
That he needs to chat.
Ribbet, ribbet, ribbet.

—Susan M. Paprocki

Cup hand behind ear.

Ten Little Frogs

One little, two little, three little frogs,
Four little, five little, six little frogs,
Seven little, eight little, nine little frogs,
Ten little frogs jumped high!
Ten little, nine little, eight little frogs,
Seven little, six little, five little frogs,
Four little, three little, two little frogs,
One little frog jumped low!

—Adapted traditional rhyme

Sung to the tune of "Ten Little Indians."
Count out on fingers for first verse.

Jump all ten fingers into the air.
Take away fingers on second verse.

Jump one finger down low.

Five Frisky Frogs

Five frisky frogs hopping all around the floor.
One hopped away and then there were four.
Four frisky frogs sitting underneath a tree.
One went to chase a bug and then there were three.
Three frisky frogs with tongues like sticky glue.
One caught some lunch and then there were two.
Two frisky frogs sitting in the shining sun.
One went to sleep and then there was one.
One frisky frog, no fun to be alone.
He went away and now there are none.

—Barbara Scott

Begin this rhyme with five fingers up.
Take away fingers as rhyme progresses.

Five Little Frogs

Five little frogs were sitting in a pond.
The first frog said, "Of flies, I'm very fond."
The second frog said, "See how high I can hop."
The third frog said, "I'll land in the water with a great, big plop!"
The fourth frog said, "I can swim very fast."
The fifth frog said, "In a race, I'd be last."

—Barbara Scott

Begin this rhyme with five fingers up.
Beginning with thumb, point to each in succession.

If You Want to Be a Frog

If you want to be a frog, jump up high.
If you want to be a frog, jump up high.
If you want to be a frog, don't just sit there on that log!
If you want to be a frog, jump up high.

ADDITIONAL VERSES:
. . . blink your eyes.
. . . stick out your tongue.
. . . say "ribbit, ribbit."
. . . do all four.

—Adapted traditional rhyme

Sung to the tune of "If You're Happy and You Know It."
Jump!
Jump!
Shake head "no."

Blink, blink.
Stick tongue in and out quickly.
"Ribbit, ribbit."
Jump, blink, stick out tongue, "ribbit."

Hungry Froggy

Hungry froggy,
Hungry froggy,
Catch that fly!
Catch that fly!
See it buzzing this way,
See it buzzing that way.
Try, try, try.
Catch that fly!

—Adapted traditional rhyme

Sung to the tune of "Frère Jacques."
Rub tummy.

Stick tongue in and out quickly, like a frog.

Point in one direction.
Point in the opposite direction.

Stick tongue in and out quickly, then smile and chew!

Little Frog, Little Frog

Little frog, little frog,
Hop around!
Little frog, little frog,
Sit on the ground.
Little frog, little frog,
Catch a fly!
Little frog, little frog,
Wink one eye.
Little frog, little frog,
Swim around.
Little frog, little frog,
Don't make a sound!
Little frog, little frog,
See the moonlight.
Little frog, little frog,
Say goodnight.

—Adapted traditional rhyme

This rhyme can be sung to the tune of "Teddy Bear, Teddy Bear" or chanted.

Hop all around.

Sit down.

Stick tongue in and out quickly.

Wink.

Swimming motions.

Make "Shhh" motion.

Point to eyes.

Put head on hands; pretend to sleep.

I'm a Hungry Little Toad

I'm a hungry little toad
Hopping fast across the road.
Searching low and searching high.
Hopping, searching for a fly.
I'm a hungry little toad
Hopping fast across the road.

—Adapted traditional rhyme

Sung to the tune of "Twinkle, Twinkle, Little Star."
Rub tummy.
Jump hand.
Point down, then up.
Look around.
Rub tummy.
Jump hand.

One Little Tadpole

One little tadpole grew and grew.
He found another tadpole and that makes two.
Two little tadpoles, they're baby frogs, you see.
Met another tadpole and that makes three.
Three little tadpoles, are you ready for some more?
Met another tadpole and that makes four.
Four little tadpoles, learning how to dive.
Met another tadpole and that makes five.
Five little tadpoles all swim away.
They'll turn into frogs some fine day!

—Barbara Scott

Begin rhyme with five fingers up.
Add fingers as rhyme progresses.

Wiggle five fingers behind back.

Jumping Frogs

Jumping frogs,
Jumping frogs,
Jumping all around!
Jumping high and
Jumping low,
Resting on the ground.
Jumping forward,
Jumping back.
Will they ever stop?
When they're tired, they will land
With a great big PLOP!

—Adapted traditional rhyme

Sung to the tune of "Jingle Bells."

Jump all around.

Jump high, then low.
Sit on floor.
Stand back up and jump forward.
Jump backward.
Continue jumping.

Clap or plop down on the ground.

Gung, Gung Went the Little Green Frog

Gung, gung went the little green frog one day.
Gung, gung went the little green frog.
Gung, gung went the little green frog one day,
And his eyes went blink, blink, blink.

—Traditional song

Stick out tongue as you say "gung, gung."

Blink eyes in an exaggerated fashion.

I'm a Frog

I'm a frog,
A fat and sassy frog.
I'm a frog,
And I know how to jump.
First I will jump really high
'Til I almost touch the sky.
Jumping high . . . touch the sky . . . oh.
I'm a frog,
A fat and sassy frog.
I'm a frog,
And I know how to jump.
I'm a frog,
A fat and sassy frog.
I'm a frog,
And I know how to jump.
Next I will jump really low,
No more higher than your toe.
Jumping low . . . by your toe . . . oh.
I'm a frog,
A fat and sassy frog.
I'm a frog,
And I know how to jump

—Adapted traditional rhyme

Sung to the tune of "Alouette."

Put hands out to show size.

Point to self.
Point up.

Point up and reach high!

Put hands out to show size.

Put hands out to show size.

Point to self.
Point down.

Point down, point to toe.

Put hands out to show size.

Point to self.

Croak, Croak Went the Little Brown Toad

Croak, croak went the little brown toad one day.
Croak, croak went the little brown toad.
Croak, croak went the little brown toad one day,
And his tongue went thwup, thwup, thwup!

—Adapted traditional rhyme

Sung to the tune of "Gung, Gung Went the Little Green Frog."

Stick tongue quickly in and out of mouth while making sound.

The Frogs in the Pond

The frogs in the pond go hop, hop, hop,
Hop, hop, hop,
Hop, hop, hop.
The frogs in the pond go hop, hop, hop,
All through the day.

ADDITIONAL VERSES:
They jump in the water with a splash, splish, splash . . .
The eyes on the frog go blink, blink, blink . . .
The frogs in the pond go swim, swim, swim . . .
The frogs in the pond catch flies all day . . .

—Adapted traditional rhyme

Sung to the tune of "The Wheels on the Bus."

Hop.

Make circle in the air with hand.

Clap or pretend to splash.
Blink eyes in an exaggerated way.
Swimming motion.
Make "thwap" sound with tongue like catching flies.

I'm a Little Froggy

I'm a little froggy
In a pond.
Hopping and swimming
All day long.
When I hear a sound
And want to dash,
I jump right in
With a great big splash!

—Adapted traditional rhyme

Sung to the tune of "I'm a Little Teapot."
Fist sits on opposite hand.

Hop fist, then make swimming motions.

Put hand to ear.

Clap.

Five Sleepy Frogs

Five sleepy frogs trying not to snore.
One fell asleep and then there were four.
Four sleepy frogs, they need a nap, you see.
Another fell asleep and then there were three.
Three sleepy frogs, yawning's what they do.
Another fell asleep and then there were two.
Two sleepy frogs lying in the sun.
Another fell asleep and now they're just one.
One sleepy frog when the day is done.
He went to sleep and now there are none.

—Barbara Scott

Begin this rhyme with five fingers up.
Take away fingers as rhyme progresses.

Froggy Fun

Counting frogs is lots of fun!
Here's a frog . . . he's number one.
See one sitting in the morning dew.
Count him also . . . he's number two.
Look there, underneath the tree.
Another frog . . . he's number three.
Sitting right outside my door
Is another . . . he's number four.
Into the pond, see him dive.
One last frog . . . he's number five.

—Barbara Scott

Hold up one finger.
Add fingers as the rhyme progresses.

The Frogs Go Hopping

The frogs go hopping one by one,
Hurrah, hurrah.
The frogs go hopping one by one,
Hurrah, hurrah.
The frogs go hopping one by one,
The little one stops to say, "Guk gung."

Sung to the tune of "The Ants Go Marching." This is another great rhyme to do with flannel or Velcro board figures! Begin with one finger up.

And they all go hopping down . . . to the pond . . . to play in the rain.

ADDITIONAL VERSES:

The frogs go hopping two by two . . .
    the little one stops to say, "Achoo!"
The frogs go hopping three by three . . .
    the little one stops to climb a tree.
The frogs go hopping four by four . . .
    the little one stops, his feet are sore.
The frogs go hopping five by five . . .
    the little one stops to take a dive.
The frogs go hopping six by six . . .
    the little one stops to jump over sticks.
The frogs go hopping seven by seven . . .
    the little one stops to look to heaven.
The frogs go hopping eight by eight . . .
    The little one stops out by the gate.
The frogs go hopping nine by nine . . .
    the little one stops to sit on a vine.
The frogs go hopping ten by ten . . .
    the little one stops to say, "The end!"

—Adapted traditional rhyme

Add fingers as rhyme progresses.

Books to Share

Arnold, Tedd. 2009. *Green Wilma, Frog in Space.* New York: Dial. ISBN: 978-0803726987.
Breen, Steve. 2007. *Stick.* New York: Dial. ISBN: 978-0803731240.
Cyrus, Kurt. 2008. *Tadpole Rex.* Boston: Harcourt Children's Books. ISBN: 978-0152059903.
Larranaga, Ana Martin. 1999. *The Big Wide-Mouthed Frog.* London: Walker Books. ISBN: 978-0744567076.
Parenteau, Shirley. 2007. *One Frog Sang.* Somerville, MA: Candlewick Press. ISBN: 978-0763623944.
Wilson, Karma. 2003. *A Frog in the Bog.* New York: Margaret K. McElderry. ISBN: 978-0689840814.

Musical Selections

"Bean Bag Hop" from *Me and My Bean Bag.* ASIN: B0001Z8VYQ.
"Can You Leap Like a Frog?" from *Kids in Action* by Greg and Steve. ASIN: B0000A8XP8.
"Five Little Frogs" from *Singable Songs for the Very Young* by Raffi. ASIN: B0010VNFW8.
"Froggie Went A'Courtin'" from *Victor Vito* by Laurie Berkner. ASIN: B002HHY5DM.
"Mr. Froggie Went A-Courtin'" from *Burl Ives Sings Little White Duck* by Burl Ives. ASIN: B00138H0F6.
"The Little Green Frogs" from *It's Toddler Time* by Carol Hammet and Elaine Bueffel. ASIN: B0001CVE7A.

Sources

Anonymous. 1902. *Nursery Rhymes from Mother Goose with Alphabet*. Philadelphia: W.W. Houston. Available: www.childrenslibrary.org (accessed March 10, 2010).

Carle, Eric. 1989. *Eric Carle's Animals, Animals*. New York: Philomel.

"Children's Nursery Rhymes." Available: www.zelo.com/family/nursery (accessed March 10, 2010).

Dailey, Susan M. 2001. *A Storytime Year*. New York: Neal-Schuman.

———. 2007. *Sing a Song of Storytime*. New York: Neal-Schuman.

Grayson, Marion. 1962. *Let's Do Fingerplays*. Fairfield, CT: R.B. Luce.

Headland, Isaac Taylor. 1900. *Chinese Mother Goose Rhymes*. Grand Rapids, MI: Fleming R. Revell.

Hummingbird Educational Resources: Resources for Early Childhood and Kindergarten Educators. Available: www.hummingbirded.com (accessed March 10, 2010).

Index of Rhymes. Available: www.kidsnurseryrhymes.co.uk/rhymes (accessed March 10, 2010).

Irving, Jan, and Robin Currie. 1993. *Straw into Gold: Books and Activities about Folktales*. Santa Barbara, CA: Teacher Ideas Press.

McKinnon, Elizabeth, and Gayle Bittinger. 1994. *Busy Bees Spring: Fun for Two's and Three's*. Everett, WA: Warren Publishing House.

North Central Library Co-operative. n.d. *Storytime Booklet* [out of print].

Rhymes.org. Available: www.rhymes.org/uk (accessed March 10, 2010).

Roberts, Lynda. 1985. *Mitt Magic: Fingerplays for Finger Puppets*. Silver Spring, MD: Gryphon House.

Scott, Louise B. 1960. *Rhymes for Fingers and Flannelboards*. New York: McGraw-Hill.

———. 1983. *Rhymes for Learning Times*. Minneapolis: T.S. Denison & Co.

Totline Staff, comp. 1994. *1001 Rhymes and Fingerplays*. Everett, WA: Warren Publishing House.

Warren, Jean. 1990. *Theme-a-Saurus II*. Everett, WA: Warren Publishing House.

Ice Cream
You scream, I scream, we all scream for ice cream!

Rhyme

How Do You Eat an Ice Cream Cone?

Some folks taste it daintily,
Others gulp it down quick-ily.
Some lick around and round,
So it never, ever comes dripping down.
Some shove the ice cream
Down with their tongue,
So at the bottom of the cone,
You're left with some.
But some lick in just one place
So it gets sort of sloppy,
And the top plops off
In a great big bloppy!

—Jan Irving and Robin Currie

I Love Ice Cream

I love ice cream,
I love ice cream!
How about you?
How about you?
Fill my cone with one scoop,
Fill my cone with two scoops.
Sprinkles, too,
For me and you!

—Barbara Scott

You Scream, I Scream

You scream,
I scream,
We all scream for

ICE CREAM!

—Traditional rhyme

Ice Cream a Penny a Lump

Ice cream,
A penny a lump.

The more you eat,
The more you jump.

—Traditional rhyme

Telling Guide

Everyone should do appropriate actions as you read this poem.

This rhyme can be sung to the tune of "Frère Jacques" or chanted.
Place hands over heart.

Point to child.
Point to another child.
Hold out one fist.
Hold out two fists.
Motion of putting sprinkles on ice cream.
Point to self, then children.

Point to children.
Point to self.
Move hands out to indicate group, then cup hands around mouth.
Shout!

Make small circle with thumb and index finger to represent coin.
Pretend to lick cone.
Jump!!!

Five Hungry Little Pigs

Five hungry little pigs	Hold up five fingers.
Went to find something to eat.	Rub stomach.
They went to an ice cream store	Walk fingers.
To get a tasty treat.	Lick lips.
The first little pig said,	Hold up one finger.
"I think I will take	
A great, big enormous	Hold arms out wide.
Chocolate milk shake."	Pretend to drink through straw.
The second little pig said,	Hold up two fingers.
"Give me two scoops of cherry."	Pretend to dip scoops.
The third little pig said,	Hold up three fingers.
"I'll take a sundae with strawberries."	Pretend to make sundae.
The fourth little pig said,	Hold up four fingers.
"Give me four scoops of peach."	Pretend to dip scoops.
The fifth little pig said,	Hold up five fingers.
"I can't decide. Just give me one of each!"	Spread out both hands with palms up.

—Susan M. Dailey

Five Scoops of Ice Cream

Five scoops of ice cream	Begin this rhyme with five fingers up.
Sitting in a bowl.	
The first scoop said, "I'm nice and cold."	Beginning with thumb, point to each in succession.
The second scoop said, "I'm nice and crunchy."	
The third scoop said, "I'm sweet and munchy."	
The fourth scoop said, "I'm delicious, too."	
The fifth scoop said, "We're scooped just for you."	Point to children.

—Barbara Scott

Counting Cones

I have a bunch of ice cream cones,	
A lot, as you will see!	
And I would like it very much	
If you would count with me.	Proceed to count cones on fingers.
Here's number one, butter pecan.	
Here's number two, vanilla cashew.	
Here's number three, black raspberry.	
Here's number four, chocolate with chips galore!	
Here's number five, pumpkin pie.	
Here's number six, peppermint stick.	
Here's number seven, strawberry heaven.	
Here's number eight, banana parfait.	
Here's number nine, cookies and cream so fine!	
Here's number ten, apple cinnamon.	

—Barbara Scott

Ice Cream, Ice Cream

Ice cream, ice cream	
In a bowl.	Make circle with hands.
Ice cream, ice cream,	
Nice and cold!	Shivering motion.
Ice cream, ice cream,	
What a treat!	Clap three times.
Ice cream, ice cream,	
Good to eat!	Rub tummy.

—Barbara Scott

Books to Share

Henkes, Kevin. 2003. *Wemberley's Ice Cream Star*. New York: Greenwillow Books. ISBN: 978-0060504052.

McEvoy, Greg. 1998. *The Ice Cream King*. Markham, Ontario: Fitzhenry and Whiteside. ISBN: 978-0773730694.

Murphy, Stuart. 2002. *The Sundae Scoop*. New York: HarperCollins. ISBN: 978-0060289249.

Pinkwater, Daniel. 1999. *Ice Cream Larry*. Tarrytown, NY: Marshall Cavendish Children's Books. ISBN: 978-0761450436.

———. 2002. *Cone Kong*. New York: Cartwheel Books. ISBN: 978-0439216784.

Santoro, Scott. 1999. *Isaac the Ice Cream Truck*. New York: Henry Holt and Company. ISBN: 978-0805052961.

Musical Selections

"Ice Cream" from *Skinnamarink TV* by Sharon, Lois, and Bram. ASIN: B000065FY4.

"Ice Cream Cone" from *Buzz, Buzz* by Laurie Berkner. ASIN: B00004S36S.

"Ice Cream Man" from *Jumpin' on the Bed* by Geof Johnson. ASIN: B000V02ODA.

"Ice Cream Truck" from *Daniel Kirk and The Chowhounds* by Daniel Kirk. ASIN: B000CA8YZQ.

"Scoops of Ice Cream" from *Very Derryberry* by Debi Derryberry. ASIN: B00112XSI2.

"She Likes Ice Cream" from *You're Really Movin!* by The Rocking Rockets. Available: www.songsforteaching.com (accessed March 9, 2010).

Sources

Dailey, Susan M. 2001. *A Storytime Year*. New York: Neal-Schuman.

Index of Rhymes. Available: www.kidsnurseryrhymes.co.uk/rhymes (accessed March 10, 2010).

Irving, Jan, and Robin Currie. 1986. *Mudlicious: Stories and Activities Featuring Food for Preschool Children*. Santa Barbara, CA: Libraries Unlimited.

Kings, Queens, and Other Royalty
You never know whom you will find wandering around the castle!

Rhyme

Old King Cole

Old King Cole was a merry old soul.
And a merry old soul was he.
He called for his pipe.
And he called for his bowl.
And he called for his fiddlers three.
Every fiddler had a fine fiddle.
And a very fine fiddle had he.
Oh, there's none so rare as can compare,
With King Cole and his fiddlers three.

—Traditional rhyme

The King's in Town

Oh, do you know the king's in town?
The king's in town, the king's in town?
Oh, do you know the king's in town?
Everybody bow down.

—Kathy Ross

Noble Duke of York

The noble Duke of York,
He had ten thousand men.
He marched them up the hill,
And then he marched them down again.
When you're up—you're up,
When you're down—you're down.
And when you're only half-way up,
You're neither up nor down.

—Traditional rhyme

Where Is the Prince?

Where is the Prince?
I've looked both near and far.
The King and Queen are looking for you.
I wonder where you are.

—Kathy Ross

Telling Guide

Hands make circle above head to represent crown. / Laugh.

Motion of putting pipe to mouth.
Make circle in front of body for bowl.
Hold up three fingers.
Make fiddling motions.

Shake head.
Hold up three fingers.

Sung to the tune of "Do You Know the Muffin Man?"

Repeat and add on other gestures such as "Take off your hats," "Wave to him now," "Let's go see him now," "Let's all sit down," etc.

March forward.
March backward.
Stand up tall.
Squat down.
Neither squat nor fully stand.

Shrug shoulders and hold out hands.
Shelter eyes as if looking for something.
Place hands on head to form a crown.
Shrug shoulders and hold out hands.

Five Queens

There were five queens on a quest.
To see who was the very best!
The first queen went to take a test.
The second queen said, "I'll go out west."
The third queen climbed Mount Everest.
The fourth queen made a beautiful vest.
The fifth queen said, "I'll just take a rest."

—From Natural Learning

Hold up five fingers.
Wiggle all five.
Touch thumb.
Touch index finger.
Touch middle finger.
Touch ring finger.
Touch little finger.

All the King's Knights

All the king's knights,
On a warm sunny day,
Hopped on their horses
And galloped away.
They galloped 'round the castle.
Then they galloped through the town.
They galloped so fast,
That they all fell down!
Clank!

—Kathy Ross

Have each child find a partner. The child in front will be the horse. The child in the back takes the hands of the child in front to be the knight rider. Each horse and knight gallop around the room and then fall down at the end of the rhyme. Do this at least twice so the children can switch places.

Knight Song

I'll be wearing iron plates upon my chest.
I'll be wearing an iron helmet and a vest.
Oh, I'll carry a shield and dagger.
When I walk I nearly stagger.
'Cause a suit of armor
Isn't really light,
"For a knight!"

—Jan Irving and Robin Currie

Sung to the tune of "She'll Be Comin' 'Round the Mountain."
Pound chest.
Pull on "helmet" over head.
Lift arms to hold "shield" and "dagger."
Walk haltingly, as if wearing heavy armor.

Speak this line; point to self.

Put Your Crown on Your Head

Put your crown on your head, on your head.
Put your crown on your head, on your head.
Put your crown on your head,
Don't put it on your feet instead.
Put your crown on your head, on your head.

—Kathy Ross

Sung to the tune of "Put Your Finger in the Air." For this rhyme, you can use small crown cutouts attached to craft sticks. Substitute other body parts, the sillier the better.

If I Were a Queen

If I were a queen,
What would I do?
I'd make you king,
And I'd wait on you.

Hands make circle on top of head to indicate crown.
Put index finger to cheek, questioning.
Motion of "knighting."

If I were a king,
What would I do?
I'd make you queen,
For I'd marry you.

—Traditional rhyme

Hands make circle on top of head to indicate crown.
Put index finger to cheek, questioning.
Bow down.

Rock-a-Bye Baby, Thy Cradle Is Green

Rock-a-bye baby,
Thy cradle is green.
Father's a nobleman,
Mother's a queen.
Betty's a lady
Who wears a gold ring.
Johnny's a drummer
Who drums for the king!

—Traditional rhyme

Motion of rocking baby in arms.

Bow.
Hands make circle on top of head to indicate crown.

Point to finger.

Motion of drumming.

Doodle Doodle Doo

Doodle doodle doo,
The princess lost her shoe;
Her Highness hopped,
The fiddler stopped,
Not knowing what to do.

—Traditional rhyme

Clap three times.
Point to shoe.
Hop in place.
Pretend to fiddle, then stop.
Shrug shoulders.

When Good King Arthur

When good King Arthur ruled the land,
He was a goodly king.
He stole three pecks of barley-meal
To make a bag-pudding.
A bag-pudding the king did make
And stuffed it well with plums.
And in it put great lumps of fat
As big as my two thumbs.
The king and queen did eat thereof
And noblemen beside;
And what they could not eat that night,
The queen next morning fried.

—Traditional rhyme

Hands make circle on top of head to indicate crown.
Nod head "yes."
Hold up three fingers.

Motion of stirring.
Motion of sprinkling in fruit.

Hold up both thumbs.
Pretend to eat.

Shake head "no."
Motion of using a spatula to turn something, such as a pancake.

Little Girl, Little Girl

"Little girl, little girl,	
Where have you been?"	Put hands to the sides, questioning.
"Gathering roses to give	Motion of picking flowers.
To the queen."	Bow.
"Little girl, little girl,	
What gave she you?"	Put hands to the sides, questioning.
"She gave me a diamond	Make circle in front of body with fingers.
As big as my shoe."	Point to shoe.

—Traditional rhyme

King Boggen

King Boggen,	
He built a fine new hall;	Put hands over head, fingertips together to form roof.
Pastry and piecrust,	Pretend to mix in bowl.
That was the wall.	
The windows were made	Put hands on either side of head; pretend to look through "window."
Of black pudding and white,	
Roofed with pancakes,	Motion of pounding nail with hammer.
You never saw the like!	Shake head "no."

—Traditional rhyme

Royalty

	Begin this rhyme with all standing.
This is the king,	Boys point to themselves.
And here is his crown.	Place pretend crown on head.
Here is his throne,	
So let's sit down.	Boys sit down on floor.
This is the queen,	Girls point to themselves.
And here is her crown.	Place pretend crown on head.
Here is her throne,	
So let's sit down.	Girls sit down on the floor.

—Carolyn N. Cullum

Books to Share

Dodds, Dayle Ann. 2007. *The Prince Won't Go to Bed.* New York: Farrar, Straus, and Giroux. ISBN: 978-0374361082.

Ellis, Sarah. 2006. *The Queen's Feet.* Markham, Ontario: Red Deer Press. ISBN: 978-0889953208.

Funke, Cornelia. 2007. *Princess Pigsty.* Somerset, England: The Chicken House. ISBN: 978-0439885546.

Gibert, Bruno. 2004. *The King Is Naked!* New York: Clarion Books. ISBN: 978-0618410675.

Katz, Karen. 2008. *Princess Baby.* New York: Schwartz and Wade Books. ISBN: 978-0375841194.

Melling, David. 2001. *The Kiss That Missed.* Hauppauge, NY: Barron's Educational Series. ISBN: 978-0764154515.

Musical Selections

"Follow Me, I Am the Leader" from *Get Funky and Musical Fun* by The Learning Station. ASIN: B0001CJ8KU.

"Jump Start for the Queen of Hearts," "Five Brave Knights," and "Poor Princess Polly" from *Castles, Knights, and Unicorns* by Ronno. ASIN: B00019PVO0.

"Old King Cole" from *Rhymin' to the Beat*, vol. 2, by Jack Hartmann and Friends. ASIN: B0026EIIRU.

"Pineapple Princess" from *Lilo and Stitch Island Favorites, Featuring Songs from Lilo and Stitch 2* by Disney. ASIN: B000AA7HYC.

"Princess Di's Distress" from *Moonboat* by Tom Chapin. ASIN: B000050KSS.

Sources

Anonymous. 2001. *Baby's First Nursery Treasury*. Fairfield, IA: Books Are Fun.

Cullum, Carolyn N. 2007. *The Storytime Sourcebook II*. New York: Neal-Schuman.

"Fingerplays." Natural Learning. Available: www.naturallearning.com/fingerplays.html (accessed March 11, 2010).

Index of Rhymes. Available: www.kidsnurseryrhymes.co.uk/rhymes (accessed March 10, 2010).

Irving, Jan, and Robin Currie. 1987. *Glad Rags: Stories and Activities Featuring Clothes for Children*. Santa Barbara, CA: Libraries Unlimited.

Lang, Andrew, ed. 1897. *The Nursery Rhyme Book*. London: Frederick Warne & Co.

"The Mother Goose Pages." Mama Lisa's World of Children & International Culture. Available: www.mamalisa.com (accessed March 4, 2010).

Rhymes.org. Available: www.rhymes.org (accessed March 11, 2010).

Rosetti, Christina G. 1893. *Sing-Song: A Nursery Rhyme Book*. New York: Macmillan and Company.

Sinclair, Patti, Tami Chumbley, and Kathy Ross. 2005. *Collaborative Summer Library Program Manual*. Mason City, IA: Collaborative Summer Library Program.

Sitarz, Paula Gaj. 1987. *Picture Book Story Hours: From Birthdays to Bears*. Santa Barbara, CA: Libraries Unlimited.

Songs for Teaching: Using Music to Promote Learning. Available: www.songsforteaching.com (accessed March 11, 2010).

Wiggin, Kate Douglas, and Nora Archibald Smith. 1907. *Pinafore Palace*. New York: Grosset & Dunlap. Available: www.gutenberg.org (accessed March 11, 2010).

Kites

The theme of kites, and the wind that guides them, is just perfect for spring!

Rhyme

Telling Guide

Come Fly a Kite

Come fly a kite
And watch it sail   Hold hand high.
Across the sky,
Waving its tail!   Wave hand back and forth.

—Jean Warren

Kite Friends

One little kite in the sky so blue,
Along came another, then there were two.   Hold up one finger, then two fingers.
Two little kites flying high above me,
Along came another, then there were three. Hold up three fingers.
Three little kites, just watch how they soar.
Along came another, then there were four.   Hold up four fingers.
Four little kites, so high and alive,
Along came another, then there were five.   Hold up five fingers.
Five little kites dancing 'cross the sky,
What a sight to see, way up high!   Dance all five fingers in air.

—Jean Warren

I See the Wind

I see the wind when the leaves dance by,   Dance hands around.
I see the wind when the clothes wave "Hi!" Wave hand.
I see the wind when the trees bend low,   Bend arms over and down.
I see the wind when the flags all blow.   Wave arms high.
I see the wind when the kites fly high,   Raise arms high.
I see the wind when the clouds float by.   Gently wave hands.
I see the wind when it blows my hair,   Lift hair with hands.
I see the wind 'most everywhere!   Hold hands out, palms up.

—Jean Warren

Wind Tricks

The wind is full of tricks today,
It blew our newspaper away.   Sweep arms to one side.
It chased the trash can down the street,
It almost blew us off our feet.   Stumble and almost fall.
It makes the trees and bushes dance,
Just listen to it howl and prance!   Cup hand behind ear.

—Adapted traditional rhyme

The Wind

The wind came out to play one day.
He swept the clouds out of his way.
He blew the leaves and away they flew.
The trees bend low, and their branches did, too.
He blew the great big ships at sea.
And he blew my kite away from me.

—Author unknown

Make sweeping motion with arms.
Make fluttering motion with fingers.
Lift arms and lower them.
Repeat sweeping motions.
Hide hands.

Kite Flying

There were two little sisters
Went walking one day,
Partly for exercise, partly for play.
Their kites they took with them,
They wanted to fly,
Were a big centipede,
And a big butterfly.
In a very few moments,
They floated up high,
Like a dragon that sccmcd to be
Touching the sky.

—Traditional Chinese rhyme

ASL sign for kite: hands in fists, one higher than the other, action of tugging up and down on kite string.
Hold up two fingers.
Walk two fingers of one hand on palm of other hand.

Use ASL sign for kite.

Wiggle index finger like worm.
Cross hands, lock thumbs, wiggle fingers for wings.

Point up.

Reach up high!

Kites

Five little kites flying high in the sky,
Said, "Hi!" to the cloud as it passed by.
Said, "Hi!" to the bird,
Said, "Hi!" to the sun,
Said, "Hi!" to an airplane—oh what fun!
Then whish went the wind
And they all took a dive.
One, two, three, four, five.

—Lynda Roberts

Hold up five fingers.
Wave hello.

Blow.
Take hand down low.

One Little Kite

One little kite in the sky so blue
Was joined by another and then there were two.
Two little kites sailing in the breeze
Were joined by another and then there were three.
Three little kites, just watch them soar!
Were joined by another and then there were four.
Four little kites, see them dip and dive,
Were joined by another and that makes five.

Begin this rhyme with one finger up.
Add fingers as rhyme progresses.

Five little kites, oh what fun!
Watch them rise and fly in the sun!

—Barbara Scott

Raise all five fingers into the air and move around like a kite.

Five Little Kites

Five little kites were sailing in the breeze.
The first kite said, "Watch out for those trees!"
The second kite said, "I love to fly high!"
The third kite said, "Let's try to touch the sky."
The fourth kite said, "My tail is very long."
The fifth kite said, "The wind is very strong."

—Barbara Scott

Begin this rhyme with five fingers up.
Starting with thumb, point to each in succession.

My Kites

Here are my kites.
Let's count them one by one.
Watching them soar and dive
Is really lots of fun!
The first little kite has a long, long tail.
The second little kite really knows how to sail.
The third little kite has a design of blue.
The fourth little kite can fly high, too.
The fifth little kite is really the best.
It flies higher than all the rest!

—Barbara Scott

This is a great rhyme to do on the flannel or Velcro board as well!

Hold up index finger.
Hold up other fingers in succession.

Blow, Wind, Blow

Blow, wind, blow.
Move the kites to and fro.
Up and down,
And 'round and 'round.
Finally bring them
To the ground.
Blow, wind, blow.
Move the kites to and fro.

—Barbara Scott

Blow.
Put hand in air; move in "s" motion.
Move hand up and down.
Make circle with hand.

Land hand on ground.

Put hand in air; move in "s" motion from side to side.

This Is My Kite

This is my kite.
It flies so high.
It kisses the clouds
Up in the sky.
Flying my kite
Is lots of fun!
See it soar
Up toward the sun.

Hold up one hand to represent kite.
Fly hand into the air.
Blow a kiss.

Put hand over eyes; peer into the air.

My kite, it has
A very long tail.
It helps my kite
To really sail.
I move my kite
With a heavy string.
To fly it high,
It's just the thing!

—Barbara Scott

If You'd Like to Fly a Kite

If you'd like to fly a kite,
Clap your hands.
If you'd like to fly a kite,
Clap your hands.
If you'd like to fly a kite, then clap with all your might!
If you'd like to fly a kite,
Clap your hands.

ADDITIONAL VERSES:
. . . stomp your feet . . . then stomp with all your might.
. . . shout "hooray" . . . then shout with all your might.
. . . do all three . . . do all three with all your might.

—Adapted traditional rhyme

The Wind

The wind blows the leaves around,
And hardly ever makes a sound.
Wind keeps my kite up in the air,
And doesn't even have a care.
It bends the branches of trees, you see,
And helps the ships as they sail the sea.

—Barbara Scott

Ten Little Kites

One little, two little, three little kites,
Four little, five little, six little kites,
Seven little, eight little, nine little kites,
Ten little kites on strings.
Ten little, nine little, eight little kites,
Seven little, six little, five little kites,
Four little, three little, two little kites,
One little kite on a string!

—Adapted traditional rhyme

Move hands to indicate size.

Nod head "yes."
Move hand from side to side.

Clap three times.

Sung to the tune of "If You're Happy and You Know It."

Clap, clap.

Clap, clap.

Clap, clap.

Make "Shhh!" motion.

Shake head "no."
Bend from side to side.
Hand makes wave motions.

Sung to the tune of "Ten Little Indians." This is a super rhyme to do with the flannel or Velcro board as well!
Count out on fingers for first verse.

Take away fingers in second verse.

My Kite

	Sung to the tune of "On Top of Old Smokey."
One day I was flying	
My kite in the wind.	Put hand in air to represent kite.
It was really blowing,	Move hand from side to side.
The trees they did bend.	Bend from side to side.
I thought I was holding	Hold "string" tight.
My kite really tight.	
It slipped from my fingers	Let go of "string."
And flew out of sight.	Put hand over eyes; peer into the air.
If you see my kite,	Point to children on "you."
This message do send:	
Please come back to me.	Beckon.
I miss you, my friend.	Place hand over heart.

—Barbara Scott

Books to Share

Berenstain, Stan. 2004. *We Like Kites*. Logan, IA: Perfection Learning. ISBN: 978-0756956363.
Lin, Grace. 2002. *Kite Flying*. New York: Knopf Books for Young Readers. ISBN: 978-0375815201.
Murphy, Stuart. 2000. *Let's Fly a Kite*. New York: HarperCollins. ISBN: 978-0060280345.
Packard, Mary. 2004. *The Kite*. Danbury, CT: Children's Press. ISBN: 978-0516246321.
Rey, Margaret. 2007. *Curious George Flies a Kite*. Boston: Houghton Mifflin Books for Children. ISBN: 978-0618723966.

Musical Selections

"Five Little Kites" from *Happy Everything* by Dr. Jean. ASIN: B000SM3N0E.
"I Am the Wind" from *Fred's Favorites* by Fred Penner. ASIN: B000065SFL.
"If I Were a Kite" from *Making Moosic* by Anna Moo. Available: www.songsforteaching.com (accessed March 10, 2010).
"Let's Go Fly a Kite" from *Musical Scarves and Activities* by Georgiana Stewart. ASIN: B0001AC3KO.
"Wind Is Blowing" from *Janet's Planet* by Janet Scarloff. Available: www.songsforteaching.com (accessed March 10, 2010).
"Wonderful Wind" from *Geography, Geology, and Meteorology* by Intelli-Tunes. Available: www.songsforteaching.com (accessed March 10, 2010).

Sources

Hansen, Charles, and Cynthia Stilley. 1996. *Ring a Ring O'Roses*. Flint, MI: Flint Public Library.
Headland, Isaac Taylor. 1900. *Chinese Mother Goose Rhymes*. Grand Rapids, MI: Fleming H. Revell.
Indenbaum, Valerie, and Marcia Shapiro. 1983. *The Everything Book for Teachers of Young Children*. El Cajon, CA: Partner Press.
McKinnon, Elizabeth, and Gayle Bittinger. 1994. *Busy Bees Spring: Fun for Two's and Three's*. Everett, WA: Warren Publishing House.
Roberts, Lynda. 1985. *Mitt Magic: Fingerplays for Finger Puppets*. Silver Spring, MD: Gryphon House.
Totline Staff, comp. 1994. *1001 Rhymes and Fingerplays*. Everett, WA: Warren Publishing House.
Warren, Jean, comp. 1990. *Theme-a-Saurus II*. Everett, WA: Warren Publishing House.

Mice
Mice are creeping, creeping all about!

Rhyme | **Telling Guide**

Little Mousie

See the little mousie

Creeping up the stair,
Looking for a warm nest.
There—Oh! There.

—From *Let's Do Fingerplays*

Telling Guide:
Put index and middle finger on thumb for "mouse."
Creep mouse slowly up other forearm, bent at elbow.

Let mouse spring into elbow corner.

Hickory Dickory Dock

Hickory, dickory dock,
The mouse ran up the clock.
The clock struck one.
The mouse ran down,
Hickory, dickory dock!

—Traditional rhyme

Telling Guide:
Bend at waist and swing arms.
"Run" fingers up arm.
Clap on one.
Run fingers down arm.

Hurry, Scurry, Little Mouse

Hurry, scurry, little mouse,
Start down at your toes.
Hurry, scurry, little mouse,
Past your knees he goes.
Hurry, scurry, little mouse,
Past where your tummy is.
Hurry, scurry, little mouse,
Give you a mousie kiss.

—Traditional rhyme

Telling Guide:
Wiggle fingers on one hand.
Point to toes.
Wiggle fingers up leg.

Wiggle fingers up body.
Wiggle fingers up chest.
Fingers on cheek.
Make kissing sound and open hand wide.

Five Little Mice

Five little mice on the pantry floor,
This little mouse peeked behind the door.
This little mouse nibbled at the cake.
This little mouse not a sound did make.
This little mouse took a bite of cheese.
This little mouse heard the kitten sneeze.
"Ah choo!" sneezed the kitten,
And "Squeak!" they cried,
As they found a hole and ran inside.

—Traditional rhyme

Telling Guide:
Hold up five fingers.
Cup hands around face.
Pretend to eat.
Hold finger in front of mouth, "Shhh."
Pretend to eat.
Cup hand around ear.

Hold hands up as if surprised.
Run in place.

Little Mousie

Here's a little mousie,
Peeking through a hole.
Peek to the left.
Peek to the right.
Pull your head back in.
There's a cat in sight!

—From Pennsylvania Center for the Book

Poke index finger of one hand through fist of the other.

Wiggle finger to the left.
Wiggle finger to the right.
Pull finger in fist.

There Was a Little Mouse

There was a little mouse,
And he lived in a hole.
And when everything was quiet, as quiet as can be,
Shhh—shhh—shhh—
Out popped he!

—Traditional rhyme

Stick up right thumb.
Insert right thumb into left fist.

Pop out thumb.

Little Mouse

This rhyme can be sung to the tune of "Teddy Bear, Teddy Bear" or chanted.

Little mouse, little mouse,
Stand on tiptoes!
Little mouse, little mouse,
Wiggle your nose!
Little mouse, little mouse,
Wiggle your ears, if you please.
Little mouse, little mouse,
Nibble your cheese.
Little mouse, little mouse,
Lift your tail up and down.
Little mouse, little mouse,
Scurry around!
Little mouse, little mouse,
Rest your head.
Little mouse, little mouse,
Go to bed.

—Barbara Scott

Stand on toes.

Wiggle nose.

Wiggle ears.

Pretend to eat cheese.

Bend knees and go up and down.

Run in circle.

Head on hands.

Close eyes and begin to snore.

Five Busy Mice

Sung to the tune of "One Elephant."

Five busy mice went out to seek
Crunchy, munchy morsels to eat, eat, eat.
Along came a cat and scared one away.
Four little mice returned that day.

—Barbara Scott

Begin the rhyme with five fingers up.

Take away fingers as rhyme progresses.
Repeat for four, three, two, one.

Little Bitty Frisky Mouse

Little bitty frisky mouse	Fingers show size.
Running all around the house!	Run in place.
First you're up,	Point up.
And then you're down.	Point down.
Then you're running 'round and 'round.	Run in a circle.
Running here,	Point in one direction.
And running there.	Point in the opposite direction.
Now you're running everywhere!	Hands make circles in the air.
Little bitty frisky mouse	Use fingers to show size.
Running all around the house.	Run in place.

—Barbara Scott

Mousie

Mousie comes a-creeping, creeping.	Close fist and push index finger of other hand through.
Mousie comes a-peeping, peeping.	Push finger through until tip of index finger just appears.
Mousie says, "I'd like to stay,	
But I haven't time today."	Shake head "no."
Mousie popped into his hole	Pull finger back into hole.
And said, "Achoo!	Pretend to sneeze.
I've got a cold!"	

—Traditional rhyme

The City Mouse

The city mouse lives in a house.	Put fingertips together over head to form roof.
The garden mouse lives in a bower.	Spread fingers apart, hands overhead, to form the garden shelter.
He's friendly with the frogs and toads	Shake hands.
And sees pretty plants in flower.	Put hands in front of body, palms together; move palms apart to represent flower opening.
The city mouse eats bread and cheese.	Pretend to eat.
The garden mouse eats what he can.	Shrug shoulders.
We will not grudge him seeds and stalks,	Shake head "no."
Poor little timid furry man.	

—Traditional rhyme

The Mice

Five little mice on the pantry floor,	Hold up five fingers.
Seeking for bread crumbs or something more.	Put hand over eyes, searching.
Five little mice on a shelf up high,	Five fingers rest on palm of other hand.
Feasting so daintily on a pie—	Hands make circle.
But the big round eyes of the wise old cat	Put fingers around eyes.

See what the little mice are at.

Quickly she jumps!—but the mice run away
And hide in their snug little holes all day.
"Feasting in pantries may be very nice,
But home is the best!" say the five little mice.

—Emilie Poulsson

Left hand, the cat, pounces on right hand, the mice.
Hide fingers behind back.

Hide five fingers inside other cupped hand.

Little Mouse

He climbed up the candlestick,
The little mousy brown.
To steal and eat tallow
And he could not get down.
He called for his grandma,
But his grandma was in town.
So he doubled up into a wheel,
And rolled himself down.

—Traditional Chinese rhyme

Motion of climbing hand over hand.

Pretend to eat.
Shake head "no."
Cup hands around mouth.

Roll hands around each other.

The Little Mouse

I have seen you, little mouse,
Running all around the house.
Through the hole, your little eye
In the wainscot peeping sly.
Hoping soon some crumbs to steal,
To make quite a hearty meal.
Look before you venture out,
See if pussy is about.
If she's gone, you'll quickly run
To the larder for some fun;
'Round about the dishes creep,
Taking into each a peep,
To choose the daintiest that's there,
Spoiling things, you do not care.

—Traditional rhyme

Point to eyes.
Run in place.
Make circle with fingers in front of eye and peek through.

Pretend to take and eat food.
Rub tummy.

Put hand over eyes, searching.
Run in place.

Tiptoe in place.
Pretend to look into dishes.

Shake head "no."

Where Are the Baby Mice?

Where are the baby mice?
Squeak, squeak, squeak,
I can't see them.
Peek, peek, peek.
Here they come out of their hole in the wall,
One, two, three, four, five and that's all.

—Traditional rhyme

Hide fist behind back.

Peek-a-boo motion.
Show fist.
Show fingers one at a time.

Five Little Mice

Five little mice went out to play,
Gathering crumbs along the way.
Out came pussycat, sleek and fat.
Four little mice came scampering back.
Four little mice went out to play. . . .
Three little mice went out to play. . . .
Two little mice went out to play. . . .
One little mouse went out to play,
Gathering crumbs along the way.
Out came pussycat, sleek and fat.
No little mice and that was that!

—Traditional rhyme

Begin this rhyme with five fingers up.

Take away fingers as rhyme progresses.

Clap on "that was that."

Mouse, Get Out of Our House

What do I hear rustling around
Making that squeak, squeak, squeaking sound?
I think it has a tail that is long,
Tiny feet and teeth that are strong.

Do you think it could be a mouse?
Tell it to get out of our house!

—Susan M. Dailey

Cup ear with hand; rub fingers together.
Squeak.
Hold hand far from body for long tail.
Hold up hand with thumb and index finger close together; chomp teeth.
Hold out hands, questioning.
Gesture with thumb over shoulder.

Three Blind Mice

Three blind mice, three blind mice,
See how they run, see how they run.
They all ran after the farmer's wife,
Who cut off their tails with a carving knife.

Did you ever see such a sight in your life
As three blind mice?

—Adapted traditional rhyme

Hold up three fingers, then cover eyes with hands.
Hold hand above eye and look around.
Run fingers.
Hold out one palm; make chopping motion with other hand into palm.
Hold out hands, questioning.
Hold up three fingers, then cover eyes with hands.

Five Little Mice

Five little mice
Went out to play,
Through the fields
And far away.
Mama mouse called,
"Squeak, squeak, squeak!"
But one little mouse
Played hide-and-seek.
Five little mice

Sung to the tune of "Six Little Ducks."
Hold up five fingers.
Wiggle fingers.
Move hand in zigzag motion.
Move hand away from body.
Put thumb and index finger together; move apart like mouth moving.

Put down one finger.
Repeat with four, three, two, one. Then sing:

Played hide-and-seek.
Didn't come home
When their mama squeaked.
But when the big cat
Started to hiss,
They ran home
As quick as this.

—Susan M. Dailey

Mouse Hunt

I am a brave little mouse.
I roam bravely through my house.
I'm going hunting for a cat.
Well, what do you think of that?
Do you want to come along?
OK, let's go on a cat hunt!
Oh, look
Here's a cupboard. Let's climb up it.
Oh, look
Here's a sink. Let's swim across it.
Oh, look
Here's an oven. Let's run across it.
Oh, look

Here's the end of the cupboard. Let's slide down it.
Oh, look
Here's a trap. Let's tiptoe around it.
Oh, look
Here's some tall carpet. Let's push through it.
Oh, look
Here's something dark.
Here's something big.
Here's something furry.
Here's something purry.
IT'S A CAT! RUN!
Through the carpet
Around the trap
Up the cupboard
Across the oven
Across the sink
Down the cupboard
Back in our hole
Safe at last.
I wasn't afraid. Were you?

—Adapted traditional rhyme by Susan M. Dailey

Snap fingers.

This is a variation of "Going on a Bear Hunt."

Slap lightly, alternating hands on legs in rhythm. / Point.

Pretend to climb. Return to slapping hands on legs. / Point.

Pretend to swim. Return to slapping hands on legs. / Point.

Slap hands quickly on legs. Return to slapping hands on legs more slowly. / Point.

Pretend to slide. Return to slapping hands on legs. / Point.

Tiptoe. Return to slapping hands on legs. Point.

Pretend to push aside with arms. Return to slapping hands on legs. / Point.

Slap hands on legs quickly.

Pant; place hand over heart.
Shake head.

'Round and 'Round the Haystack

'Round and 'round the haystack
Goes the little mouse.
One step, two steps,
In his little house.

—Traditional rhyme

Make circle with index finger in the air.

Hold up one finger, then two.
Raise arms over head, fingertips together to form roof.

Five Little Mice

Five little mice on the old barn floor.
One ran away and then there were four.
Four little mice, two and two, you see.
One ran away and then there were three.
Three little mice chewing on a shoe.
One ran away and then there were two.
Two little mice playing with beams from the sun.
One ran away and then there was one.
One little mouse, not having much fun.
He ran away and now there are none.

—Barbara Scott

Begin this rhyme with five fingers up.
Take away fingers as rhyme progresses.

Are You Sleeping?

Are you sleeping,
Are you sleeping,
Little Mouse,
Little Mouse?
Hurry scurry this way,
Hurry scurry that way,
'Round the house,
'Round the house.

—Adapted traditional rhyme

Sung to the tune of "Frère Jacques."
Put head on hands; pretend to sleep.

Point in one direction.
Point in the other direction.
Make circle in the air with finger.

Five Tired Mice

Five tired mice were headed to bed.
The first one said, "Here's a pillow for my head."
The second one said, "This bed is nice and comfy."
The third one said, "My bed is hard and lumpy."
The fourth tired mouse let out a great big sigh.
The fifth tired mouse nodded off and closed his eyes.

—Barbara Scott

Begin this rhyme with five fingers up.
Starting with thumb, point to each in succession.

A Little Mouse Goes Out of the Cave

A little mouse goes out of the cave.
It's moving its nose
And playing a game.

—Traditional Spanish rhyme

Wiggle nose.

Have children move in a circle.
Continue counting up to the number
of children you have in your
storyhour group.

*Sung to the tune of "Bingo." This is a
great rhyme to use with letters on a hand
mitt or larger letters on a flannel or
Velcro board.*

Mouse

I know an animal that's small and runs around the house.
M-O-U-S-E,
M-O-U-S-E,
M-O-U-S-E,
And Mouse is its name-o!

—Adapted traditional rhyme

Continue the song as in the original,
taking away letters and replacing them
with clapping.

Five Pieces of Cheese

Five pieces of cheese on the pantry floor.
A little mouse took one and now there are four.
Four pieces of cheese, yellow as you can see.
A little mouse took one and now there are three.
Three pieces of cheese, just a yummy few.
A little mouse took one and now there are two.
Two pieces of cheese sitting in the sun.
A little mouse took one and now there's just one.
One piece of cheese, yes, just one.
A little mouse took it and now there are none.

—Barbara Scott

Begin this rhyme with five fingers up.

Take away fingers as rhyme progresses.

This Little Mouse

This little mouse wiggled under the door.
This little mouse made a leap to the floor.
This little mouse ran out to play.
This little mouse ran far, far away.
And this little mouse ate cheese all day!

—Barbara Scott

Begin this rhyme with five fingers up.

Starting with thumb, point to each in
succession.

Ten Little Mice

Ten little mice were out in the field,
Out in the field at play.
One little mouse found some corn,
And he ran away.
Nine little mice were out in the field,
Out in the field at play.
One little mouse found some nuts,
And he ran away.

*This is also a fun rhyme to do on the
flannel or Velcro board with mice figures!*
Begin this rhyme with ten fingers up.

Take away fingers as rhyme progresses.

Eight little mice were out in the field,
Out in the field at play.
One little mouse found some seeds,
And he ran away.
Seven little mice were out in the field,
Out in the field at play.
One little mouse found some beans,
And he ran away.
Six little mice were out in the field,
Out in the field at play.
One little mouse found some carrots,
And he ran away.
Five little mice were out in the field,
Out in the field at play.
One little mouse found some wheat,
And he ran away.
Four little mice were out in the field,
Out in the field at play.
One little mouse found some berries,
And he ran away.
Three little mice were out in the field,
Out in the field at play.
One little mouse found some grapes.
And he ran away.
Two little mice were out in the field,
Out in the field at play.
One little mouse found some cherries,
And he ran away.
One little mouse was out in the field,
Out in the field at play.
That little mouse missed all his friends,
And he ran away.

—Barbara Scott

Baby Mice

Baby mice are creeping,   Wiggle all fingers on thighs.
Creeping all around.
How many baby mice
Are there to be found?   Nod head to one side, questioning.
One, two, three,   Count fingers.
Four, five, six,
Seven, eight, nine, and ten.
Baby mice are creeping   Wiggle all fingers on thighs.
All around again!

—Barbara Scott

Hungry Mice

Mice are nibbling,
Mice are nibbling,
Lots of cheese,
Lots of cheese!
Yummy and delicious,
Good and so nutritious.
Eating cheese,
Lots of cheese!

—Adapted traditional rhyme

Sung to the tune of "Frère Jacques." ASL sign for mouse: hold index finger to nose, then brush nose, moving finger to side.
Use ASL sign for mouse.
Use ASL sign.
Nibbling motion.

Rub tummy.

Nibbling motions.

Five Hungry Mice

Five hungry mice stood outside the kitchen door.
One ran inside the cupboard and now there are four.
Four hungry mice seeing all there is to see.
One ran inside the pantry and now there are three.
Three hungry mice, not just any food will do.
One ran under the sink and now there are two.
Two hungry mice know there's eating to be done.
One ran across the counter and now there's just one.
One hungry mouse, all by himself,
Found the popcorn hidden on the very top shelf!

—Barbara Scott

Begin this rhyme with five fingers up.
Take away fingers as rhyme progresses.

The Mouse and the Cat

The little mouse goes creeping
Softly around the cat.
The sleeping kitty opens his eyes,
And pounces just like that!

—Barbara Scott

Creeping motion.
Make "Shhh" motion.
Close, then open eyes quickly.
Pouncing motion.

Quiet Little Mouse

I'm a quiet little mouse,
Tip-toeing around the house.
If a cat I chance to meet
I'll scurry away on my four little feet.

—Barbara Scott

ASL sign for cat: make "OK" sign with fingers beside nose, then pull outward as if pulling on whiskers.
Make "Shhh" motion.
Tiptoe fingers of one hand on palm of other. / Use ASL sign for cat.

Running motion.

Where Are the Baby Mice?

Where are the baby mice?
In their nest, you see.
How many baby mice are there?
Count them now with me.

—Barbara Scott

Look around.
Lay one cupped hand on palm of other hand.

Count fingers of the hand on top, one to five.

I'm a Lonely Little Mouse

I'm a lonely little mouse,
Hiding all around the house.
I can disappear just like that,
Especially when I see the cat!

—Barbara Scott

This Little Mousie

This little mousie peeked in the door.
This little mousie jumped to the floor.
This little mousie came out to play.
This little mousie ran away.
This little mousie said, "Dear me,
Dinner is over and it's time for tea!"

—Adapted traditional rhyme

ASL sign for cat: make "OK" sign with fingers beside nose, then pull outward as if pulling on whiskers.

Point to self.

Hide eyes.

Snap fingers or clap once.

Use ASL sign for cat.

Point to thumb.

Point to index finger.

Point to middle finger.

Point to ring finger.

Point to little finger.

Books to Share

Aylesworth, Jim. 2007. *Little Bitty Mousie*. London: Walker Books for Young Readers. ISBN: 978-0802796370.

Donofrio, Beverly. 2007. *Mary and the Mouse, the Mouse and Mary*. New York: Schwartz and Wade. ISBN: 978-0375836091.

Garland, Michael. 2007. *How Many Mice?* New York: Dutton Juvenile. ISBN: 978-0525478331.

Kirk, Daniel. 2009. *Library Mouse: A Friend's Tale*. New York: Abrams Books for Young Readers. ISBN: 978-0810989276.

Riley, Linnea. 1997. *Mouse Mess*. New York: Blue Sky Press. ISBN: 978-0590100489.

Urban, Linda. 2009. *Mouse Was Mad*. Boston: Houghton Mifflin. ISBN: 978-0152053376.

Musical Selections

"Grey Little Mouse" from *Sing It! Say It! Stamp It! Sway It!*, vol. 3, by Peter and Ellen Allard. Available: www.cdbaby.com (accessed March 12, 2010).

"Hickory Dickory Dock" from *Pop Go The Wiggles: Nursery Rhymes and Songs* by The Wiggles. ASIN: B0012OVFSE.

"The Mice Go Marching" from *Rhythms on Parade* by Hap Palmer. Available: www.happalmer.com (March 12, 2010).

"Mickey Mouse March" from *Simplified Rhythm Stick Activities*. Available: www.kimboed.com (accessed March 10, 2010).

"The Tailor and the Mouse" from *Burl Ives Sings Little White Duck* by Burl Ives. ASIN: B00000253F.

"Three Blind Mice" from *Sing Along with Bob #2*. ASIN: B0026OZJCC.

Sources

Activity Village. Available: www.activityvillage.co.uk/chinese_nursery_rhymes.htm (accessed April 9, 2010).

Briggs, Diane. 1999. *101 Fingerplays, Stories, and Songs to Use with Finger Puppets*. Chicago: American Library Association.

Fun Baby Games Online. Available: www.fun-baby-games-online.com (accessed March 12, 2010).

Grayson, Marion. 1962. *Let's Do Fingerplays*. Fairfield, CT: R.B. Luce.

Index of Rhymes. Available: www.kidsnurseryrhymes.co.uk/rhymes (accessed March 10, 2010).

Kindermusik. Available: www.kindermusikeducators.com (accessed March 12, 2010).

Mama Lisa's World of Children & International Culture. Available: www.mamalisa.com (accessed March 4, 2010).

Mother Goose Nursery Rhymes. Available: www.mothergoose.com (accessed March 12, 2010).

"Music Fun for Infants & Toddlers." Center of Excellence for Early Childhood Learning and Development. Available: child.etsu.edu/news/conf2009/Infant%20Toddler.pdf (accessed March 12, 2010).

North Central Library Co-operative. n.d. *Storytime Booklet* [out of print].

Pennsylvania Center for the Book. Available: www.pabook.libraries.psu.edu (accessed March 12, 2010).

Poulsson, Emilie. 1893. *Fingerplays for Nursery and Kindergarten*. New York: Lothrop, Lee, and Shepard, reprinted 1921.

Rossetti, Christina G. 1893. *Sing-Song: A Nursery Rhyme Book*. New York: Macmillan and Company.

Totline Staff, comp. 1994. *1001 Rhymes and Fingerplays*. Everett, WA: Warren Publishing House.

Chapter 6

Monkeys and Crocodiles
to Pigs

Monkeys and Crocodiles

Feel free to use the word "alligator" in place of "crocodile"!

These two themes appear together because of the great fables and folktales that feature both animals.

Rhyme

Five Little Monkeys Jumping on the Bed

Five little monkeys jumping on the bed.
One fell off and bumped his head.
His mother called the doctor
And the doctor said,
"No more monkeys jumping the bed!"

—Traditional rhyme

Monkeys in a Tree

Five little monkeys
Sitting in a tree,
Teasing Mr. Crocodile,
"You can't catch me."
Along comes Mr. Crocodile,
As quiet as can be—
SNAP!!!
Away swims Mr. Crocodile
As full as he can be!!!!

—Lynda Roberts

Just Like Me

Monkeys all stand up, just like me.
Monkeys all wiggle, just like me.
Monkeys all jump up, just like me.
Monkeys all make faces, just like me.
Monkeys all stretch high, just like me.
Monkeys all sit down, quietly.

—Traditional rhyme

Five Little Monkeys

Five little monkeys went out to play.
In the trees, they swung far away.
Mother Monkey said, "Ee, ee, ee, ee!"
Four little monkeys came back to the tree.

—Barbara Scott

Telling Guide

This is an old stand-by, tried and true! Some kits provide props for this rhyme, such as the Monkey Mitt and individual monkeys. Childcraft offers a kit with plush monkeys and a bed.
Begin with five fingers up.
Bump self on head.
Motion of dialing phone or holding receiver to ear.

Continue with four, three, two, one. Take away fingers as rhyme progresses.

Another tried-and-true rhyme! This is a fun flannel or Velcro board activity. Childcraft also offers a kit with plush tree, monkeys, and alligator.
Stick fingers in ear, teasing motion.

With fingers together and thumbs out, snap hands shut. Continue until all monkeys are gone.

Finish with . . .

Match actions to words; point to self on "just like me."

This rhyme can be sung to the tune of "Six Little Ducks" or chanted.
Begin rhyme with five fingers up.

Take away fingers as rhyme progresses. Repeat for four, three, two, one.

Monkeys

The monkeys climb up the trees
To see what they can see.
A snake slithers round
The monkeys run down
As fast as they can flee!

—Carolyn N. Cullum

One Little Crocodile

One little crocodile out in the swamp,
Looking around to see what he could chomp.
He snapped at a monkey,
But the monkey got away,
And the crocodile went home hungry that day.
One little crocodile out in the swamp,
Looking around to see what he could chomp.
He snapped at a frog,
But the frog got away,
And the crocodile went home hungry that day.
One little crocodile out in the swamp,
Looking around to see what he could chomp.
He snapped at a turtle,
But the turtle got away,
And the crocodile went home hungry that day.
One little crocodile out in the swamp,
Looking around to see what he could chomp.
But all the little animals got away, and he didn't catch a thing.
So he had to get his dinner at Burger King.

—Kay Lincycomb

I'm a Little Crocodile

I'm a little crocodile, long and green.
I've the longest tail you have ever seen.
If you go swimming in my swamp,
Look out for my teeth,
So you don't get a chomp!

—Kay Lincycomb

Baby Crocodile

Oh, I'm bringing home a baby crocodile.
Won't that really make my mommy smile?
Oh, I'm bringing home a baby crocodile.
"Ouch! It bit me!"
Oh, I'm throwing down a baby crocodile.
Won't that really make my mommy smile?

Sung to the tune of "Hickory Dickory Dock."
Pretend to climb up tree.
Put hand above eyes; look around.
Slide arms across body like a snake.
Run in place.

This rhyme can also be sung to the tune of "Six Little Ducks."

Slap hands together.
Slap again.

Hold tummy.

Slap.
Slap.

Hold tummy.

Slap.
Slap.

Hold tummy.

Slap.

Repeat with other animals if you wish.

Sung to the tune of "I'm a Little Teapot."
Hold hands apart to indicate long.
Turn and wiggle.
Make swimming motion.
Point to teeth.
Clap hands.

Sung to the tune "I'm Bringing Home a Baby Bumblebee."
Hold hands as if holding a crocodile.

Shake hand.
Act like you are throwing it.

Oh, I'm throwing down a baby crocodile.
"Because it bit me!"

—Kay Lincycomb

Monkeys Swinging

Monkeys swinging, swinging all day.
Monkeys swinging, swinging all day.
Monkeys swinging, swinging all day.
Swinging, swinging 'til I say,
"Stop!"

ADDITIONAL VERSES:
Monkeys eating, eating all day . . .
Monkeys scratching, scratching all day . . .
Monkeys chatter, chatter all day . . .

—Susan M. Dailey

I'm a Little Monkey

I'm a little monkey in a tree,
Swinging by my tail so merrily.
I can leap and fly from tree to tree,
I have lots of fun, you see.
I'm a little monkey, watch me play,
Munching on bananas every day.
Lots of monkey friends to play with me,
We have fun up in the tree.

—Carla C. Skjong

Monkey, Monkey

Monkey, monkey,
Jump all around.
Monkey, monkey,
Sit on the ground.
Monkey, monkey,
A banana eat.
Monkey, monkey,
Tastes so sweet!
Monkey, monkey,
Swing in the trees!
Monkey, monkey,
Great big sneeze!
Monkey, monkey,
No more light.
Monkey, monkey,
Say good night.

—Adapted traditional rhyme

Shake hand.

Sung to the tune of "Skip to My Lou." Do motions as indicated.

Speak this line.

Sung to the tune of "I'm a Little Teapot." ASL sign for monkey: with hands on both sides of chest, pretend to scratch up and down.
Use ASL sign for monkey.
Swing back and forth.
Continue to swing.

Use ASL sign again.
Pretend to eat.
Indicate children in front of you.
Point up.

This rhyme can be sung to the tune of "Teddy Bear, Teddy Bear" or chanted.

Jump like a monkey.

Sit.

Pretend to peel a banana and eat.

Rub tummy.

Swing back and forth.

"Achoo!"

Shake head "no."

Put head on hands; pretend to sleep.

Five Little Monkeys

Five little monkeys and not one more.
One found a banana and now there are four.
Four little monkeys swinging in the trees.
One fell down and now there are three.
Three little monkeys, they're looking right at you!
One went to sleep and now there are two.
Two little monkeys were playing in the sun.
One wandered off and now there's just one.
One little monkey, yes, there's only one.
He went home and now there are none.

—Barbara Scott

Begin rhyme with five fingers up.
Take away fingers as rhyme progresses.

I'm a Little Monkey

I'm a little monkey
In a tree.
I love to eat
Bananas, you see.
I have lots of friends
Who come to play.
We have fun
Ev'ry day!

—Adapted traditional rhyme

Sung to the tune of "I'm a Little Teapot." ASL sign for monkey: with hands on both sides of chest, pretend to scratch up and down.
Use ASL sign for monkey.

Motion of eating.

Wiggle fingers.

Clap three times on syllables.

The Monkey Hokey Pokey

You put your monkey ears in,
You put your monkey ears out,
You put your monkey ears in
And you shake them all about.
You do the monkey pokey and you turn yourself around.
That's what it's all about!

ADDITIONAL VERSES:
. . . monkey nose.
. . . monkey paws.
. . . monkey toes (or feet).
. . . monkey tail.

—Adapted traditional rhyme

Sung to the tune of "The Hokey Pokey." Do motions as indicated.

Clap.

Monkey See and Monkey Do

Monkey, monkey, see what I do?
Monkey, monkey, can you do it, too?
I clap, clap, clap my monkey hands.
Can you clap, clap, clap your monkey hands?

Clap hands.

I scratch, scratch, scratch my monkey head.

Scratch head.

Can you scratch, scratch, scratch your monkey head?

I beat, beat, beat my monkey chest.

Beat on chest with hands.

Can you beat, beat, beat your monkey chest?

I jump, jump, jump up and down.

Jump around like a monkey.

Can you jump, jump, jump up and down?

I make, make, make a monkey sound.

Chatter like a monkey.

Can you make, make, make a monkey sound?

—Barbara Scott

Silly Monkeys

Sung to the tune of "Alouette."

Silly monkeys,
Lots of silly monkeys.

Wiggle ten fingers.

Silly monkeys,
High up in the tree.

Point up.

They make faces
All day long.

Make a silly face.

Watch them while I
Sing this song.

Point to eyes.

All day long, sing this song . . . oh.

Silly monkeys,
Lots of silly monkeys.

Wiggle ten fingers.

Silly monkeys
High up in the tree.

Point up.

—Adapted traditional rhyme

Five Little Crocodiles

Five little crocodiles wading by the shore.

Begin rhyme with five fingers up.

One went to chase some food and now there are four.

Take away fingers as rhyme progresses.

Four little crocodiles were sleeping 'neath a tree.
One woke up and now there are three.
Three little crocodiles with nothing much to do.
One slid into the water and now there are two.
Two little crocodiles basking in the sun.
One found some tasty fish and now there is one.
One little crocodile, just a lonely one.
He went home and now there are none.

—Barbara Scott

Beware the Smile

Beware the smile
Of the crocodile!

Smile a big smile, or use hands on top of each other for "mouth" and "teeth."

Don't go near the swamp,

Shake head "no."

Or you'll hear a big CHOMP!

Big bite or use hands to chomp.

—Barbara Scott

The Crocodile Goes

The crocodile's legs go crawl, crawl, crawl,
Crawl, crawl, crawl,
Crawl, crawl, crawl.
The crocodile's legs go crawl, crawl, crawl
All through the swamp.
The crocodile's tail goes swish, swish, swish,
Swish, swish, swish,
Swish, swish, swish.
The crocodile's tail goes swish, swish, swish
All through the swamp.
The crocodile's eyes go blink, blink, blink,
Blink, blink, blink,
Blink, blink, blink.
The crocodile's eyes go blink, blink, blink
All through the swamp.
The crocodile's teeth go chomp, chomp, chomp,
Chomp, chomp, chomp,
Chomp, chomp, chomp.
The crocodile's teeth go chomp, chomp, chomp
All through the swamp.

—Adapted traditional rhyme

Sung to the tune of "The Wheels on the Bus."
Crawling motion with hands.

Make circle in the air with pointer finger. / Move arm back and forth.

Move arm back and forth.
Blink eyes slowly.

Blink eyes slowly.
Hands form mouth; fingers are teeth. Open and shut hands.

Hands form mouth; fingers are teeth. Open and shut hands.

Five Hungry Crocodiles

Five hungry crocodiles were waiting in the swamp.
The first one said, "See my teeth? Chomp, chomp!"
The second one said, "Quiet we must stay."
The third one said, "We're waiting for our prey."
The fourth one said, "We are all colored green."
The fifth one said, "We look very mean."

—Barbara Scott

Begin this rhyme with five fingers up.

Starting with thumb, point to each in succession.

Oh, Crocodile

Oh crocodile, oh crocodile,
How scary are your teeth!
Oh crocodile, oh crocodile,
How scary are your teeth!
You have a great big toothy smile
That makes me want to run a mile!
Oh crocodile, oh crocodile,
How scary are your teeth!
Oh crocodile, oh crocodile,
How scary are your teeth!
Oh crocodile, oh crocodile,

Sung to the tune of "O Christmas Tree."

Hands are mouth; fingers are teeth. Open and shut hands.

Make crocodile teeth motion.
Point to smile.
Motion of running.

Make crocodile teeth motion.

Make crocodile teeth motion.

How scary are your teeth!	Make crocodile teeth motion.
I am afraid of great big crocs.	Point to self.
They scare me right out of my socks!	Point to feet.
Oh crocodile, oh crocodile,	
How scary are your teeth!	Make crocodile teeth motion.

—Barbara Scott

Crocodile, Crocodile

	This rhyme can be sung to the tune of "Teddy Bear, Teddy Bear" or chanted.
Crocodile, crocodile,	
Roll around.	Roll hands.
Crocodile, crocodile,	
Rest on the ground.	Sit.
Crocodile, crocodile,	
Snap at a fly.	Snap hands as mouth.
Crocodile, crocodile,	
Blink one eye.	Blink an eye.
Crocodile, crocodile,	
Do not fail!	Shake head "no."
Crocodile, crocodile,	
Swish your tail.	Move arm or bottom back and forth.
Crocodile, crocodile,	
In the moonlight.	Make circle in air with hands to represent moon.
Crocodile, crocodile,	
Say goodnight.	Put head on hands; pretend to sleep.

—Adapted traditional rhyme

Books to Share

Bell, Cece. 2006. *Sock Monkey Rides Again.* Somerville, MA: Candlewick Press. ISBN: 978-0763630898. (This is one of a series of books by this author.)

Donaldson, Julia. 2008. *Where's My Mom?* New York: Dial. ISBN: 978-0803732285.

Monroe, Chris. 2007. *Monkey with a Tool Belt.* Minneapolis: Carolrhoda Books. ISBN: 978-0822576310.

Ochiltree, Dianne. 2002. *Ten Monkey Jamboree.* New York: Simon & Schuster. ISBN: 978-0689836206.

Sierra, Judy. 1997. *Counting Crocodiles.* Fairbanks, AK: Gulliver Books. ISBN: 978-0152001926.

———. 2004. *What Time Is It, Mr. Crocodile?* Boston: Harcourt Children's Books. ISBN: 978-0152164454.

Musical Selections

"The Castle Croc" from *Castles, Knights, and Unicorns* by Ronno. ASIN: B00019PVO0.

"Five Little Monkeys" from *Greg and Steve: Ready . . . Set . . . Move* by Greg and Steve. ASIN: B000153K1U.

"Matthew the Monkey" from *Animals at the Zoo* by Bobby Susser. ASIN: B00005BABL.

"Monkey Fun" from *Debbie's Ditties 3: At the Library* by Debbie Clement). Available: www.rainbowswithinreach.com (accessed March 13, 2010).

"Never Smile at a Crocodile" from *Animal Rock*. ASIN: B00005B6CG.
"See You Later, Alligator" from *Bean Bag Rock and Roll*. ASIN: B00019PVO0.

Sources

Cullum, Carolyn N. 2007. *The Storytime Sourcebook II*. New York: Neal-Schuman.

Dailey, Susan M. 2001. *A Storytime Year*. New York: Neal-Schuman.

Lincycomb, Kay. 2007. *Storytimes . . . Plus!* New York: Neal-Schuman.

North Central Library Co-operative. n.d. *Storytime Booklet* [out of print].

Roberts, Lynda. 1985. *Mitt Magic: Fingerplays for Finger Puppets*. Silver Spring, MD: Gryphon House.

Warren, Jean. 1990. *Theme-a-Saurus II*. Everett, WA: Warren Publishing House.

———. 1991. *Alphabet Theme-a-Saurus*. Everett, WA: Warren Publishing House.

Outer Space

Enjoy these rhymes about planets, the moon, stars, and riding in a rocket ship!

Rhyme	**Telling Guide**

A Tiny Little Star

There's a tiny little star	
Way up in the sky,	Raise fist high.
A tiny little star,	
Up so very high.	Raise fist even higher.
She twinkles brightly	
Through the night,	Open fist and wiggle fingers.
But during the day	
She's out of sight.	Close hand back into fist.

—Jean Warren

Four Little Stars

Four little stars winking at me,	Hold up four fingers.
One shot off, then there were three.	Bend down first finger.
Three little stars with nothing to do,	
One shot off, then there were two.	Bend down second finger.
Two little stars afraid of the sun,	
One shot off, then there was one.	Bend down third finger.
One little star, alone is no fun,	
It shot off, then there were none.	Bend down fourth finger.

—Jean Warren

Sally Go 'Round the Sun

Sally go 'round the sun,	
Sally go 'round the moon,	
Sally go 'round the stars,	
Every afternoon.	Have children hold hands and walk in a circle.

—Traditional rhyme

Twinkle, Twinkle, Little Star

Twinkle, twinkle, little star,	Flutter fingers of one hand to represent star twinkling.
How I wonder what you are.	Put index finger to cheek, wondering.
When the blazing sun is gone,	Raise arms over head to form circle.
When he nothing shines upon,	Shake head "no."
Then your show your little light.	
Twinkle, twinkle all the night.	Flutter fingers again for twinkle.
Then the traveler in the dark	

Thanks you for your little spark.
He could not see which way to go,
If you did not twinkle so.
In the dark blue sky you keep,
And often through my curtains peep.
For you never shut your eye,
'Til the sun is in the sky.

—Traditional rhyme

Blast Off: A Participatory Story

Ready?
We're going on a moon walk.
We are all set to go!
Climb up to the spaceship.
Count backwards:
Ten, nine, eight, seven,
WAIT!
Have you got your moon gloves?
Here—put them on.
Ready?
We're going on a moon walk.
We are all set to go!
Count backwards:
Ten, nine, eight, seven, six, five,
WAIT!
Have you zipped up your space suit?
Altogether—ZIP.
Ready?
We're going on a moon walk.
We are all set to go!
Count backwards:
Ten, nine, eight, seven, six, five, four,
WAIT!
Have you got on your moon boots?
Here—put them on.
Left.
Right.
Ready?
We're going on a moon walk.
We are all set to go!
Count backwards:
Ten, nine, eight, seven, six, five, four, three, two,
WAIT!
Have you got your helmet?

Look left, then right.
Flutter fingers for twinkle.
Point to sky.

Shake head "no."
Raise arms over head to form circle.

Have children repeat each line after the leader. Set an even rhythm by tapping knees. Do actions as indicated.

Here—put it on.
NOW we are ready!
Count backwards:
Ten, nine, eight, seven, six, five, four, three, two, one, zero,
BLAST OFF!

—Jan Irving

Ten Little Spaceships

One little, two little,
Three little spaceships,
Four little, five little,
Six little spaceships,
Seven little, eight little,
Nine little spaceships,
Ten little spaceships go.
"Countdown? Ready?"
"Ten, nine, eight, seven, six, five, four, three, two, one, zero."

"BLAST OFF!"

—Robin Currie

Sung to the tune of "Ten Little Indians."

Hold up one finger for each ship.

Speak remaining lines.
Everyone crouches down lower and lower during the count.
Jump up, thrusting arms above head.

We're Flying to the Moon

We're flying to the moon,
We're flying to the moon,
We've left the earth in a rocket ship,
And we're flying to the moon.
Ten, nine, eight, seven, six, five, four, three, two, one, zero!

—Kathy Ross

Sung to the tune of "The Farmer in the Dell." Have children extend arms upward to form nose of rocket ship, and walk around in a circle as they sing. They can crouch down for the countdown, and pop up for the blast off!

Blast Off!

Walk around the moon,
And try to grab a star.
Stardust! Stardust!
Fall where you are!

—Kathy Ross

Sung to the tune of "Ring Around the Rosy."

For additional verses, replace the word "walk" with "skip," "run," "twirl," "tiptoe," "skate," and "hop."

Five Little Stars

Five little stars twinkling in the sky.
Five little stars, see them oh, so high!
One little star from the sky did fall.
Now four little stars twinkle . . . that is all.

—Barbara Scott

Sung to the tune of "Six Little Ducks." Begin rhyme with five fingers up; wiggle fingers for "twinkle."

Take away fingers as rhyme progresses.

Repeat for four, three, two, one.

Counting Stars

Count, count, let's count the stars

Way up in the sky.
See them sparkle, see them shine,

This can be sung to the tune of "Row, Row, Row Your Boat" or chanted. This rhyme also works well as a flannel board activity!
Point upward.

Wiggle fingers.

Glowing in the night.
One . . . two . . . three . . . four . . . five.

—Barbara Scott

Put up fingers and count in succession.

Star Light, Star Bright

Star light, star bright,

First star I see tonight.
I wish I may,
I wish I might,

Have the wish
I wish tonight!

—Traditional rhyme

Flutter fingers to represent twinkling star.
Hold up one finger.
Put right hand over heart.
Put left hand over heart on top of right hand.
Close eyes.

I See the Moon

I see the moon,
And the moon sees me.
God bless the moon,
And God bless me!

—Traditional rhyme

Point up.
Point to self.
Put hands up in the air.
Put both hands on chest.

The Man in the Moon

The man in the moon
Looked out of the moon,
And this is what he said:
"'Tis time that now I'm getting up,
All babies went to bed."

—Traditional rhyme

Make circle with hands around face.
Point to eyes.

Point to wrist, indicating watch.
Fold hands by side of head; pretend to sleep.

Off We Go

Ten . . . nine . . . eight,
The rockets are ready to detonate.
Seven . . . six . . . five,
Let's take this ship for a test drive.
Four . . . three,
I forgot my helmet, pardon me.
Two . . . one,
BLAST OFF! See you when we get home!

—Carolyn N. Cullum

Use fingers to count down.

Moon, So Round and Yellow

Moon, so round and yellow,
Looking from on high,
How I love to see you
Shining in the sky.
Oft and oft I wonder,

Make circle with fingers.
Point to eyes.

Point up.
Put finger on cheek, tilt head, thinking.

When I see you there,
How they get to light you,
Hanging in the air.
Where you go at morning
When the night is past,
And the sun comes peeping
O'er the hills at last.
Sometimes I still watch you
Slyly overhead.
When you think I'm sleeping
Snugly in my bed.

—Matthias Barr

Sun, Sun, Shining Down

Sun, sun, shining down
Gives us lots of light.
You shine brightly through the day,
Then go to bed at night.

—Barbara Scott

The Earth Goes 'Round and 'Round

The earth goes 'round and 'round,
The earth goes 'round and 'round.
Heigh-ho the derry-o,
The earth goes 'round and 'round.
It orbits 'round the sun,
It orbits 'round the sun.
Heigh-ho the derry-o,
It orbits 'round the sun.
The earth is where we live,
The earth is where we live.
Heigh-ho the derry-o,
The earth is where we live.

—Barbara Scott

Five Little Stars

Five little stars and not one more.
One blinked off and then there were four.
Four little stars are shining through the tree.
One blinked off and then there were three.
Three little stars, twinkling like they do.
One blinked off and then there were two.
Two little stars not having any fun.
One blinked off and then there was one.

Shrug shoulders.

Arms make large circle; start down by side; move arms up until over head.

Point to eyes.

Put hands to side of head.

Sung to the tune of "Row, Row, Row Your Boat."
Make sun above head with arms.

Wiggle fingers in air for sun's rays.
Head on hands, pretend to sleep.

Sung to the tune of "The Farmer in the Dell."
Make circle in the air representing earth rotating around.

Clap in rhythm to this line.
Make rotating earth motion.
Roll hands.

Clap in rhythm.
Roll hands.
Point to self.

Clap in rhythm.
Point to self.

Begin rhyme with five fingers up.
Take away fingers as rhyme progresses.

One little star, afraid to be a hero.
He blinked off and then there were zero.

—Barbara Scott

If You'd Like to Fly in Space

If you'd like to fly in space, clap your hands.
If you'd like to fly in space, clap your hands.
If you'd like to fly in space, then put on a happy face!
If you'd like to fly in space, clap your hands.

ADDITIONAL VERSES:

. . . stomp your feet.
. . . nod your head.
. . . shout "Hooray!"
. . . do all four.

—Adapted traditional rhyme

Sung to the tune of "If You're Happy and You Know It."
Clap, clap.
Clap, clap.
Smile.
Clap, clap.

Clap, stomp, nod, and shout.

Twinkling Stars

Twinkling stars are all around.
Shine their light upon the ground.
Watch them sparkle, see them shine.
The one I wish on, I call mine.
Twinkling stars are all around.
Shine their light upon the ground.

—Adapted traditional rhyme

Sung to the tune of "Twinkle, Twinkle, Little Star."
Wiggle fingers to represent twinkling.
Point to ground.
Point to eyes.
Hold up one finger.
Wiggle fingers as before.
Point to ground.

I'm a Little Rocket Ship

I'm a little rocket ship,
Tall and sleek.
Here are my fins,

And here is my peak.
When the countdown starts,
My engines roar.
Up and away,
Now watch me soar!

—Adapted traditional rhyme

Sung to the tune of "I'm a Little Teapot."

Move hands to indicate size.
Hold arms close to body on sides, hands out.
Make point with arms together overhead.

Wiggle side to side.

Jump up into the air.

Five Little Shooting Stars

Five little shooting stars sitting in the sky.
The first one said, "I'm up so high."
The second one said, "To the ground I'll fall."
The third one said, "I'll land on that wall."
The fourth one said, "Ready? Let's go!"
The fifth one said, "Hurry! Don't be slow!"

—Barbara Scott

Begin rhyme with five fingers up.
Starting with thumb, point to each in succession.

Our Solar System

Our solar system's
Made up of nine planets
That we know:
Mercury, Venus, Earth, Mars,
Jupiter, Saturn, Uranus, and Pluto.
These nine planets,
They all orbit 'round the Sun.
Some are near,
Some are far.
Some just right for everyone!

—Barbara Scott

Move hands to show expanse.

Count out on fingers.

Hold up nine fingers.
Make circle in the air.

Use hands to show near and far.
Use hands to show expanse again.

The Lights on the Rocket

The lights on the rocket blink on and off,
On and off, on and off.
The lights on the rocket blink on and off,
All the way to space.
ADDITIONAL VERSES:
The dials on the rocket turn left, then right . . .
The alarms on the rocket go beep, beep, beep . . .
The engines on the rocket go roar, roar, roar . . .

—Adapted traditional rhyme

Sung to the tune of "The Wheels on the Bus."
Hands in air, open for "on" and close for "off."

Point up.

Pretend to turn dials left and right.
Pretend to push button.
Shake from side to side.

Let's Put on Our Space Suits

This is the way we zip our suit,
Zip our suit, zip our suit.
This is the way we zip our suit
On our way to space!
This is the way we pull on our boots,
Pull on our boots, pull on our boots.
This is the way we pull on our boots
On our way to space!
This is the way we put on our gloves,
Put on our gloves, put on our gloves.
This is the way we put on our gloves
On our way to space!
This is the way our helmet fits,
Helmet fits, helmet fits.
This is the way our helmet fits
On our way to space!
"Ready? Let's count down . . ."
"Ten, nine, eight, seven, six, five, four, three, two, one . . ."
"Blast off!"

—Adapted traditional rhyme

Sung to the tune of "The Mulberry Bush."
Pretend to zip space suit.

Pretend to pull boots on feet.

Pretend to put gloves on hands.

Pretend to position helmet on head.

Speak remaining lines.

Books to Share

Carle, Eric. 1991. *Papa, Please Get the Moon for Me.* New York: Simon & Schuster Children's Publishing. ISBN: 978-0887081774. (One of my favorites—this is a classic! Children love the fold-out pages!)

Dahl, Michael. 2004. *On the Launch Pad: A Counting Book about Rockets.* Mankato, MN: Picture Window Books. ISBN: 978-1404805811.

Landry, Leo. 2007. *Space Boy.* Boston: Houghton Mifflin Books for Children. ISBN: 978-0618605682.

Mitton, Tony. 1997. *Roaring Rockets.* Ashmore City, Qld: Kingfisher Publishing. ISBN: 978-0753451069.

Puttock, Simon. 2006. *Earth to Stella!* New York: Clarion Books. ISBN: 978-0618585359.

Yaccarino, Dan. 1997. *Zoom! Zoom! Zoom! I'm Off to the Moon.* New York: Scholastic. ISBN: 978-0590956109.

Musical Selections

"Good Morning Starshine" from *Let's Dance* by Sharon, Lois, and Bram. ASIN: B00000DCJW.

"Grocery—Space Trip" from *Debbie's Dillies: 2 Much Fun* by Debbie Clement. Available: www.rainbowswithinreach.com (accessed March 13, 2010).

Journey into Space. CD available: www.kimboed.com (accessed March 10, 2010).

"The Planet Song" from *Dance and Sing: The Best of Nick Jr.* ASIN: B00005Q3AT.

"Rockin' Rockets" from *Wiggle, Giggle, and Shake* by Rae Pica and Richard Gardzina. ASIN: B000X038IS.

"Twinkle, Twinkle, Little Star" from *Sing Along with Bob #2.* ASIN: B000QZYBMW.

Sources

Anonymous. 2001. *Baby's First Nursery Treasury.* Fairfield, IA: Books Are Fun.

Cullum, Carolyn N. 2007. *The Storytime Sourcebook II.* New York: Neal-Schuman.

Findlay, Diane, Susan Mast, Kathy Ross, and Patti Sinclair. 2007. *Collaborative Summer Library Program Manual.* Mason City, IA: Collaborative Summer Library Program.

Irving, Jan and Robin Currie. 1988. *Full Speed Ahead: Stories and Activities for Children on Transportation.* Santa Barbara: Teacher Ideas Press.

"Man in the Moon." Available: www.zelo.com/family/nursery/maninmoon.asp (accessed April 9, 2010).

Moffat, Alfred. 1911. *Our Old Nursery Rhymes.* New York: G. Schirmer.

Sinclair, Patti, Tami Chumbley, Geri Cupery, Diane Findlay, and Jerri J. Heid. 2004. *Collaborative Summer Library Program Manual.* Mason City, IA: Collaborative Summer Library Program.

Stevenson, Burton E. 1915. *The Home Book of Verse for Young Folks.* New York: Henry Holt and Company.

Totline Staff, comp. 1994. *1001 Rhymes and Fingerplays.* Everett, WA: Warren Publishing House.

Warren, Jean, comp. 1993. *Nursery Rhyme Theme-a-Saurus.* Everett, WA: Warren Publishing House.

Owls

Here's hoping you find these rhymes to be a real hoot!

Rhyme	Telling Guide
### The Owl and the Brownies	
An owl sat on the branch of a tree,	Owl is right forefinger; branch is left forefinger. / Make "Shhh" motion.
And he was as quiet as quiet could be.	
'Twas night and his eyes were open like this,	Circle eyes with thumb and forefinger.
And he looked all around; not a thing did he miss.	Look about, shake head "no."
Some brownies climbed up the trunk of the tree,	Put owl back on perch.
And sat on a branch as quiet as he.	Move middle, ring, and little fingers of right hand next to owl.
Said the solemn old owl, "Hoo! Hoo! Hoo! Hoo!"	
Up jumped the brownies and away they all flew.	Make brownies back away from perch, leaving only the owl sitting on his perch.
—From Rhymes for Little Hands	

Five Little Owls

Rhyme	Telling Guide
Five little owls and not one more.	Hold up five fingers.
This one went to chase a mouse.	Point to thumb.
Then there were four.	Take away thumb; four fingers remain.
Four little owls sitting in a tree.	
This one went to chase a rabbit.	Point to index finger.
Then there were three.	Three fingers remain.
Three little owls saying, "Hoo, hoo!"	Hold up three fingers.
This one went to chase a snake.	Point to middle finger.
Then there were two.	Hold up two fingers.
Two little owls, waiting for the sun.	
This one went to chase a skunk.	Point to ring finger, then hold nose.
Now there's just one.	Hold up one finger.
One little owl, afraid to be a hero.	
He flew away and now there are zero!	
—Barbara Scott	

Hoot Owl, Hoot Owl

Rhyme	Telling Guide
	This rhyme can be sung to the tune of "Teddy Bear, Teddy Bear" or chanted.
Hoot owl, hoot owl,	
Flap your wings.	Flap arms.
Hoot owl, hoot owl,	
Let's hear you sing!	Children say, "Hoo! Hoo!"
Hoot owl, hoot owl,	
Blink your eyes.	Exaggerated blinking of eyes.
Hoot owl, hoot owl,	
Reach for the sky.	Reach upward.
Hoot owl, hoot owl,	
Sit right down.	Sit on the floor.

Hoot owl, hoot owl, Turn your head around.	Turn head from side to side.
Hoot owl, hoot owl, Dance and sway.	Dance and sway in place.
Hoot owl, hoot owl, Fly away!	Fly around the room.

—Barbara Scott

One Little Owl 💿

One little owl flew and flew. He met another owl and that makes two.	Begin rhyme holding one finger up. Add other fingers as rhyme progresses.
Two little owls sitting in a tree. Were joined by another owl And that makes three. Three little owls . . . wait, there's one more! Count them now . . . one, two, three, four! Four little owls, Watch them swoop and dive. Found another owl and that makes five!	

—Barbara Scott

A Wise Old Owl

A wise old owl sat in an oak.	Children and leader are seated.
The more he heard,	Point to ears.
The less he spoke.	Point to mouth.
The less he spoke,	Continue to point to mouth.
The more he heard.	Point to ears.
Why aren't we all like that wise old bird?	Hands out to the sides, wondering.

—Traditional rhyme

The Little Brown Owl

The little brown owl sits	Thumb and index finger indicate size.
Up in the tree.	Point up.
And if you look well,	Point to eyes.
His big eyes you may see.	Make big circles around eyes with fingers.
He says "What-a-whoo" When the night grows dark,	
And he hears the dogs howl,	Howl.
And the little fox bark.	Bark.

—Traditional rhyme

There Was a Little Boy

There was a little boy Went into a barn, And lay down On some hay.	Raise arms overheard, fingertips together to form roof.
An owl came out	Put hands to side of head; pretend to sleep.

And flew about
And the little boy
Ran away.

Flap arms.

Running motion.

—Traditional rhyme

Wise Mr. Owl

Wise Mr. Owl
Sitting in a tree,
Turns his head
All ways to see
Everything that comes and goes,
Sneaking through the garden rows.
He sees rabbits in their house,
And spots his dinner . . . it's a mouse!

Hands make circles around eyes.

Turn head from side to side as far as you can.

Motion of sneaking, "Shhh" motion.
Point to eyes.
Point, then clap three times.

—Barbara Scott

On a Dark and Windy Night

On a dark and windy night
The owl is ready to take flight.
He looks about with eyes so round,
And spies some food on the ground.
He spreads his wings . . . away he flies,
And soars across the moonlight sky.

Blow for wind.

Turn head from side to side.
Point to eyes.
Arms out to sides; flap.
Hold arms out straight; pretend to soar up and down.

—Barbara Scott

Five Little Owls

Five little owls having fun galore.

One danced off and then there were four.
Four little owls were sitting in the tree.
One fell off the branch and then there were three.
Three little owls, each saying, "Hoo, hoo!"
One saw a tasty mouse and then there were two.
Two little owls in the setting sun.
One got tired and now there's just one.
One little owl, sitting all alone.
He flew away and then there were none.

Begin rhyme with five fingers up; wiggle fingers.
Take away fingers as rhyme progresses.

—Barbara Scott

Five Little Owls

Five little owls went out to play
In the forest one fine day.
Mother Owl said, "Hoo, hoo, hoo, hoo!"
Only four little owls came back, it's true.
No little owls went out to play
In the forest one fine day.

Sung to the tune of "Five Little Ducks."
Begin rhyme with five fingers up.

Take away fingers as rhyme progresses.
Continue with four, three, two, one, until . . .

Mother Owl said, "Hoo, hoo, hoo, hoo!"
And all the little owls came back, it's true!

—Adapted traditional rhyme

I'm a Little Brown Owl

I'm a little brown owl
In a tree.
I build my nest up high, you see.
All I do is work,
No time to play.
I hunt at night and sleep all day!

—Adapted traditional rhyme

Sung to the tune of "I'm a Little Teapot."
Use hands to indicate size.

Point up.

Shake head "no."
Put head on hands; pretend to sleep.

Owl Count

Counting owls is so much fun!
Here is owl number one.
The fun's begun, we're far from through.
Here is owl number two.
I see one now, up in that tree!
Here is owl number three.
The next one's standing by the door.
Here is owl number four.
Watch him swoop and watch him dive.
Here is owl number five.
This one's doing lots of tricks.
Here is owl number six.
Watch him soar straight up to heaven.
Here is owl number seven.
The next one's sitting on the gate.
Here is owl number eight.
The next one's fit and looking fine.
Here is owl number nine.
See him fly in from the glen.
Here is owl number ten.

—Barbara Scott

This is a perfect rhyme to do on the flannel or Velcro board with owl figures. It can just as easily be done on the fingers!

Five Little Owls

Five little owls on a dark, dark night,
With big round eyes, they're quite a sight.
The first little owl has a pointed nose.
The second little owl has claws for toes.
The third little owl has feathers on his back.
The fourth little owl is speckled gray and black.

Circle fingers around eyes; then hold up five fingers.
Beginning with thumb, point to each in succession.

The fifth little owl winks one big eye.
Then all the little owls let out a cry.

          —Barbara Scott

Say, "Hoo, hoo!"

At Night

At night when you have gone to bed,
And you are fast asleep,
The hoot owl flies and dines upon
Anything that creeps.
He may be looking for a mouse,
A rabbit or a frog.
But if there are none to be found,
There's lots of tasty bugs!

          —Barbara Scott

Put head on hands; pretend to sleep.
Flap arms.

Fingers make circles around eyes.
Say, "Ribbet."
Shrug shoulders.
Rub tummy.

Wise Old Owl

Wise old owl
In the tree,
Whoo-oo are you winking at?
Is it me?

          —Jean Warren

Wink eye.

Five Little Owls

This little owl has great, round eyes.
This little owl is of very small size.
This little owl can turn her head.
This little owl likes mice, she said.
This little owl flies all around,
And her wings make hardly a single sound.

          —Author unknown

Point to one finger at a time, or make five owl cutouts and use this as a flannel or Velcro board activity.

Little Owl

Little owl in the tree,
He is winking down at me.
As he winks all through the night,
Little owl is quite a sight!
Little owl in the tree,
He is hooting down at me.
As he hoots all through the night,
Little owl is quite a sight!

          —Jean Warren

Sung to the tune of "This Old Man."

Wink eye.

Make hooting sound.

Books to Share

Allen, Jonathan. 2006. *I'm Not Cute!* New York: Hyperion. ISBN: 978-0786837205.
———. 2007. *I'm Not Scared!* New York: Hyperion. ISBN: 978-0786837229.

Hopgood, Tim. 2009. *Wow! Said the Owl: A Book about Colors.* New York: Farrar, Straus, and Giroux. ISBN: 978-0374385187.

Manning, Mick. 2007. *Cock-a-Doodle-Hooooo!* Intercourse, PA: Good Books. ISBN: 978-1561485680.

Serfozo, Mary. 2007. *Whooo's There?* New York: Random House Books for Young Readers. ISBN: 978-0375840500.

Waddell, Martin. 1992. *Owl Babies.* Somerville, MA: Candlewick Press. ISBN: 978-1564021014. (My library owns this in big book format—great for group sharing!)

Musical Selections

"Owl Lullaby" from *Sharon, Lois, and Bram Sing A to Z.* Available: www.songsforteaching.com (accessed March 10, 2010).

"Snowy Owl" from *Debbie's Ditties: 2 Much Fun* by Debbie Clement. Available: www.rainbowswithinreach.com (accessed March 13, 2010).

"Two Little Owls" from *Burl Ives Sings Little White Duck.* ASIN: B000V97WQA.

"Up All Night" by Zach Burba. Available: www.songsforteaching.com (accessed March 10, 2010).

Sources

Bates, Clara Doty. 1881. *On the Tree Top.* Available: www.gutenberg.org/etext/24530 (accessed March 13, 2010).

Burnham, Maude. 1910. *Rhymes for Little Hands.* East Longmeadow, MA: Milton Bradley Company.

Flora, Sherrill. 1987. *The Preschool Calendar.* Minneapolis, MN: T.S. Denison & Co.

Lang, Andrew, ed. 1897. *The Nursery Rhyme Book.* London: Frederick Warne & Co.

McKinnon, Elizabeth, and Gayle Bittinger. 1994. *Busy Bees Fall: Fun for Two's and Three's.* Everett, WA: Warren Publishing House.

"Nursery Rhymes." The Mother Goose Pages. Available: www-personal.umich.edu/~pfa/dreamhouse/nursery/rhymes.html (accessed March 13, 2010).

Scott, Louise B. 1993. *Rhymes for Learning Times.* Minneapolis, MN: T.S. Denison & Co.

Totline Staff, comp. 1994. *1001 Rhymes and Fingerplays.* Everett, WA: Warren Publishing House.

Penguins

A plethora of penguin rhymes for your enjoyment!

Rhyme

Penguin, Penguin

Penguin, penguin, turn around.
Penguin, penguin, touch the ground.
Penguin, penguin, waddle in place.
Penguin, penguin, make a funny face!
Penguin, penguin, flap your wings.
Penguin, penguin, dance and sing!
Penguin, penguin, slide on ice.
Penguin, penguin, dressed so nice!

—Adapted traditional rhyme

Five Little Penguins

Five little penguins on the icy shore.
One dove in the water and now there are four.

Four little penguins standing near the sea.
One dove in the water and now there are three.
Three little penguins with nothing to do.
One dove into the water and now there are two.
Two little penguins, see them run!
One dove into the water and now there's just one.
One little penguin, not having any fun.
He dove into the water and now there are none!

—Barbara Scott

Five Little Penguins

Five little penguins sliding on the ice.
Five little penguins, isn't that nice!
One little penguin lost his balance and fell.
Now there are four little penguins . . . oh well.

—Barbara Scott

Little Penguins

Five little penguins standing on the shore.
One went to chase a fish, then there were four.
Four little penguins, two and two, you see.
One went to find some krill, then there were three.
Three little penguins wondering what to do.
One got scared off by a seal, then there were two.

Telling Guide

This rhyme can be sung to the tune of "Teddy Bear, Teddy Bear" or chanted.
Do actions as indicated in the rhyme.

Fix "coat" and "tie."

Begin rhyme with five fingers up.
Dive fingers toward floor as penguins dive.
Take away fingers as the rhyme progresses.

This is a great rhyme to use with small finger puppets!
Begin with five fingers up; slide fingers over palm of other hand.

Take away fingers as rhyme progresses.
Shrug shoulders. Continue for four, three, two, one.

This is another great rhyme to use with small finger puppets!
Begin rhyme with five fingers up.
Take away fingers as rhyme progresses.

Two little penguins looking for some fun.
One went to chase a polar bear, then there was one.
One little penguin, not having any fun.
He waddled off and now there are none!

—Barbara Scott

One Little Penguin, One

One little penguin, one.
Slipping and sliding, oh what fun!
Two little penguins, two.
All dressed up and looking at you!
Three little penguins, three.
Jumping and splashing in the sea!
Four little penguins, four.
Eat some fish and want some more!
Five little penguins, five.
It's so much fun to watch them dive!

—Barbara Scott

This rhyme also works well as a flannel or Velcro board activity!
Begin rhyme with one finger up.

Add fingers as rhyme progresses.

Penguins Jump!

Penguins jump, penguins dive,
OK, penguins, look alive!
Penguins waddle, penguins walk,
We don't have any time to talk!
Penguins slip, penguins slide,
Come on, penguins, show some pride!
Penguins snooze, penguins snore,
Wake right up and play some more!

—Barbara Scott

Jump fingers, then dive them to the floor.
Stand or sit at attention.
Waddle in place; walk in place.
Shake head "no."
Slip and slide side to side.
Puff out chest.
Put hands to side of head; pretend to sleep, then snore! / Wake up and wiggle all over.

One Little Penguin

One little penguin in the snow
Waddles fast and waddles slow,
Flaps his wings and calls, "Come on,
Join me in this winter fun!"

—Adapted from a song by Susan M. Dailey

Sung to the tune of "Five Little Ducks."
You can do this counting to five or ten!

Waddle.
Flap arms; put hand to mouth, calling.
Beckon with hand. Continue to whatever number you wish!

Waddle, Little Penguin

Waddle, little penguin,
Waddle to and fro.
Waddle in a circle
As over the ice you go!

—Barbara Scott

Waddle in place.
Waddle forward and back.
Waddle around in a circle.

Five Little Penguins

Five little penguins went out to play,
Over the ice cap far away.
Mother Penguin said, "Eep, eep, eep, eep!"
Four little penguins came back to sleep.
No little penguins went out to play,
Over the ice cap far away.
Mother Penguin said, "Eep, eep, eep, eep!"
And all the little penguins came back to sleep!

—Adapted traditional rhyme

Sung to the tune of "Six Little Ducks."
Begin rhyme with five fingers up.

Take away fingers as rhyme progresses.
Continue with four, three, two, one, then . . .

Five Little Penguins

Five little penguins were out for a sail.
The first one said, "Hey! Look at that whale!"
The second one said, "Wow! Look at him go!"
The third one said, "He's getting ready to blow."
The fourth one said, "I think his eyes are green."
The fifth one said, "Biggest whale I've ever seen!"

—Barbara Scott

Begin rhyme with five fingers up.
Beginning with thumb, point to each in succession.

Penguin Hokey Pokey

You put your right flipper in,
You pull your right flipper out.
You put your right flipper in and you shake it all about.
You do the penguin pokey and you waddle all around.
That's what it's all about!

ADDITIONAL VERSES:
. . . left flipper in.
. . . penguin foot in.
. . . other foot in.
. . . penguin beak in.
. . . penguin tail in.

—Adapted traditional rhyme

Sung to the tune of "The Hokey Pokey."
Do motions as indicated.

Waddle in a circle.
Clap.

The Itsy Bitsy Penguin

The itsy bitsy penguin
Lives where it's nice and cold.
He has two wings,
But cannot fly, I'm told.
He waddles around
On frozen land all day.
'Til he finds a group of friends
And they all go off to play.

—Adapted traditional rhyme

Sung to the tune of "The Eensy Weensy Spider."

Shiver.

Flap arms; shake head "no."
Waddle.

Put hands in the air; have them "talk" to each other.

See the Penguins

See the penguins
Dressed in white and black.
They waddle, waddle forward,
And they waddle, waddle back.
They flap their wings
As they move about.
They jump in the water,
Then they jump back out!

—Barbara Scott

Point to eyes.

Waddle forward.
Waddle backward.
Flap arms.

Jump forward.
Jump backward.

Sung to the tune of "The Ants Go Marching."

The Penguins Go Waddling

The penguins go waddling one by one,
Hurrah, hurrah.
The penguins go waddling one by one,
Hurrah, hurrah.
The penguins go waddling one by one.
The little one stops to look at the sun,
And they all go waddling down to the cave, to get out of
the snow.

ADDITIONAL VERSES:
The penguins go waddling two by two . . .
the little one stops to say, "Achoo!"
The penguins go waddling three by three . . .
the little one stops, a snack he sees.
The penguins go waddling four by four . . .
the little one stops to eat some more.
The penguins go waddling five by five . . .
the little one stops to take a dive.
The penguins go waddling six by six . . .
the little one stops to play with sticks.
The penguins go waddling seven by seven . . .
the little one stops to look to heaven.
The penguins go waddling eight by eight . . .
the little one stops a while to wait.
The penguins go waddling nine by nine . . .
the little one stops 'cause he fell behind.
The penguins go waddling ten by ten . . .
the little one stops to say, "The end!"

—Adapted traditional rhyme

Little Penguins

Little penguins, little penguins,
Diving here,
Diving there.

Sung to the tune of "Frère Jacques."

Motion of diving.

Catching fish and krill,	Motion of catching.
'Til you get your fill.	
Yum, yum, yum.	Rub tummy.
Yum, yum, yum.	

—Adapted traditional rhyme

Little Penguin

	Sung to the tune of "Alouette."
Little penguin,	Use hands to indicate size.
Funny little penguin.	
Little penguin,	
Dressed in black and white.	Point to clothes.
Fish is what you love to eat.	Rub tummy.
At catching them you can't be beat!	Shake head "no."
Love to eat, can't be beat . . . oh.	Shake head "no."
Little penguin,	Use hands to indicate size.
Funny little penguin.	
Little penguin,	
Dressed in black and white.	Point to clothes.

—Adapted traditional rhyme

Going on a Penguin Hunt!

We're going on a penguin hunt!	
We're going to catch a penguin to take to the zoo!	
Are you ready?	
Let's go!	Beckon; slap thighs as if walking.
Oh, look!	Put hand over eyes.
There's a huge snow bank.	Use hands to indicate size.
Can't go over it,	Shake head "no."
Can't go under it.	
Gotta shovel through it!	Make shoveling motions.
We're through!	
Let's go!	Slap thighs in walking motion.
Oh, look!	Put hand over eyes.
There's an icy river.	
Can't go over it,	Shake head "no."
Can't go under it.	
Gotta paddle through it.	Paddling motion. Say, "Watch out for the ice!"
We're across!	
Let's go!	Slap thighs in walking motion.
Oh, look!	Put hand over eyes.
I see an icy windstorm.	
Can't go over it,	Shake head "no."
Can't go under it.	
Gotta go through it.	Motion of grabbing coat to brace self, walking slowly. Say, "Brrrr! It's freezing!"
We're through!	

Let's go! — Slap thighs in walking motion.

Oh, look! — Put hand above eyes.

I see a cave!

Maybe there are some penguins there.

Let's go inside. — Walk slowly.

Wow . . . it's dark in here and I didn't bring my flashlight.

What's that in the corner? — Feel around.

It doesn't feel like a penguin. — Continue feeling around.

Penguins have feathers.

This doesn't have feathers. — Shake head "no."

It has fur . . . — Keep feeling.

. . . and claws, — Keep feeling.

. . . and a big nose and sharp teeth. — Keep feeling.

It's a POLAR BEAR!

RUN!!! — Slap thighs fast in running motion. Then do all motions again, only in opposite order: Grab coat and walk fast; say, "Brrrr! It's cold!" Paddle fast back across the icy river; say, "Watch out for the ice!" Shovel back through snow bank.

Whew! We made it! — Wipe brow.

I think we'll go looking for penguins another day! — Nod head "yes."

—Adapted traditional rhyme

The Penguin Is a Bird

Sung to the tune of "The Farmer in the Dell."

The penguin is a bird, — Flap arms.

The penguin is a bird.

Hi-ho the derry-o,

The penguin is a bird. — Continue to flap arms.

He has wings but can't fly, — Shake head "no."

He has wings but can't fly.

Hi-ho, the derry-o,

He has wings but can't fly. — Shake head "no."

—Adapted traditional rhyme

Five Little Penguins

Sung to the tune of "Michael Finnegan."

Five little penguins swimming in the ocean, — Begin rhyme with five fingers up.

Five little penguins swimming in the ocean.

Five little penguins swimming in the ocean,

Then one jumps right out! — Take away fingers as rhyme progresses. Continue four, three, two, one, until . . .

No little penguins swimming in the ocean, — Shake head "no."

No little penguins swimming in the ocean.

No little penguins swimming in the ocean,

They've all jumped right out!

—Adapted traditional rhyme

The Emperor

In the land of ice and snow,	Wiggle fingers downward.
Where temperatures drop to 80 below,	Hug self and shiver.
The Emperor penguin stands proud and tall.	Sit up straight.
The cold doesn't bother him at all!	Shake head "no."
The Emperor has spots around his ears.	Point to ears.
They are orange and yellow.	
He likes to eat fish and squid.	Motion of eating.
He's a very dapper fellow!	Nod head "yes."

—Barbara Scott

Plenty of Penguins

Ten little penguins standing in a line.	Begin rhyme with ten fingers up.
One waddled off and now there are nine.	Take away fingers as rhyme progresses.
Nine little penguins, trying hard to wait.	
Another waddled off and now there are eight.	
Eight little penguins looking toward heaven.	
Another waddled off and now there are seven.	
Seven little penguins doing silly tricks.	
Another waddled off and now there are six.	
Six little penguins ready to take a dive.	
Another waddled off and now there are five.	
Five little penguins standing on the shore.	
Another waddled off and now there are four.	
Four little penguins, cute as can be	
Another waddled off and now there are three.	
Three little penguins happy through and through.	
Another waddled off and now there are two.	
Two little penguins, not having so much fun.	
Another waddled off and now there's just one.	
One little penguin alone in the sun.	
He waddled off and now there are none.	

—Barbara Scott

Books to Share

Chester, Jonathan. 1997. *Splash! A Penguin Counting Book.* Berkeley, CA: Tricycle Press. ISBN: 978-1883672560.

Dunbar, Polly. 2007. *Penguin.* Somerville, MA: Candlewick Press. ISBN: 978-0763634049.

Gorbachev, Valerie. 2008. *Turtle's Penguin Day.* New York: Knopf Books for Young Readers. ISBN: 978-0375843747.

Kimmel, Elizabeth Cody. 2004. *My Penguin Osbert.* Somerville, MA: Candlewick Press. ISBN: 978-0763616991.

Lester, Helen. 2009. *Tacky Goes to Camp*. Boston: Houghton Mifflin Books for Children. ISBN: 978-0618988129. (This is part of a series of books about this fun character. He is one my favorites!)

Minor, Wendell. 2008. *If You Were a Penguin*. New York: Katherine Tegen Books. ISBN: 978-0061130977.

Musical Selections

"The Freeze" from *Kids in Motion* by Greg and Steve. ASIN: B00000AG63.

"I'm a Little Penguin," "Seven Penguins," "Five Little Penguins," "Penguin Poem," "Adelie Penguins," "Peter Peter Penguin," and "The Penguin Egg" from *Antarctica* by Mr. I. Available: www.songsforteaching.com (accessed March 10, 2010).

"Penguin Parade" from *Penguin Parade* by The Banana Slug String Band. Available: www.songsforteaching.com (accessed March 10, 2010).

"Penguin Parade," "Pondering Penguins," and "Penguin Ball" from *Computer Cat* by Donna Rhodenizer and Andy Duinker with The Relative Minors. Available: www.songsforteaching.com (accessed March 10, 2010).

"The Penguin Polka" from *Dance and Sing: The Best of Nick Jr.* ASIN: B00005Q3AT.

"Penguin's Tuxedo" from *(Almost) Two Much* by Nan Hoffman. Available: www.nanhoffman.com (accessed March 10, 2010).

Sources

Dailey, Susan M. 2007. *Sing a Song of Storytime*. New York: Neal-Schuman.

Pigs

Oink oink here, oink oink there, piggies are everywhere!

Rhyme | **Telling Guide**

Tom, Tom, the Piper's Son

Tom Tom, the Piper's son,
Stole a pig and away he run. — Make grabbing motion, then run in place.
The pig got eat. — Pretend to eat.
And Tom got beat. — Clap hands.
And he went crying down the street. — Hands to eyes, crying motions.

—Traditional rhyme

Five Little Pigs

The first little pig danced a merry, merry jig. — Begin rhyme with five fingers up.
The second little pig ate candy. — Beginning with thumb, point to each in succession.
The third little pig wore a blue and yellow wig.
The fourth little pig was dandy.
The fifth little pig never grew very big,
So they called him "Tiny Little Andy."

—From Mama Lisa's World of Children

This Little Pig

This little pig went to market, — Point to one finger at a time, beginning with the thumb.
This little pig stayed home,
This little pig had roast beef,
This little pig had none,
This little pig cried, "Wee, wee, wee,"
And ran all the way home.

—From Mama Lisa's World of Children

Two Mother Pigs

Two mother pigs lived in a pen, — Show thumbs.
Each had four babies and that made ten. — Show fingers and thumbs.
These four babies were black as night, — Hold one hand up, thumb in palm.
These four babies were black and white. — Hold other hand up, thumb in palm.
But all eight babies loved to play
And they rolled and rolled in the mud all day. — Roll hands over each other.
At night, with their mother, they curled up in a heap, — Make fists, palms up.
And squealed and squealed 'til they went to sleep.

—From *Let's Do Fingerplays*

To Market, To Market

To market, to market to buy a fat pig. — Either gallop around room or in place.
Home again, home again, jiggety-jig.
To market, to market to buy a fat hog.

Home again, home again, jiggety-jog.

—Traditional rhyme

Five Little Piggies

Five little piggies went out to play,
In the mud one summer day.
They rolled, and they rolled, and they rolled all day.
One little piggie rolled away,
And only four came back to play.

—Barbara Scott

Piggies in the Barnyard

Ten little piggies,
They live in the barnyard.
Ten little piggies
Standing in a row.
Ten little piggies
See the farmer coming.
Oink! Oink! Oink! Oink!
Watch them go!

—Barbara Scott

This Little Pig

This little pig eats corn and this little pig eats hay.
This little pig eats pizza every other day.
This little pig eats ice cream while shopping at the mall.
And this little pig was sleeping and had no lunch at all!

—Barbara Scott

Ten Little Piggies

Ten little piggies in the barn
Squealing as they play!
Ten little piggies in the barn.
Count them, if you may.
One, two, three . . . four, five, six . . . seven, eight, nine,
    ten piggies in the pigpen.
Ten little piggies in the barn.
Watch them run away!

—Barbara Scott

Five Little Pigs

"It's time for my piggies to go to bed,"
The great big mother piggy said.
"So I will count them first to see
If all my piggies came back to me.
One little piggie, two little piggies,
Three little piggies dear.

Begin rhyme with five fingers up.

Roll hands one over the other.
Take away fingers as rhyme progresses.
Repeat for four, three, two, one.

Sung to the tune of "Down by the Station."

Hold up ten fingers.

Hold all fingers straight up.

Put hand over eyes, watching.

Wiggle fingers, then hide them behind back.

Begin rhyme with five fingers up.
Starting with thumb, point to each in succession.

Sung to the tune of "Old McDonald."
Hold up ten fingers.
Say, "Oink, oink."

Hold up ten fingers.
Wiggle fingers, and then hide them behind back.

Clasp hands at side of head.

Hold up one hand; count fingers individually.

Four little piggies, five little piggies.

Yes, they're all here."   Nod head "yes."

                    —Traditional rhyme

If a Pig Wore a Wig

If a pig wore a wig,   Point to head.

What could we say?   Shrug shoulders.

Treat him as a gentleman,

And say "Good day."   Bow at waist.

If his tail chanced to fail   Move index finger in circular motion.

What could we do?   Shrug shoulders again.

Send him to the tailoress   Pretend to sew.

And get one new.   Make circular motion with index finger.

                    —Christina Rossetti

Jack Sprat's Pig

Jack Sprat's pig,

He was not very little,   Use hands to show small height.

Nor yet very big.   Move hands far apart to show tallness.

He was not very lean.   Move hands together to show skinny.

He was not very fat.   Move hands far apart to show width.

He'll do well for a grunt,   Cross arms in front of body; nod

Says little Jack Sprat.   head "yes."

                    —Traditional rhyme

Little Pig

Little pig, little pig,

Turn around.   Turn in place.

Little pig, little pig,

Roll on the ground.   Roll hands.

Little pig, little pig,

Please don't cry.   Shake head "no."

Little pig, little pig,

Wink one eye.   Wink.

Little pig, little pig,

Eat sweet corn.   Pretend to eat.

Little pig, little pig,

'Til the early morn.   Raise hands above head in circle for sun.

Little pig, little pig,

Hide out of sight.   Put hands over eyes.

Little pig, little pig,

Say goodnight!   Wave and say, "Goodnight."

                    —Barbara Scott

Five Little Pigs

Five little pigs ran around the barn floor.
One fell down and then there were four.
Four little pigs underneath the tree.
One fell asleep and then there were three.
Three little pigs eating sloppy stew.
One ran away and then there were two.
Two little pigs sitting in the sun.
One got sunburned and now there's just one.
One little pig standing all alone.
He trotted away and then there were none.

—Barbara Scott

Begin rhyme with five fingers up.
Take away fingers as rhyme progresses.

Books to Share

Bailey, Linda. 2007. *Goodnight, Sweet Pig.* Tonawanda, NY: Kids Can Press. ISBN: 978-1553378440.

DiPucchio, Kelly S. 2004. *Bed Hogs.* New York: Hyperion. ISBN: 978-0786818846.

Muntean, Michaela. 2006. *Do Not Open This Book.* New York: Scholastic. ISBN: 978-0439698399.

Numeroff, Laura. 2005. *If You Give a Pig a Party.* New York: HarperCollins. ISBN: 978-0060283261.

Saltzberg, Barney. 2009. *Cornelius P. Mud, Are You Ready for Baby?* Somerville, MA: Candlewick Press. ISBN: 978-0763635961. (This is part of a series of books by this author.)

Weeks, Sarah. 2005. *I'm a Pig.* New York: HarperCollins. ISBN: 978-0694010752.

Musical Selections

"Party Time in the Mud" from *We're on Our Way* by Hap Palmer. ASIN: B00000JXNG.

"Pig Rap" from *Animal Rock.* ASIN: B00005B6CG.

"Piggly Wiggly" from *Sing It! Say It! Stamp It! Sway It!* by Peter and Ellen Allard. Available: www.cdbaby.com (accessed March 13, 2010).

"Piggy Rap" from *Debbie's Ditties: 2 Much Fun* by Debbie Clement. Available: www.rainbowswithinreach.com (accessed March 13, 2010).

"This Little Pig" from *Rhymin' to the Beat*, vol. 2, by Jack Hartman and Friends. ASIN: B0026EIIRU.

"This Little Piggy" from *Plant a Little Seed* by Prairie Orchid. ASIN: B001R0KB6U.

Sources

Grayson, Marion. 1962. *Let's Do Fingerplays.* Fairfield, CT: R.B. Luce.

Mama Lisa's World of Children & International Culture. Available: www.mamalisa.com (accessed March 4, 2010).

Rossetti, Christina. 1872. *Sing-Song.* New York: MacMillan and Company.

Sinclair, Patti, Tami Chumbley, Geri Cupery, Diane Findlay, and Jerri J. Heid. 2004. "Discover New Trails @ Your Library." *Collaborative Summer Library Program Manual.* Mason City, IA: Collaborative Summer Library Program.

Pizza to Scarecrows

Pizza

Enjoy these rhymes about a treat we all love to eat!

Rhyme	Telling Guide
### Hand-Me-Down Food	
Five leftover pizza pieces	Hold up one hand.
From the night before.	
Dad came and ate one,	
Gulp!	
And then there were . . .	Lower one finger.
Four leftover pizza pieces,	
One with anchovies.	
Mom came and ate one,	
Gulp!	
And then there were . . .	Lower another finger.
Three leftover pizza pieces,	
Cheese like sticky glue.	
Brother came and ate one,	
Gulp!	
And then there were . . .	Lower another finger.
Two leftover pizza pieces,	
Not having any fun.	
Sister came to take one,	
Gulp!	
And then there was . . .	Lower another finger.
One leftover pizza piece,	Hold one finger up.
But I don't wanna be a hog,	
So I went and got it,	
And split it with the dog!	Lower last finger.
Arf!	

— Jan Irving and Robin Currie

### Pizza	*Sung to the tune of "Bingo."*
I had a pizza all my own	
And all of it was mine-o.	
P-I-Z-Z-A, P-I-Z-Z-A, P-I-Z-Z-A,	
And all of it was mine-o!	
I had a pizza that I shared.	
One piece went to my brothers.	
P-I-Z-Z—, P-I-Z-Z—, P-I-Z-Z-,	Clap on the A.
But all the rest of it was mine-o!	
I had a pizza that I shared.	
One piece went to my sister.	

P-I-Z—, P-I-Z—, P-I-Z—,
But all the rest of it was mine-o!
I had a pizza that I shared.
One piece went to my mother.
P-I—, P-I—, P-I—,
But all the rest of it was mine-o!
I had a pizza that I shared.
One piece went to my father.
P—, P—, P—,
But all the rest of it was mine-o!
I had a pizza that I shared.
One piece is all I'm left-o,
And now that piece is gone-o!

—Jan Irving and Robin Currie

Clap on the Z and A.

Clap on the Z, Z, and A.

Clap on the I, Z, Z, and A.

Clap on all letters for three rounds.

Pizza, Pizza

Pizza, pizza, what a treat!
Pizza, pizza, good to eat!
Pizza, pizza, round and chewy!
Pizza, pizza, nice and gooey!
Pizza, pizza, toss that dough!
Pizza, pizza, don't be slow!
Pizza, pizza, with lots of cheese!
Give me pizza, if you please!

—Barbara Scott

Clap.
Rub tummy.
Arms make circle.
Fingers make motions of pulling cheese.
Pretend to toss dough up and catch.
Shake finger, admonishingly.
Hands make motion of sprinkling cheese.
Point to self.

I Love Pizza

CHORUS:
I love pizza, yummy, yummy pizza.
I love pizza. I really do.
I love pizza, yummy, yummy pizza.
I love pizza. Do you love it, too?

VERSE 1:
Make the dough and spread it thin.
Toss it up and make it spin.
Spread it thin. Make it spin . . . oh.
CHORUS

VERSE 2:
Top with sausage, sauce, and cheese,
Mushrooms, peppers, if you please.
Sauce and cheese, pepper please . . . oh.
CHORUS

Sung to the tune of "Alouette."

Rub stomach.
Nod head "yes."
Rub stomach.
Point outward.

Pretend to mix and roll dough.
Twist hand.

Pretend to sprinkle toppings around.

VERSE 3:
Any time of any day,
"I want pizza" is what I say.
Any time, any day . . . oh.
CHORUS

—Susan M. Dailey

Pretend to point to watch.
Point to self.

Making Pizza

Stretch the dough.
Spread the sauce.
Sprinkle on the cheese.
Cook the pizza.
Cut the pizza.
I'll have a big slice please!

—Gail Benton

Use both hands to stretch dough.
Use open hand to spread sauce.
Wiggle fingers to sprinkle cheese.
Use open hand palm up to slide pizza in oven. / Pretend to cut pizza.
Hold hand out, palm up.

Five Little Pizzas

Five little pizzas in the pizza shop.
The first little pizza had mushrooms on top.
The second little pizza was topped with lots of cheese.
The third little pizza was as plain as you please.
The fourth little pizza had lots of pepperoni.
But the fifth little pizza tasted just like macaroni!
Five little pizzas in the pizza shop,
Where making yummy pizzas
Never, ever stops!

—Barbara Scott

Begin rhyme with five fingers up.
Starting with thumb, point to each in succession.

Shake head "no."

Five Yummy Pizzas

Five yummy pizzas with toppings galore.
One of them got eaten and then there were four.
Four yummy pizzas, the best you'll ever see.
One of them got eaten and then there were three.
Three yummy pizzas with sticky, cheesy goo.
Another one got eaten and then there were two.
Two yummy pizzas with sauce that likes to run.
Another one got eaten and then there was one.
One yummy pizza, nice and brown and done.
The last one got eaten and now there are none!

—Barbara Scott

Begin rhyme with five fingers up.
Take away fingers as rhyme progresses.

Please, Mr. Pizza Man

Please, Mr. Pizza Man,
Spinning pizza dough.
Make me a pizza,
A pizza to go!
Top it with sauce,
And lots of meat!
Sprinkle on the cheese.
The taste can't be beat!

Motion of throwing and spinning dough overhead.

Motion of pouring sauce.
Motion of placing meat.
Motion of sprinkling cheese.
Rub tummy.

—Barbara Scott

Books to Share

Boniface, William. 2000. *What Do You Want on Your Pizza?* New York: Price, Stern, Sloan. ISBN: 978-0843174731.
Castaldo, Nancy. 2005. *Pizza for the Queen.* New York: Holiday House. ISBN: 978-0823418657.
Dobson, Christina. 2003. *Pizza Counting.* Watertown, MA: Charlesbridge Publishing. ISBN: 978-0881063387.
Morgan, Mary. 2008. *Dragon Pizzeria.* New York: Knopf Books for Young Readers. ISBN: 978-0375823091.
Sturges, Philemon. 1999. *The Little Red Hen Makes a Pizza.* New York: Dutton Juvenile. ISBN: 978-0525459538
Wellington, Monica. 2006. *Pizza at Sally's.* New York: Dutton Juvenile, ISBN: 978-0525477150.

Musical Selections

"Fraction Pizza" from *Totally Math* by Dr. Jean. ASIN: B000JELRJU.
"I Am a Pizza" from *10 Carrot Diamond* by Charlotte Diamond. ASIN: B0000683V4.
"Make a Pizza" from *Circle Time Activities* by Georgiana Stewart. ASIN: B000231GNU.
"Make a Pizza Pie" from *Sing Along and Learn* by Ken Shelton. ISBN: 978-0439665391 (book and CD set).
"Pizza, Pizza, Pizza" from *Jump and Jive with Hi-5.* ASIN: B0002006X0. (A songlet on this CD, but cute nonetheless!)
"Pizza Pizzazz" from *Pizza Pizzazz* by Peter and Ellen Allard. ASIN: B000GETZH4.

Sources

Benton, Gail, and Trisha Waichulaitis. 2003. *Ready-to-Go Storytimes: Fingerplays, Scripts, Patterns, Music, and More.* New York: Neal-Schuman.
Dailey, Susan M. 2001. *A Storytime Year.* New York: Neal-Schuman.
Irving, Jan, and Robin Currie. 1986. *Mudlicious: Stories and Activities Featuring Food for Preschool Children.* Santa Barbara, CA: Libraries Unlimited.
———. 1994. *Second Helpings: Books and Activities about Food.* Santa Barbara, CA: Teacher Ideas Press.

Popcorn

Hopping, popping, it's a yummy treat!

Rhyme	**Telling Guide**
Popcorn	
Pop! Pop! Pop!	Clap hands.
Pour the corn into the pot.	
Pop! Pop! Pop!	Clap hands.
Take and shake it 'til it's hot.	
Pop! Pop! Pop!	Clap hands.
Lift the lid—what have we got?	
Pop! Pop! Pop!	Clap hands.
POPCORN!	Say loudly.
—From *Busy Fingers, Growing Minds*	
Popcorn	
Open the door.	Pretend to pull door open.
Put the bag in.	Lay one hand out, palm up.
Then push the button.	Pretend to push.
Watch it spin.	Move finger in circle.
Listen and soon	Put hand to ear.
You'll hear a pop.	Clap hands on "pop."
Pop . . .	Say "pop" many times, faster and faster, then say "stop."
. . . Pop, stop!	Hold up one hand, palm out.
Smells so delicious.	Sniff air.
Yummy to eat.	Pretend to put kernels in mouth and gulp.
Say, do you know	Point to kids.
This tasty treat?	Rub stomach.
"It's popcorn!"	Speak this line.
—Adapted from a song by Susan M. Dailey	
Yummy Popcorn	
Yummy popcorn,	
What a treat!	Clap three times.
Fluffy and so	
Good to eat!	Rub tummy.
Pour the kernels in the pot.	Pouring motion.
Can you wait for the pop?	
I know you can!	Nod head "yes."
There it goes!	
Pop! Pop! Pop! Pop!	Clap on each "pop."
The yummy fun just never stops!	Shake head "no."
—Barbara Scott	

Popcorn, Popcorn

Popcorn, popcorn
In the pot.
Heat it 'til
It's nice and hot!
See it hop!
Hear it pop!
Popcorn, popcorn.
Pop! Pop! Pop!

—Barbara Scott

Clap three times.
Motion of turning on stove burner.

Point to eyes.
Point to ears.

Clap three times.

Popcorn, Popcorn

Popcorn, popcorn,

Pop around!
Popcorn, popcorn,
Pop to the ground.
Popcorn, popcorn,
Pop up high.
Popcorn, popcorn,
Reach for the sky!
Popcorn, popcorn,
Smells so good!
Popcorn, popcorn,
Yummy food.
Popcorn, popcorn,
Pop, pop, pop!
Popcorn, popcorn,
Get ready to . . . STOP!

—Adapted traditional rhyme

This rhyme can be sung to the tune of "Teddy Bear, Teddy Bear" or chanted. Begin the rhyme with children standing up.
Jump around.

Squat down.

Stand up.

Reach up high.

Point to nose.

Rub tummy.

Jump around and continue jumping.

Hold up hand, palm out; stop jumping.

Popping Popcorn

Popping popcorn,
Popping popcorn,
In the pot
In the pot.
Watch it go a' hopping.
Hear it go a' popping.
Pop! Pop! Pop!
Pop! Pop! Pop!

—Adapted traditional rhyme

Sung to the tune of "Frère Jacques."
Open and close hands.

Make circle in front of body with hands.

Point to eyes.
Point to ears.
Clap three times.
Clap three times.

Five Popcorn Kernels

Five popcorn kernels sitting in a pot.
The first one said, "It's getting hot."
The second said, "I feel the heat."

Begin this rhyme with five fingers up.
Starting with thumb, point to each in succession.

The third one said, "We're a tasty treat."
The fourth one said, "Now I'm big and white."
The fifth one said, "Are you ready to take a bite?"
—Barbara Scott

At the end of this rhyme, ask children: "Would you like to eat that popcorn?" The answer is likely to be a resounding "YES"!

Five Pieces of Popcorn

Five pieces of popcorn and not one more.
Daddy came and ate one and now there are four.
Four pieces of popcorn, quite yummy, you see.
Mommy came and ate one and now there are three.
Three pieces of popcorn, just a tasty few.
My sister came and ate one and now there are two.
Two pieces of popcorn and we're almost done.
My brother came and ate one and now there's just one.
One piece of popcorn, missing all the fun.
I came and ate it and now there are none.
—Barbara Scott

Begin this rhyme with five fingers up.
Take away fingers as rhyme progresses.

Popcorn

I'm a bunch of popcorn in a pot.
I wiggle around when the heat's turned up.
I sizzle and I pop, and then I'm done.
Popping corn is so much fun!
—Barbara Scott

Sung to the tune of "I'm a Little Teapot."
Make circle in front of body with hands.
Wiggle!
Clap on the word "pop."
Clap three times on "so much fun."

Pop! Pop! Pop!

Pop! Pop! Pop!
Pop! Pop! Pop!
Popcorn in the pan.
Popping here and popping there,
Watch it if you can!
Pop! Pop! Pop!
Pop! Pop! Pop!
Listen now . . . it's stopped.
Look closely, right before our eyes
The popcorn kernels popped!
—Adapted traditional rhyme

Sung to the tune of "Jingle Bells."
Open and close left hand, then right; repeat.
Make circle in front of body with hands.
Point one direction, then the other.
Point to eyes.
Open and close left hand, then right; repeat.
Point to ears.
Point to eyes.

I Love Popcorn

I love popcorn,
I love popcorn!
Yes, I do!
Yes, I do!
I love to watch it hopping.

Sung to the tune of "Frère Jacques."
Place one hand over heart.
Place other hand over heart.
Nod head "yes."

Point to eyes.

I love to hear it popping.

Point to ears.

Yum, yum yum!

Rub tummy.

Yum, yum, yum!

— Adapted traditional rhyme

If You Want to Pop Some Popcorn

Sung to the tune of "If You're Happy and You Know It."

If you want to pop some popcorn,

Clap your hands.

Clap, clap.

If you want to pop some popcorn,

Clap your hands.

Clap, clap.

If you really want to pop, then never ever stop!

If you want to pop some popcorn,

Clap your hands.

Clap, clap.

ADDITIONAL VERSES:

. . . stomp your feet.

Stomp, stomp.

. . . nod your head.

Nod head.

. . . shout "Hooray!"

Shout and pump fist in the air.

. . . do all four!

Clap, stomp, nod, and shout.

— Adapted traditional rhyme

Pop and Spin

Little yellow kernels,

Indicate size with fingers.

Sitting in the pot.

Make circle with hands.

Waiting for the oil

To get hot.

Motion of turning knob on stove.

Hear that sizzling?

Point to ears.

The fun will soon begin!

Watch the little kernels

Pop and spin!

On "pop," clap; on "spin," circle one finger around in the air.

— Barbara Scott

Popping Popcorn

Sung to the tune of "Old McDonald."

Popping popcorn is such fun,

I'd do it every day.

Move hands to show expanse.

A treat to eat when we're done.

It's not work, it's play!

Shake head "no."

With a pop, pop here,

Clap on all "pops."

And a pop, pop there.

Here a pop, there a pop,

Everywhere a pop, pop!

Popcorn popping is such fun,

I'd do it every day!

Move hands to show expanse.

— Adapted traditional rhyme

Five Little Kernels

Five little kernels
Dancing in the pot.
The oil got hot and one went POP!
No little kernels
Dancing in the pot.
That's it, now it's time to stop!

—Barbara Scott

Begin this rhyme with five fingers up.

Wiggle fingers.

Clap on the word "pop." Take away fingers as rhyme progresses. Continue with four, three, two, one, until . . .

Put hand out in "stop" motion.

Let's Pretend

Let's pretend we're popcorn kernels.
Ready? Let's begin!
The oil is waiting in the pot.
C'mon, let's jump in!
Can you feel it heating up?
It's beginning to get hot.
Sizzle, sizzle, sizzle.
Sizzle 'til you pop!

—Barbara Scott

Begin this rhyme standing up.

Beckon, then crouch on the floor.

Fan self.

Slowly rise up from crouched position.

Jump!

Here's a Bowl of Popcorn

Here's a bowl of popcorn,
Big and fluffy white!
Scoop it up with your hands
And take a great, big bite!

—Barbara Scott

Make circle in front of body with hands.

Scooping motion.

Pretend to eat and chew.

Books to Share

Asch, Frank. 1992. *Popcorn: A Frank Asch Bear Story*. New York: Parent's Magazine Press. ISBN: 978-0440847434. (This Trumpet Book Club book is probably my favorite popcorn book of all time!)
Low, Alice. 1994. *The Popcorn Shop*. New York: Scholastic. ISBN: 978-0590471213.
Moran, Alex. 2003. *Popcorn*. A Green Light Reader. Orlando, FL: Houghton Mifflin Harcourt. ISBN: 978-0152048211.
Thayer, Jane. 1989. *The Popcorn Dragon*. New York: HarperCollins. ISBN: 978-0688083403.

Musical Selections

"Popcorn" from *The Corner Grocery Store and Other Songs* by Raffi. ASIN: B0000003HA.
"Popcorn" from *We All Live Together*, vol. 2, by Greg and Steve. ASIN: B00000AG62.
"Popcorn Calling Me" from *Buzz Buzz* by Laurie Berkner. ASIN: B00004S36S.
"Popcorn Chant" from *Sing It! Say It! Dance It! Sway It!*, vol.1, by Peter and Ellen Allard. Available: www.cdbaby.com (accessed March 13, 2010).
"Popcorn Chant" from *Stinky Cake* by Carole Peterson. ASIN: B000CAKRTW.
"Popcorn Party" from *Silly Willy Moves through the ABCs* by Brenda Colgate. ASIN: B00004TVSJ.

Sources

Dailey, Susan M. 2007. *Sing a Song of Storytime*. New York: Neal-Schuman.
Redleaf, Rhonda. 1983. *Busy Fingers, Growing Minds*. St. Paul, MN: Redleaf Press.

Rain, Puddles, Umbrellas, and Rainbows
This is a great theme for the month of April (with its showers) or for spring in general!

Rhyme	Telling Guide
### Pitter-Pat	
Pitter-pat, pitter-pat, oh so many hours,	Let fingers patter on floor, table, hand, etc.
Although it keeps me in the house,	
It's very good for flowers.	Cup hands and extend slowly upward.
—From *Let's Do Fingerplays*	
### Raindrops	
Rain is falling down, rain is falling down.	Raise arms; flutter fingers down.
Pitter-patter, pitter-patter,	Tap fingers on floor or palm of hand.
Rain is falling down.	
—From *Let's Do Fingerplays*	
### The Rain Is Falling Everywhere	
The rain is falling everywhere.	Hold arms overhead; wiggle fingers down into squatting position.
The flowers start to grow,	Stand slowly, raising hands with palms together.
And later when the sun comes out,	Circle arms overhead, fingertips touching.
Then we can see a rainbow.	Let arms fall open in an arc.
—Traditional rhyme	
### Rain on the Green Grass	
Rain on the green grass,	Put ten fingers up, spread out to represent grass. / Raise arms over head to represent branches.
Rain on the tree,	
Rain on the housetop,	Put hands overhead, fingertips touching.
But not upon me!	Point to self and shake head "no."
—Traditional rhyme	
### Rain House	
I've got a little house to keep me dry,	Point two hands over head.
When raindrops fall down from the sky.	Wiggle fingers down as rain falls.
My umbrella is just the thing	Point two hands over head.
To hide me from the rains of spring.	Pull arms together; move down to hide face.
—Jan Irving	
### Rain, Rain, Go to Spain	
Rain, rain, go to Spain.	Flutter fingers down.
Never show your face again.	Shake head "no."
—Traditional rhyme	

Rain, Rain Falling Down

Rain, rain falling down,
Landing on the ground.
What a lovely sound you make
Splashing on the ground.

—Susan L. Moon

Sung to the tune of "Row, Row, Row Your Boat."
Wiggle fingers downward.
Move arms out to sides.

Wiggle fingers up and down.

Raindrops

Ten little raindrops dancing on the walk,
Pitter patter, pitter patter, that's the way they talk.
Out comes the yellow sun shining in the sky,
And away all the raindrops fly, fly, fly.

—Traditional rhyme

Hold up ten fingers.
Wiggle fingers in the air.
Make large circle above head with arms.
Hide fingers behind back.

Rain, Rain

Rain, rain falling down,
Falling on the ground.
Pitter-patter, pitter-patter,
What a lovely sound!

—Susan A. Miller

Flutter fingers downward.

Cup hand behind ear.

Rainbow Over the Waterfall

Rainbow over the waterfall,
Rainbow over the tree,
Rainbow over the mountains,
Rainbow over the sea.
Rainbow over the flowers,
Rainbow over the bee,
Rainbow over the dancers,
Rainbow over me!

—Jean Warren

Form arc, then dip hands downward.
Form arc, then a tree shape, with hands.
Form arc, then draw mountains in air.
Form arc, then rock hands like waves.
Form arc, then cup hands for flower.
Form arc, then fly finger around.
Form arc, then sway body.
Form arc, then point to self.

One Misty, Moisty Morning

One misty, moisty morning,
When cloudy was the weather,
There I met an old man,
All clothed in leather.
All clothed in leather,
With a cap under his chin.
How do you do and how do you do,
And how do you do again.

—Traditional rhyme

Point up to sky.
Put hand on back; hunch over.
Point to clothes.

Point under chin.
Shake hands with those around.
Continue to shake hands.

If All Were Rain

If all were rain and never sun,

No bow could span the hill.

Flutter fingers down for rain; make large circle over head for sun.
Move index finger from left to right in the air, making a rainbow arch.

If all were sun and never rain,

There'd be no rainbow still.

—Christina G. Rossetti

Raise arms over head for sun; fingers flutter down again for rain.
Shake head "no."

Rain, Rain Go Away

Rain, rain, go away.
Come again another day.
Little Johnny wants to play.

—Traditional rhyme

Shake hands to both sides, dismissing.
Nod head "yes."
Hold left palm out; index and middle fingers of right hand jump and run on it.

The Rain

The rain is falling all around.
It falls on field and tree.

It rains on the umbrella here,

And on the ships at sea.

—Robert L. Stevenson

Flutter fingers down.
Put palm out in front for field; hands over head for tree branches
Put hands over head, fingertips together for umbrella.
Make wave motion with hand and arm.

Rain in Spring

So soft and gentle falls the rain,
You cannot hear it on the pane;
For if it came in pelting showers,
'Twould hurt the budding leaves and flowers.

—Gabriel Setoun

Flutter fingers down.
Shake head "no."
Pound fists on legs.
Put hands in front, palms together; move palms apart for opening flower.

It's Raining, It's Pouring

It's raining, it's pouring,
The old man is snoring.
He went to bed,
And he bumped his head,
And he couldn't get up in the morning!

—Traditional rhyme

Flutter fingers down.
Put hands to side of head; pretend to sleep, and snore!
Tap top of head with fist.
Shake head "no."

Counting Raindrops

This is a fun rhyme to do with a flannel or Velcro board. Do the raindrop shapes in different colors! In addition to the raindrop shapes, have a numeral on each to reinforce numbers.
Begin rhyme with one finger up.
Add fingers as rhyme progresses.

Raindrop one and raindrop two,
You see me and I see you!
Raindrop three and raindrop four,
Are you knocking at my door?
Raindrop five and raindrop six,
Are you playing lots of tricks?
Raindrop seven and raindrop eight,
Falling on my garden gate.
Raindrop nine and raindrop ten,
Now it's time to begin again!

—Barbara Scott

A Rainy Day

"Rain, rain, go away!"	Flutter fingers down.
The children at the window say.	
Splash, splash through	Slap hands on legs.
Many a pool.	
The small folk make	Walk index and middle finger of right hand on palm of left for children.
Their way to school.	
"Hip! Hip! Hurrah!" cries Jack.	Pump fist in the air.
And all the ducklings	Make right hand head of duck; open fingers to speak.
Answer, "Quack!"	

—Traditional rhyme

Little Raindrops

Oh, where do you come from,	Put index finger on cheek, wondering.
You little drops of rain,	
Pitter-patter, pitter-patter,	Drum fingers on legs or floor.
Down the window pane?	
They won't let me walk,	Shake head "no" throughout next lines.
They won't let me play,	
And they won't let me go	
Out of doors at all today.	
They put away my playthings	Motion of putting things away.
Because I broke them all,	
And then they locked up all my bricks,	Motion of turning a key in a lock.
And took away my ball.	
Tell me, little raindrops,	Put index finger on cheek, wondering.
Is that the way you play,	
Pitter-patter, pitter-patter,	Drum fingers on legs or floor.
All the rainy day?	
They say I'm very naughty,	Shake index finger, admonishing.
But I've nothing else to do,	Put hands on either side of head.
But sit here at the window;	Pretend to look out window.
I should like to play with you.	
The little raindrops cannot speak,	Shake head "no."
But "Pitter-pitter-pat"	
Means "We can play on this side;	Point one way.
Why can't you play on that?"	Point the opposite way.

—Traditional rhyme

Millions of Rain Drops

Millions of massive rain drops	Wiggle fingers down.
Have fallen all around;	
They have danced on the housetops,	Point to the sky.
They have hidden in the ground.	Point to the ground.

They were liquid-like musicians,
With anything for keys,
Beating tunes upon the windows,
Keeping time upon the trees.

—Traditional rhyme

Rainwear

It's raining, it's pouring.
The puddles are now forming.
I pulled on my boots
And ran hot foot
To jump in the puddles this morning.
It's raining, it's pouring.
This umbrella is so boring,
When I hold it up high.
But it drips down my back
When it's pouring.

—Carolyn N. Cullum

The Rain Comes Down

The rain comes down,

The flowers grow up.

The rain comes down,
The umbrellas go up.
The rain comes down,
And we all dress up in
Boots, coat, and rain cap.

—Carolyn N. Cullum

Storm

Thunder booms,
Lightning bolts flash.
A storm is coming,
So inside I'll dash.

—Susan M. Dailey

The Raindrops

When the flowers are thirsty
And the grass is dry,
Merry little raindrops
Tumble from the sky.
All around they patter,
In their happy play,

Pretend to "play" piano.

Put arms up for branches; sway back and forth in time.

Sung to the tune of "It's Raining, It's Pouring."
Flutter fingers downward like rain.

Pull on boots.

Jump into puddles.
Flutter fingers like rain.
Hold up umbrella.

Sung to the tune of "The Mulberry Bush."

Fingers float down like rain.
Push one hand through circle of other hand, pantomiming flower growing.
Fingers float down like rain.
Open the umbrella.
Fingers float down like rain.

Put on each piece of clothing.

Stomp foot on ground.
Make zigzag motion with hand.
Place hand over eyes, looking around.
Slap hands on thighs quickly.

Put hands together at wrists, cupped to resemble flower.
Hold up ten fingers in front.

Wiggle fingers in a downward motion.

Wiggle fingers all around.

'Til some little sunbeams
Chase them all away!

Make circle above head with hands.
Wiggle fingers up.

— Maude Burnham

Little Raindrops

Oh, where do you come from,
You little drops of rain,
Pitter patter, pitter patter,
Down the window pane?
They won't let me walk,
And they won't let me play,
And they won't let me go
Out of doors at all today.
They put away my playthings
Because I broke them all.
And then they locked up all my bricks
And took away my ball.
Tell me, little raindrops,
Is that the way you play,
Pitter patter, pitter patter
All the rainy day?
They say I'm very naughty
But I've nothing else to do
But sit here at the window.
I should like to play with you.
The little raindrops cannot speak
But "Pitter, patter pat"
Means "We can play on this side;
Why can't you play on that?"

Flutter fingers down.

Walk fingers of one hand on the opposite hand.
Shake head "no."

Action of putting things away.

Motion of turning a key in a lock.
Make circle with hands.

Wiggle fingers down.

Shake head "no."
Rest hand on fist.

Shake head "no."

Shrug shoulders.

— Mrs. Hawkshaw

Rainbow Colors

Rainbow purple, rainbow blue,
Rainbow green and yellow too.
Rainbow orange, rainbow red,
Rainbow smiling overhead.
Come and count the colors with me,
How many colors do you see?
One, two, three, up to green,
Four, five, six colors can be seen.

Count on fingers as the colors are mentioned in this rhyme. This can also be sung to the tune of "Hush, Little Baby."

Point to smile.

— Jean Warren

A Rainbow Gay

From big gray clouds
The raindrops fell,
Drip, drip, drip, one day,
Until the sunlight
Changed them all
Into a rainbow gay.

—Adapted traditional rhyme

Flutter fingers downward.

Form arc above head with arms.

Five Little Umbrellas

Five little umbrellas were waiting by the door.
Dad took the red one and then there were four.
Four little umbrellas by the hall tree.
Mom took the purple one and then there were three.
Three little umbrellas, one of them is blue.
My brother took that one and then there were two.
Two little umbrellas, our rhyme is almost done.
My sister took the yellow one and now there's just one.
One little umbrella, a lonely orange one.
I took that umbrella and now there are none.

—Barbara Scott

This is a great rhyme to do on your flannel or Velcro board with umbrellas in the colors mentioned.
Begin this rhyme with five fingers up.
Take away fingers as rhyme progresses.

I Am an Umbrella

I am an umbrella,
Watch me now.
I can do a trick,
I'll show you how.
When I open up
I make a way
For you to be dry
On a rainy day!

—Adapted traditional rhyme

Sung to the tune of "I'm a Little Teapot."
Stand straight, arms down at sides.

Bring arms up on either side.

Point to children.
Wiggle fingers in the air for rain.

This Is the Way We Walk in the Rain

This is the way we walk in the rain,
Walk in the rain, walk in the rain.
This is the way we walk in the rain,
With our big umbrella.
This is the way we splash in the rain,
Splash in the rain, splash in the rain.
This is the way we splash in the rain,
With our big umbrella.
This is the way we dance in the rain,

Sung to the tune of "The Mulberry Bush."
Motion of walking.

Put hands over head, fingertips touching. / Pretend to splash.

Put hands over head, fingertips touching. / Motion of dancing.

Dance in the rain, dance in the rain.
This is the way we dance in the rain,
With our big umbrella.

Put hands over head, fingertips touching.

—Adapted traditional rhyme

Rain Is Falling

Sung to the tune of "Frère Jacques."

Rain is falling,
Rain is falling,

Wiggle fingers in the air.

From the sky,
From the sky.

Point up.

Hand me my umbrella,
Hand me my umbrella.

Make umbrella over head with arms, fingertips touching.

Now I'm dry,
Now I'm dry.

Nod head "yes."

—Adapted traditional rhyme

Rainy

Sung to the tune of "Bingo." Do it as the original, taking away letters and replacing them with claps on verses. It's also a great rhyme to do with a hand mitt or with the flannel or Velcro board!

I carry my umbrella when rainy is the weather.
R-A-I-N-Y,
R-A-I-N-Y,
R-A-I-N-Y,
When rainy is the weather!

—Adapted traditional rhyme

Rain Is Falling

Sung to the tune of "London Bridge."

Rain is falling to the ground,
To the ground, to the ground.

Wiggle fingers from up to down.

Rain is falling to the ground.
See it rain!

Point to eyes.

Pitter pat the rain comes down,
Rain comes down, rain comes down.

Pat thighs in rhythm to the words "pitter pat."

Pitter pat the rain comes down.
See it rain!

—Adapted traditional rhyme

If You Have a Red Umbrella

Sung to the tune of "If You're Happy and You Know It." Have umbrellas done up ahead of time in all different colors, several of each. You may wish to laminate them for durability. When the color is mentioned in the song, have children hold up their umbrellas!

If you have a red umbrella, hold it up.
If you have a red umbrella, hold it up.
If you have one that is red,
Hold it high above your head.
If you have a red umbrella, hold it up.

Continue with other colors.

—Adapted traditional rhyme

I Have an Umbrella

I see the clouds.

Point to eyes.

I hear the thunder.

Point to ears.

Good thing I have an umbrella
That I can stand under!

—Barbara Scott

Put hands over head, fingertips touching.

Books to Share

Bullock, Kathleen. 1989. *It Chanced to Rain.* New York: Simon & Schuster Children's Publishing. ISBN: 978-0671660055.
Gorbachev, Valeri. 2002. *One Rainy Day.* New York: Philomel. ISBN: 978-0399236280.
Hest, Amy. 1999. *In the Rain with Baby Duck.* Somerville, MA: Candlewick Press. ISBN: 978-0763606978.
Lewison, Wendy C. 2004. *Raindrop, Plop!* New York: Viking Juvenile. ISBN: 978-0670059508.
London, Jonathan. 1997. *Puddles.* New York: Viking Juvenile. ISBN: 978-0670872183.
Wells, Rosemary. 2004. *Ruby's Rainy Day.* New York: Grosset & Dunlap. ISBN: 978-0448431840.

Musical Selections

"If All the Raindrops" from *Barney's Greatest Hits: The Early Years.* ASIN: B00004W55I.
"Leaky Umbrella" from *Jim Gill Sings The Sneezing Song and Other Contagious Rhymes.* Available: www.jimgill.com (accessed March 13, 2010).
"Over the Rainbow" from *Musical Scarves and Activities.* ASIN: B0001AC3KO.
"Polka Dot Umbrella" from *Pop Goes the Octopus* by Oswald. ASIN: B000084TUP.
"Singin' in the Rain" from *Rock and Roll Songs That Teach* by The Learning Station. ASIN: B00004RDLE.
"Umbrella" and "Cross under the Umbrella" from *Rhythmic Parachute Play* by Joann Seker and George Jones. ASIN: B001E0GNAG. (Using a parachute with your group, if you have a big enough area, is a great activity!)

Sources

Anonymous. 1902. *Nursery Rhymes from Mother Goose with Alphabet.* Philadelphia: W.W. Houston. Available: www.childrenslibrary.org (accessed March 10, 2010).
Anonymous. 2001. *Baby's First Nursery Treasury.* Fairfield, IA: Books Are Fun.
Burnham, Maude. 1910. *Rhymes for Little Hands.* East Longmeadow, MA: Milton Bradley Company.
Cullum, Carolyn N. 2007. *The Storytime Sourcebook II.* New York: Neal-Schuman.
Dailey, Susan M. 2001. *A Storytime Year.* New York: Neal-Schuman.
Grayson, Marion. 1962. *Let's Do Fingerplays.* Fairfield, CT: R.B. Luce.
Index of Rhymes. Available: www.kidsnurseryrhymes.co.uk/rhymes (accessed March 10, 2010).
Irving, Jan, and Robin Currie. 1991. *Raising the Roof: Children's Stories and Activities on Houses.* Santa Barbara, CA: Teacher Ideas Press.
McKinnon, Elizabeth, and Gayle Bittinger. 1994. *Busy Bees Spring: Fun for Two's and Three's.* Everett, WA: Warren Publishing House.
"Nursery Rhymes." The Mother Goose Pages. Available: www-personal.umich.edu/~pfa/dreamhouse/nursery/rhymes.html (accessed March 13, 2010).
Nursery Rhymes—Lyrics, Origins & History. Available: www.rhymes.org.uk (accessed March 13, 2010).
Rossetti, Christina G. 1893. *Sing-Song: A Nursery Rhyme Book.* New York: Macmillan and Company.
Songs for Teaching: Using Music to Promote Learning. Available: www.songsforteaching.com (accessed March 11, 2010).

Stevenson, Burton E. 1915. *The Home Book of Verse for Young Folks*. New York: Henry Holt and Company.

Totline Staff, comp. 1994. *1001 Rhymes and Fingerplays*. Everett, WA: Warren Publishing House.

Warren, Jean. 1990. *Theme-a-Saurus II*. Everett, WA: Warren Publishing House.

Warren, Jean, comp. 1989. *Theme-a-Saurus*. Everett, WA: Warren Publishing House.

Wiggin, Kate Douglas, and Nora Archibald Smith. 1907. *Pinafore Palace*. New York: Grosset & Dunlap. Available: www.gutenberg.org (accessed March 10, 2010).

Robots

Beep, beep, beep, beep . . . here they come marching down the street!

	Telling Guide

Rhyme

Counting Robots

Ten blinking robots were standing in a line.
One turned off and then there were nine.
Nine blinking robots looking oh so great.
One turned off and then there were eight.
Eight blinking robots looking up to heaven.
One turned off and then there were seven.
Seven blinking robots doing fancy tricks.
One turned off and then there were six.
Six blinking robots looking so alive.
One turned off and then there were five.
Five blinking robots waiting at the door.
One turned off and then there were four.
Four blinking robots underneath the tree.
One turned off and then there were three.
Three blinking robots wondering what to do.
One turned off and then there were two.
Two blinking robots standing in the sun.
One turned off and then there was one.
One blinking robot, we're almost done.
He turned off and then there were none.

—Barbara Scott

Telling Guide

This is a fun rhyme to do with flannel or Velcro board figures!
Begin this rhyme with five fingers up.
Take away fingers as rhyme progresses.

How Many Robots?

How many robots do you see?
Come on now and count with me!
Here's a robot that's lots of fun.
He is robot number one.
Here's a robot that is new.
He is robot number two.
Here's a robot taller than me.
He is robot number three.
Here's a robot walking across the floor.
He is robot number four.
Here's a robot that seems so alive.
He is robot number five.

—Barbara Scott

Beckon.

Hold up index finger.

Add middle finger.

Add ring finger.

Add pinkie.

Add thumb.

Meet My Robot

Meet my robot!   Beckon.
He's really neat!
Watch him as he
Moves his feet.   Walk stiffly.
Up and down go his arms.   Move arms up and down stiffly.
He won't do you any harm.   Shake head "no."
His head he moves
From side to side.   Move head side to side in a jerky
                                                  motion.
He is searching far and wide.
Watch his eyes
As they go blink.   Do exaggerated blinking.
Tap his head,   Tap lightly on head.
You'll hear a clink!
I'm glad you've met
My robot friend.
The fun with him
Will never end!   Shake head "no."

—Barbara Scott

Robot, Robot

This rhyme can be sung to the tune of "Teddy Bear, Teddy Bear" or chanted. All motions should be done like a robot would, with jerky, exaggerated movements.

Robot, robot,
Turn around.   Turn in place.
Robot, robot,
Touch the ground.   Lean over and touch ground.
Robot, robot,
Pat your head.   Pat head.
Robot, robot,
Walk instead.   Walk in a circle.
Robot, robot,
Move your arms.   Move arms.
Robot, robot,
Smile with charm.   Smile.
Robot, robot,
Blink your eyes.   Blink.
Robot, robot,
Wave goodbye.   Wave.

—Adapted traditional rhyme

The Lights on the Robot

Sung to the tune of "The Wheels on the Bus."

The lights on the robot blink on and off,   Open hands, then close them; repeat.
On and off, on and off.
The lights on the robot blink on and off,

All around the rocket ship.
The arms on the robot go up and down,
Up and down, up and down.
The arms on the robot go up and down,
All around the rocket ship.
The dials on the robot turn left and right,
Left and right, left and right.
The dials on the robot turn left and right,
All around the rocket ship.
The legs on the robot step back and forth,
Back and forth, back and forth.
The legs on the robot move back and forth,
All around the rocket ship.
The mouth on the robot goes "Beep, blip, beep,
Beep, blip, beep, beep, blip, beep."
The mouth on the robot goes "Beep, blip, beep,"
All around the rocket ship!

> Move arms up and down in a jerky motion.

> Pretend to turn dial left, then right.

> Move backward and forward in a jerky motion.

> Say these in an exaggerated manner.

—Adapted traditional rhyme

Five Little Robots

The first little robot went beep, beep, beep.
The second little robot wanted to sleep.
The third little robot marched in place.
The fourth little robot floated in space.
The fifth little robot sang a silly song.
Five little robots keep going all night long!

> Begin this rhyme with five fingers up.
> Beginning with thumb, point to each in succession.

> Wiggle all fingers.

—Barbara Scott

Robots Everywhere

Robots here,
Robots there.
I see robots everywhere!
Robots driving robot cars,
Robots flying to the stars.
Robots sweeping up the floor,
Robots knocking at the door.
Robots here,
Robots there,
I see robots everywhere!

> Point in one direction.
> Point in opposite direction.
> Gesture all around.
> Pretend to drive.
> Point to the sky.
> Pretend to sweep.
> Pretend to knock.

> Point in one direction, then in opposite direction.

—Barbara Scott

Five Noisy Robots

Five noisy robots in a toy store.
This one drained his battery and now there are four.
Four noisy robots, shiny as can be.

> Begin this rhyme with five fingers up.
> Take away fingers as rhyme progresses.

This one got all rusty and now there are three.
Three noisy robots, a very loud few.
This one got stuck and now there are two.
Two noisy robots with nowhere to run.
This one wandered off and now there is one.
One noisy robot, left all alone.
He ran away and now there are none.

—Barbara Scott

Books to Share

Carrick, Paul. 2009. *Watch Out for Wolfgang!* Watertown, MA: Charlesbridge Publishing. ISBN: 978-1570916892.

Gritton, Steve. 2009. *The Trouble with Sisters and Robots.* Morton Grove, IL: Albert Whitman & Co. ISBN: 978-0807580905.

James, Simon. 2008. *Baby Brains and RoboMom.* Somerville, MA: Candlewick Press. ISBN: 978-0763634636.

Kuszyk, R. Nicholas. 2009. *R Robot Saves Lunch.* New York: Putnam Juvenile. ISBN: 978-0399247576.

Scieszka, Jon. 2009. *Robot Zot.* New York: Simon & Schuster Children's Publishing. ISBN: 978-1416963943.

Staake, Bob. 2004. *Hello, Robots.* New York: Viking Juvenile. ISBN: 978-0670059058.

Musical Selections

"Dancin' Machine" from *Rockin' Down the Road* by Greg and Steve. ASIN: B00000DGMU.

"Dancing Robots" from *You Can Dance!* by The Learning Station. ASIN: B000WGTOI6.

"Move Like a Machine" from *Perceptual Motor Rhythm Games* by Jack Capon and Rosemary Hallum. ASIN: B0002GFMJG.

"Robot" from *Action!* by The Blankies. ASIN: B000OYC8UW.

"Robot #1" from *Jump and Jive with Hi-5.* ASIN: B0002O06X0.

"Sam the Robot Man" from *Movement Songs Children Love.* Book with CD. Available: www.songsforteaching.com (accessed March 13, 2010).

Scarecrows (and Crows Too!)
Scarecrows are a great theme for autumn!

Rhyme

Scarecrow

Scarecrow, scarecrow, turn around.
Scarecrow, scarecrow, jump up and down.
Scarecrow, scarecrow, arms up high.
Scarecrow, scarecrow, wink one eye.
Scarecrow, scarecrow, bend your knees.
Scarecrow, scarecrow, flap in the breeze.
Scarecrow, scarecrow, climb into bed.
Scarecrow, scarecrow, rest your head.

—From *Busy Fingers, Growing Minds*

I'm a Little Scarecrow

I'm a little scarecrow,
Raggedy and worn.
I wear a hat,
And a shirt that's torn.
When the crows come,
I wave and shout,
"Away from my garden—
Get on out!"

—From Hummingbird Educational Resources

Scarecrow

The floppy, floppy scarecrow
Stands in the field all day.
His job is to scare the birds away.
Up on a pole as high as he can be
And away fly those black crows,
One, two, three.

—From Hummingbird Educational Resources

Five Crows All Shiny Black

Five crows all shiny black,
Sat on a scarecrow's back,
Eating some most delicious corn . . .
Yum, yum!
Scarecrow winked and shouted, "Boo!"
Scared one crow, and away he flew.
Now there are four black shiny crows,
Caw, caw!

—From Laurabaas.com

Telling Guide

This rhyme can be sung to the tune of "Teddy Bear, Teddy Bear" or chanted.
Imitate all actions.

Sung to the tune of "I'm a Little Teapot."
Stretch out arms on either side.

Touch head with hands.
Point to shirt.

Wave, and shout next lines.

Sung to the tune of "The Itsy Bitsy Spider."

Stretch out arms at sides.
Wave arms.
Point up.

Count on three fingers.

This rhyme can be sung to the tune of "Five Green and Speckled Frogs" or chanted.
Begin rhyme with five fingers up.

Rub tummy.
Shout.
Take away fingers as rhyme progresses.

Repeat verses taking away one crow each time.

Jingle Jangle Scarecrow

When all the birds are sleeping and the sun has gone to bed,
Up jumps the scarecrow and this is what he said,
"I'm a jingle jangle scarecrow
With a flippy-floppy hat.
I shake my feet like this
And I shake my hands like that!"
When all the crows were sleeping and the sun was behind a cloud,
Up jumped the scarecrow and shouted very LOUD,
"I'm a jingle jangle scarecrow
With a flippy-floppy hat.
I can shake my arms like this,
And shake my arms like that!"

—From Laurabaas.com

Sung to the tune of "The Itsy Bitsy Spider." Have children begin the rhyme by kneeling and placing their heads on the floor, covering their eyes and singing quietly.

Jump up.

Stretch way up tall.

Use hand movement for hat.

Shake feet alternately.

Shake hands.

Begin as you did for first verse.

Stretch way up tall.

Use hand movement for hat.

Shake arms up and down.

Shake arms from side to side.

Scarecrow Fingerplay

I'm a scary scarecrow made of straw,
Listening for the crows to caw.
I watch the field all day and all night, too.
If a crow comes by, I just say "Boo!"

—From Laurabaas.com

Sung to the tune of "I'm a Little Teapot."

Stand tall and stretch out arms.

Cup hands to ears.

Hand to brow, searching motion.

Put hands on hips and shout "BOO."

Two Blackbirds

There were two blackbirds
Sitting on a hill,
The one named Jack,
The other named Jill.
Fly away, Jack!
Fly away, Jill!
Come back, Jack!
Come back, Jill!

—Traditional rhyme

Hold up both hands, thumbs erect, fingers bent.

Wiggle one thumb.

Wiggle the other thumb.

Bend down or hide one thumb.

Bend down or hide other thumb.

Raise or bring back one thumb erect.

Raise other thumb erect or bring back.

One Little Scarecrow

One little scarecrow
To chase off the crows.
When the wind blows
This is how he goes:
He flops to the left.
He flaps to the right.
He spins all around.
Oh, what a silly sight!

—Susan M. Dailey

Hold up one finger.

Blow.

Flop body toward left side.

Flap arms to right.

Spin around.

The Old Black Crow

Sung to the tune of "The Mulberry Bush." Children should be standing up for this rhyme.

The old black crow is flying around,
Flying around, flying around.
The old back crow is flying around,
Flying around my garden.

Flap arms leisurely; fly around in a circle.

So then I put my scarecrow up,
My scarecrow up, my scarecrow up.
So then I put my scarecrow up,
To scare the old black crow.

Put arms out to sides, pretending to be a scarecrow.

It's working now, 'cause he's on the run,
He's on the run, he's on the run.
It's working now, 'cause he's on the run.

Make scary face and wiggle hands.
Flap arms fast.

Goodbye, you old black crow!

Wave goodbye.

—Adapted traditional rhyme

The Lonely Scarecrow

The scarecrow looks so lonely,
Out standing in his field.

Put arms out to sides, pretending to be a scarecrow.

But as he stands and guards the rows,
A great harvest it will yield!

Wiggle fingers up to represent crops growing.

—Barbara Scott

Three Crows

Sung to the tune of "The Mulberry Bush."

Three crows sat upon a wall,
Sat upon a wall, sat upon a wall.
Three crows sat upon a wall,

Sit three fingers on opposite arm.

On a cold and frosty morning.

Hug self and shiver.

The first crow was waving at his ma,
At his ma, at his ma.

Wave.

The first crow was waving at his ma,

Wave.

On a cold and frosty morning.

Hug self and shiver.

The second crow fell and hurt his claw,
Hur his claw, hurt his claw.

Hold one "injured" hand in the other.

The second crow fell and hurt his claw,

Hold one "injured" hand in the other.

On a cold and frosty morning.

Hug self and shiver.

The third crow couldn't caw at all,
Caw at all, caw at all.

Shake head "no."

The third crow couldn't caw at all,

Shake head "no."

On a cold and frosty morning.

Hug self and shiver.

—Adapted traditional Scottish rhyme

Silly Scarecrow

Silly scarecrow,
Silly dancing scarecrow.
Silly scarecrow,
Dance around all day!
First you flop your arm like this,
Then flop your other arm like this.
Arm like this, arm like this . . . oh.
Silly scarecrow,
Silly dancing scarecrow.
Silly scarecrow,
Dance around all day!

ADDITIONAL VERSES:
First you bend your leg like this,
Then bend your other leg like this. . . .
First you nod your head like this,
Then you nod your head like this. . . .

             —Adapted traditional rhyme

Sung to the tune of "Alouette."
Sway side to side in rhythm.

Flop arm.
Flop other arm.
Flop one arm, then the other.
Sway side to side.

Bending motion.
Another bending motion.
Nod front to back.
Shake side to side.

Flippy-Floppy Scarecrow

I'm a flippy-floppy scarecrow.
I'm stuffed with lots of hay.
I take a stand out in the field,
And scare all the crows away . . . "BOO!"

             —Barbara Scott

Flap in the wind like a scarecrow.
Nod head "yes."
Stand still.
Make a scary face, flap arms, and shout "boo."

Five Hungry Crows

Five hungry crows eating corn galore.
One got full and flew away and then there were four.
Four hungry crows eating rows of peas.
One got full and flew away and then there were three.
Three hungry crows eating lettuce, too.
One got full and flew away and then there were two.
Two hungry crows eating carrots in the sun.
One got full and flew away and then there was one.
One hungry crow eating beans all alone.
He got full and flew away and now there are none.

             —Barbara Scott

Begin this rhyme with five fingers up.
Take away fingers as rhyme progresses.

Five Little Scarecrows

Five little scarecrows, scaring crows away,
Were talking in the corn field one fine day.
The first one said, "I like my hat!"
The second one said, "I see a cat!"

Begin rhyme with five fingers up.

Starting with thumb, point to each in succession.

The third one said, "I have a button for a nose."
The fourth one said, "Boots cover my toes."
The fifth one said, "I'm stuffed with hay."
Five scarecrows talking, one fine day!

Wiggle all five fingers.

—Barbara Scott

Sleepy Little Scarecrow

Sleepy little scarecrow,
It's time to go to bed.
On your pillow,
Lay your head.
Close your eyes
While the cold wind blows,
And dream all night
About scaring crows.

Rub eyes.
Point to wrist, showing time.

Lay head on hands.
Close eyes.

Motion of shooing crows away.

—Barbara Scott

Scarecrow Counting

Swaying in the autumn breeze,
Stands the scarecrow, counting leaves.
Goodness gracious, sakes alive!
There go one, two, three, four, five,
Six, seven, eight, nine, and ten.
He is ready to count leaves again!

Hold arms out to sides, pretending to be a scarecrow.

Count out on fingers of one hand.
Count out on fingers of other hand.

—Barbara Scott

Books to Share

Brown, Ken. 2001. *The Scarecrow's Hat*. Atlanta, GA: Peachtree Publishers. ISBN: 978-1561452408.
Brown, Margaret Wise. 1998. *The Little Scarecrow Boy*. New York: HarperCollins. ISBN: 978-0060262846.
Cazet, Denys. 1994. *Nothing at All*. New York: Scholastic. ISBN: 978-0531068229.
Martin, Bill. Jr. 1986. *Barn Dance*. New York: Henry Holt and Company. ISBN: 978-0805000894.
Preston, Tim. 1999. *The Lonely Scarecrow*. New York: Dutton Juvenile. ISBN: 978-0525460800.
Rex, Michael. 2003. *Scarecrow*. Madison, WI: Turtleback Books. ISBN: 978-0613988032.

Musical Selections

"Scarecrow" from *Happy Everything* by Dr. Jean. Available: www.drjean.org (accessed March 14, 2010).
"Scarecrow" from *Songs for All Seasons* by Geof Johnson. ASIN: B0000E2FRS.
"Scarecrow Song" from *Listen and Learn Fall*. Available: www.songsforteaching.com (accessed March 10, 2010).
"The Scarecrow Song" from *Learning the Four Seasons*. Available: www.songsforteaching.com (accessed March 10, 2010).

Sources

Dailey, Susan M. 2001. *A Storytime Year*. New York: Neal-Schuman.

Laurabaas.com. Available: laurabaas.com/2007/10/02/time-for-stories-scarecrows-storytime-plan/ (accessed May 14, 2010).

"Lotsa Lesson Plans—Scarecrows." Hummingbird Educational Resources. Available: www.hummingbirded.com/scarecrows.html (accessed March 14, 2010).

Redleaf, Rhonda. 1983. *Busy Fingers, Growing Minds*. St. Paul, MN: Redleaf Press.

Scott, Louise Binder. 1960. *Rhymes for Fingers and Flannelboards*. New York: McGraw-Hill.

Chapter **8**

Shapes to Teeth

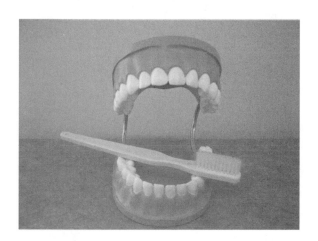

Shapes

There are so many shapes—circles, squares, rectangles, triangles, and more!

Rhyme	**Telling Guide**

The Circle

The circle is a shape
That's easy to be found.
It has no corners on it
And is completely round.

                         —Author unknown

Form circle with fingers.

A Square Is Its Name

Here's a shape that you should know.
A square is its name.
It has four corners and four sides
That measure all the same.

                         —Author unknown

Form square with fingers.

Sally the Square

When Sally the Square
Went to the fair,
She was all alone and blue.
Then she found a square cat
To be her friend,
And now the squares are two.
When Sally the Square
Went to the fair,
She was all alone, you see.
But she found a square cat
And then a square pig,
And now the squares are three.
When Sally the Square
Went to the fair,
She wanted to see more.
She found a square cat,
A square pig, then a duck,
And now the squares are four.

                         —Jean Woods

This is also a great rhyme to do as a flannel or Velcro board activity!
Let index finger represent Sally.

As friends are added, add fingers.

The Square Song

I am a square, a lovely square,
I have four sides, they're all the same,
I have four corners, four lovely corners,
I am a square, that is my name.

—Rita J. Galloway

Sung to the tune of "You Are My Sunshine." You can have children hold up construction paper squares instead of using fingers to make the square shape. Make square shape with fingers.
Show four fingers.

Make square shape with fingers.

The Triangle Song

I am a small triangle.
I have three sides, you see.
I also have three corners.
They're just right for me!

—Rita J. Galloway

Sung to the tune of "Pop Goes the Weasel." You can have children hold up construction paper triangles instead of using fingers to make the triangle shape. Make triangle shape with hands.
Hold up three fingers.

Make a Shape

Make a circle,
Make a circle.
Draw it now, draw it now.
A circle has no corners,
A circle has no corners.
It is round, it is round.
Make a square,
Make a square.
Draw it now, draw it now.
A square has four corners,
And its sides are equal.
All the same, all the same.
Make a triangle,
Make a triangle.
Draw it now, draw it now.
A triangle has three corners,
Two sides and a bottom.
Two sides down, one across.
Make a rectangle,
Make a rectangle.
Draw it now, draw it now.
A rectangle has four sides,
Two long and two short ones.
Long and short, long and short.

—Adapted traditional rhyme

Sung to the tune of "Frère Jacques."
Draw circle in the air.

Draw square in the air.

Draw triangle in the air.

Draw rectangle in the air.

I Know a Shape

I know a shape and it is round,
And circle is its name-o.
C-I-R C-L-E,
C-I-R C-L-E,
C-I-R C-L-E,
And circle is its name-o.
I know a shape that has four sides,
And square is its name-o.
S-Q-U A-R-E,
S-Q-U A-R-E,
S-Q-U A-R-E,
And square is its name-o.
I know a shape that has three sides,
Triangle is its name-o.
T-R-I- A-N G-L-E,
T-R-I- A-N G-L-E,
T-R-I- A-N G-L-E,
And triangle is its name-o.
I know a shape that's like a kite,
And diamond is its name-o.
D-I-A-M-O-N-D,
D-I-A-M-O-N-D,
D-I-A-M-O-N-D,
And diamond is its name-o.

—Adapted traditional rhyme

Sung to the tune of "Bingo." To help with recognition of letters in the song, use a hand mitt with letters attached or place large letters on a flannel or Velcro board. To further reinforce the concept of each shape, provide multiple copies of the shapes for children to hold up as they sing the verses.

I'm a Little Square

I'm a little square,
As you can see.
With four equal sides,
I'll always be.
I can be a box or
Maybe a block.
The fun with me
Just never stops!

—Adapted traditional rhyme

Sung to the tune of "I'm a Little Teapot."

Make a square.

Show four fingers.

Make square shape.

Shake head "no."

I'm a Circle

I'm a circle,
A big and bouncy circle.
I'm a circle,
Just watch what I can do!
I can roll all around.

Sung to the tune of "Alouette."

Make a circle with hands.

Roll hands.

I have no sides to be found.
To be found, roll around . . . oh.
I'm a circle,
A big and bouncy circle.
I'm a circle,
Come and play with me.

—Adapted traditional rhyme

Shake head "no."
Roll hands.
Make circle with hands.

Beckon.

I'm a Diamond

Sung to the tune of "Camptown Races."
Draw diamond shape in the air.

I'm a diamond,
Yes I am.
Diamond, diamond.
I'm a shape that's lots of fun,
A diamond is my name.
I can be a kite,
I can be a sign.
I'm a diamond, yes I am,
I'm a diamond shape.

—Adapted traditional rhyme

Nod head "yes."

Hold out one hand to the side.
Hold out other hand to the side.
Nod head "yes."

Shapes Hokey Pokey

Sung to the tune of "The Hokey Pokey." Have one of each shape mentioned in the song cut out for each child. You can laminate them for durability and reuse. For extra fun, make the shapes different colors and do the song as a color-and-shape Hokey Pokey!
Do motions as directed.

You put your circle in,
You put your circle out,
You put your circle in and you shake it all about.
You do the shape pokey and you turn yourself around.
That's what it's all about!

—Adapted traditional rhyme

Turn in place.
Clap. *Continue the song with square, triangle, rectangle, oval, diamond, star, etc.*

I'm a Little Triangle

Sung to the tune of "I'm a Little Teapot."
Make triangle shape with fingers.

I'm a little triangle,
Yes, siree.
I have three sides,
As you can see.
I can be a tree,
Or a slice of pie.
I'm lots of fun.
Give me a try!

—Adapted traditional rhyme

Hold up three fingers.

Hold out hand to one side, then other hand to opposite side.

Clap three times.
Point to self.

If You Like a Shape

If you like a shape that's round, clap your hands.
If you like a shape that's round, clap your hands.
If you like a shape that's round and rolls along the ground,
If you like a shape that's round, clap your hands.
If you like a shape that's square, stomp your feet.
If you like a shape that's square, stomp your feet.
If you like a shape that's square, like that window over there,
If you like a shape that's square, stomp your feet.
If you like a shape that's rectangle, shout "Hooray"!
If you like a shape that's rectangle, shout "Hooray"!
If you like rectangle shapes, we should see it on your face!
If you like a shape that's rectangle, shout "Hooray"!
If you like all kinds of shapes, do all three!
If you like all kinds of shapes, do all three!
If you like all kinds of shapes, c'mon, let's celebrate!
If you like all kinds of shapes, do all three!

—Adapted traditional rhyme

Sung to the tune of "If You're Happy and You Know It."
Clap, clap.
Clap, clap.
Roll hands.
Clap, clap.
Stomp, stomp.
Stomp, stomp.
Point.
Stomp, stomp.
Shout and pump fist in the air.

Clap, clap, stomp, stomp, shout "Hooray"!

Beckon.

Ten Little Shapes

One little, two little, three little shapes,
Four little, five little, six little shapes,
Seven little, eight little, nine little shapes,
Ten little shapes I see.
Ten little, nine little, eight little shapes,
Seven little, six little, five little shapes,
Four little, three little, two little shapes,
One little shape I see.

—Adapted traditional rhyme

Sung to the tune of "Ten Little Indians." Use different colored shapes for this, and place them on your flannel or Velcro board. Talk about what types of shapes they are, and identify colors before removing them in the second verse.

I'm an Oval

I'm an oval,
I'm an oval.
Long and round,
Long and round.
I'm shaped like an egg,
I'm shaped like an egg.
Long and round,
Long and round.

—Adapted traditional rhyme

Sung to the tune of "Frère Jacques."

Make an oval shape.

Books to Share

Charles, N.N. 1994. *Looking through Shapes at Apples and Grapes*. New York: Blue Sky Press. ISBN: 978-0590478854.

Emberley, Ed. 2001. *The Wing on a Flea: A Book about Shapes*. New York: Little, Brown Young Readers. ISBN: 978-0316234870.

Emberley, Rebecca. 2000. *My Shapes/Mis Formas*. New York: LB Kids. ISBN: 978-0316233552.

Greene, Rhonda G. 2001. *Where a Line Bends . . . A Shape Begins*. Mooloolaba, Qld: Sandpiper. ISBN: 978-0618152414.

MacKinnon, Debbie. 2000. *Eye Spy Shapes*. Watertown, MA: Charlesbridge Publishing. ISBN: 978-0881061352.

Walsh, Ellen S. 2007. *Mouse Shapes*. Boston: Harcourt Children's Books. ISBN: 978-0152060916. (This is just one in a series of wonderful concept books by this author starring the mice!)

Musical Selections

"Circles" from *C Is For Cookie: Cookie's Favorite Songs*. ASIN: B000002BBC.

"I'll Be a Circle" from *Sing Along and Learn* by Ken Sheldon. Book and CD set. ISBN: 978-0439665391.

"Round in a Circle" from *We All Live Together*, vol. 1, by Greg and Steve. ASIN: B00000DGMR.

"Shape Man" from *Get Ready, Get Set, Sing!* by Sarah Barchas. Available: www.cduniverse.com (accessed March 15, 2010).

"The Shape Song" from *Sing to Learn* by Dr. Jean. ASIN: B000F8R7J4.

"Tracing Shapes" from *Dance and Sing: The Best of Nick Jr*. ASIN: B00005Q3AT.

Sources

McKinnon, Elizabeth, and Gayle Bittinger. 1994. *Busy Bees Fall: Fun for Two's and Three's*. Everett, WA: Warren Publishing House.

———. 1995. *Busy Bees Winter: Fun for Two's and Three's*. Everett, WA: Warren Publishing House.

Totline Staff, comp. 1994. *1001 Rhymes and Fingerplays*. Everett, WA: Warren Publishing House.

Warren, Jean. 1990. *Theme-a-Saurus II*. Everett, WA: Warren Publishing House.

———. 1991. *Piggyback Songs for School*. Everett, WA: Warren Publishing House.

Spiders

This is a great theme for Halloween or for anytime!

Rhyme	Telling Guide

Spider Web

I'm a big spider,
I spin, I spin.
I spin big webs,
To catch flies in.

—Author unknown

Hold up arms and open hands.
Turn in place.
Hold up arms and open hands.
Fold arms tightly to chest.

The Eency Weency Spider ⊙

Eency, weency spider
Climbed up the waterspout.
Down came the rain
And washed the spider out.
Out came the sun
And dried up all the rain.
And the eency, weency spider
Climbed up the spout again.

—Traditional rhyme

Use one hand as spider; wiggle fingers to climb.
Bend other arm at elbow for water spout.

Sweep hands downward.
Form circle over head with arms.
Wiggle fingers up.
Use one hand as spider; wiggle fingers to climb.
Bend other arm at elbow for water spout.

Five Little Spiders

Five little spiders crawling all around
The first one said, "See the bug I found?"
The second one said, "My web is neat."
The third one said, "I have eight feet."
The fourth one said, "We're all so small."
The fifth one said, "Time for autumn leaves to fall."
Then whoosh went the wind and out went the light,
And the five little spiders crawled out of sight.

—Stephanie Stokes, LibraryPalooza

Begin rhyme with five fingers up.
Point to each in succession as rhyme progresses.

Clap loudly.
Make fingers crawl behind back.

Put Your Spider on Your Nose

Put your spider on your nose, on your nose.
Put your spider on your nose, on your nose.
Put your spider on your nose,
And watch where it goes.
Put your spider on your nose, on your nose.

ADDITIONAL VERSES:
Put your spider on your ear . . . oh dear, oh dear.

Sung to the tune of "If You're Happy and You Know It." Use your hand as a wiggly spider, or give each child a spider ring to use.

Put your spider on your head . . . I need to go to bed.
Put your spider on your knee . . . oh woe is me!

—Stephanie Stokes, LibraryPalooza

Little Miss Muffet

Little Miss Muffet sat on a tuffet,
Eating her curds and whey.
Down came a spider,
Which sat down beside her,
And frightened Miss Muffet away.

—Traditional rhyme

Children sit cross-legged.

Pretend to eat.

Put one arm in the air; wiggle other hand down it.

Put hands on either side of face, surprised look.

The Spider

Oh, my dear brother spider,
With your stomach big and red,
From the eaves you are hanging
On a single little thread.

—Traditional Chinese rhyme

ASL sign for spider: with hands crossed at wrists, wiggle fingers on both hands.
Use ASL sign for spider.

Put arms out in front of stomach to show size.

Hold up one finger.

The Spider Spins a Web

The spider spins a web,
The spider spins a web.
Heigh-ho, just watch him go!
The spider spins a web.
The spider traps a _____.
The spider traps a _____.
Heigh-ho, just watch him go!
The spider traps a _____.
The spider lets them go,
The spider lets them go.
Heigh-ho, just watch him go!
The spider lets them go!

—Adapted traditional rhyme

Sung to the tune of "The Farmer in the Dell." Use ASL sign detailed above for this rhyme too. You can let children supply bug names for you where indicated.
Use ASL sign for spider.

Use ASL sign.
Insert the name of any type of bug.
Make fists as if grabbing something.

Open fists.

Five Little Spiders

Five little spiders crawling on the floor.
One fell asleep and now there are four.
Four little spiders spinning webs in the tree.
One wandered off and now there are three.
Three little spiders sitting in the morning dew.
One saw some breakfast and then there were two.
Two little spiders enjoying the sun.
One ran away and now there's just one.

Begin this rhyme with five fingers up.
Take away fingers as rhyme progresses.

One little spider not having any fun.
He went away and now there are none.

—Barbara Scott

Ten Little Spiders

Ten little spiders,
Wiggle all around.   Wiggle all fingers in the air.
Ten little spiders,
Wiggle on the ground.   Touch the floor with wiggling fingers.
Ten little spiders,
Wiggle up high.   Wiggle fingers up in the air.
Ten little spiders,
Wiggle toward the sky.   Wiggle fingers even higher!
Ten little spiders,
Wiggle on my nose.   Wiggle fingers on nose.
Ten little spiders,
Wiggle on my toes.   Wiggle fingers on toes.
Ten little spiders,
Wiggle on my head.   Wiggle fingers on head.
Ten little spiders,
Wiggle on to bed.   Wiggle fingers and put behind back.

—Adapted traditional rhyme

Ten Little Spiders

*Sung to the tune of "Ten Little Indians."
This is also a great rhyme to do with
flannel or Velcro board visuals!*
Count out on fingers for first verse.

One little, two little, three little spiders,
Four little, five little, six little spiders,
Seven little, eight little, nine little spiders,
Ten little spiders on a web.
Ten little, nine little, eight little spiders,   Take away fingers in second verse.
Seven little, six little, five little spiders,
Four little, three little, two little spiders,
One little spider on a web.

—Adapted traditional rhyme

Silly Little Spider

*ASL sign for spider: with hands crossed at
wrists, wiggle fingers on both hands.*
Use ASL sign for spider.

Silly little spider
Jumping all around.   Using ASL sign, make hands jump in
                                      the air.
Where, oh where
Can your friends be found?   Tap temple, wondering.
They're spinning webs
High up in the trees.   Hold arms out to sides for trees.
Watch them sway,   Sway back and forth.
Blowing in the breeze.

—Barbara Scott

Spider

I know a friend who has eight legs,
And spins a pretty web.
SP-I-D-E-R,
SP-I-D-E-R,
SP-I-D-E-R,
And spider is his name-o.
The tiny hairs upon his legs
Allow him to hear.
SP-I-D-E-R,
SP-I-D-E-R,
SP-I-D-E-R,
And spider is his name-o.
Some are fuzzy,
Some are smooth,
Some come in different colors.
SP-I-D-E-R,
SP-I-D-E-R,
SP-I-D-E-R,
And spider is his name-o.

—Adapted traditional rhyme

Sung to the tune of "Bingo." This version does not take away letters in the name. It simply presents some simple facts about the spider!

Say the "SP" letters together.

Wiggle fingers with palms up.
Stroke back of hand.

The Creepy-Crawly Spider

The creepy-crawly spider
Crawled up the hollow tree.
He spins a beautiful web
For all the world to see.
When the morning came,
It was covered all in dew,
And the creepy-crawly spider
Will spin again anew!

—Adapted traditional rhyme

Sung to the tune of "The Eensy Weensy Spider."
Use one hand for spider, fingers wiggling; crawl it up opposite arm.

Point to eyes.
Raise arms over head, making sun.
Wiggle fingers down to represent rain.

Nod head "yes."

See the Spider

See the spider spin his web,
Spin his web,
Spin his web.
See the spider spin his web.
Go, spider, go!
Spin it up and spin it down,
Spin it up,
Spin it down.
Spin it up and spin it down.

Sung to the tune of "London Bridge." ASL sign for spider: with hands crossed at wrists, wiggle fingers on both hands.
Use ASL sign for spider.

Clap three times.
Use ASL sign; go up in the air first, then down.

Go, spider, go!   Clap three times.
Now the spider's web is spun.   Use ASL sign.
It is finished,
It is done.   Wipe hands off, as if finishing a job.
Now the spider's web is spun.
Good job, spider!   Give thumbs-up sign.

—Adapted traditional rhyme

Spider Movement

Sung to the tune of "The Farmer in the Dell."

Crawl, spider, crawl.   Crawling motion.
Crawl, spider, crawl.
Creep and crawl up the wall.
Crawl, spider, crawl.
Jump, spider, jump.   Pretend to jump.
Jump, spider, jump.
Give your legs a great big thump!
Jump, spider, jump.
Run, spider, run.   Pretend to run in place.
Run, spider, run.
Now that your web is spun.
Run, spider, run.
Swim, spider, swim.   Swimming motion.
Swim, spider, swim.
Take a dive right off that limb.
Swim, spider, swim.

—Adapted traditional rhyme

Books to Share

Basic, Zdenko. 2008. *The Cleverest Spider.* New York: Sterling. ISBN: 978-1402752445.
Cronin, Doreen. 2005. *Diary of a Spider.* New York: HarperCollins. ISBN: 978-0060001537.
Harper, Charise M. 2004. *Itsy Bitsy, The Smart Spider.* New York: Dial. ISBN: 978-0803729018.
Kirk, David. 1998. *Miss Spider's ABC.* New York: Scholastic. ISBN: 978-0590282796.
London, Jonathan. 1998. *Dream Weaver.* Boston: Silver Whistle. ISBN: 978-0152009441.
Monks, Lydia. 2004. *Aaaarrgghh! Spider!* Boston: Houghton Mifflin Books for Children. ISBN: 978-0618432509.

Musical Selections

"Eency Weency Spider" from *Get Ready, Get Set, Sing!* by Sarah Barchas. Book and CD set. ISBN: 978-0963262110.
"Itsy Bitsy Spider" from *Big Fun* by Greg and Steve. ASIN: B00000AG60.
"Little Miss Muffet" from *Rhymin' to the Beat*, vol. 2, by Jack Hartman and Friends. ASIN: B0026EIIRU.
"Spider on the Floor" from *Singable Songs for the Very Young* by Raffi. ASIN: B00000DDEX.
"The Spider's Web" from *Bloom* by Zak Morgan. B0001ARHAU.

"Spunky Spider" from *Songs about Insects, Bugs, and Squiggly Things.* ASIN: B00000DARQ.

Sources

Headland, Isaac Taylor. 1900. *Chinese Mother Goose Rhymes.* Grand Rapids, MI: Fleming H. Revell.

LibraryPalooza. Available: www.librarypalooza.com (accessed April 9, 2010).

Moffat, Alfred. 1911. *Our Old Nursery Rhymes.* New York: G. Schirmer.

"Nursery Rhymes." The Mother Goose Pages. Available: www-personal.umich.edu/~pfa/dreamhouse/nursery/rhymes.html (accessed March 13, 2010).

Squirrels and Nuts
Squirrels are a great theme for fall!

Rhyme

Telling Guide

Squirrels

Five little squirrels sitting in a tree.
The first little squirrel said, "What do I see?"
The second little squirrel said, "I see a gun."
The third little squirrel said, "Oh let's run."
The fourth little squirrel said, "Let's hide in the shade."
The fifth little squirrel said, "I'm not afraid."
Then bang went the gun and away they did run.

—Author unknown

Begin rhyme with five fingers in the air.
Starting with thumb, point to each in succession.

Whisky, Frisky

Whisky, frisky, hippity hop,
Up he goes, to the tree-top.
Whirly, twirly, round and round,
Down he scampers to the ground.
Furly, curly, what a tail,
Tall as a feather, broad as a sail.

Where's his supper? In the shell.
Snappy, cracky, out it fell.

—Author unknown

Raise left arm; run up to hand with fingers of right hand.
Roll hand back down arm.

Spread fingers of right hand; move hand back and forth.
Make hollow ball using both hands.
Let hands fall apart, as nut broken in half.

Four Busy Squirrels

Four busy squirrels
Scamper all around.
One finds a nut
To bury underground.
One gnaws an acorn
And doesn't make a sound.
One goes to sleep
High in a leafy nest.
One climbs a tree
That's what it likes best.
Whoosh goes the wind
Leaves swirl round and round.
Four busy squirrels
Scamper through the forest ground.

—From KinderNature

Hold up four fingers.
Wiggle fingers.
Hold up one finger.
Pretend to dig.
Pretend to chew.
Hold finger in front of lips.
Pretend to sleep.
Point upward.
Pretend to climb tree.
Nod head.
Wave arms.
Turn around.
Hold up four fingers.
Wiggle fingers.

The Squirrel

These are the brown leaves	Flutter hands to ground.
Fluttering down.	
And this is the tall tree	Hold up right arm.
Bare and brown.	
This is the squirrel	Form fist with left hand, thumb up.
With eyes so bright;	Form two circles.
Hunting for nuts	
With all his might.	
This is the hole	Form hole with fingers.
Where day by day,	
Nut after nut	
He stores away.	Pretend to place nuts in hole.
When winter comes	
With its cold and storm,	
He'll sleep curled up	Circle right hand around left fist.
All snug and warm.	

—From Better Kid Care

Five Little Squirrels

Five little squirrels scamper up a tree.	Begin rhyme with five fingers up; wiggle fingers up opposite arm.
The first one said, "Lots of nuts I see!"	Starting with thumb, point to each in succession.
The second one said, "They're nice and round."	
The third one said, "There are more on the ground."	
The fourth one said, "Here's a handful for me."	
The fifth one said, "Hungry we will not be!"	Shake head "no."

—Barbara Scott

The Squirrel

Little squirrel living there	
In the hollow tree,	Hands make a hole.
I've a pretty cage for you;	Put fingertips of both hands together in front.
Come and live with me.	
You may turn the little wheel—	Rotate index fingers around each other.
That will be great fun!	
Slowly 'round or very fast,	Rotate fingers slow, then fast.
If you faster run.	
Little squirrel, I will bring	
In my basket here,	Cup hands in front. / Make circles with thumbs and index fingers.
Every day a feast of nuts!	
Come then, squirrel dear.	Beckon.
But the little squirrel said,	
From his hollow tree:	

"Oh! No, no! I'd rather far
Live here and be free."
So my cage is empty yet,
And the wheel is still;
But my little basket here
Oft with nuts I fill.
If you like, I'll crack the nuts,
Some for you and me.
For the squirrel has enough
In his hollow tree.

—Emilie Poulsson

Shake head "no."

Put fingertips of both hands together in front.

Cup hands in front. / Put thumbs and fingertips together in circles.

Pound one fist on top of the other.

Point to self, then children.

Hands make hole.

Squirrels

Five little squirrels sitting in a tree.
The first one said, "What do I see?"
The second one said, "Some nuts on the ground."
The third one said, "Those are nuts I found."
The fourth one said, "I'll race you there."
The fifth one said, "All right, that's fair."
So they shook their tails and ran with glee!
To the nuts that lay at the foot of the tree.

—Lynda Roberts

Begin this rhyme with five fingers up.

Starting with thumb, point to each in succession.

Wiggle bottom and run in place.

Make small circles with thumbs and index fingers to represent nuts.

Nuts to You!

One nut, two nuts, three nuts, four.
See them rolling out the door!
Five nuts, six nuts, seven nuts, eight.
Now they're rolling out the gate!
Nine nuts . . . wait . . . and now there's ten!
Roll away and begin again!

—Barbara Scott

Count out the nuts on your fingers.
Roll hands over each other.
Continue to count out on fingers.
Put hands with fingertips together; open as a gate.

Roll hands again.

The Busy Little Squirrel

The busy little squirrel
Is gathering nuts all day.
The busy little squirrel
Has no time to play.
Up and down the tree he runs,
A mission on his mind!
The busy little squirrel looks
For tasty nuts to find!

—Barbara Scott

Gathering motion.

Shake head "no."
Point up, then down.
Point to head.
Point to eyes.
Rub tummy.

Five Little Squirrels

Five little squirrels with lots of nuts to store.
One ran away and then there were four.
Four little squirrels sitting in the tree.
One ran away and then there were three.
Three little squirrels wondering what to do.
One ran away and then there were two.
Two little squirrels not having much fun.
One ran away and now there's just one.
Little squirrel in the tree all alone.
He ran away and then there were none.

—Barbara Scott

Begin this rhyme with five fingers up.
Take away fingers as rhyme progresses.

Two Little Squirrels

Two little squirrels
Sitting in a tree.
One named Golly,
And the other named Gee.
Run away, Golly.
Run away, Gee.
Come back, Golly.
Come back, Gee.

—Adapted traditional rhyme

Hold up two thumbs.

Wiggle one thumb.
Wiggle other thumb.
Put one thumb behind back.
Put other thumb behind back.
Bring one thumb back to the front.
Bring other thumb back to the front.

Little Squirrel, Little Squirrel

Little squirrel, little squirrel,
Turn around.
Little squirrel, little squirrel,
Gather nuts on the ground.
Little squirrel, little squirrel,
Scamper up the tree.
Little squirrel, little squirrel,
Look and see.
Little squirrel, little squirrel,
Hiding in the trees.
Little squirrel, little squirrel,
There behind the leaves.
Little squirrel, little squirrel,
Scamper on down.
Little squirrel, little squirrel,
Rest on the ground.

—Adapted traditional rhyme

This rhyme can be sung to the tune of "Teddy Bear, Teddy Bear" or chanted.

Turn around in a circle.

Gathering motion.

Climbing motions.

Put hand over eyes; look around.

Point up.

Hold hands in front of face; peek around.

Motion of climbing down.

Put head on hands; snore.

Squirrel Friends

One little squirrel, lonely and blue,
Met another squirrel and that makes two.
Two little squirrels sitting in a tree,
Met another squirrel and that makes three.
Three little squirrels having fun galore,
Met another squirrel and that makes four.
Four little squirrels near the old beehive,
Met another squirrel and that makes five.
Run, little squirrel friends,
Scamper and play.
Have lots of fun every day!

—Barbara Scott

Begin this rhyme with one finger up.
Add fingers as rhyme progresses.

Wiggle all five fingers.

The Little Squirrel

The little squirrel gathers nuts
That fall upon the ground.
He buries them
And knows just where
They're later to be found!

—Barbara Scott

Gathering motion.
Wiggle fingers up in air, then move them down.
Tap head.
Digging motion.

I'm a Squirrel

I'm a squirrel,
I'm a squirrel,
In a tree,
In a tree.
Running, jumping, playing
On the branches swaying.
Look at me!
In the tree!

—Barbara Scott

Sung to the tune of "Frère Jacques."
Point to self.

Hold arms out for branches.

Run and jump.
Sway from side to side.
Point to eyes.

I'm a Nut

I'm an acorn, small and round,
Lying on the cold, cold ground.
Everybody walks over me.
That is why I'm cracked, you see.
I'm a nut!
I'm a nut!
I'm a nut!

—Adapted traditional rhyme

Make small circle.
Shiver.
Move hands to show expanse.
Shrug shoulders.
Make "click, click" sound with tongue.
Make "click, click" sound with tongue.
Make "click, click" sound with tongue.

Five Little Nuts

Five little nuts lying on the ground.
The first one said, "What's that sound?"
The second one said, "A squirrel I see."

Begin rhyme with five fingers up.
Starting with thumb, point to each in succession.

The third one said, "He's hunting for me."
The fourth one said, "He's hungry for lunch."
The fifth one said, "We'll make a tasty bunch."

—Barbara Scott

Acorn

I know what squirrels just love to eat,
And acorn is its name-o!
A-C-O-R-N,
A-C-O-R-N,
A-C-O-R-N,
And acorn is its name-o!

—Adapted traditional rhyme

Sung to the tune of "Bingo." As with the original song, take away letters each time, replacing them with clapping. It's also a fun rhyme to do with a hand mitt and the letters, or you could do the letters on your flannel or Velcro board.

An Evening Visitor

Late in the evening,
When the sun goes down,
The little brown squirrel
Scampers to the ground.
He runs into my garden
To find food, you see.
He gathers corn, berries, and more
To take back to his tree.
There he stores the food he finds
In a hole safe and sound.
For in this spot, he always knows
There's food to be found.

—Barbara Scott

Raise arms above head.
Bring arms down slowly to represent setting sun.
Climbing motion.
Run in place.

Gathering motion.

Make hole with fingers.
Tap temple.
Rub tummy.

The Squirrel's Tail

There are many uses
For the tail of a squirrel.
When it rains, he has a
Built-in umbrella to unfurl!

In the sun, his tail provides
An awful lot of shade.
It also helps him balance
When jumps from branches need to be made!

—Barbara Scott

Wiggle bottom.
Flutter fingers down for rain.
Make umbrella shape over head with arms.
Circle arms over head to represent sun.
Put hands above eyes, shading.
Motion of balancing.

I'm a Little Acorn

I'm a little acorn, small and round.
You'll find me in a tree,
Or on the ground.
Squirrels think I am

Sung to the tune of "I'm a Little Teapot."
Make circle with index finger and thumb.
Point up.
Point down.

A tasty lunch.

They gather and store me

By the bunch!

—Adapted traditional rhyme

Rub tummy.

Gathering motion.

Squirrels, They Love Acorns

Sung to the tune of "Peanut Butter and Jelly."

First you take an acorn

And you find it, you find it.

Put hand over eyes, searching.

First you take an acorn

And you find it, you find it.

Squirrels, they love acorns!

They're yummy!

Rub tummy.

Squirrels, they love acorns!

They're yummy!

Rub tummy.

Then you make a hole,

And you dig it, you dig it.

Both hands do a digging motion.

Then you make a hole,

And you dig it, you dig it.

Squirrels, they love acorns!

They're yummy!

Rub tummy.

Squirrels, they love acorns!

They're yummy!

Rub tummy.

Then you take the acorn,

And you drop it, you drop it.

Motion of dropping acorn into hole.

Then you take the acorn,

And you drop it, you drop it.

Squirrels, they love acorns!

They're yummy!

Rub tummy.

Squirrels, they love acorns!

They're yummy!

Rub tummy.

Then you take the dirt,

And you cover it, you cover it.

Motion of covering up hole with dirt.

Then you take the dirt,

And you cover it, you cover it.

Squirrels, they love acorns!

They're yummy!

Rub tummy.

Squirrels, they love acorns!

They're yummy!

Rub tummy.

—Adapted traditional rhyme

Five Little Squirrels Went Out to Play

Sung to the tune of "Five Little Ducks."

Five little squirrels went out to play

Begin rhyme with five fingers up.

In the forest one fine day.

Mother Squirrel said, "Chi, chi, chi, chi."

Take fingers away as rhyme progresses.

Only four little squirrels came back to eat.
No little squirrels went out to play
In the forest one fine day.
Mother Squirrel said, "Chi, chi, chi, chi."
And all the little squirrels came back to eat!

—Adapted traditional rhyme

| | Continue four, three, two, one, until . . . |
| | Shake head "no." |

Acorn Rain

First one little acorn hit the ground.
Then another little acorn hit the ground.
Mr. Squirrel thought it strange.
It was an acorn rain!
Look! It's raining acorns all around!

—Barbara Scott

Bring back fingers at end of rhyme; wiggle all fingers.
Sung to the tune of "If You're Happy and You Know It."
Tap the floor two times.
Tap the floor two times.
Tap temple, questioning look.

Tap on floor many times with both hands.

The Little Squirrel

Hush, little children,
I've something to say.
There's a dear little squirrel,
So bushy and gray.
He peeps through the branches
And plays day by day.
Now don't make a noise
And scare him away.

—Barbara Scott

Make "Shhh" motion.

Use hands to indicate size.

Peep through fingers.

Make "Shhh" motion.

Books to Share

Ehlert, Lois. 1993. *Nuts to You.* Boston: Harcourt Children's Books. ISBN: 978-0152576479.
Fowler, Richard. 1984. *A Squirrel's Tale.* Tulsa, OK: Educational Development Corporation. ISBN: 978-0881101577.
Freeman, Don. 2005. *Earl the Squirrel.* New York: Viking Juvenile. ISBN: 978-0670060191.
Sherry, Kevin. 2009. *Acorns Everywhere!* New York: Dial Books for Young Readers. ISBN: 978-0803732568.
Tafuri, Nancy. 2007. *The Busy Little Squirrel.* New York: Simon & Schuster Children's Publishing. ISBN: 978-0689873416.
Watt, Melanie. 2006. *Scaredy Squirrel.* Tonawanda, NY: Kids Can Press. ISBN: 978-1553379591. (This is one of a series of books about this great character!)

Musical Selections

"Furry Squirrel" from *Touched by a Song* by Miss Jackie Silberg. ASIN: B002K74FCK.
"Gray Squirrel" from *Happy Everything* by Dr. Jean. Available: www.drjean.org (accessed March 14, 2010).
"Grey Squirrel" from *Sing It! Say It! Stamp It! Sway It!*, vol. 3, by Peter and Ellen Allard. Available: www.songsforteaching.com (accessed March 11, 2010).
"Peep Squirrel" from *Dancing through the Seasons* by Joanie Calum. Available: www.songsforteaching.com (accessed March 11, 2010).

"Poor Baby Squirrel" from *Wonder Pets! Wonder Pets!* by The Wonder Pets. ASIN: B000NOKBF2.
"Trading Squirrels" from *Animal House* by Recess Monkey. ASIN: B000NQPWUY.

Sources

Better Kid Care. Available: betterkidcare.psu.edu (accessed March 15, 2010).

"Four Busy Squirrels." KinderNature: A Resource for Early Childhood Educators. Available: kindernature.storycounty.com/display.aspx?DocID=2005929102 (accessed March 15, 2010).

Poulsson, Emilie. 1893. *Fingerplays for Nursery and Kindergarten.* New York: Lothrop, Lee, and Shepard, reprinted 1921.

Roberts, Lynda. 1985. *Mitt Magic: Fingerplays for Finger Puppets.* Silver Spring, MD: Gryphon House.

Traditional Music Library. Available: www.traditionalmusic.co.uk (accessed March 10, 2010).

Stir and Bake

Bread, cookies, cakes, and pies . . . mmmmmm . . . are you getting hungry?

Rhyme	**Telling Guide**
### Making Bread	
"The farmer and the miller	
Have worked," the mother said,	
"And got the flour ready,	
So I will make the bread."	
She scooped from out of the barrel	Make scoop with both hands.
The flour white as snow,	Make "sieve" with fingertips of both hands together.
And in her sieve she put it	
And shook it to and fro.	Shake hands up and down.
Then in the pan of flour	Make circle in front with arms.
A little salt she threw;	Pinch salt with fingers and throw.
A cup of yeast she added,	Cup hand.
And poured in water too.	Action of pouring.
To mix them all together	
She stirred with busy might,	Action of stirring.
Then covered it and left it	
Until the bread was light.	Action of covering and patting bread loaf.
More flour then she sifted	
And kneaded well the dough,	Action of kneading, fists up and down.
And in the waiting oven	
The loaves of bread did go.	
The mother watched the baking,	
And turned the loaves, each one,	Hands in fists, turn them right, then left.
Until at last, rejoicing,	
She said, "My bread is done!"	
—Emilie Poulsson	
### Mix a Pancake	
Mix a pancake,	Do actions as indicated.
Stir a pancake,	
Pop it in the pan.	
Fry the pancake,	
Toss the pancake,	
Catch it if you can!	
—Traditional rhyme	

Pat-a-Cake

Pat-a-cake, pat-a-cake, baker's man.	Slap legs, then clap.
Bake me a cake as fast as you can.	Continue to slap legs and clap.
Roll it and pat it and mark it with a "B,"	Rolling and patting motions; make a "B."
And put it in the oven for Baby and me.	Motion of sliding cake in oven.

—Traditional rhyme

Pancakes, What a Treat!

Flapjacks	Clap.
Flapjacks	Clap.
Hot-on-the-griddle cake!	Throw arms in air.
Pancakes	Clap.
Pancakes	Clap.
Flip-over-easy cakes!	Turn hands, palms up, then down.
Blueberry	Squat lower on each word.
Buckwheat	
Buttermilk	
What a treat!	Jump high with arms raised.

—Jan Irving and Robin Currie

Pancake Stack

Have children form a semicircle around the leader, who does actions of pouring the batter and flipping the pancakes with an imaginary spatula. The "inside circle" is the space in the middle of the circle of children.

Is everybody ready to make pancakes?	
Here's our pan.	Motion to the "inside circle."
First, I'll pour in the batter.	Make pouring motion.
Everybody put in two round spoonfuls.	Prompt children to put out two rounded fists.
Good. Just right.	
Look at that! You're starting to spread.	Have children spread out fists to show two flat palms.
You're GOOD LOOKING PANCAKES!	
I can see lots of bubbles coming.	Have children wiggle fingers.
You're ready to turn over.	
Pancakes, flip!	Have children flip palms over.
Pancake one—stack.	
Two—stack.	Count as each child stacks a hand on top of another's until everyone has made one big pancake stack.
Three—stack.	
Just what I wanted for a morning snack!	
I LOVE PANCAKES!	Leader hugs the pancake hand stack.

—Jan Irving and Robin Currie

Cookie Jar

I looked in the cookie jar and what did I see?	Pretend to look.
A big fat cookie Mother put there for me!	Make big circle with hands.
Mother looked in the cookie jar	Pretend to look.

But she did not see
The big fat cookie she put there for me!

—From *Busy Fingers, Growing Minds*

Shake head "no."

Going to the Market

Come to the market
Just down the street.
We don't need a coach.
We can go on our feet.
Papa wants cherries,
And apples and steak.
Mama wants bread
And chocolate cake.

—Traditional rhyme

Beckon with your finger.
Point off to the side.
Pretend to hold horse's reins.
Tap feet in place.
Make small circles with fingers.
Make a big circle for steak.
Make long shape for loaf.
Rub tummy and smack lips.

To Market, To Market

To market, to market,
To buy a fat pig.
Home again, home again,
Jiggety jig.
To market, to market,
To buy a fat hog.
Home again, home again,
Jiggety jog.
To market, to market,
To buy a plum bun.
Home again, home again,
Shopping is done.

—Traditional rhyme

Clap it out, or pretend you are holding reins, riding a pig!

Counting Cookies

Cookies, cookies in a jar.
Let's count them, counting really far!
One gingerbread man with a raisin nose.
One sugar cookie, shaped like a rose.
One chocolate chip, all nice and crunchy.
One macaroon, nice and munchy!
One almond drop that tastes so sweet.
One double fudge that can't be beat!
One peanut butter that tastes really yummy.
One oatmeal raisin for my tummy.
One chewy coconut, we're almost done.
And one pecan sandie, the very last one.
How many cookies do you see?
Come and count them now with me!

—Barbara Scott

This rhyme also makes a great flannel or Velcro board activity!

Begin with one finger up.
Add fingers as the rhyme progresses.

Count all ten fingers.

Body Bread

Stir, stir, stir the dough.

Knead it, knead it.

Punch it down, punch it down.

Shape it, bake it.

Eat it up!

—Jan Irving and Robin Currie

This whole-body action chant can be done several ways. Divide children into five groups; teach one line of the chant and its accompanying actions to each group, and let them practice. Then do the chant with each group saying only the line they have practiced. As they know their parts better, say the chant faster. When they are secure with their words, have them do all five lines at the same time. After the children are familiar with the words and actions to the whole chant, do it as a round.

Said briskly; children seated performing stirring actions.

Elongate the "e" sound in the word "knead"; children on their knees performing kneading actions.

Say "punch" emphatically as children stand up and punch one fist into their other palm. Say "down" as children squat.

Children seated, curling their arms around their bodies and tucking their heads in.

Children jump up with their arms raised.

Pat-a-Cake

Pat-a-cake, pat-a-cake,
Baker's man.
That I will master as quick as I can.
Prick it and nick it,
And mark it with a "T,"
And there will be plenty
For baby and me.

—Traditional rhyme

Slap hands on thighs and clap in rhythm for the first three lines.

Point an index finger with emphasis; make a comma in the air. / Make letter "T" in the air.

Point to children, then self.

Do You Know the Muffin Man?

Do you know the muffin man,
The muffin man, the muffin man?
Do you know the muffin man,
Who lives on Drury Lane?
Yes, I know the muffin man,
The muffin man, the muffin man.
Yes, I know the muffin man,
Who lives on Drury Lane.

—Traditional rhyme

This is a super rhyme to do with just a clapping rhythm. Or, to change it up a bit, use rhythm instruments such as lummi sticks or sand blocks to pound out the rhythm!

Handy Spandy

Handy Spandy,
Jack, a-dandy,
Loves plum cake and sugar candy.
He bought some at the baker's shop,
And away he went, hop, hop, hop.

—Traditional rhyme

Clap in rhythm for first two lines.

Make circle with hands for cake.
Motion of handing over money.
Hop in place.

Blow, Wind, Blow

Blow, wind, blow,
And go, mill, go!
That the baker may take it,
And into rolls make it,
And bring us some hot in the morn.

—Traditional rhyme

Blow.
Roll hands around each other.

Motion of putting pan in oven.
Spread arms over head to represent sun.

Five Currant Buns

Five currant buns in a baker's shop.
Round and fat with a cherry on top.
Along came (child's name) with a penny one day.
Bought a currant bun and took it away.

—Author unknown

Begin this rhyme with five fingers up.

Take fingers away as rhyme progresses.
Continue for four, three, two, one.

Grinding Flour

We push the mill,
The flour we make.
And then for grandma,
A cake we'll bake.

—Traditional Chinese rhyme

Walk in circle, hands in front.

Make circle with hands.

Cake Baking

We turn the cake,
The cake we bake.
We put in oil, or pork, or steak.
And when 'tis done,
We'll have some fun,
And give a piece to everyone.

—Traditional Chinese rhyme

Make circle in front of body with hands.
Count off ingredients on fingers.
Action of taking cake out of oven.

Action of passing out pieces.

Bake, Bake the Cake

Bake, bake the cake,
The baker has declared.
If one wants to bake a fine cake,
He has to have these seven things:
Sugar and salt,
Butter and lard,

Put index finger in the air.

Make circle in front of body with hands.
Count off seven ingredients on fingers.

Eggs and flour,
Saffron makes the cake yellow.
Push it into the oven.

                    —Traditional German rhyme

Motion of putting cake in oven.

Five Donuts

Five little donuts in a bakery shop,
Sprinkled with powdered sugar on top.
Along comes (child's name) with a penny to pay.
He/she buys a donut and takes it away.

                    —Lynda Roberts

This is also a great rhyme to do as a flannel or Velcro board activity!
Begin this rhyme with five fingers up.

Take away fingers as rhyme progresses.
Continue with four, three, two, one.

Five Little Cookies: A Countdown Rhyme

Five little cookies were sitting on a plate.
All the little children thought they looked just great.
One child picked a chocolate chip, and wished he could
    have more.
When that child was finished, there were only four.
Four little cookies were sitting on a plate.
All the little children thought they looked just great.
One child picked a pink one, and sat down beneath a tree.
When that child was finished, there were only three.
Three little cookies were sitting on a plate.
All the little children thought they looked just great.
One child picked a peanut butter, and he began to chew.
When that child was finished, there were only two.
Two little cookies were sitting on a plate.
All the little children thought they looked just great.
One child picked an oatmeal, because the raisins looked
    like fun.
When that child was finished, there was only one.
One little cookie was sitting on a plate.
All the little children thought it looked just great.
One child picked the last one, and when that child was done,
Mother looked at the plate and saw there were none.
No more cookies sitting on the plate.
All the little children thought they had tasted great.
Now all the little children were sitting by the door,
And Mother thought that she had better bake some more.

                    —Kay Lincycomb

This rhyme also works well as a flannel or Velcro board activity!
Begin this rhyme with five fingers up.

Take away fingers as rhyme progresses.

Rub tummy.

There's a Cookie on My Plate

There's a cookie on my plate, on my plate, on my plate.
There's a cookie on my plate, a cookie right here.

Sung to the tune of "There's a Hole in My Bucket."
Use one hand flat like a plate, and point to it.

I'm ready to eat it, to eat it, to eat it.
I'm ready to eat it, to eat it right now.
That cookie's so yummy,
So yummy, so yummy.
That cookie's so yummy, it tasted so good.
Now the plate is so empty, so empty, so empty.
Now the plate is so empty.
Please, Mom, bake some more!

Act as if eating.

Rub tummy.

Put hands out and open them.
Say loudly.

—Kay Lincycomb

The Little Bitty Cookie: An Action Song

Sung to the tune of "The Itsy Bitsy Spider."
Rolling hands.

A little bitty cookie rolled across the floor.
I tried to catch it, but it rolled right out the door.
I was so hungry; I could not let it go.
I chased that little cookie, but I was too slow.
That little bitty cookie rolled across the yard.
I tried to catch it, but it was so hard.
I finally caught the cookie, when it jumped into the lake.
And that soggy little cookie, tasted oh so great!

Rub tummy.
Move arms as if running.

Rolling hands.
Jump.
Rub tummy.

—Kay Lincycomb

Ten Little Pancakes

Sung to the tune of "Ten Little Indians."

Count out the pancakes on your fingers.

One little, two little, three little pancakes,
Four little, five little, six little pancakes,
Seven, eight, nine, ten little pancakes,
Piled on my plate.
Ten little, nine little, eight little pancakes,
Seven little, six little, five little pancakes,
Four, three, two, one little pancake,
They all went down just great!

Hand showing tall

—Kay Lincycomb

Five Little Pies

Begin this rhyme with five fingers up.
Take away fingers as rhyme progresses.

Five little pies in the grocery store.
(Child's name) bought one, and then there were four.
Four little pies displayed for all to see.
(Child's name) bought one, and then there were three.
Three little pies, but before I knew,
(Child's name) bought one, and then there were two.
Two little pies, oh what fun!
(Child's name) bought one, and then there was one.
One little pie, sitting all alone.
(Child's name) bought that pie and then there were none.

—Barbara Scott

Ten Little Cookies

Ten little cookies laying on a plate.
Mom eats two, then there were eight.
When Dad comes home, two cookies he picks.
Leaving on the plate only six.
Brother comes home, slamming the door.
He eats two cookies, then there are four.
When Sister comes come, there are still a few.
She eats a couple, then there are two.
Baby wakes up. His nap is done.
He eats a cookie, then there is one.
The cat jumps on the table and eats the last one.
The poor dog is too late. He only gets a crumb.

—Susan Dailey

This rhyme is great to do with visuals on a flannel or Velcro board.
Begin rhyme with ten fingers up.
Take away fingers in twos as rhyme progresses.

We Are Gonna Bake a Cake

We are gonna bake a cake,
Bake a cake, bake a cake.
We are gonna bake a cake.
Let's get started!
Pour the cake mix in the bowl,
In the bowl, in the bowl.
Pour the cake mix in the bowl.
Keep on pouring!
Add the eggs and oil, too,
Oil, too, oil, too.
Add the eggs and oil, too
To the cake mix!
Mix it, mix it really well,
Really well, really well.
Mix it, mix it really well.
Fill the cake pan!
In the oven it will go,
It will go, it will go.
In the oven it will go.
Set the timer!
Take it out, it sure smells good,
Sure smells good, sure smells good.
Take it out, it sure smells good.
Smells so yummy!

Sung to the tune of "London Bridge." To mix batter in the bowl, either pretend to have a big stirring spoon or put one arm in a semicircle at the waist to represent a bowl and the other hand stirs.
Point to self.

Action of pouring out mix.

Motion of cracking eggs and pouring oil.

Motion of mixing batter in bowl.

Motion of sliding pan in oven.

Motion of setting timer.
Sniff.

Action of inhaling aroma.

Spread the icing on the top,
On the top, on the top.
Spread the icing on the top.
Makes me hungry!
All the cake has disappeared,
Disappeared, disappeared.
All the cake has disappeared.
"Where? In my tummy!"

—Barbara Scott

Motion of icing cake.

Rub tummy.

Speak this line; point to stomach and pat.

This fingerplay can also be done as a flannel or Velcro board activity.

Muffin Count!

Counting muffins can be fun!
Here's cinnamon . . . it's number one!
This one has berries that are blue.
Here's blueberry . . . it's number two!
This one comes from a fruit on a tree.
Here's apple . . . it's number three!
This one's yummy, that's for sure.
Here's chocolate chip . . . it's number four!
This one is as good as sweetness from the hive.
It's oatmeal honey . . . it's number five!

—Barbara Scott

Hold up one finger.

Hold up two fingers.

Hold up three fingers.

Hold up four fingers.

Baker Man, Baker Man

Baker man, baker man,
Turn around.
Baker man, baker man,
Touch the ground.
Baker man, baker man,
Cut the dough.
Baker man, baker man,
Don't be slow.
Baker man, baker man,
Roll it out.
Baker man, baker man,
Please don't pout!
Baker man, baker man,
Add those sprinkles.
Baker man, baker man,
Don't get the giggles!

—Adapted traditional rhyme

Do motions as indicated.

Motion of cutting with cookie cutter.

Shake finger, admonishingly.

Motion of rolling dough.

Stick out lower lip.

Wiggle fingers in air.

Put hand over mouth; pretend to laugh.

Five Delicious Cookies

Five delicious cookies,
We bought them at the store.

Begin rhyme with five fingers up.

My little brother ate one;
Now there are four.   *Take away fingers as rhyme progresses.*
Four delicious cookies,
With a cup of tea.
My little sister ate one;
Now there are three.
Three delicious cookies,
I would love to chew!
My daddy came and ate one;
Now there are two.
Two delicious cookies,
This really is no fun!
My mommy came and ate one,
And now there's just one.
One delicious cookie
Disappearing fast!
Now it's in MY tummy!   *Rub tummy.*
They're all gone at last!

—Barbara Scott

Five Little Cupcakes

Five little cupcakes in a bakery shop,   *Begin this rhyme with five fingers up.*
Round and fat with frosting on top.
Along came (child's name) with her quarter one day,
And bought a cupcake and ran away.   *Take away fingers as rhyme progresses.*
Four little cupcakes. . . .
Three little cupcakes. . . .
Two little cupcakes. . . .
One little cupcake. . . .

—Stephanie Stokes, LibraryPalooza

Books to Share

Beaumont, Karen. 2008. *Who Ate All the Cookie Dough?* New York: Henry Holt and Company. ISBN: 978-0805082678.
Miranda, Anne. 2001. *To Market, To Market.* Logan, IA: Perfection Learning. ISBN: 978-0756906672.
Nakagawa, Chihiro. 2008. *Who Made This Cake?* Honesdale, PA: Front Street. ISBN: 978-1590785959.
Staake, Bob. 2008. *The Donut Chef.* New York: Golden Books. ISBN: 978-0375844034.
Wellington, Monica. 2006. *Mr. Cookie Baker.* New York: Dutton Juvenile. ISBN: 978-0525477631.
Wilson, Karma. 2006. *Whopper Cake.* New York: Margaret K. McElderry. ISBN: 978-0689838446.

Musical Selections

"C Is for Cookie" from *C Is for Cookie: Cookie's Favorite Songs.* ASIN: B000002BBC. (This CD has lots of other cool cookie-themed songs on it as well!)

"Doughnuts" from *Jim Gill Makes It Noisy in Boise, Idaho* by Jim Gill. Available: www.jimgill.com (accessed March 15, 2010).

"Five Brown Buns" from *Great Big Hits* by Sharon, Lois, and Bram. ASIN: B000008KML.

"I'm a Pretzel" from *So Big: Activity Songs for Little Ones* by Hap Palmer. ASIN: B0000690AD.

"Let's Go to the Market" from *We All Live Together*, vol. 5, by Greg and Steve. ASIN: B00000DGMT.

"Muffin Man" from *We All Live Together*, vol. 2, by Greg and Steve. ASIN: B00000AG62.

Sources

Anonymous. 1902. *Nursery Rhymes from Mother Goose with Alphabet.* Philadelphia: W.W. Houston. Available: www.childrenslibrary.org (accessed March 10, 2010).

BBC School Radio. "Early Learning: Listen and Play." Available: www.bbc.co.uk/schoolradio/earlylearning/listenandplay_autumn06_prog09.shtml (accessed April 9, 2010).

Dailey, Susan M. 2001. *A Storytime Year.* New York: Neal-Schuman.

Headland, Isaac Taylor. 1900. *Chinese Mother Goose Rhymes.* Grand Rapids, MI: Fleming H. Revell.

Irving, Jan. 1994. *Second Helpings: Books and Activities about Food.* Santa Barbara, CA: Teacher Ideas Press.

Irving, Jan, and Robin Currie. 1986. *Mudlicious: Stories and Activities Featuring Food for Preschool Children.* Santa Barbara, CA: Libraries Unlimited.

LibraryPalooza. Available: www.librarypalooza.net (accessed March 15, 2010).

Lincycomb, Kay. 2007. *Storytimes . . . Plus!* New York: Neal-Schuman.

Mama Lisa's World of Children & International Culture. Available: www.mamalisa.com (accessed March 4, 2010).

McKinnon, Elizabeth, and Gayle Bittinger. 1994. *Busy Bees Fall: Fun for Two's and Three's.* Everett, WA: Warren Publishing House.

"Nursery Rhymes." The Mother Goose Pages. Available: www-personal.umich.edu/~pfa/dreamhouse/nursery/rhymes.html (accessed March 13, 2010).

Poulsson, Emilie. 1921. *Fingerplays for Nursery and Kindergarten.* New York: Lothrop, Lee, and Shepard.

Redleaf, Rhonda. 1983. *Busy Fingers, Growing Minds.* St. Paul, MN: Redleaf Press.

Roberts, Lynda. 1985. *Mitt Magic: Fingerplays for Finger Puppets.* Silver Spring, MD: Gryphon House.

Rossetti, Christina. 1893. *Sing-Song: A Nursery Rhyme Book.* New York: Macmillan and Company. Available: http://digital.library.upenn.edu/women/rossetti/singsong/singsong.html#mix (accessed April 9, 2010).

Sinclair, Patti, Tami Chumbley, and Kathy Ross. 2005. *Collaborative Summer Library Program Manual.* Mason City, IA: Collaborative Summer Library Program.

Wiggin, Kate Douglas, and Nora Archibald Smith. 1907. *Pinafore Palace.* New York: Grosset & Dunlap. Available: www.gutenberg.org (accessed March 15, 2010).

Teeth

These rhymes let you have fun showing those pearly whites!

Rhyme	Telling Guide

My Teeth

There are teeth in my mouth
That are shiny and white.
I brush them carefully morning and night.
They help me chew and keep my smile bright.
Even though now they fit snug and tight,
One of these days I may feel one wiggle.
Then my tooth will get loose and jiggle and jiggle.
And my tooth will fall out and what do you know?
In the very same spot a new tooth will grow.
—From *Busy Fingers, Growing Minds*

Telling Guide:
Point to teeth.
Imitate brushing.
Make chewing motions and smile.

Pretend to wiggle a tooth.
Pretend to pull tooth out.

Toothbrush Song

Brush your teeth,
Brush your teeth.
It's a quarter to one,
And you want to have a little fun . . .
You brush your teeth.
When you wake up in the morning,
It's a quarter to two,
And you're looking around for something to do . . .
You brush your teeth.
When you wake up in the morning,
It's a quarter to three,
And your mind is humming twiddledeedee . . .
You brush your teeth.
When you wake up in the morning,
It's a quarter to four,
And you think you hear a knock at your door . . .
You brush your teeth.
When you wake up in the morning,
It's a quarter to five,
And you just can't wait to come alive . . .
You brush your teeth.
You brush your teeth.
You brush your teeth.
You brush your teeth.
—From ChildFun

Telling Guide:
Make "chchch, chchchchchchchhhh" sound; repeat.

Make "chchch, chchchchchchchhhh" sound.

Make "chchch, chchchchchchchhhh" sound.

Make "chchch, chchchchchchchhhh" sound.

Make "chchch, chchchchchchchhhh" sound.

Make "chchch, chchchchchchchhhh" sound; repeat more quietly.

Repeat sound even more quietly.

Say the last line in a whisper.

Got My Toothbrush 💿

Got my toothpaste,
Got my brush.
I won't hurry, I won't rush.
Making sure my teeth are clean
Front and back and in between.
When I brush for quite a while,
I will have a happy smile!

—From Laurabaas.com

The Dentist

The dentist cleans my teeth.
The dentist cleans my teeth.
He scrubs them clean,
I rinse them out.

We make a real great team!

—Carolyn N. Cullum

Where's My Tooth? An Action Rhyme

My tooth is loose, see it wiggle.
Uh-oh!
My tooth is gone.
Now where did it go?
It could be here.
It could be there.
It could be just about anywhere.
Who can find my tooth?
Is this my tooth?
"No!"

LAST VERSE:
Well my tooth is back, and I won't tarry.
It'll go under my pillow for the tooth fairy!

—Kay Lincycomb

I Have a Loose Tooth

I have a loose tooth,
I have a loose tooth.
See it move, see it move.
Wiggle, wiggle, wiggle,

Sung to the tune of "Twinkle, Twinkle, Little Star."

Hold imaginary toothpaste in one hand.

Hold imaginary toothbrush in other hand. / Shake head "no."

Point to teeth.

Brushing motion.

Smile.

Sung to the tune of "The Farmer in the Dell."

Brushing motions.

Vigorous brushing motions.

Pantomime swishing water around in mouth.

Cross arms in front of body and nod head.

Look around.

Point.

Point.

Put animal tooth on flannel board.

Ask audience.

Repeat verse but with different animal teeth. For the last tooth, use one that looks like a human tooth so that the answer is "Yes!"

Sung to the tune of "Frère Jacques."

Pretend to wiggle tooth.

Wiggle, wiggle wiggle.
'Til it's out, 'til it's out.
I have a loose tooth,
I have a loose tooth.
It's in my hand, it's in my hand.   Hold out hand and point.
Wiggle, wiggle wiggle,
Wiggle, wiggle, wiggle.
Now it's out, now it's out.
I have a loose tooth,
I have a loose tooth.
What do I do? What do I do?   Shrug.
Put it under my pillow, put it under my pillow.
And go to sleep, and go to sleep.   Hand on hand.
I have a loose tooth,
I have a loose tooth.
Now it's gone! Now it's gone!   Hold up empty hand.
Wiggle, wiggle, wiggle,
Wiggle, wiggle, wiggle.
Tooth fairy came. Tooth fairy came.   Hold up a quarter in hand.

—Kay Lincycomb

I'm a Toothbrush: An Action Rhyme

I'm a toothbrush. Just watch me go.
I am brushing to and fro.   Jump side to side.
I'm a toothbrush. The best you've ever found.
I am brushing around and around.   Turn around.
I'm a toothbrush. I'll keep away the plaque.
I am brushing in the front, then the back.   Jump forward and backward.
I'm a toothbrush. Now don't you frown.
I am brushing up and down.   Jump up and down.
I'm a toothbrush. If you brush awhile,
I will give you a pretty smile.   Smile; point to mouth.

—Kay Lincycomb

Brush, Brush, Brush

Sung to the tune of "Row, Row, Row Your Boat."

Brush, brush, brush your teeth,   Motion of brushing teeth.
Brush them every day,
And you will have no cavities,   Shake head "no."
So shout "hip, hip, hooray"!   Pump fist in the air.

—Adapted traditional rhyme

When You Get Up in the Morning

When you get up in the morning, brush your teeth.
When you get up in the morning, brush your teeth.
It's a habit that is right.
Brush them morning, noon, and night.
When you get up in the morning, brush your teeth.
When you get up in the morning, brush your teeth.
When you get up in the morning, brush your teeth.
When you get up in the morning,
Even though you may be yawnin'
When you get up in the morning, brush your teeth.

—Adapted traditional rhyme

Sung to the tune of "If You're Happy and You Know It."
Motion of brushing.

Nod head "yes."
Count out on three fingers.
Motion of brushing.
Motion of brushing.

Stretch.
Big yawn.
Motion of brushing.

Brushing Teeth

Brush your teeth,
Brush your teeth,
Morning, noon, and night.
Brush your teeth until they shine,
Nice and pearly white!
Brush your teeth,
Brush your teeth,
Brush them 'til they glow.
You want your teeth to look their best,
When you smile and say hello!

—Adapted traditional rhyme

Sung to the tune of "Jingle Bells."

Motion of brushing.

Pretend to spit!

Motion of brushing.

Nod head "yes."
Big smile!

Types of Teeth

I know a type of tooth you have that's used to tear your food.
IN-CI-S-O-R,
IN-CI-S-O-R,
IN-CI-S-O-R,
Incisor is its name-o!
I know a type of tooth you have that's used to grasp your food.
CA-N-I-N-E,
CA-N-I-N-E,
CA-N-I-N-E,
And canine is its name-o!
I know a type of tooth you have that's used to grind your food.
M-O-L-A-R,
M-O-L-A-R,
M-O-L-A-R,
And molar is its name-o!

—Adapted traditional rhyme

Sung to the tune of "Bingo."

Say the "IN" and "CI" letters together.

Say the "CA" letters together.

Toothbrush, Toothbrush

Toothbrush, toothbrush,
Brush around.

Toothbrush, toothbrush,
Brush up and down.

Toothbrush, toothbrush,
Mouth's open wide.

Toothbrush, toothbrush,
Brush side to side.

Toothbrush, toothbrush,
Brush in the back.

Toothbrush, toothbrush,
Brush away that snack.

Toothbrush, toothbrush,
Almost done!

Toothbrush, toothbrush,
That was fun!

—Adapted traditional rhyme

Brushing motion.

Do motion as indicated.

Open mouth wide.

Do motion as indicated.

Open and brush those back teeth!

Nod head "yes."

Clap three times.

Wiggly Tooth

Have you seen my wiggly tooth,
My wiggly tooth, my wiggly tooth?
Have you seen my wiggly tooth?
It moves this way and that!
"Hey! It came out!"
My tooth goes under my pillow,
My pillow, my pillow.
My tooth goes under my pillow,
And now I go to sleep!
Hooray, the tooth fairy has come,
She has come, she has come.
Hooray, the tooth fairy has come.
She left me lots of cash!
"See?"

—Adapted traditional rhyme

Sung to the tune of "The Muffin Man."
Put hands out to sides, questioning.

Move finger back and forth by mouth.
Speak this line; hold imaginary tooth.
One hand, palm down, is pillow; slide other hand under it.

Put head on hands; pretend to sleep.
Pump fist in the air in excitement.

Speak this line; show play money to the children.

Brushing Teeth

Brushing teeth is fun,
Brushing teeth is fun.
Hi ho the derry-o,
Brushing teeth is fun.
I take my favorite paste,
And squeeze it on my brush.

Sung to the tune of "The Farmer in the Dell."
Motion of brushing.

Nod head "yes."
Motion of holding tube of toothpaste.
Motion of putting toothpaste on brush.

I take the time to really clean.	Brushing motion.
I'm never in a rush!	Shake head "no."
And now my brushing's done.	
My teeth are nice and clean.	Smile!
Remember to brush up and down	Put hand to head; tap temple as if thinking.
And even in between!	

—Adapted traditional rhyme

This Is the Way

Sung to the tune of "The Mulberry Bush."

This is the way we brush our teeth,	Motion of brushing.
Brush our teeth, brush our teeth.	
This is the way we brush our teeth,	
So early in the morning.	
This is the way we floss our teeth,	Motion of flossing.
Floss our teeth, floss our teeth.	
This is the way we floss our teeth,	
So early in the morning.	

—Adapted traditional rhyme

These Are My Teeth

These are my teeth.	Point to teeth.
I open them wide,	Open mouth wide.
For the dentist	
To look inside.	Hand over eyes, peer.
He checks each tooth	
With patience and care,	Nod head "yes."
And fixes the cavities	
That might be hiding there.	Hand over eyes, hiding.

—Barbara Scott

Books to Share

Child, Lauren. 2006. *My Wobbly Tooth Must Not Ever Never Fall Out.* London: Puffin Books. ISBN: 978-0141382401.

Faulker, Keith. 2002. *The Mixed-Up Tooth Fairy.* New York: Cartwheel Books. ISBN: 978-0439356091.

Palatini, Margie. 2004. *The Sweet Tooth.* New York: Simon & Schuster Children's Publishing. ISBN: 978-0689851599.

Schaefer, Lola. 2004. *Loose Tooth.* New York: HarperCollins. ISBN: 978-0060527761.

Van Leeuwen, Jean. 2009. *Amanda Pig and the Wobbly Tooth.* London: Puffin Books. ISBN: 978-0142412909.

Wing, Natasha. 2003. *The Night before the Tooth Fairy.* New York: Grosset & Dunlap. ISBN: 978-0448432526.

Musical Selections

"Brush Your Teeth" from *Singable Songs for the Very Young* by Raffi. ASIN: B0000003H4.

"Clean My Teeth" from *Jump and Jive with Hi-5*. ASIN: B0002O06X0.

"Loose Tooth" from *Sing It! Say It! Stamp It! Sway It!*, vol. 2, by Peter and Ellen Allard. ASIN: B000056IIN.

"My Tooth It Is Wiggling" from *Pizza Pizzazz* by Peter and Ellen Allard. ASIN: B000GETZH4.

"Tiger with a Toothbrush" from *We're on Our Way* by Hap Palmer. ASIN: B00000JXNG.

"Wiggly Tooth" from *Don't Forget the Donut* by Wayne Potash. ASIN: B000BP2Y26.

Sources

ChildFun. Available: www.childfun.com/themes.dental.shtml (accessed April 9, 2010).

Cullum, Carolyn N. 2007. *The Storytime Sourcebook II*. New York: Neal-Schuman.

Laurabaas.com. Available: laurabaas.com/2008/02/17/all-about-teeth-storytime/ (accessed May 15, 2010).

Lincycomb, Kay. 2007. *Storytimes . . . Plus!* New York: Neal-Schuman.

Redleaf, Rhonda. 1983. *Busy Fingers, Growing Minds*. St. Paul, MN: Redleaf Press.

Songs for Teaching. "You Brush Your Teeth." Available: www.songsforteaching.com/healthyhabits/brushyourteeth.htm (accessed April 9, 2010).

Chapter 9

Transportation to Zoo

Transportation: Boats, Trains, Planes, and Automobiles
Enjoy these rhymes that celebrate all of the ways we go, go, go!

Rhyme	Telling Guide
### Row Your Boat Some More 💿	*Sung to the tune of "Row, Row, Row Your Boat."*
Row, row, row your boat Gently down the stream. Merrily, merrily, merrily, merrily, Life is but a dream.	Pretend to row slowly.
Row, row, row your boat Slowly down the creek. Lazily, lazily, lazily, lazily, Slowly down the creek.	Pretend to row slowly.
Row, row, row your boat Quickly down the river. Faster, faster, faster, faster, Quickly down the river.	Pretend to row quickly.
Row, row, row your boat All around the lake. Circle, circle, circle, circle, All around the lake.	Turn in circles while rowing.
Row, row, row your boat Through the sticky swamp. Slugging, slugging, slugging, slugging, Stuck there in the mud. UGH!	Sink quietly to seated position.
—Jan Irving	
### All Hands on Deck	
One fat sailor called to the crew.	Hold up thumb.
Next came sailor number two.	Hold up index finger.
Number three was tall as the mast.	Hold up middle finger.
Number four came running fast.	Hold up ring finger.
Number five was not too tall—	Hold up smallest finger.
But he was captain of them all.	
He called six, seven, and eight	Hold up thumb, index, middle, ring, and smallest fingers of other hand.
Nine and ten came a little late.	
"All hands on deck," the captain said.	Hold up all ten fingers.
"Hoist the anchor. Full speed ahead!"	
—Jan Irving	

Motor Boat, Motor Boat

Motor boat, motor boat,
Go so slow.
Motor boat, motor boat,
Go so fast.
Motor boat, motor boat, step on the gas!

—Traditional rhyme

Steer boat very slowly.

Steer boat fast.
Foot makes motion of pushing imaginary gas pedal.

The Boats

This is the way, all the long day,
The boats go sailing by,

To and fro, in a row,
Under the bridge so high.

—From *Let's Do Fingerplays*

Use one hand as a boat and the other as a bridge.
Move hand back and forth under bridge.

Row, Row, Row Your Boat

Row, row, row your boat,
Gently down the stream.
Merrily, merrily, merrily, merrily,
Life is but a dream.

—Traditional rhyme

To do the rowing motion, fold arms high in front of chest, with elbows extending out and fisted hands meeting; reach forward and pull back as if rowing.

The Sailboat

The sailboat has a very tall mast
That holds its sail in place.
When the wind blows, the boat goes fast,
And I feel the wind on my face.

—From *Busy Fingers, Growing Minds*

Hold arm up high.
Raise arms over head to form a triangle.
Pretend to blow and move arms fast.
Rub face.

A Boxcar Countdown

Clickety clack clickety clack—
Hear the train come down the track,
Puffing 'cause it's going fast.
Count the cars as they go past.
Clickety-one, clickety-one,
Here comes boxcar number one.
Clickety-two, clickety-two,
Here comes boxcar number two.
Clickety-three, clickety-three,
Here comes boxcar number three.
Clickety-four, clickety-four,
Here comes boxcar number four.
Clickety-five, clickety-five,
Here comes boxcar number five.

Hold up one finger.

Add fingers as rhyme progresses.

Clickety-six, clickety-six,
Here comes boxcar number six.
Clickety-seven, clickety-seven,
Here comes boxcar number seven.
Clickety-eight, clickety-eight,
Here comes boxcar number eight.
Clickety-nine, clickety-nine,
Here comes boxcar number nine.
Clickety-ten, clickety-ten,
Here comes boxcar number ten.
Clickety clack, clickety clack—
The train has gone on down the track.
Puffing 'cause it's going fast.
Wave good-bye 'cause it's all past.   Wave goodbye.

—Jan Irving

The Train

The train goes chugging up and down,   Chug back and forth.
Carrying goods from town to town.
It carries corn and new cars, too,
And as it goes, it says, "Choo-choo."

—Elizabeth McKinnon

The Train

Choo, choo, choo,   Slide hands together.
The train runs down the track.   Run fingers down arm.
Choo, choo, choo,   Slide hands together.
And then it runs right back.   Run fingers up arm.

—From *Let's Do Fingerplays*

Down by the Station

Down by the station, early in the morning,   Tap legs or clap hands.
Do you see the engines standing in a row?
Do you see the engineer pull the big whistle?   Close fist; raise high; pull forward.
Toot, toot, choo, choo, off we go.   Blow for "toot"; slide palms together
                                                       for "choo."

—Traditional rhyme

An Airplane

To make the airplane, extend right hand in front of body horizontally, palm opened flat, facing down.

If I had an airplane,   Make airplane with hand.
Zum, zum, zum,
I would fly to Mexico,   Fly hand through air.
Wave my hand and off I'd go.   Wave to people.
If I had an airplane,   Make airplane with hand.
Zum, zum, zum.

—From *Let's Do Fingerplays*

Up, Up, Up

Up, up, up.

Here we go up, up, up!

Now we're flying!

Here we fly up and down, up and down.

And here we go 'round and 'round and 'round.

Now we're landing,

Fly slowly, slowly.

Now we're down, down, on the ground.

—Kathy Ross

Stand up.

Reach arms up.

Flap arms up and down.

Turn around while flapping arms.

Stop turning; flap arms slowly.

Sit down.

Uplifting Experience

I know a way you sit on the ground,

Then rise to the sky with a *zzzzzip*.

You can ride in the basket of a hot air balloon,

Or go on a helicopter trip.

—Jan Irving

Squat on ground.

Stand, saying "Zzzzzip."

Touch fingertips over head.

Cross wrists over head; wave hands.

The Wheels on My Bike

This rhyme can be sung to the tune of "The Wheels on the Bus" or chanted.

Roll hands around each other.

The wheels on my bike go 'round and 'round,

'Round and 'round, 'round and 'round.

The wheels on my bike go 'round and 'round,

All around my town.

Make big circle with hand.

ADDITIONAL VERSES:

The bell on my bike goes ring, ring, ring . . .

The pedals on my bike go up and down . . .

The handles on my bike go left and right . . .

—Kathy Ross

Pretend to ring bike bell.

Move up and down.

Move imaginary handlebars from side to side.

Pumping Gas

See the gas pumps all in a row.

Lower the hose, push the crank,

Put the nozzle in the tank,

Squeeze the handle,

And hear the gasoline flow.

"S-s-s-s-s-s."

Watch the pump,

Look at those numbers go!

—From *Busy Fingers, Growing Minds*

Imitate actions.

Gas Station Song

Sung to the tune of "Mary Had a Little Lamb."

Gas stations are fun for me,

Fun for me, fun for me.

Gas stations are fun for me,

Bring your family!

Mommy pumps the gas like this,	Mime pumping action.
Gas like this, gas like this.	
Mommy pumps the gas like this,	
Fill 'er, fill 'er up!	
Daddy squirts some air in tires	"Psssst."
Air in tires, air in tires.	
Daddy squirts some air in tires,	
So they won't go flat.	
Pop the hood up, check inside,	Clap.
Check inside, check inside.	
Pop the hood up, check inside,	
Is everything all right? Right!	
Now drive through our free car wash,	Wiggle fingers over head.
Free car wash, free car wash.	
Now drive through our free car wash,	
But roll the windows up. Yup!	

—Jan Irving

School Bus Song

Where oh where is school bus 7?	*Sung to the tune of "Paw Paw Patch."* Shade eyes and look around.
Where oh where is school bus 7?	
Where oh where is school bus 7?	
Can you see it coming down the street?	
Could it be stuck in traffic?	Pretend to steer wheel.
Could it be stuck in traffic?	
Could it be stuck in traffic?	
Can you see it coming down the street?	
Did it run out of gas?	Throw up hands in despair.
Did it run out of gas?	
Did it run out of gas?	
Can you see it coming down the street?	
Did the tires all go flat?	Clap.
Did the tires all go flat?	
Did the tires all go flat?	
Can you see it coming down the street?	
Here it comes—it's right on time.	Wave.
Here it comes—it's right on time.	
Here it comes—it's right on time.	
Hop aboard and we are off to school.	

—Jan Irving

Down by the Station

Down by the station,	
Early in the morning.	Arms make circle above head to represent sun.
See the little puffer-bellies	

All in a row.

See the engine driver
Pull his little lever.

"Puff, puff, peep, peep"
Off we go!

—Traditional rhyme

Put hands in front, about 12 inches apart, arms bent at elbows.
Or "station master."
Or "pull the little handle"; motion of pulling.
Or "Chug, chug, toot, toot!"
"Chug" around like a train.

Grandpa's Boat

Good old Grandpa built a boat,
Put it in the pond to float.
It was strong and it was light;
Nicely painted green and white.
Jack and Charley learned to row,
Did their best to make it go;
Taking turns, they tried to pull,
'Til they both could row and scull.
Soon the boys grew brown and stout,
Rowing all the girls about.
Rowing here, and rowing there,
While the summer days were fair.

—Traditional rhyme

Motion of hammering.

Put arm out in front; see-saw back and forth to indicate boat on water.

Motion of painting.

Motion of rowing.

Row some more!

Show muscles!

Point in one direction, then in other.

Hands make large circle above head.

Engine on the Track

Here is the engine on the track.
Here is the coal car, just in back.
Here is the boxcar to carry freight.
Here is the mail car. Don't be late.
Way back here at the end of the train
Rides the caboose through the sun and rain.

—Lynda Roberts

Hold up thumb.
Hold up pointer finger.
Hold up middle finger.
Hold up ring finger.
Hold up little finger.

Boats Sail On

This small boat
It has oars.
We must row to get to shore.
So let's row, row, row, row
Faster let us go.
I just found it has a hole.
This old boat
It has sails.
We pull hard to raise these sails.
And the wind blows hard,
The faster we will go.
At least this time, no one must row.

Sung to the tune of "This Old Man."

Pretend to row boat while sitting on floor.

Point to hole in bottom of boat.

Show children how to pull rope to raise sails.

This big boat
We turn it on.
It doesn't need oars or sails to run.
We just turn the key,   Pretend turning key to start engine.
And the engine starts to roar.
Watch us as we leave the shore.   Wave to everyone on the shore.

—Carolyn N. Cullum

The Wheels on the Bus

The wheels on the bus go 'round and 'round,   Roll hands around each other.
'Round and 'round, 'round and 'round.
The wheels on the bus go 'round and 'round
On the way to school.

ADDITIONAL VERSES:

The lights on the bus go blink, blink, blink . . .   Open and close fingers quickly.
The doors on the bus go open and shut . . .   Bring hands together in front of chest;
                                                          swing outward and inward.
The stop sign on the bus goes in and out . . .   Hold arm out to side; bring palm in
                                                          toward body, then away.
The driver on the bus says, "Move on back!" . . .   Hold up fist with thumb out; point
                                                          backward over shoulder.
The students on the bus go up and down . . .   Bounce up and down.

—Adapted traditional rhyme by Susan M. Dailey

Car Sounds

My car makes lots of sounds.   On "car" pretend to drive; on
My car makes lots of sounds.   "sounds" put hand to ear.
My car makes lots of sounds.
Listen while it makes these sounds.
My seat belt goes click.   Pretend to fasten seat belt.
Listen while it goes click.
My horn goes beep, beep, beep.   On "beep, beep," pretend to honk horn.
My turn light goes . . .   Make click noise with tongue; open
Listen while it goes . . .   fingers in rhythm.
My engine goes vroom, vroom.   Pretend to drive.
Listen while it goes vroom.

—Adapted from a song by Susan M. Dailey

I'm a School Bus

I am long.   Stretch arms in front of body.
And I am tall.   Stretch arms high.
And I am very, very wide.   Stretch arms to sides.
I am yellow with black numbers
And a stop arm on my side.   Palm facing out, move hand to side.
I'm a school bus.   Point to self; nod head.

I'm a school bus.
Yes, I am a school bus.
I'm a school bus.
I'm a very cool school bus.

Put two thumbs up.

—Adapted from a song by Susan M. Dailey

My Bike

Pedal 'round and 'round,
Pedal 'round and 'round.

Roll hands around each other.

I steer my bike
Anywhere I like.

Pretend to steer.

Pedal 'round and 'round.

Roll hands around each other.

—Adapted from a song by Susan M. Dailey

Washing the Car

Sung to the tune of "The Mulberry Bush."

Let's go out and wash the car,
Wash the car, wash the car.
Let's go out and wash the car,
Because it is so dirty.

Pretend to wash car.

ADDITIONAL VERSES:
Take a brush and scrub the tires . . .
Because they are so dirty.
Take a sponge and soap the car . . .
Because it is so dirty.
Take a hose and rinse the car . . .
Because it is so soapy.
Take a towel and dry the car . . .
Now the car's not dirty.

Pretend to do motions as mentioned.

—Adapted from a song by Susan M. Dailey

We Are Going on a Bike Ride

We are going on a bike ride.
Wheels on the bike go 'round and 'round.

Roll hands around each other.

Steer it straight and pedal steady.

Steer and pedal.

But now look what we found. . . .
"Some potholes"

Speak remaining lines; dip hands quickly downward. Repeat verse, replacing last line with . . .

". . . bumps"

Move hands quickly upward.

". . . branches"

Move hands to side, as if swerving from branch.

". . . hill."

Move hands upward and slow the rolling motion of hands; then move downward and speed up rolling motion.

—Adapted from a song by Susan M. Dailey

My Wagon

I have a little wagon
I pull around with me.
I fill it with my toys
So everyone can see.
I love my little wagon,
Sometimes I jump inside.
Then I push with my two feet
And give my toys a ride.

—Jean Warren

Do actions as indicated.

Five Little Boats

Five little boats were having a race.
The first one said, "I will win first place."
The second one said, "I'm moving very fast."
The third one said, "I don't want to be last."
The fourth one said, "We're running out of time."
The fifth one said, "I've crossed the finish line."

—Barbara Scott

Begin this rhyme with five fingers up.
Beginning with thumb, point to each in succession.

Ten Little Boats

Ten little boats were sailing in a line.
One floated away and then there were nine.
Nine little boats, none of them were late.
One zoomed away, and then there were eight.
Eight little boats sailing off to heaven.
One chugged away and then there were seven.
Seven little boats doing fancy tricks.
One steamed away and then there were six.
Six little boats, all ready to arrive.
One reached the dock and then there were five.
Five little boats with passengers galore.
One sailed away and then there were four.
Four little boats drifting out to sea.
One turned around and then there were three.
Three little boats, just a very few.
One stopped to fish and then there were two.
Two little boats heading into the sun.
One made a wrong turn and then there was one.
One little boat, all his friends were gone.
He dropped his anchor and then there were none.

—Barbara Scott

This rhyme also works well as a flannel or Velcro board presentation.
Begin this rhyme with ten fingers up.
Take away fingers as rhyme progresses.

The Airplane

The airplane has big wings,
The airplane has big wings.
Heigh-ho, the derry-o,
The airplane has big wings.
The propeller goes 'round and 'round,
The propeller goes 'round and 'round.
Heigh-ho the derry-o,
The propeller goes 'round and 'round.
It flies up to the sky,
It flies up to the sky.
Heigh-ho the derry-o,
It flics up to thc sky.
It lands back on the ground,
It lands back on the ground.
Heigh-ho the derry-o,
It lands back on the ground.

—Adapted traditional rhyme

Sung to the tune of "The Farmer in the Dell."
Stretch arms out to sides.

Make circle in air with hand.

Stretch arms out; dip and dive side to side.

With arms still outstretched, sit down.

I'm a Little Airplane

I'm a little airplane,
Watch me fly.
I take off from the ground,
And head to the sky.
Watch me twist and dive,
Give me a hand.
When I'm done,
It's down I'll land!

—Adapted traditional rhyme

Sung to the tune of "I'm a Little Teapot."

Stretch arms out on either side.

Point up.
Do motions.
Clap.

Sit.

If You Want to Be a Train

If you want to be a train, sound your horn.
If you want to be a train, sound your horn.
If you want to be a train, you do not have to explain.
If you want to be a train, sound your horn.
If you want to be a train, turn your wheels.
If you want to be a train, turn your wheels.
If you want to be a train, you do not have to explain.
If you want to be a train, turn your wheels.
If you want to be a train, ring your bell.
If you want to be a train, ring your bell.
If you want to be a train, you do not have to explain.
If you want to be a train, ring your bell.

Sung to the tune of "If You're Happy and You Know It."
"Toot, toot!"; motion of pulling cord.
"Toot, toot!"; do same motion.
Shake head "no."
"Toot, toot!"; do same motion.
Bicycle arms.
Bicycle arms.

Bicycle arms.
"Ding! Ding!"; "ring" hand side to side.
"Ding! Ding!"; do same motion.

"Ding! Ding!"; do same motion.

ADDITIONAL VERSE:

If you want to be a train, do all three!

—Adapted traditional rhyme

I Am a Semi Truck

I am a semi truck, black and white.
Here are my headlights
That light up the night.
My wheels go 'round,
And my horn goes beep.
I deliver goods while you
Are fast asleep!

—Adapted traditional rhyme

"Toot" and pull; bicycle arms; "Ding" and ring.

Sung to the tune of "I'm A Little Teapot."
Point to self.
Make circles with both hands.

Roll hands.
Motion of honking horn.

Put head on hands; pretend to sleep.

I Love Driving in My Car

I love driving in my car,
Going places near or far.
I get in and turn the key,
Check my mirror so I can see.
I don't leave safety to luck.
My seat belt I buckle up.

—Barbara Scott

Sung to the tune of "Twinkle, Twinkle, Little Star."
Pretend to drive.
Point left, then right.
Pretend to put key in ignition.
Pretend to adjust mirror.
Shake head "no."
Pretend to latch seat belt.

See the Little Train

See the little train,
Chugging down the track.
First it chugs forward,
Then it chugs back.
Hear the bell . . . it's ringing.
Hear the whistle blow.
Trains carry people
Everywhere they want to go!

—Barbara Scott

Bicycle arms.
Move forward.
Move backward.
Motion of ringing bell.
Pump closed fist in the air two times; "Toot, toot!"
Move arms to show expanse.

I'm a School Bus

I'm a school bus,
I'm a school bus.
Yes I am!
Yes I am!
Stopping at the bus stop,
Dropping off and picking up
At the school,
At the school.

—Adapted traditional rhyme

Sung to the tune of "Frère Jacques."
Point to self.

Nod head "yes."

"Stop" motion with hand.

Five Little Bicycles

Five little bicycles waiting to explore.
One rode away and then there were four.
Four little bicycles, two pair, you see.
One fell over and then there were three.
Three little bicycles with nothing much to do.
One went to get washed off and then there were two.
Two little bicycles saw it was time to run.
One pedaled away fast and then there was one.
One little bicycle left sitting in the sun.
He headed slowly home and then there were none.

—Barbara Scott

Begin this rhyme with five fingers up.
Take away fingers as rhyme progresses.

The Plane Song

I know a vehicle that flies
Way up in the air!
P-L-A-N-E,
P-L-A-N-E,
P-L-A-N-E,
And plane is its name-o!

—Adapted traditional rhyme

Sung to the tune of "Bingo." Visuals work well with this one, either large letters on a flannel or Velcro board or small letters affixed to plane shapes on a hand mitt! As with the original song, take away letters and replace them with clapping.

I'm a Little Car

I'm a little car,
Just watch me go!
Sometimes fast,
And sometimes slow.
I have four wheels,
And a horn that beeps.
See me going
Down the street!

—Adapted traditional rhyme

Sung to the tune of "I'm a Little Teapot."

Point to self.

Point to eyes.

Drive fast.

Drive slowly.

Show four fingers.

Pretend to honk horn; say "Honk, honk."

Wave goodbye.

Books to Share

Alborough, Jez. 1999. *Duck in the Truck*. London: Picture Lions. ISBN: 978-0001983465.

———. 2003. *Captain Duck*. New York: HarperCollins. ISBN: 978-0060521233.

Best, Cari. 2006. *Sally Jean, The Bicycle Queen*. New York: Farrar, Straus, and Giroux. ISBN: 978-0374363864.

Soto, Gary. 2006. *My Little Car*. New York: Putnam Juvenile. ISBN: 978-0399232206.

Van Dusen, Chris. 2005. *If I Built a Car*. New York: Dutton Juvenile. ISBN: 978-0525474005.

Wormell, Christopher. 2001. *Puff-Puff, Chugga-Chugga*. New York: Margaret K. McElderry. ISBN: 978-0689839863.

Musical Selections

"Driving Here, Driving There" from *Jim Gill Sings Do Re Mi on His Toe Leg Knee* by Jim Gill. Available: www.jimgill.com (accessed March 10, 2010).

"Riding in My Car" from *Rockin' Down the Road* by Greg and Steve. ASIN: B00000DGMU.

"Rock-a-Motion Choo Choo" from *We All Live Together*, vol. 1, by Greg and Steve. ASIN: B00000DGMR.

"Toy Boat" from *Jim Gill's Irrational Anthem and More Salutes to Nonsense* by Jim Gill. Available: www.jimgill.com (accessed March 10, 2010).

"Truck Driver's Song" from *We're on Our Way* by Hap Palmer. ASIN: B00000JXNG.

"Up a Lazy River" from *Musical Scarves and Activities* by Georgiana Stewart. ASIN: B0001AC3KO.

Sources

Cullum, Carolyn. 2007. *The Storytime Sourcebook II*. New York: Neal-Schuman.

Dailey, Susan M. 2001. *A Storytime Year*. New York: Neal-Schuman.

———. 2007. *Sing a Song of Storytime*. New York: Neal-Schuman.

Grayson, Marion. 1962. *Let's Do Fingerplays*. Fairfield, CT: R.B. Luce.

Irving, Jan, and Robin Currie. 1988. *Full Speed Ahead: Stories and Activities for Children on Transportation*. Santa Barbara, CA: Teacher Ideas Press.

"Nursery Rhymes." The Mother Goose Pages. Available: www-personal.umich.edu/~pfa/dreamhouse/nursery/rhymes.html (accessed March 13, 2010).

Redleaf, Rhonda. 1983. *Busy Fingers, Growing Minds*. St. Paul, MN: Redleaf Press.

Roberts, Lynda. 1985. *Mitt Magic: Fingerplays for Finger Puppets*. Silver Spring, MD: Gryphon House.

Sinclair, Patti, Tami Chumbley, Geri Cupery, Diane Findlay, and Jerri J. Heid. 2004. *Collaborative Summer Library Program Manual*. Mason City, IA: Collaborative Summer Library Program.

Totline Staff, comp. 1994. *1001 Rhymes and Fingerplays*. Everett, WA: Warren Publishing House.

Totten, Kathryn. 1998. *Storytime Crafts*. Fort Atkinson, WI: Alleyside Press.

Warren, Jean. 1991. *Toddler Theme-a-Saurus*. Everett, WA: Warren Publishing House.

Willet, Edward. 1882. *Around the House*. New York: R. Worthington.

Zoo

Everyone loves a trip to the zoo. Have lots of fun with these lively rhymes!

Rhyme	**Telling Guide**

The Zoo

This is the way the elephant goes
With curly trunk instead of nose.

Clasp hands; move dangling arms back and forth.

The buffalo all shaggy and fat
Has two sharp horns in place of hat.

Point fingers out from forehead.

The hippo with his mouth so wide
Let's you see what is inside.

Open and close hands for mouth movements.

The wiggly snake upon the ground
Crawls along without a sound.

Wave hands back and forth.

But the monkey see and monkey do
Is the funniest animal in the zoo.

Put thumbs in ears and wiggle hands.

—From Alphabet Soup

The Zoo Pokey

Sung to the tune of "The Hokey Pokey."
Do actions as indicated.

You put your tiger claws in,
You take your tiger claws out,
You put your tiger claws in
And you shake them all about.
You do the zoo pokey and you turn yourself around.
That's what it's all about!

Clap.

ADDITIONAL VERSES:
You put your giraffe neck in . . .

Stick neck way in.

You put your seal flippers in . . .

Clap hands together like a seal.

You put your snake tongue in . . .

Stick out tongue.

You put your peacock tail in . . .

Move bottom in and out.

You put your anteater nose in . . .

Put nose in.

—Barbara Scott

Zoo Antics

Sung to the tune of "The Ants Go Marching."
Do motions as indicated.

The animals were hopping through the zoo,
WATCH OUT! WATCH OUT!
The animals were hopping through the zoo,
WATCH OUT! WATCH OUT!
The animals were hopping through the zoo,
We stopped to see the kangaroos,
And we all started hopping
Down the road, to get out of the rain.

The animals were climbing up in the trees,
WATCH OUT! WATCH OUT!
The animals were climbing up in the trees,
WATCH OUT! WATCH OUT!
The animals were climbing up in the trees,
We stopped to see a lot of monkeys,
And we all started climbing
Up in the trees, to get out of the rain.
The animals were diving into the pool,
WATCH OUT! WATCH OUT!
The animals were diving into the pool,
WATCH OUT! WATCH OUT!
The animals were diving into the pool,
Penguins thought it was really cool,
When we all started diving
Down into the pool at the end of the zoo!

—Carolyn N. Cullum

Kangaroo, Kangaroo

Kangaroo, kangaroo, bounce up and down.   Do actions as indicated.
Kangaroo, kangaroo, touch the ground.
Kangaroo, kangaroo, make your ears go flop.
Kangaroo, kangaroo, now let's hop.
Kangaroo, kangaroo, bend down low.
Kangaroo, kangaroo, now jump just so.
Kangaroo, kangaroo, here are your great big toes.
Kangaroo, kangaroo, now here we go.   Jump around in a circle.

—Kay Lincycomb

Here We Go Jumping

Sung to the tune of "Here We Go Looby Loo."
Do actions as indicated.

Here we go jumping high,
Here we go jumping low.
Here we go jumping all around.
That's how the kangaroo goes.
Here we go jumping fast,
Here we go jumping slow.
Here we go jumping everywhere.
That's how the kangaroo goes.

—Kay Lincycomb

Five Baby Kangaroos

Five baby kangaroos standing in a row.   Hold up five fingers.
And when they see their mothers,
They jump just so.   Jump up and down.

They jump to the left.
They jump to the right.
One jumps in his mother's pouch,
To sleep throughout the night.
Now there's no baby kangaroos
Standing in a row.
They are all sleeping now, it's time for us to go.
They jumped to the left.
They jumped to the right.
They jumped down the road,
Until they were out of sight.

—Kay Lincycomb

Jump left.
Jump right.
Do big jump.
Put hands on cheek. Repeat verses counting down four, three, two, one.

Jump left.
Jump right.
Jump in place.
Wave.

Baby Kangaroo

Sung to the tune of "Frère Jacques."

I am a baby kangaroo.
I am a baby kangaroo.
Hopping is fun, hopping is fun.
Hopping, hopping, hopping,
Hopping, hopping, hopping.
Up and down, up and down.
I am a baby kangaroo.
I am a baby kangaroo.
Hopping is fun, hopping is fun.
Won't you please hop with me?
Won't you please hop with me?
We'll have fun. We'll have fun.
I am a baby kangaroo.
I am a baby kangaroo.
Hopping is fun, hopping is fun.
I'll hop on home to mama, I'll hop on home to mama.
When day is done, when day is done.

—Kay Lincycomb

Hop in place.
Hop around in a circle.

Hop to match the words.

Repeat actions.
Point around.

Wave and hop.

The Zoo

The sun is shining. Shout, "Hooray!"
We are going to the circus today.
We'll see parrots and kangaroos,
Elephants and lions, too.
My friend wants to see snakes that wriggle,
But I like monkeys. They make me giggle!

—Susan M. Dailey

Hold hands above head in circle; say "Hooray."

Pretend to fly, then hop fingers.
Swing arms like trunk; roar
Wriggle arm.
Act like monkey; laugh.

I'd Rather Work at the Zoo

I'm tired of dusting and sweeping.
I'd rather work at the zoo.

Pretend to dust and sweep.
Place hands on hips.

I think there'd be lots of things
That I would be able to do.
I could brush the tiger's teeth,
And comb the lion's hair.
I could iron the elephant's wrinkly skin,
And teach the monkeys to share.

I could wash the spots from the leopard,
And the stripes from the zebra, too.
Do you think that's what I'd do,
If I worked at the zoo?

—Susan M. Dailey

Tap index finger to side of forehead.
Point to self; nod head.
Pretend to brush teeth.
Pretend to comb hair.
Pretend to iron.
Pretend to hold something out, then snatch it away.
Pretend to wash.

Hold out hands in questioning gesture.

Mama Kangaroo

Mama kanga-roo-roo-roo-roo-roo
Hopping 'round the zoo-zoo-zoo-zoo-zoo,
Has big feet and big ears, too.
And a pouch for a baby.
Papa kanga-roo-roo-roo-roo-roo
Hopping 'round the zoo-zoo-zoo-zoo-zoo,
Has big feet and big ears, too.
But no pouch for a baby.

—Adapted from a rhyme by Susan M. Dailey

Sung to the tune of "Skip to My Lou."

Hop in place.
Point to feet; then to ears.
Point to tummy.

Hop in place.
Point to feet, then to ears.
Shake head "no."

Zoo Animals

Susan suggests using name tags of different animals. This would also work well with pictures (multiples of each) of the different animals or small puppets on craft sticks!

Clap your hands! Shout "Hurray!"
We are going to the zoo today, zoo today.
Clap your hands! Shout "Hurray!"
I hope we see giraffes today.
Clap your hands! Shout "Hurray!"
I hope that we'll see elephants today.
Clap your hands! Shout "Hurray!"
I hope that we will see lions today.
Clap your hands! Shout "Hurray!"
We're going to the zoo today.

—Adapted from a song by Susan M. Dailey

Clap hands; shout.

Oh, I Work at the Zoo

Oh, I work at the zoo. Yes I do. Yes I do.
Oh, I work at the zoo. Yes I do. Yes I do.
Oh, I work at the zoo. Yes I work at the zoo.
Oh, I work at the zoo. Yes I do. Yes I do.

ADDITIONAL VERSES:

Oh, I clean the lion's cages. Yes I do. Sweep, sweep . . .

Oh, I feed the penguins fish. Yes I do. Yum, yum, sweep, sweep . . .

Oh, I give the bears a bath. Yes I do. Splish, splash, yum, yum, sweep, sweep . . .

Oh, I trim the tigers' toenails. Yes I do. Clip, clip, splish, splash, yum, yum, sweep, sweep . . .

—Adapted from a song by Susan M. Dailey

Motion of sweeping.

Rub tummy; sweep.

Motion of bathing; rub tummy; sweep.

Motion of clipping nails, bathing; rub tummy; sweep.

One Elephant

The zoo has one elephant.
The zoo has two lions,
And one elephant.
The zoo has three zebras,
Two lions, and one elephant.
The zoo has four flamingos,
Three zebras, two lions, and one elephant.
The zoo has five monkeys,
Four flamingos, three zebras, two lions
And one elephant.

—Gail Benton

Place arm in front of face for elephant's trunk; make a trumpeting sound on the word "elephant."

Hold up hands to resemble lion's paws; make roaring sound on the word "lions."

Prance in place; make braying sound on the word "zebras."

Stand on one leg; make fluting sound on the word "flamingos."

Hold one hand in the air and scratch arm pit; make monkey noise on the word "monkeys." / Pause and finish slowly with emphasis.

Kangaroo

When Kangaroo goes walking,
He is just as funny as can be.
And when he's tired,
He stops right there,
Using his tail for chair.

—From *Four-Footed Folk*

Walk in place.

Hold tummy and laugh.

Yawn.

Pretend to sit on tail.

Giraffe

Here's beautiful Madame Giraffe
Who never does things by half;
She'll entertain you if you wait,
Making her neck a "figure eight"!

—From *Four-Footed Folk*

Hand makes head; hold in the air.

Shake head "no."

Make "figure eight" in the air.

Hippopotamus

Puffy old Hippopotamus,
When days are warm,
Makes such a fuss.
They pack him in chunks of ice
And so they keep him cool and nice.

—From *Four-Footed Folk*

Fan self.

Stomp feet.

Motion of packing.

Wrap arms and shiver.

The Long-Neck Giraffe

Here is the giraffe,
His long neck you can see.
He can eat all the leaves
From a very high tree.
Just look at this neck,
How it slopes straight down;
If you ride him like a horse,
You would slide off on the ground.
Now, why he was made,
There is no one that knows.
He's only seen in circuses,
Or funny side shows.

—From *Golden Playdays*

ASL sign for giraffe: right hand on chest at throat, curl fingers in slightly and bring hand up in the air.
Use ASL sign for giraffe.
Point to eyes.

Chew as if eating.
Point to neck.
Point down.
Pretend to ride horse.
Slide hand down.

Shake head "no."

Hold tummy and laugh.

Zoo Count

One tired lion, napping in the sun.
Two funny penguins, splash and have some fun.
Three silly chimpanzees swinging up so high.
Four beautiful eagles getting ready to fly.
Five sleepy leopards stretch and move and yawn.
Six beautiful deer, each one with a fawn.
Seven quacking ducks swimming in the lake.
Eight huge elephants make the ground shake.
Nine colorful parrots perched high in the tree.
Ten proud peacocks fan their tails for all to see.

—Barbara Scott

Hold up index finger; pretend to sleep. / Add fingers as rhyme progresses; pretend to splash.
Swing.
Spread arms.
Do motions as indicated.

Swim motions.
Stomp feet.
Point up.
Fingers of one hand spread out as a tail.

We're Going to the Zoo

We're going to the zoo,
We're going to the zoo!
Lots of animals to see,
We're going to the zoo!
We'll see some monkeys there,
We'll see some monkeys there.
Swinging, climbing in the trees,
We'll see some monkeys there.
We'll see some elephants there,
We'll see some elephants there.
Swinging their trunks back and forth,
We'll see some elephants there.
We'll see some turtles there,

Sung to the tune of "The Farmer in the Dell."

Swing back and forth.

Put arm to nose and swing from side to side.

We'll see some turtles there.
Walking oh so very slow,

Walk slowly.

We'll see some turtles there.
We'll see some penguins there,
We'll see some penguins there.
Waddling, waddling on the ice,

Waddle.

We'll see some penguins there.

Add other animals as you wish with appropriate motions.

— Adapted traditional rhyme

If You Live at the Zoo

Sung to the tune of "If You're Happy and You Know It."

If you live at the zoo, swing your trunk.
If you live at the zoo, swing your trunk.

Put arms, hands clasped, in front; lean over; swing arms back and forth.

If you have a trunk, you must be an _____ (elephant).

Let children fill in animal names.

If you live at the zoo, swing your trunk.

Swing trunk.

If you live at the zoo, roar out loud.

"Roar!"

If you live at the zoo, roar out loud.

"Roar!"

If you roar out load, you must be a _____ (lion) proud.
If you live at the zoo, roar out loud.

"Roar!"

If you live at the zoo, swing in a tree.

Swing back and forth.

If you live at the zoo, swing in a tree.

Swing.

If you're swinging in a tree, you must be a _____ (monkey).
If you live at the zoo, swing in a tree.

Swing.

If you live at the zoo, do all three . . .

Swing trunk; "Roar"; and swing.

— Adapted traditional rhyme

Ten Little Zebras

Sung to the tune of "Ten Little Indians."

One little, two little, three little zebras,

Count out on fingers for first verse.

Four little, five little, six little zebras,
Seven little, eight little, nine little zebras,
Ten zebras at the zoo!
Ten little, nine little, eight little zebras,

Take away fingers on second verse.

Seven little, six little, five little zebras,
Four little, three little, two little zebras,
One zebra at the zoo!

— Adapted traditional rhyme

I'm a Snake

Sung to the tune of "Alouette." ASL sign for snake: index and middle fingers up and curved down near mouth; then move away from mouth in an up-and-down motion.
Use ASL sign for snake.

I'm a snake,
A black and slithery snake.
I'm a snake,

Use ASL sign.

And I live at the zoo!
I rest up in the tree so high,

Point up.

Until some food I chance to spy.

Way up high, chance to spy . . . oh.

I'm a snake,

A black and slithery snake.

I'm a snake,

And I live at the zoo!

—Adapted traditional rhyme

Point to eyes.

Use ASL sign.

Use ASL sign.

Hippo, Hippo

This rhyme can be sung to the tune of "Teddy Bear, Teddy Bear" or chanted.

Hippo, hippo,

Turn around.

Turn in place.

Hippo, hippo,

Shake the ground!

Stomp feet.

Hippo, hippo,

Open wide!

Open mouth wide.

Hippo, hippo,

Into the mud, slide.

Slide.

Hippo, hippo,

Play with the ball.

Act as if knocking ball about with nose.

Hippo, hippo,

That's not all.

Shake head "no."

Hippo, hippo,

Yawn with might.

BIG yawn.

Hippo, hippo,

Say goodnight.

Close eyes; pretend to sleep.

—Adapted traditional rhyme

Five Pretty Peacocks

Five pretty peacocks at the zoo.

Begin rhyme with five fingers up.

The first one said, "There's nothing to do."

Beginning with thumb, point to each in succession.

The second one said, "Let's strut and prance."

The third one said, "Let's dance, dance, dance."

The fourth one said, "Listen to me squeal."

The fifth one said, "What a beautiful tail."

—Barbara Scott

Silly Seals

Sung to the tune of "Twinkle, Twinkle, Little Star."

Silly seals live at the zoo.

Here is something they can do.

They can dance and clap their flippers.

Put arms straight out in front like flippers and clap.

They honk horns for meals of kippers.

Pretend to honk rubber squeeze-ball horns.

Silly seals live at the zoo,

Waiting for a visit from you!

Point to children.

—Adapted traditional rhyme

Books to Share

Cimarusti, Marie. 2003. *Peek-a-Zoo!* New York: Dutton Juvenile. ISBN: 978-0525475071.

Mayer, Mercer. 2001. *My Trip to the Zoo.* Columbus, OH: School Specialty Publishing. ISBN: 978-1577688266.

Mora, Pat. 2006. *Marimba! Animales A to Z.* New York: Clarion Books. ISBN: 978-0618194537.

Newman, Jeff. 2006. *Hippo! No, Rhino.* New York: Little, Brown Young Readers. ISBN: 978-0316155731.

Smith, Stu. 2004. *My School's a Zoo.* New York: HarperCollins. ISBN: 978-0060285104.

Wilson, Karma. 2004. *Never Ever Shout in a Zoo.* New York: Little, Brown Young Readers. ISBN: 978-0316985642.

Musical Selections

Animals at the Zoo by Bobby Susser. ASIN: B00005BABL.

"Goin' to the Zoo" from *(Almost) Two Much* by Nan Hoffman. Available: www.nanhoffman.com (accessed March 17, 2010).

"Going to the Zoo" from *Singable Songs for the Very Young* by Raffi. ASIN: B0000003H4.

"New Zoo Review" from *Big Fun* by Greg and Steve. ASIN: B00000AG60.

"Zoo Babies" from *Debbie's Ditties for Little Kiddies!* by Debbie Clement. Available: www.songsforteaching.com/store/debbies-ditties-cd-pr-1322.html (accessed March 17, 2010).

"Zoo, Zoo, Zoo" from *Animal House* by Recess Monkey. ASIN: B000NQPWUY.

Sources

Benton, Gail and Trish Waichulaitis. 2003. *Ready-to-Go Storytimes: Fingerplays, Scripts, Patterns, Music, and More.* New York: Neal-Schuman.

Cullum, Carolyn N. 2007. *The Storytime Sourcebook II.* New York: Neal-Schuman.

Dailey, Susan M. 2001. *A Storybook Year.* New York: Neal-Schuman.

———. 2007. *Sing a Song of Storytime.* New York: Neal-Schuman.

Dorsey, C.J. 1922. *Golden Playdays.* Children's Publishing Company. Available: www.childrensbooksonline.org/golden_playdays/pages/playdays14.htm (accessed March 17, 2010).

Gordon, Elizabeth. n.d. *Four Footed Folk.* Available: www.childrensbooksonline.org/Four_Footed_Folk/index.htm (accessed March 17, 2010).

Lincycomb, Kay. 2007. *Storytimes . . . Plus!* New York: Neal-Schuman.

"Zoo Songs, Poems, and Fingerplays." Available: www.alphabet-soup.net/dir7/ zoosong.html (accessed March 17, 2010).

The Source Finder

Where to Find Puppets and Storysets

Finger puppets can be used for many of the fingerplays contained in this book. The following list of companies that provide hand and/or finger puppets is by no means exhaustive but will give the librarian or early childhood educator a good start!

ArtFelt
1102 N. Brand Blvd.
San Fernando, CA 91340
1-818-365-1021
www.artfelt.net
Judy Woodworth is the developer and owner of ArtFelt. She produces a line of beautiful finger and hand puppets. Take your time browsing her site, as there's lots to see!

Becker's School Supplies
1500 Melrose Highway
Pennsauken, NJ 08110-1410
1-800-523-1490
www.shopbecker.com
This company offers a nice selection of hand puppets.

Childcraft School Specialty
P.O. Box 3239
Lancaster, PA 17604
1-800-631-5652
www.childcraft.com
Childcraft offers a number of hand puppets.

Constructive Playthings
13201 Arrington Road
Grandview, MO 64030-2886
1-800-448-4115
www.cptoys.com
In addition to a large selection of hand puppets, Constructive Playthings also offers "Tell-a-Story Glove and Puppet" sets.

Folkmanis Puppets
1219 Park Avenue

Emeryville, CA 94608
1-800-654-8922
www.folkmanis.com
In addition to the larger stuffed puppets that they offer, Folkmanis also sells a large number of finger puppets. Thumbnail pictures are available under the "Buy Puppets" tab.

Hatch
P.O. Box 11927
Winston-Salem, NC 27116
1-800-624-7968
www.hatchearlychildhood.com
This company offers a nice selection of hand puppets. It also offers the Monkey Mitt (also sold by Teachers' Discount, listed later) as well as a larger selection of sets, such as bees, frogs, and ducks!

Little Folks Visuals
P.O. Box 14243
Palm Desert, CA 92255
1-800-537-7227
www.littlefolksvisuals.com
A great source of felt puppets and storysets. Detailing and bright colors make these a treat!

National School Products
101 East Broadway
Maryville, TN 37804
1-800-627-9393
www.NationalSchoolProducts.com
In addition to hand puppets to supplement books, this company also offers some small finger puppets, for example, mice.

Oriental Trading Company
P.O. Box 2308
Omaha, NE 68103-2308
1-800-228-2269
www.orientaltrading.com
Among its extensive offerings, Oriental Trading Company sells small finger puppets that fit on the fingertips, including frogs, insects, and horses.

Puppet.com
24876 Apple Street
San Clarita, CA 91321
1-800-718-4171
www.puppet.com
This site offers a nice selection of both hand and finger puppets.

Puppet Revelation
c/o Kids and Youth Ministry Superstore
954-C NE Pine Island Road

Cape Coral, FL 33909
1-239-829-0832
www.puppetrevelation.com
This company manufactures, retails, and wholesales high-end quality puppets. Click on the "Finger Puppets" tab on the left side of the homepage. It also sells a large number of Folkmanis finger puppets.

Rhode Island Novelty

5 Industrial Road
Cumberland, RI 02864
1-800-528-5599
www.rinovelty.com
You will find this catalog as daunting as Oriental Trading's. But some careful perusing will uncover finger puppet sets, including horses, monkeys, and zoo animals.

SkyScopes Space Toys

32 North Road
East Windsor, CT 06088
1-877-623-4624
www.spacetoys.com
This site offers cool alien finger puppets!

Teachers' Discount

P.O. Box 365
Landisville, PA 17538
1-800-470-7616
www.tdbestprice.com
This is a source for Monkey Mitt sets with the fingerplay "Five Little Monkeys." The Monkey Mitt is a fuzzy hand glove with Velcro pads on the fingers. I have used other Monkey Mitt sets available with this glove, as well as rhymes I have produced with clip art and laminated for durability.

U.S. Toy Company, Inc.

13201 Arrington Road
Grandview, MO 64030-2886
1-800-255-6124
www.ustoy.com
U.S. Toy Company sells several sets of animal finger puppets, among them dinosaurs and dogs!

Websites

A Place of Our Own

aplaceofourown.org/activity.php?id=474
Instructions to make tooth finger puppets with an old glove!

Alphabet Soup

www.alphabet-soup.net/firesafety/firesafety.html
Rhymes and instructions for easy-to-make firefighter finger puppets.

BillyBear4Kids.com

www.billybear4kids.com/FingerPuppets/MakeEm.shtml

Several templates and instructions for felt finger puppets.

Disney Family Fun

familyfun.go.com/printables/craft-templates/printable/finger-puppets

Ready-to-print templates for a number of finger puppets.

DLTK's Growing Together

www.dltk-holidays.com/xmas/mouse_finger_puppet.htm

Pattern for a cute mouse finger puppet.

eHow

www.ehow.com/how_2218892_felt-finger-puppets.html

Simple instructions to make your own felt finger puppets!

Enchanted Learning Software

www.enchantedlearning.com/crafts/puppets/twofinger

Some really cute dinosaur finger puppets. Enchanted Learning is a membership-based website, but the fee is only $20.00 per year.

FreeKidsCrafts.com

www.freekidcrafts.com/finger-puppets.html

Several patterns for printable finger puppets, including finger puppets from empty plastic film canisters. Templates are included.

Martha Stewart.com

www.marthastewart.com/article/insect-finger-puppets

From Martha Stewart's site, some easy-to-make insect finger puppets!

wikiHow

www.wikihow.com/Make-Finger-Puppets

Instructions to make finger puppets out of old gloves.

Where to Find Multimedia Resources

This list provides the addresses of companies where the majority of the music listed in the "Musical Selections" can be found. While it is not exhaustive, it is a great start!

Becker's School Supplies

1500 Melrose Highway

Pennsauken, NJ 08110-1410

1-800-523-1490

www.shopbecker.com

Source for parachutes and bean bags! Check out the frog, turtle, and bug bean bags as well as those with different colors, shapes, and concepts!

Childcraft School Specialty

P.O. Box 3239

Lancaster, PA 17604

1-800-631-5652

www.childcraft.com

This company sells a limited number of music CDs but has several sets of rhythm instruments available to purchase. Sets come in 15-, 25-, and 30-player sets. It's also a source for parachutes, rainbow ribbons, and scarves!

Constructive Playthings

13201 Arrington Road

Grandview, MO 64030-2886

1-800-448-4115

www.cptoys.com

This company offers a small selection of music CDs. Also available are parachutes, scarves (both smaller and extra-large!), rainbow ribbons, and rhythm band instruments. In addition to 12-, 25-, and 30-player band sets, more instruments can be bought separately. I purchased my rhythm band set from one of its sales catalogs, so keep an eye out for that!

Educational Record Center

3233 Burnt Mill Road, Suite 100

Wilmington, NC 28403-2698

1-800-372-4543

www.erckids.com

This company is a super resource of audio CDs! Just a glance through its catalog shows lots of the CDs I mentioned in the chapters, as well as some that were not available through Amazon.

Kimbo Educational

P.O. Box 477X

Long Branch, NJ 07440-0477

1-800-631-2187

www.kimboed.com

Kimbo is a great source of audio CDs. It bills itself as "the children's music company" (it's been around since 1954) and certainly lives up to that name! With just a quick scan through the latest catalog, I saw many, many of the CDs listed in my "Musical Selections" categories.

Melody House

819 N.W. 92nd Street

Oklahoma City, OK 73114

1-800-234-9228

www.melodyhousemusic.com

Just a quick look through the offerings shows many of the CDs I've listed in the "Musical Selections" are available here. And check it out—the on-line section of $2.00 CDs! The Monkey Mitt (mentioned earlier) is also available here.

Music for Little People

P.O. Box 323

Louisiana, MO 63353

1-800-409-2457

www.musicforlittlepeople.com

This is another source for music CDs. Although it does offer some musical instruments, its selection is somewhat limited. An added bonus: selected MP3 downloads are available!

Music in Motion

P. O. Box 869231

Plano, TX 75086-9231

1-800-445-0649

www.musicmotion.com

This is a source for music CDs as well as rhythm band instruments, rainbow hoops (plastic handheld hoops with ribbon streamers attached), and streamers (sticks with ribbon streamers attached). The hoops and streamers are wonderful additions to music!

S&S Education

P.O. Box 513

Colchester, CT 06415-0513

1-800-243-9232

www.ssww.com

Sources for several different parachutes (in sizes from 6 feet to 30 feet across) as well as a parachute accessories pack that features beach balls, foam balls, toss bags, and much more. I used inflatable smiley-face balls on my parachute when we did the song "Five Little Monkeys." It was great fun!

Songs for Teaching

6632 Telegraph Road #242

Bloomfield Hills, MI 48301

1-800-649-5514

www.songsforteaching.com

Wow! What a great music resource! In addition to its catalog, it also has an online one-stop music resource. You can order CDs or download entire CDs or MP3s of individual songs. Song lyrics are also available.

Teacher's Discount

P.O. Box 365

Landisville, PA 17538

1-800-470-7616

www.tdbestprice.com

Source for bean bags, parachutes, rhythm band instruments, scarves, and rainbow ribbons. It does offer a small selection of audio CDs.

Websites

Amazon.com

www.amazon.com

The granddaddy of all sites! Once you've done a general search on your CD title, you can purchase, listen to snippets, or download songs!

Barnes & Noble

www.bn.com

Click on either "Kids" or "Music" in the tabbed area and then select "Music for Kids" on the left. Many CDs allow you to preview the songs, as well as read both editorial and customer reviews. Music is divided into the following age categories: 0–2, 3–5, 6–8, and 9–12; some seasonal music is also included.

CDBaby

www.cdbaby.com

Click on "Genres," then "Kids/Family" to be taken to a page where you can search "Children's Pop," "Children's Storytelling," "Educational," "General Children's Music," "Kid-Friendly," "Lullabies," and "Sing-Along/Interactive" areas. This site gives you the ability to preview and purchase the CD or download a song or the entire album in MP3 format! Album notes and reviews are also available.

CD Universe

www.cduniverse.com

On the left side of the site's screen, hit the "More" tab in "Browse," and then find "Children's Collections." Songs can be previewed. Especially helpful are the Customer Reviews.

Children's Music Portal

www.childrens-music.org

Home of Children's Music Portal. Areas include "Cool Recordings," "Cool Bands," "Classroom Cool," and "Story Cool." Recordings featured are available for purchase. Links take you to track listings, artist biographies and sites, and listening samples.

Kids CDs

www.kidscds.org

This site offers 16 different genres of kids' music from lullabies to jazz to sing-along. Best Sellers as well as Recently Added titles are featured on the homepage. Even their sale section features some great artists!

Kidsongs

www.kidsongs.com

The CDs here are songs that have been featured on the PBS kids' show of the same name. Offers a limited number of music CDs based on the show.

Walmart

www.walmart.com

On the left-hand menu, click on "Movies, Music & Books," then "Music CDs," and then "Children's Music." Product details give individual track listings, and you can also listen to snippets of songs. Go back to the "Movies, Music & Books" tab, and then click "MP3 Downloads" to go to a separate area. Under the tab "Genres," scroll down to "Children's." Select a type of music to see the songs that are available to download.

Index

About the Author

Barbara Scott has been the Children's Librarian at the Bucyrus Public Library in Bucyrus, Ohio, for 25 years. During this time, she has been responsible for creating pre-school storytimes, as well as administering the state summer reading program and ordering materials for the Children's Department. Additionally, she has been active in the Ohio Library Council, serving on various committees. She holds a Bachelor of Science degree from the University of Rio Grande, where she double-majored in Library Science and English.